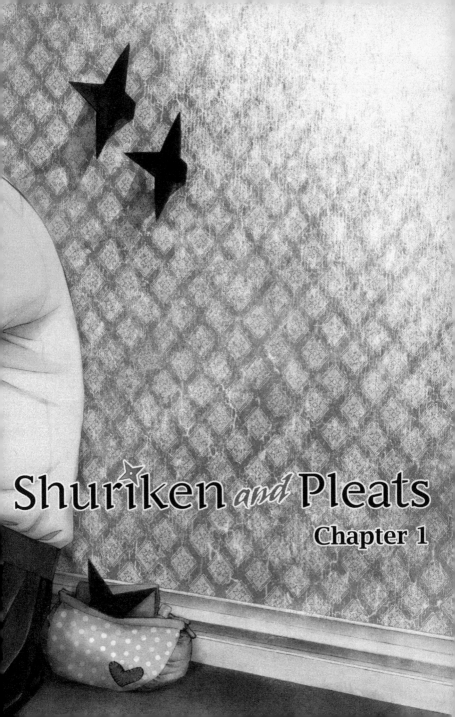

Shuriken *and* Pleats

Chapter 1

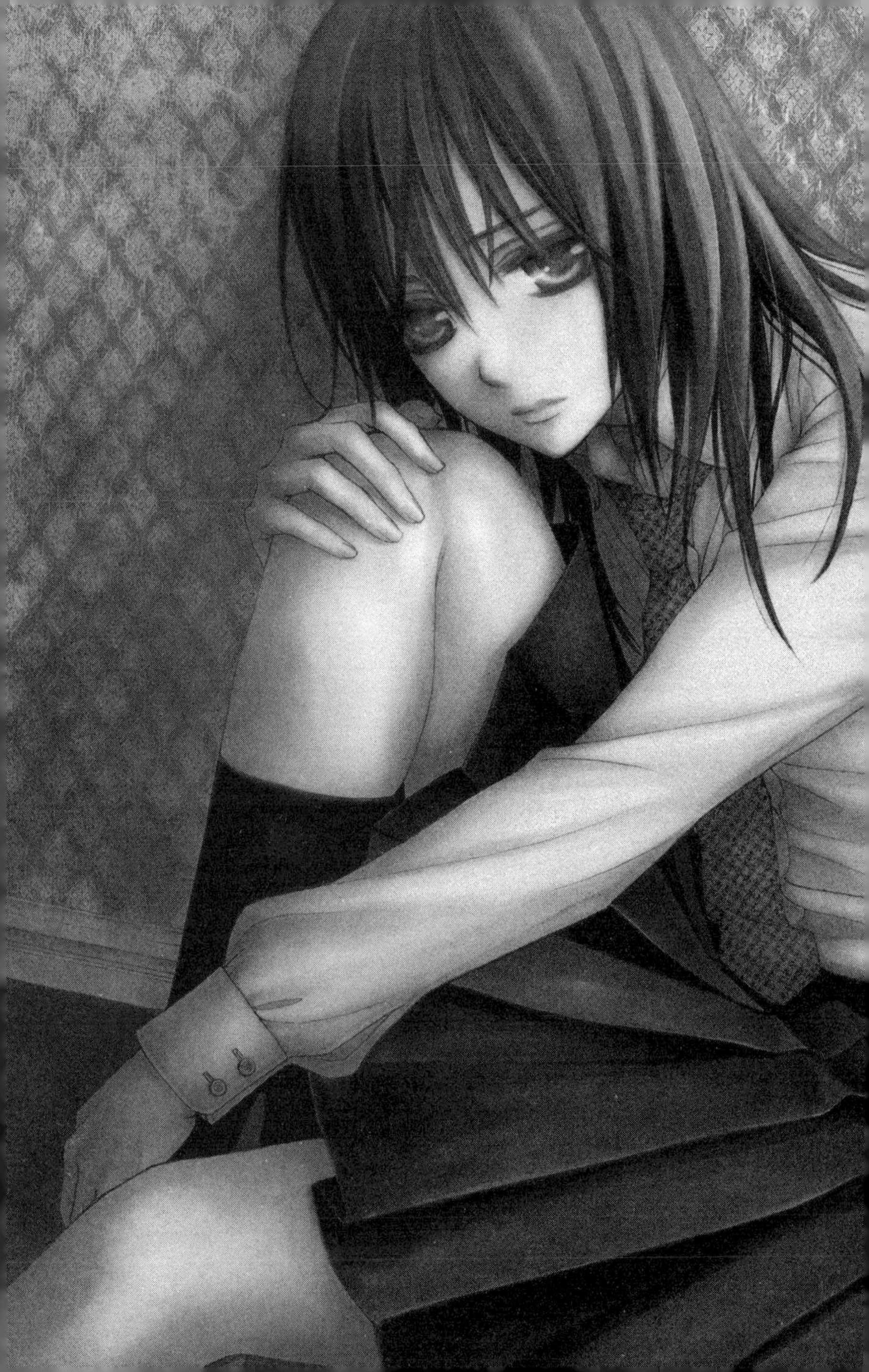

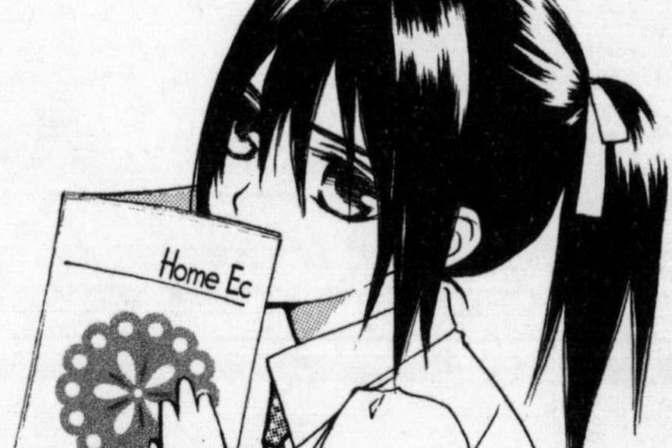
Home Ec

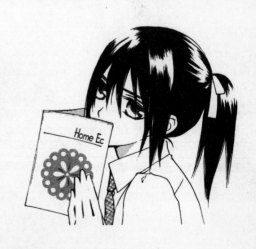

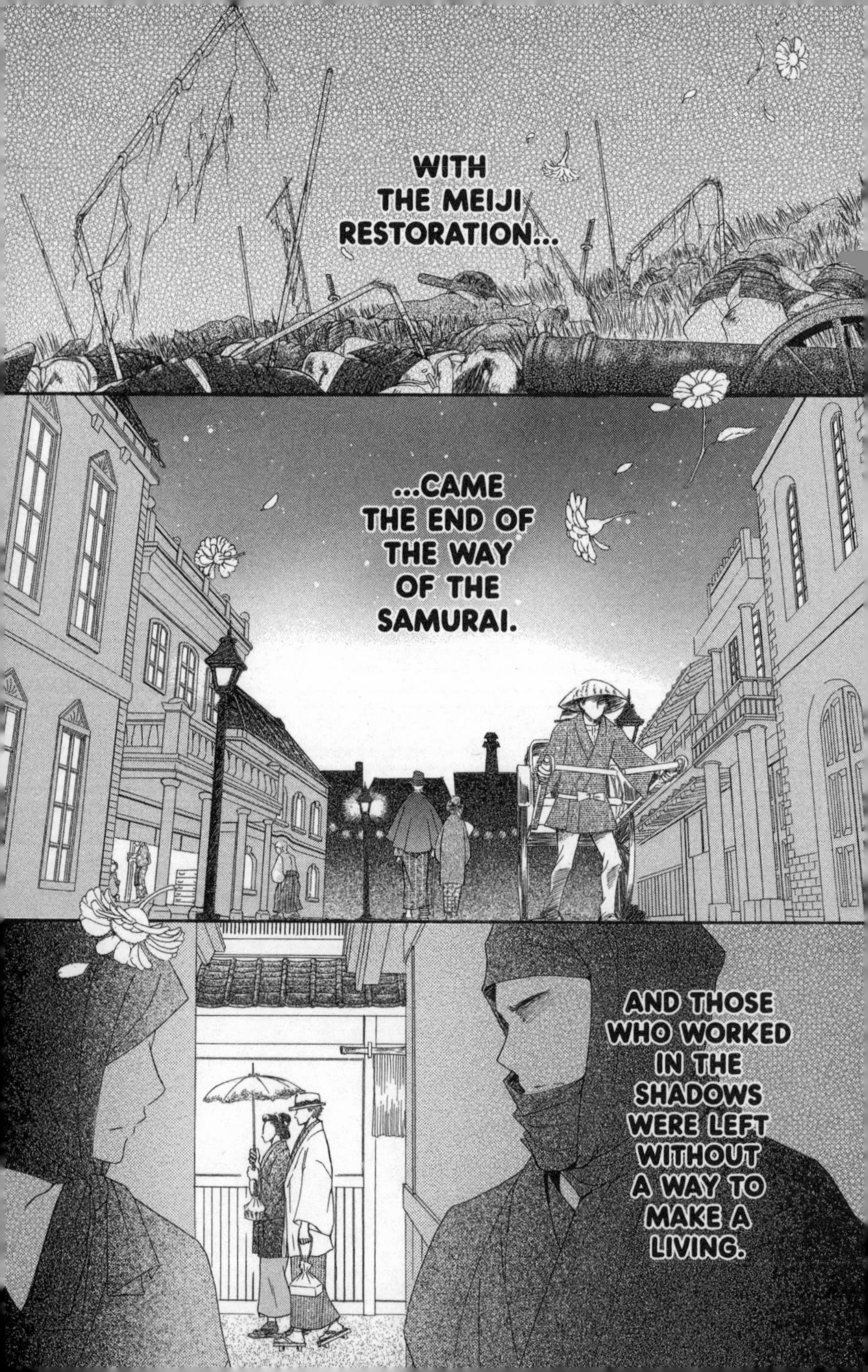
WITH THE MEIJI RESTORATION...
...CAME THE END OF THE WAY OF THE SAMURAI.
AND THOSE WHO WORKED IN THE SHADOWS WERE LEFT WITHOUT A WAY TO MAKE A LIVING.

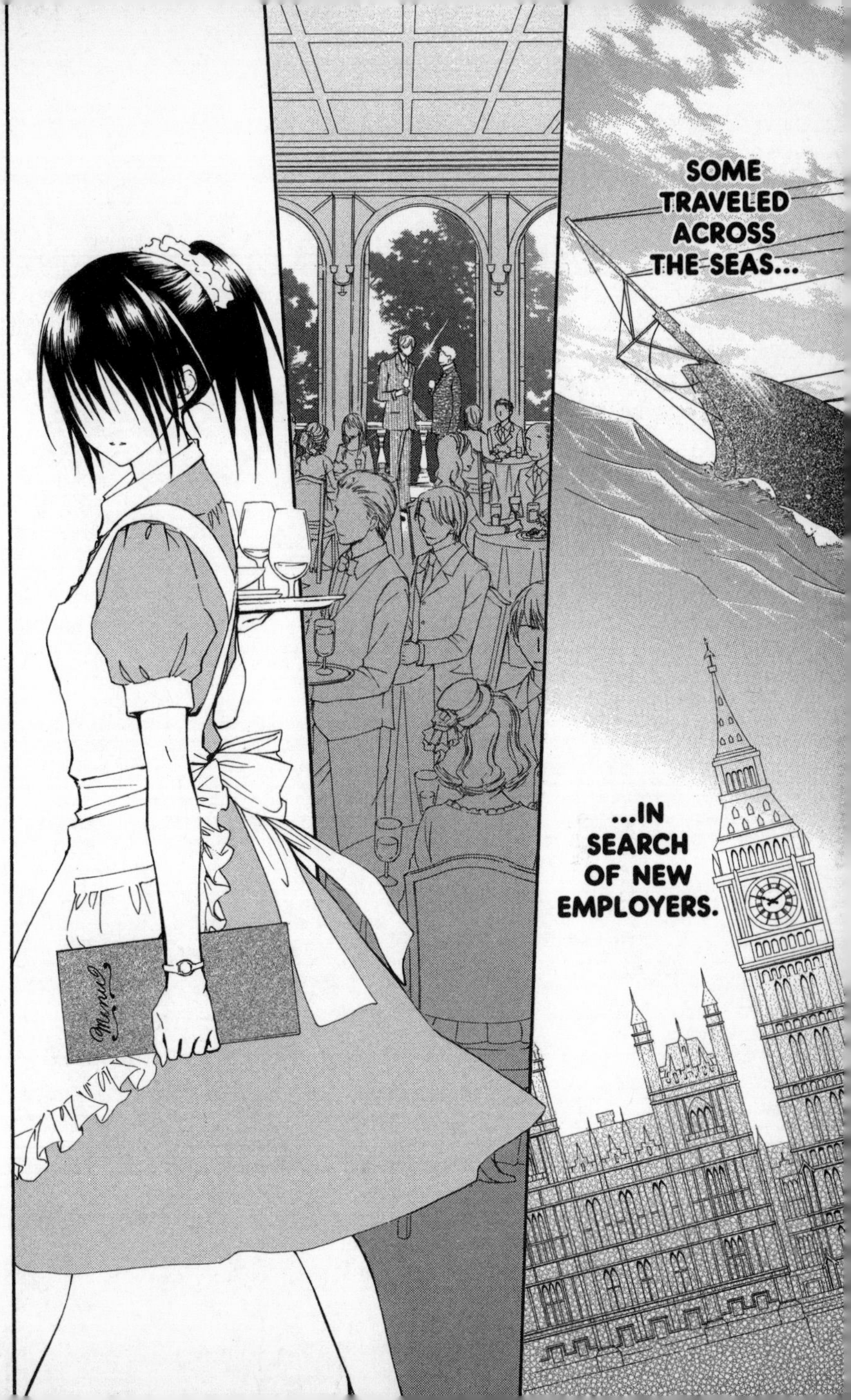
SOME TRAVELED ACROSS THE SEAS...
...IN SEARCH OF NEW EMPLOYERS.

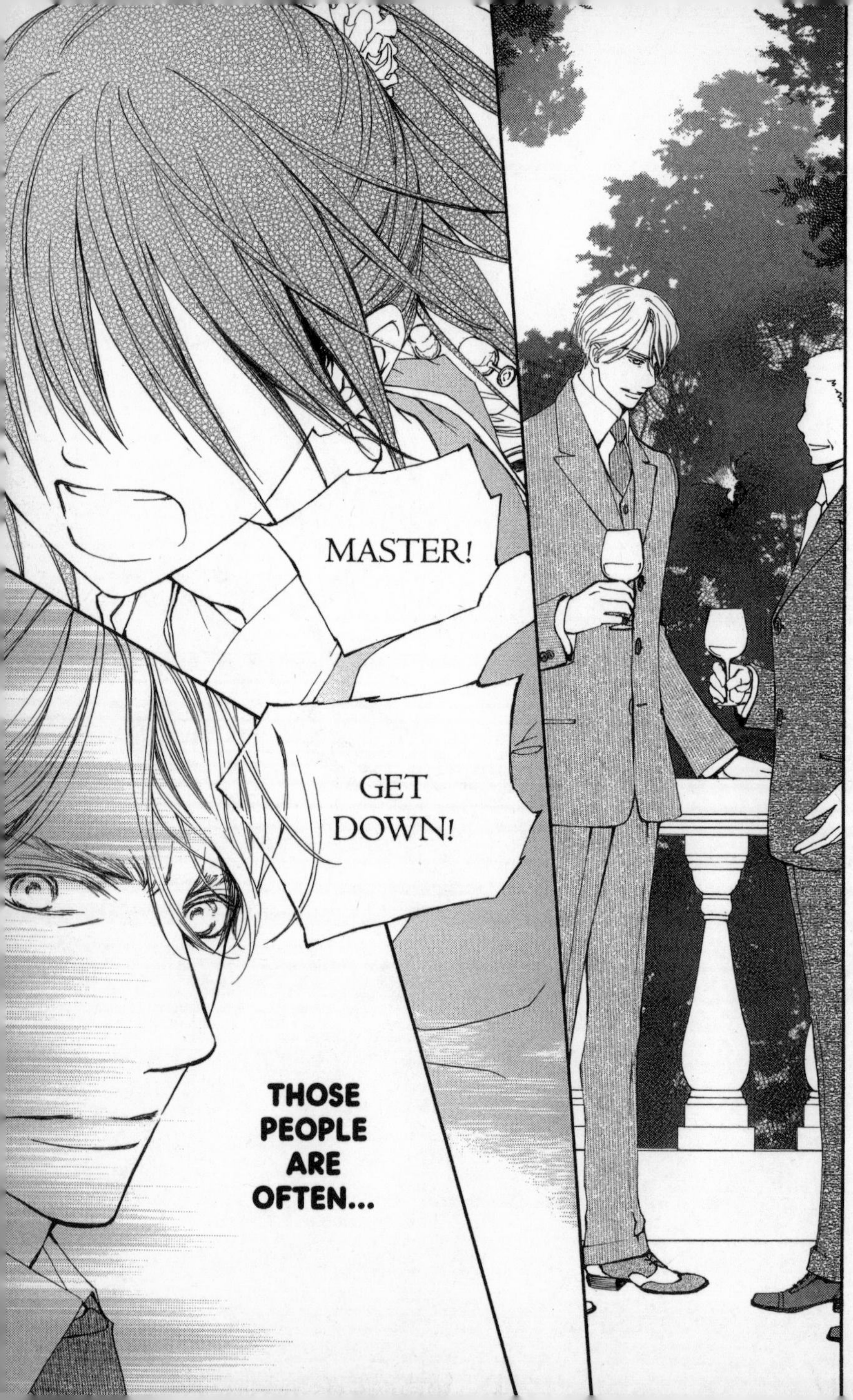
MASTER!
GET DOWN!
THOSE PEOPLE ARE OFTEN...

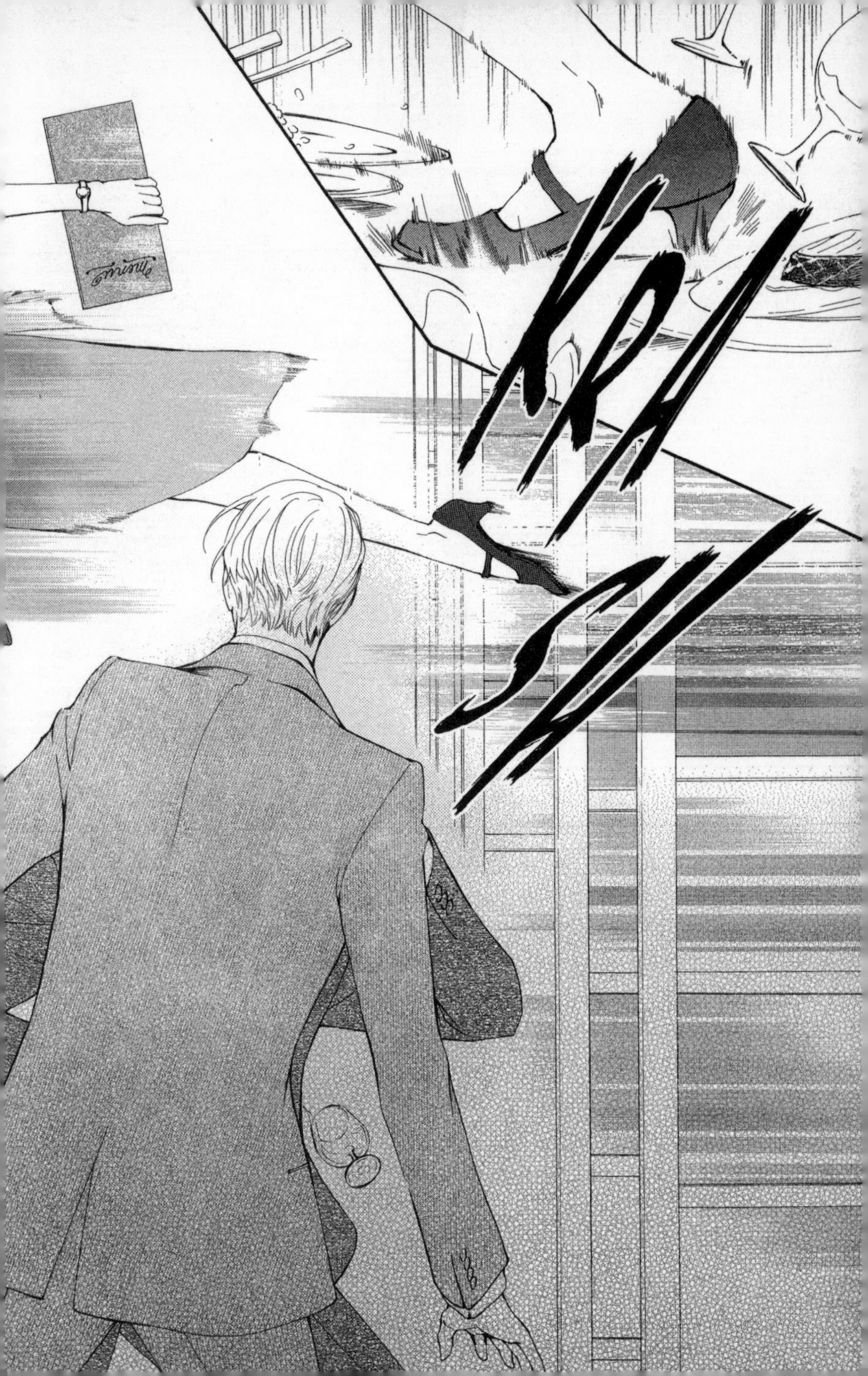
KRASH

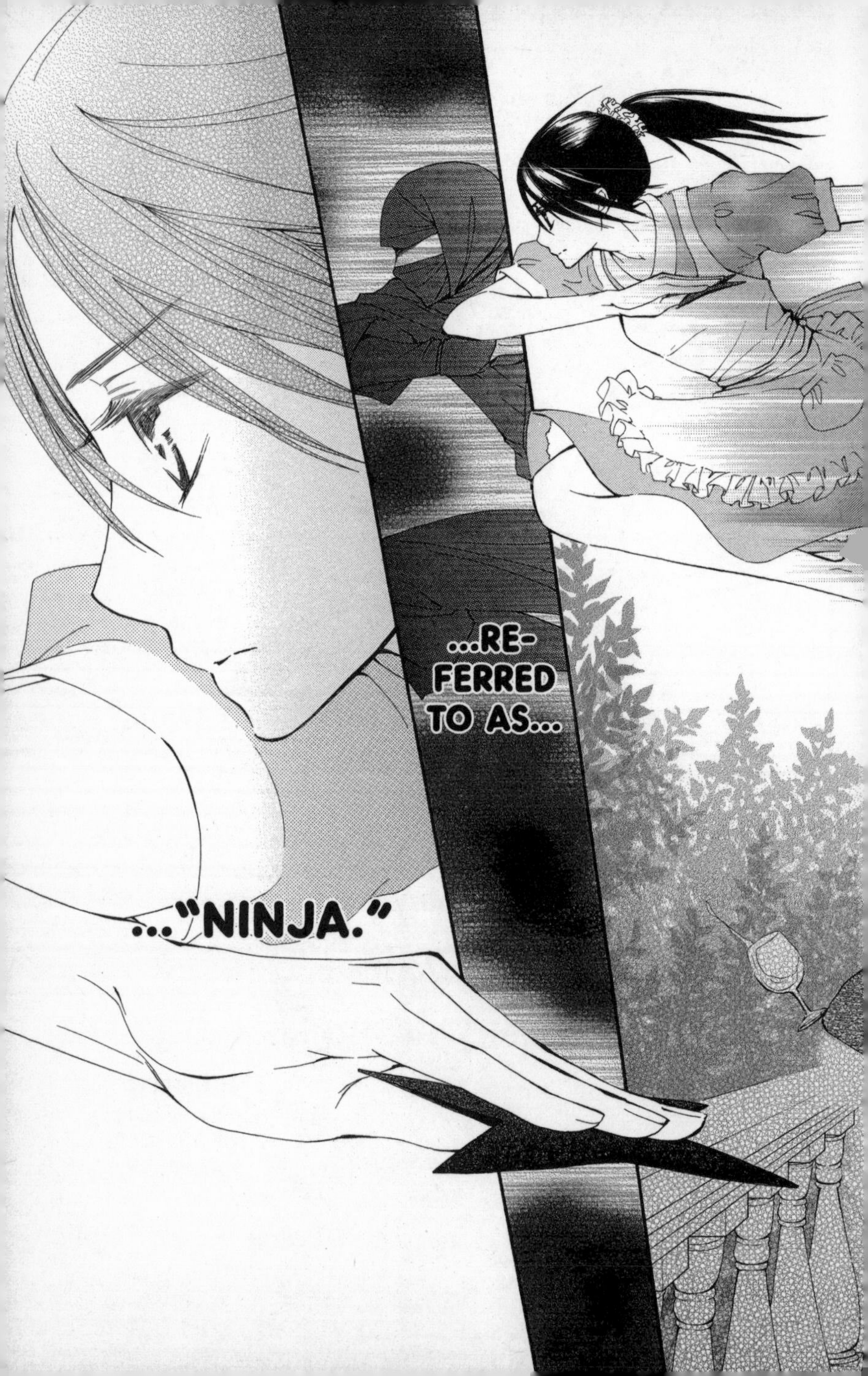
...RE-
FERRED
TO AS...
..."NINJA."

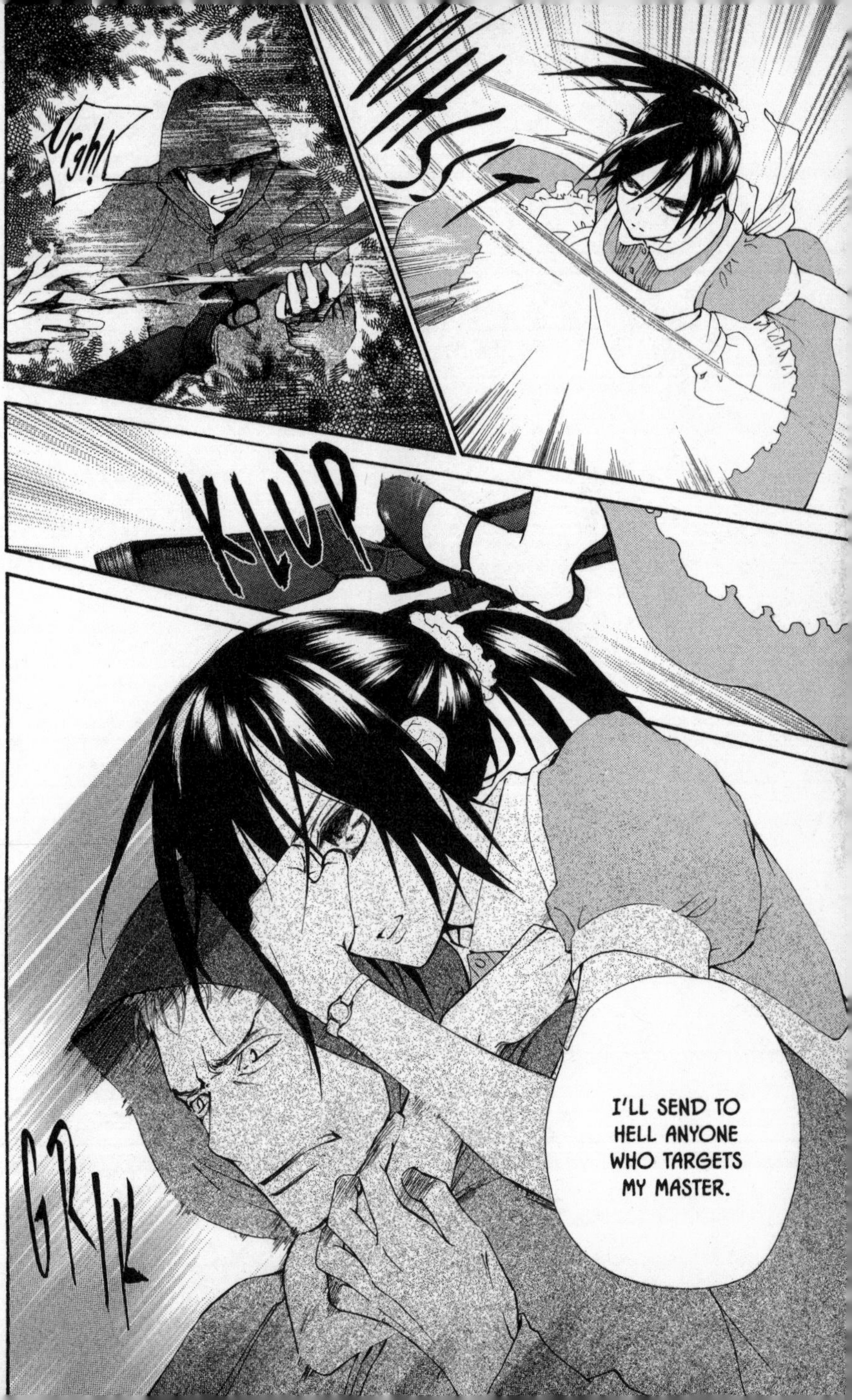
WHSST
Urgh!!
KLUP
I'LL SEND TO HELL ANYONE WHO TARGETS MY MASTER.
GRIK

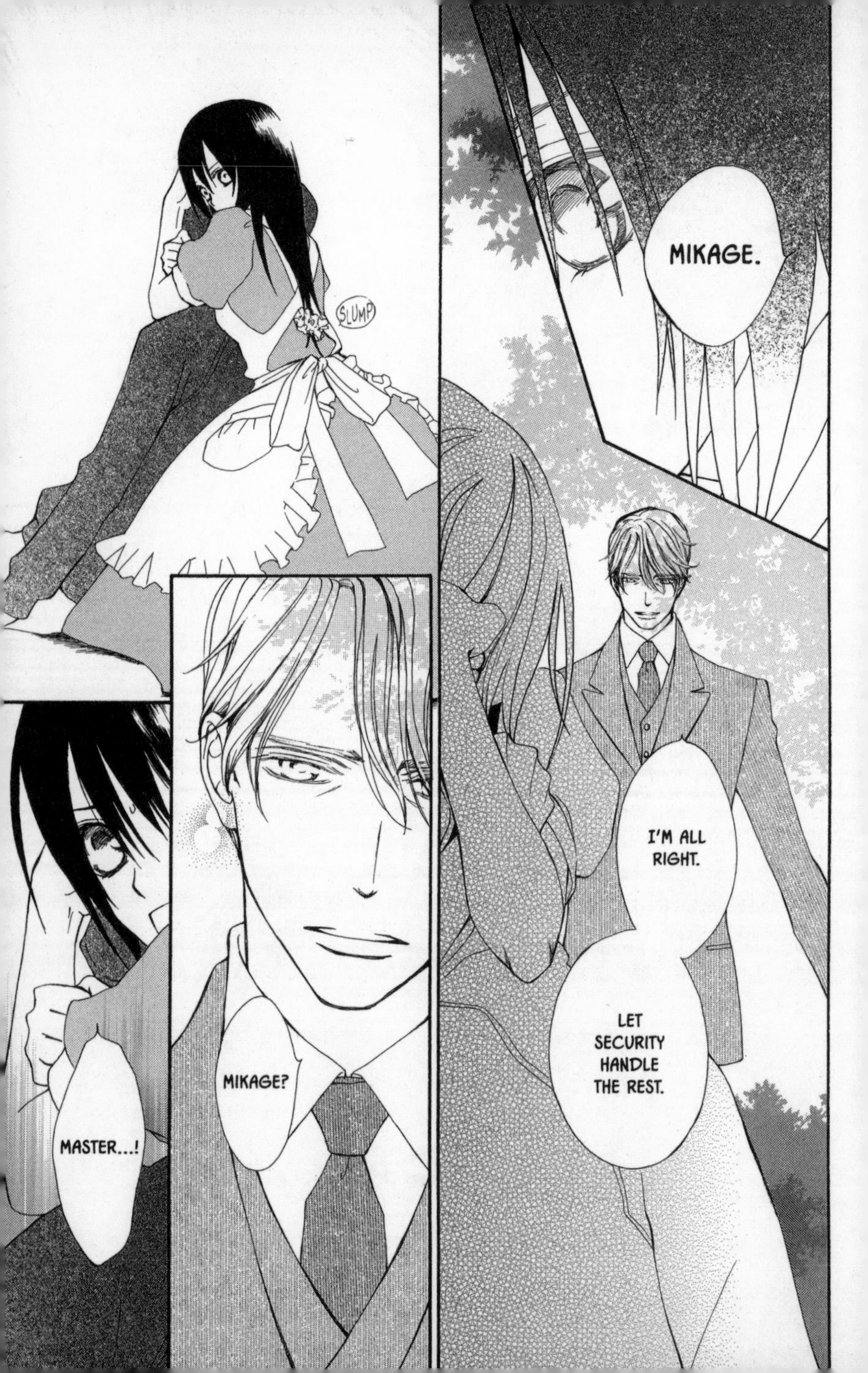
MIKAGE.
I'M ALL RIGHT.
LET SECURITY HANDLE THE REST.
SLUMP
MIKAGE?
MASTER...!

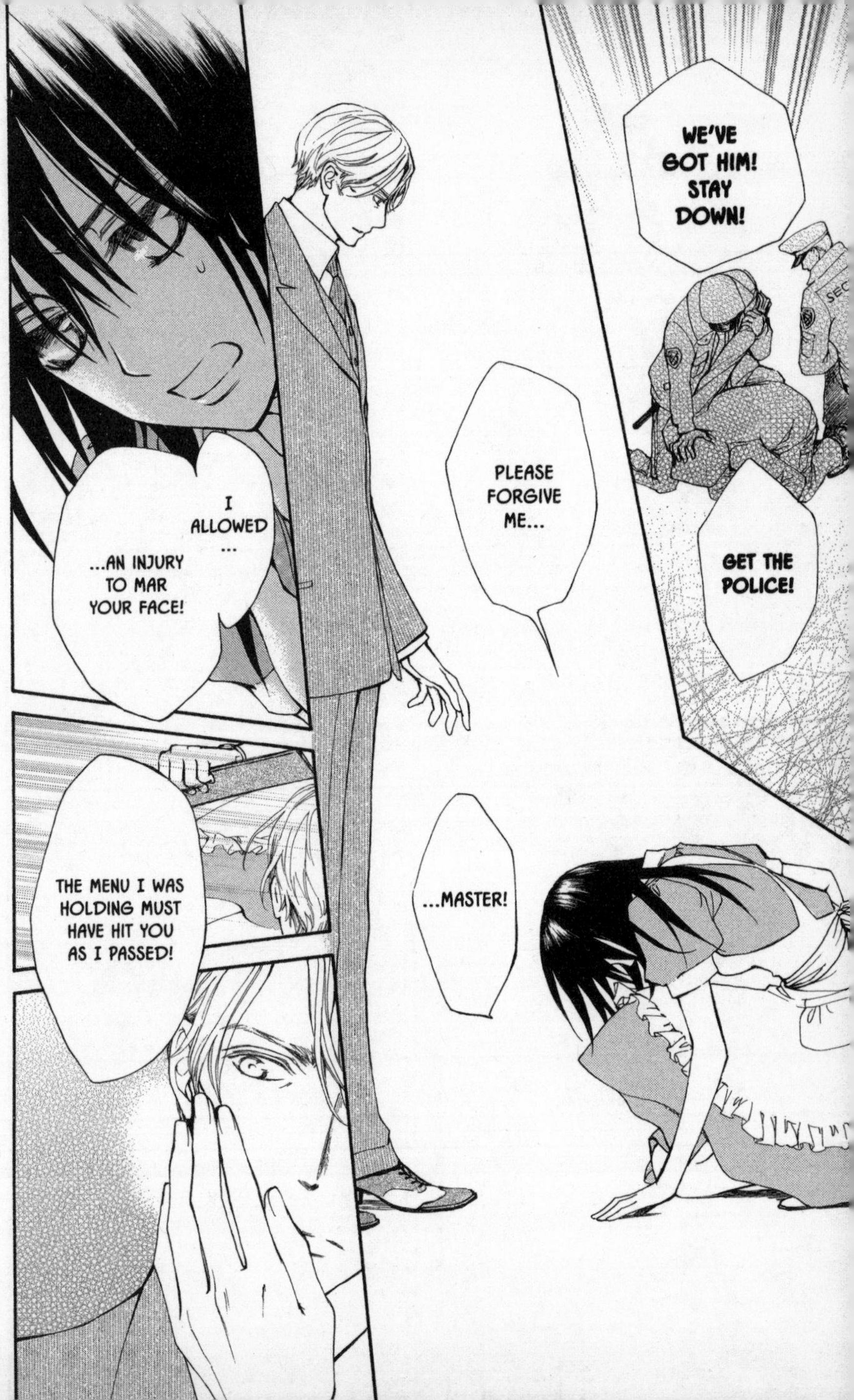
WE'VE GOT HIM! STAY DOWN!
GET THE POLICE!
PLEASE FORGIVE ME...
...MASTER!
I ALLOWED ...
...AN INJURY TO MAR YOUR FACE!
THE MENU I WAS HOLDING MUST HAVE HIT YOU AS I PASSED!

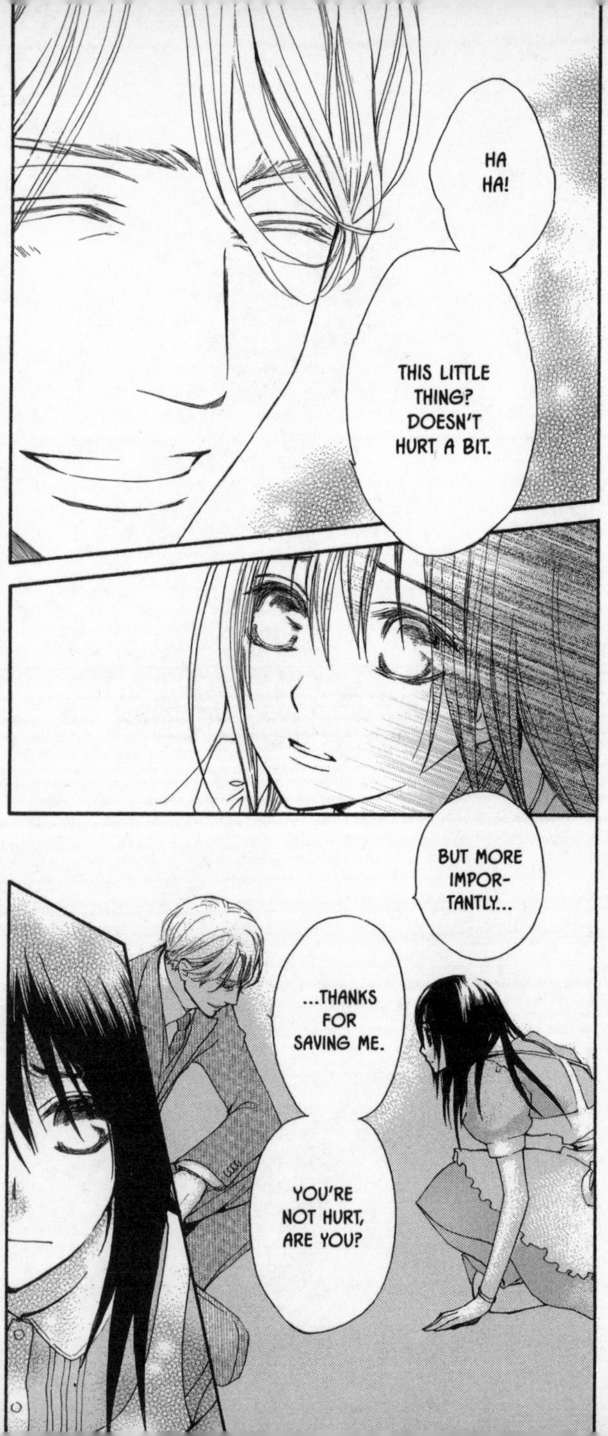
HA HA!
THIS LITTLE THING? DOESN'T HURT A BIT.
BUT MORE IMPOR-TANTLY...
...THANKS FOR SAVING ME.
YOU'RE NOT HURT, ARE YOU?

Hello to new and old readers alike. Thank you very much for picking up *Shuriken and Pleats* volume 1. What inspired me to write this manga was that I wanted to try creating a heroine who was levelheaded and cool, but also a little bit quirky. The only kind of character I could think of that'd fit the bill was...none other than a ninja. So based on the limited knowledge I possessed, Mikage was born. Being that she's a ninja, naturally I wanted the kanji for *kage*, or "shadow," in her name. [The kanji for *Mi* means "beautiful." -Ed.] And of course I also wanted her to have a master. That was where it all started. (Yes, speaking of master-slave relationships, please see my other work *Captive Hearts*. Though in this series our protagonist is a girl.) It'll be a short series, but I'll put my heart into it. I'll see you again in the second volume! I hope you have fun!

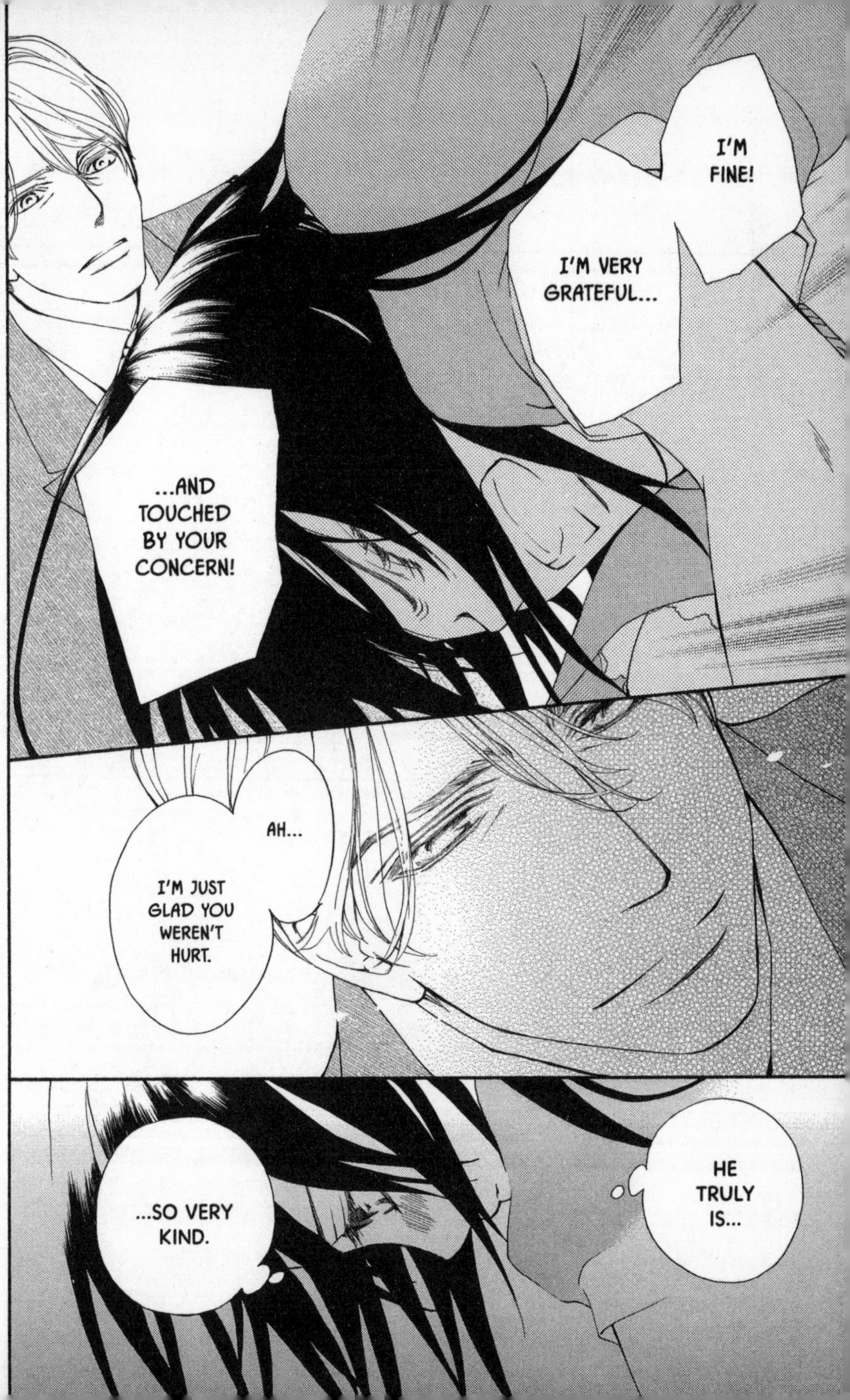
I'M FINE!
I'M VERY GRATEFUL...
...AND TOUCHED BY YOUR CONCERN!
AH...
I'M JUST GLAD YOU WEREN'T HURT.
HE TRULY IS...
...SO VERY KIND.

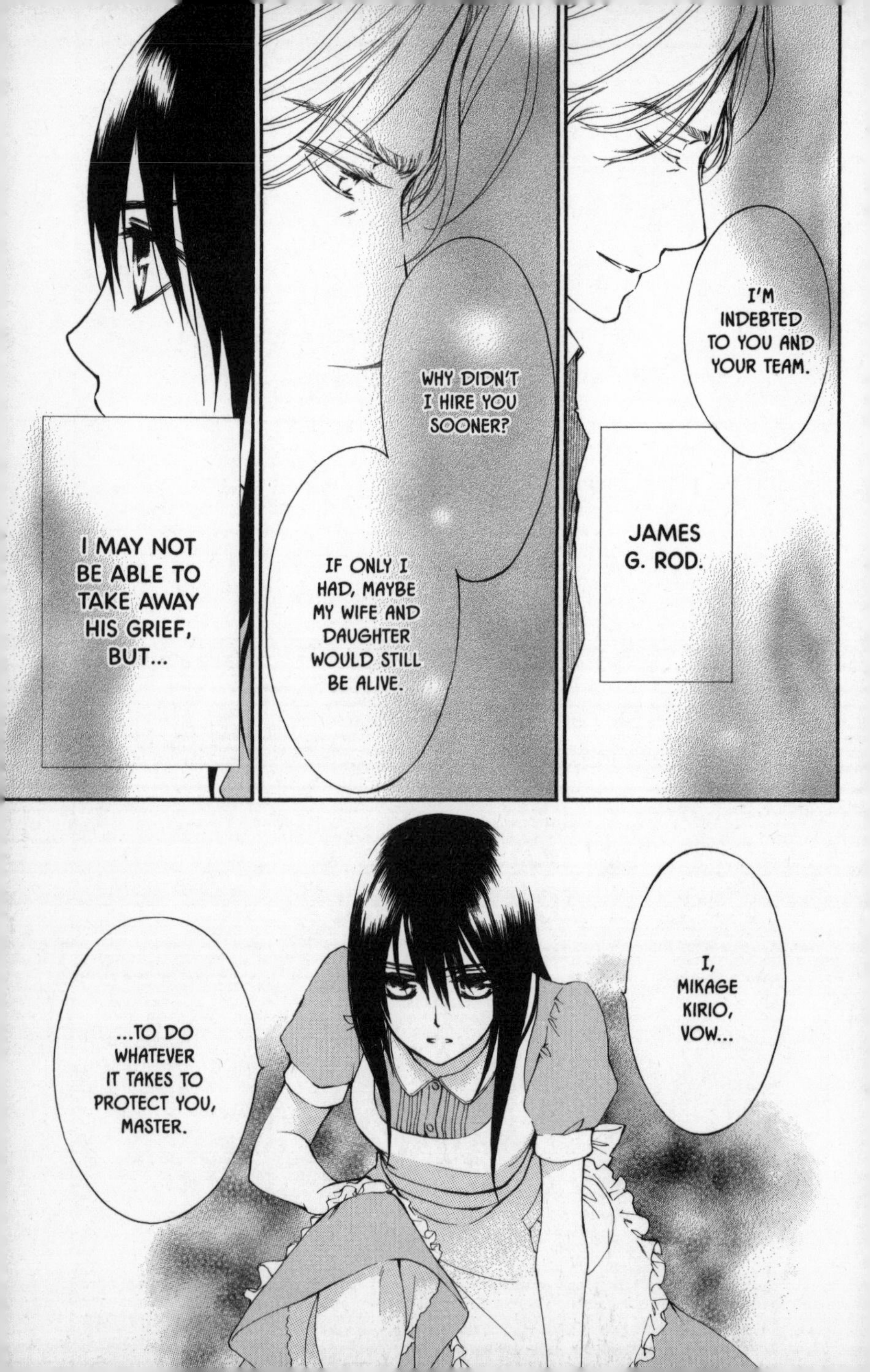
I'M INDEBTED TO YOU AND YOUR TEAM.
JAMES G. ROD.
WHY DIDN'T I HIRE YOU SOONER?
IF ONLY I HAD, MAYBE MY WIFE AND DAUGHTER WOULD STILL BE ALIVE.
I MAY NOT BE ABLE TO TAKE AWAY HIS GRIEF, BUT...
I, MIKAGE KIRIO, VOW...
...TO DO WHATEVER IT TAKES TO PROTECT YOU, MASTER.

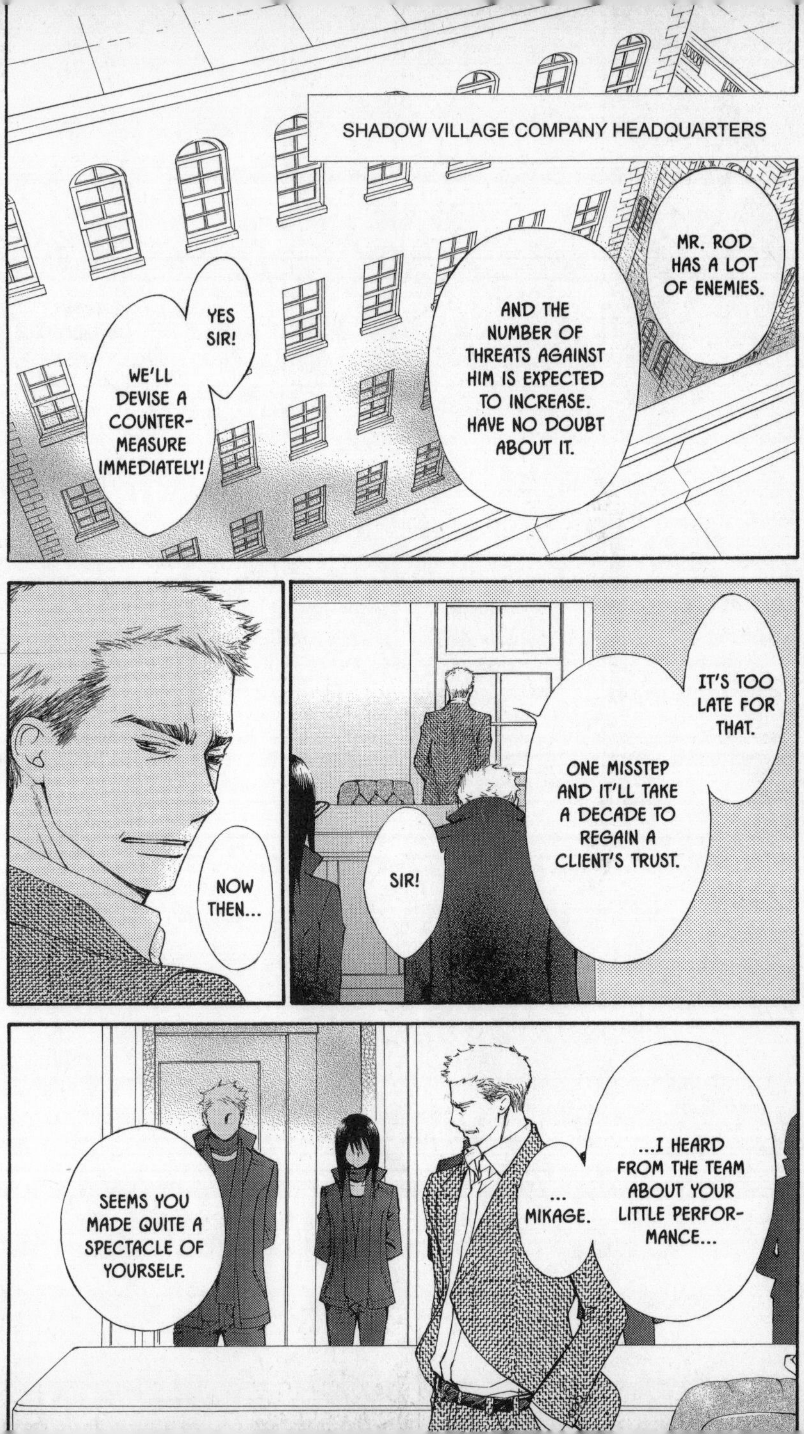
SHADOW VILLAGE COMPANY HEADQUARTERS
MR. ROD HAS A LOT OF ENEMIES.
AND THE NUMBER OF THREATS AGAINST HIM IS EXPECTED TO INCREASE. HAVE NO DOUBT ABOUT IT.
YES SIR!
WE'LL DEVISE A COUNTER-MEASURE IMMEDIATELY!
IT'S TOO LATE FOR THAT.
ONE MISSTEP AND IT'LL TAKE A DECADE TO REGAIN A CLIENT'S TRUST.
SIR!
NOW THEN...
...I HEARD FROM THE TEAM ABOUT YOUR LITTLE PERFORMANCE...
... MIKAGE.
SEEMS YOU MADE QUITE A SPECTACLE OF YOURSELF.

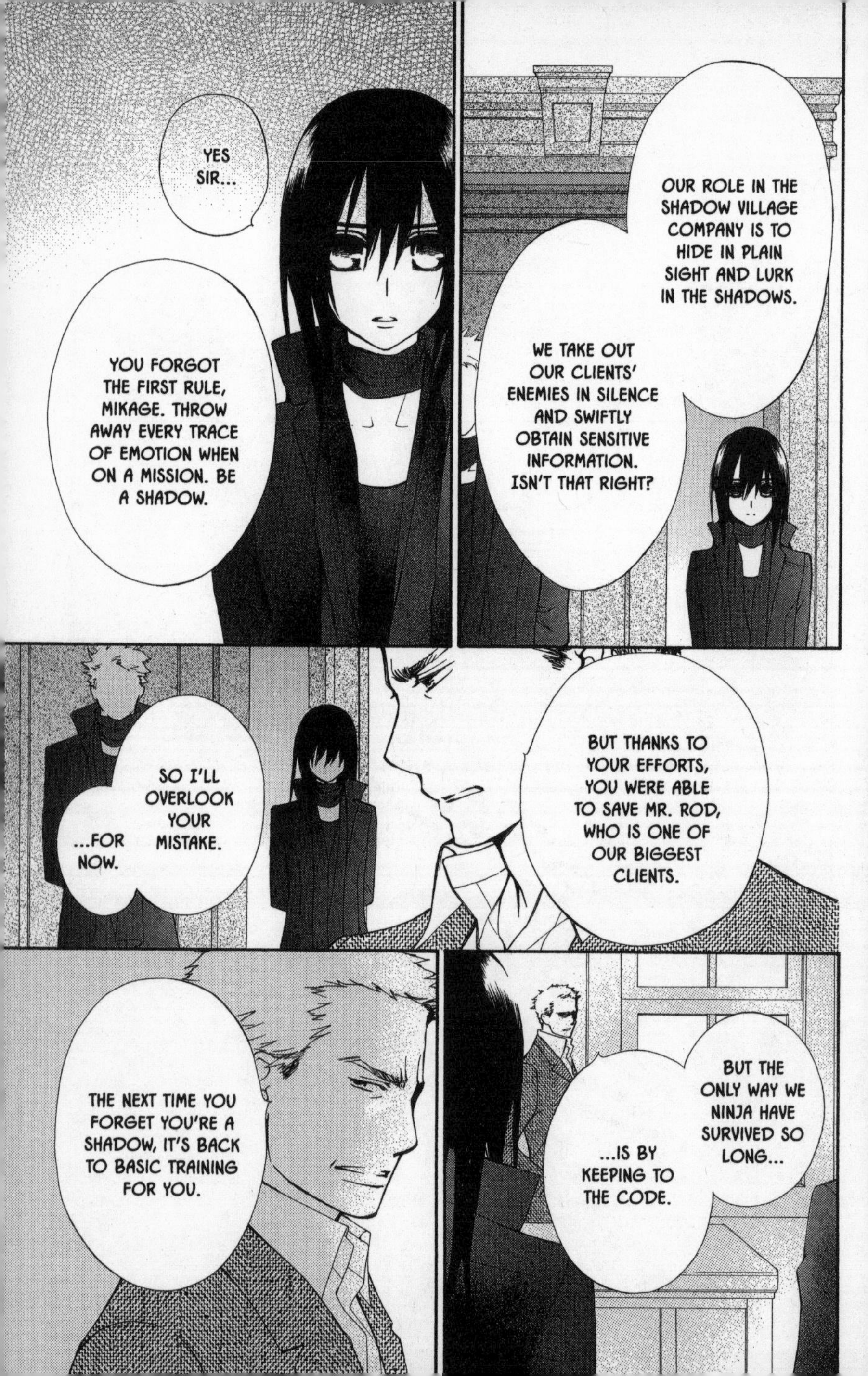
OUR ROLE IN THE SHADOW VILLAGE COMPANY IS TO HIDE IN PLAIN SIGHT AND LURK IN THE SHADOWS.
WE TAKE OUT OUR CLIENTS' ENEMIES IN SILENCE AND SWIFTLY OBTAIN SENSITIVE INFORMATION. ISN'T THAT RIGHT?
YES SIR...
YOU FORGOT THE FIRST RULE, MIKAGE. THROW AWAY EVERY TRACE OF EMOTION WHEN ON A MISSION. BE A SHADOW.
BUT THANKS TO YOUR EFFORTS, YOU WERE ABLE TO SAVE MR. ROD, WHO IS ONE OF OUR BIGGEST CLIENTS.
SO I'LL OVERLOOK YOUR MISTAKE.
...FOR NOW.
BUT THE ONLY WAY WE NINJA HAVE SURVIVED SO LONG...
...IS BY KEEPING TO THE CODE.
THE NEXT TIME YOU FORGET YOU'RE A SHADOW, IT'S BACK TO BASIC TRAINING FOR YOU.

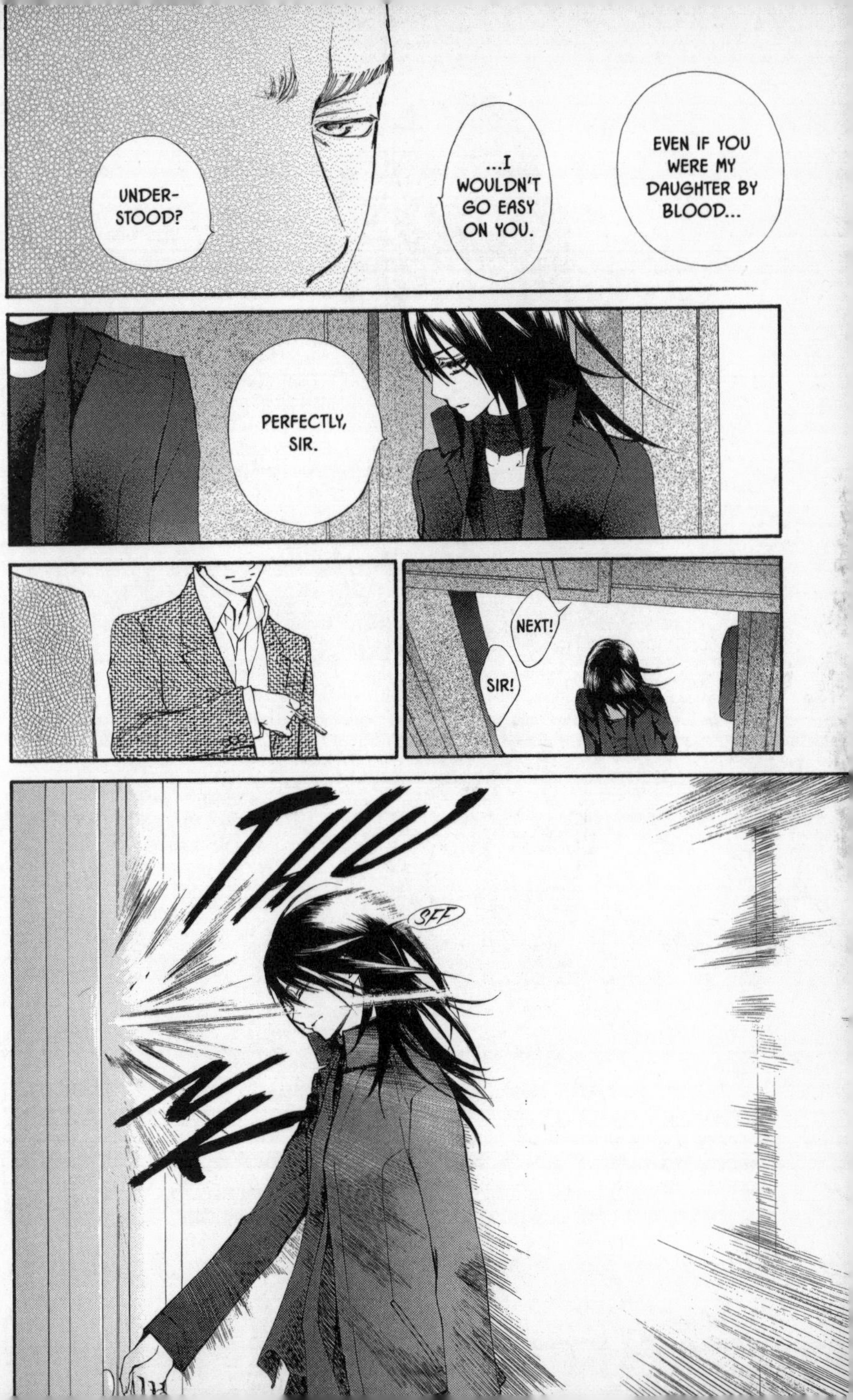
EVEN IF YOU WERE MY DAUGHTER BY BLOOD...
...I WOULDN'T GO EASY ON YOU.
UNDER-STOOD?
PERFECTLY, SIR.
NEXT!
SIR!
SFF
THUNK

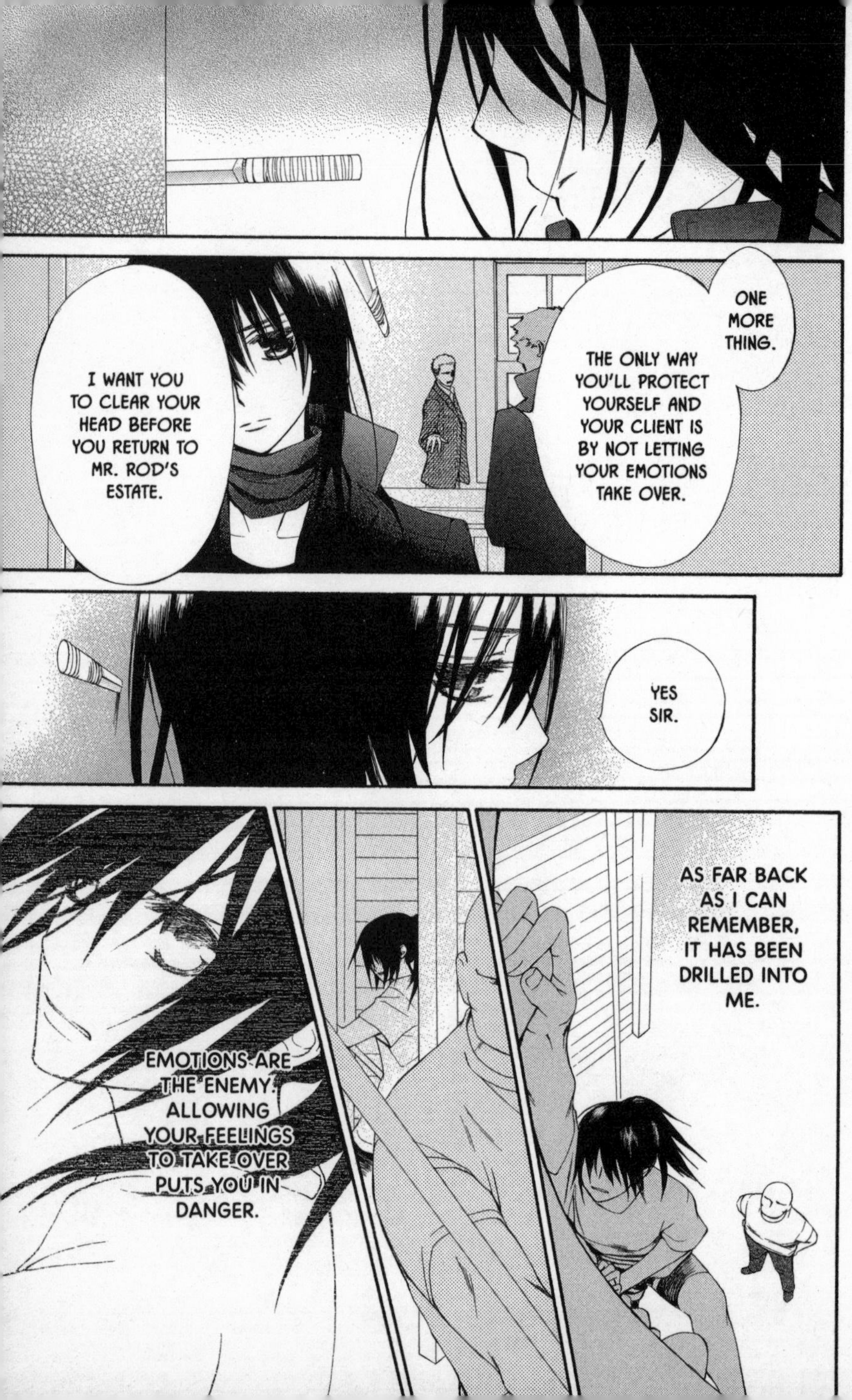
ONE MORE THING.
THE ONLY WAY YOU'LL PROTECT YOURSELF AND YOUR CLIENT IS BY NOT LETTING YOUR EMOTIONS TAKE OVER.
I WANT YOU TO CLEAR YOUR HEAD BEFORE YOU RETURN TO MR. ROD'S ESTATE.
YES SIR.
AS FAR BACK AS I CAN REMEMBER, IT HAS BEEN DRILLED INTO ME.
EMOTIONS ARE THE ENEMY. ALLOWING YOUR FEELINGS TO TAKE OVER PUTS YOU IN DANGER.

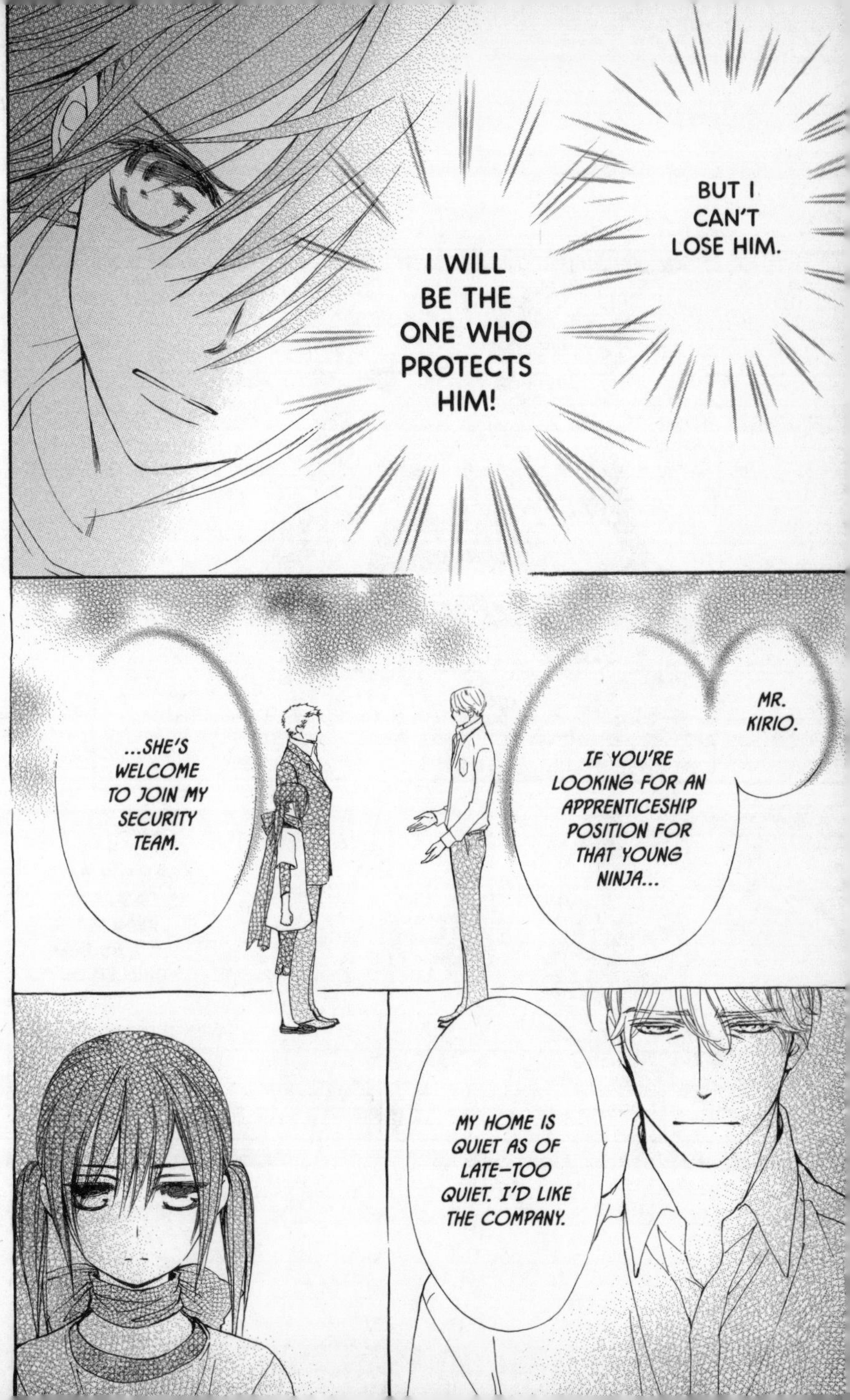
BUT I CAN'T LOSE HIM.
I WILL BE THE ONE WHO PROTECTS HIM!
MR. KIRIO.
IF YOU'RE LOOKING FOR AN APPRENTICESHIP POSITION FOR THAT YOUNG NINJA...
...SHE'S WELCOME TO JOIN MY SECURITY TEAM.
MY HOME IS QUIET AS OF LATE—TOO QUIET. I'D LIKE THE COMPANY.

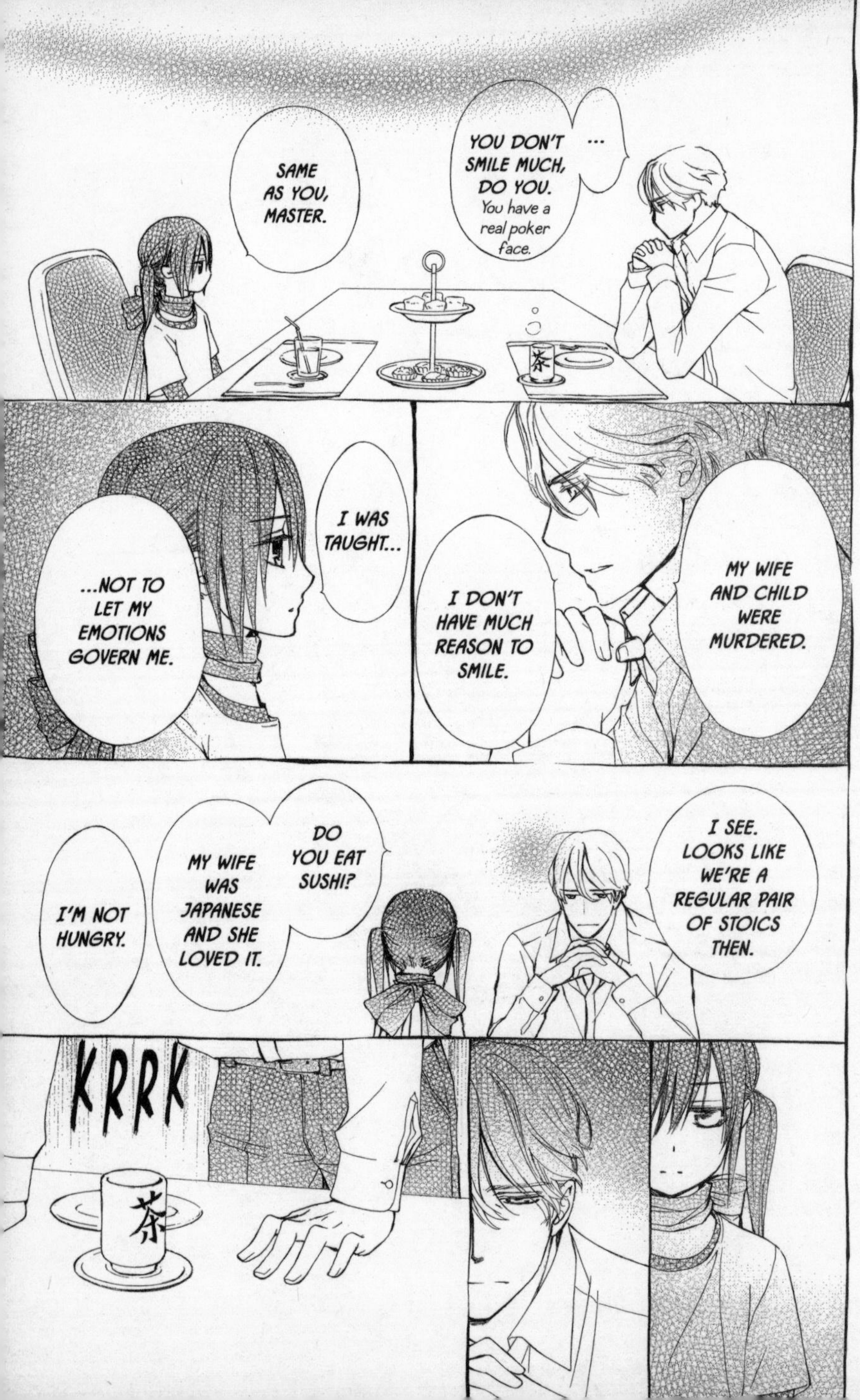
...
YOU DON'T SMILE MUCH, DO YOU. You have a real poker face.
SAME AS YOU, MASTER.
MY WIFE AND CHILD WERE MURDERED.
I DON'T HAVE MUCH REASON TO SMILE.
I WAS TAUGHT...
...NOT TO LET MY EMOTIONS GOVERN ME.
I SEE. LOOKS LIKE WE'RE A REGULAR PAIR OF STOICS THEN.
DO YOU EAT SUSHI?
MY WIFE WAS JAPANESE AND SHE LOVED IT.
I'M NOT HUNGRY.
KRRK

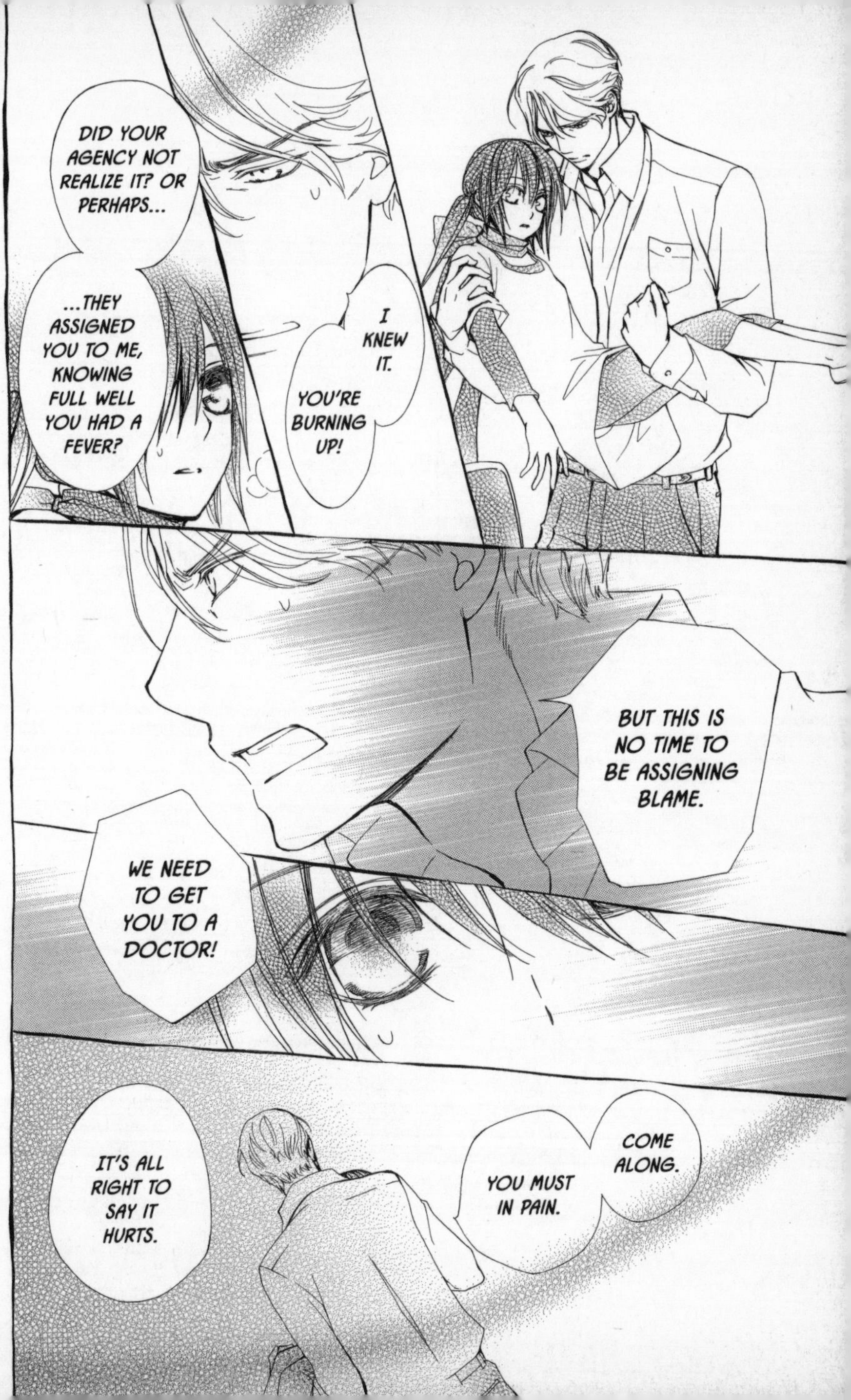
I KNEW IT.
YOU'RE BURNING UP!
DID YOUR AGENCY NOT REALIZE IT? OR PERHAPS...
...THEY ASSIGNED YOU TO ME, KNOWING FULL WELL YOU HAD A FEVER?
BUT THIS IS NO TIME TO BE ASSIGNING BLAME.
WE NEED TO GET YOU TO A DOCTOR!
COME ALONG.
YOU MUST IN PAIN.
IT'S ALL RIGHT TO SAY IT HURTS.

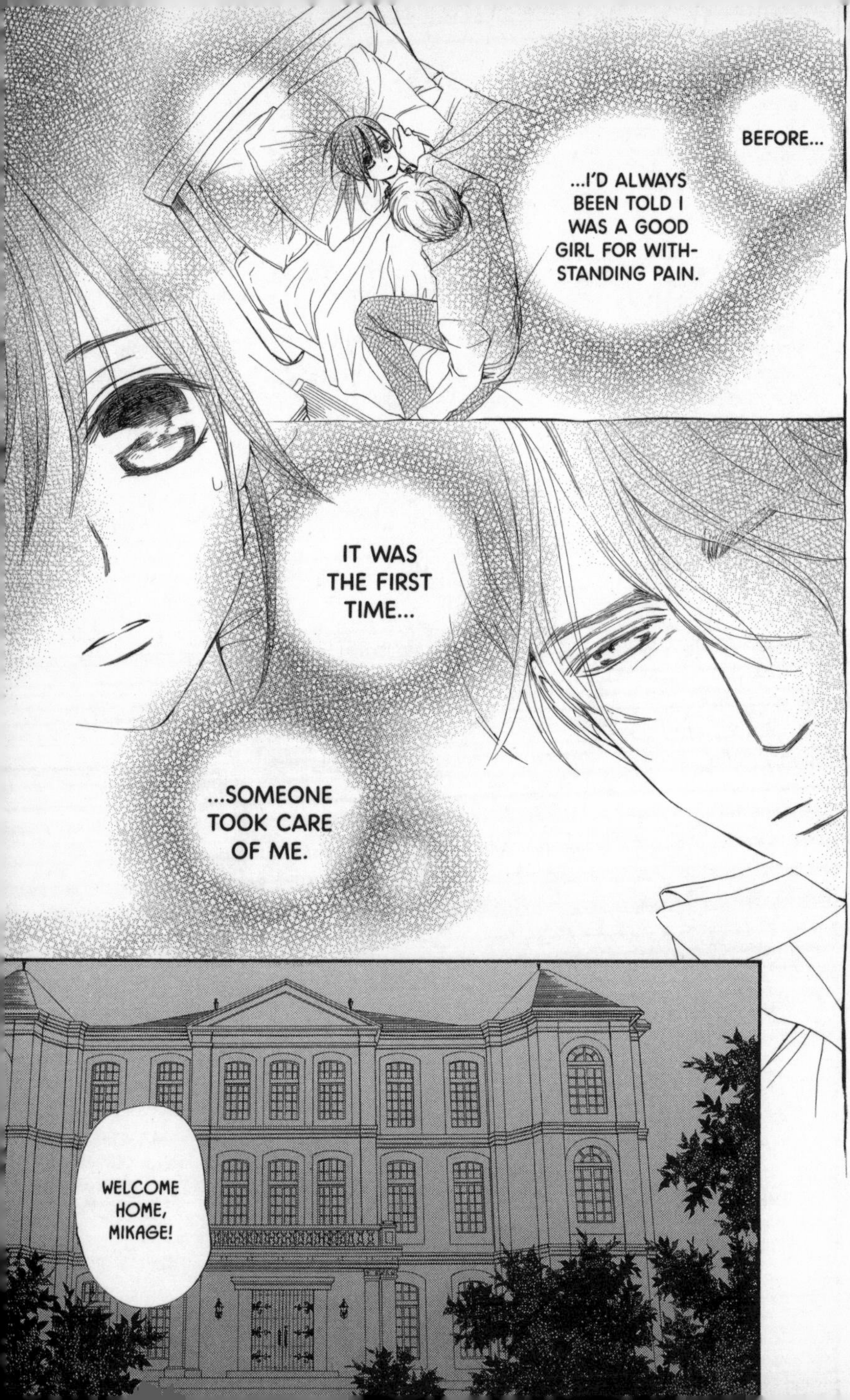
BEFORE...
...I'D ALWAYS BEEN TOLD I WAS A GOOD GIRL FOR WITH-STANDING PAIN.
IT WAS THE FIRST TIME...
...SOMEONE TOOK CARE OF ME.
WELCOME HOME, MIKAGE!

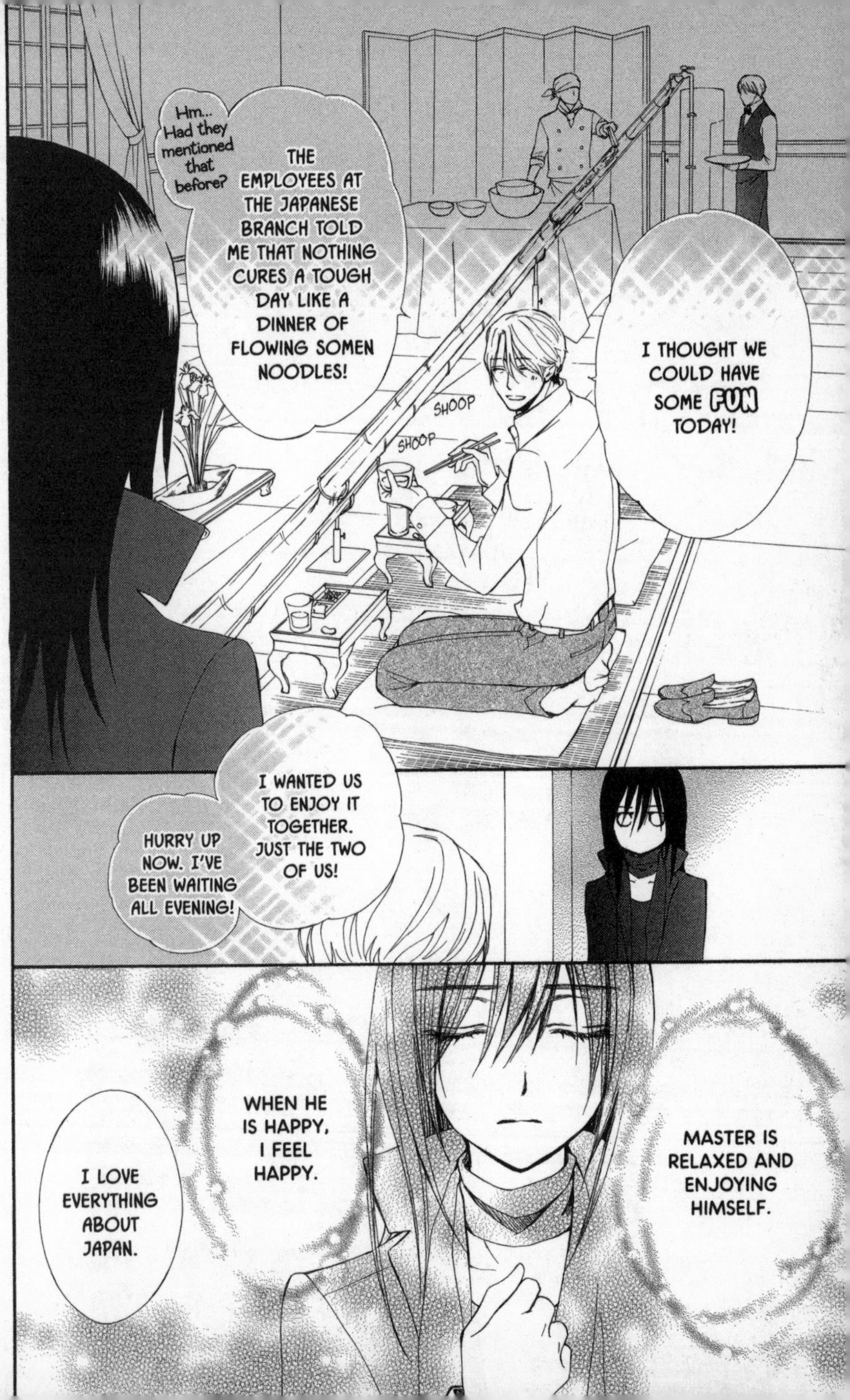
THE EMPLOYEES AT THE JAPANESE BRANCH TOLD ME THAT NOTHING CURES A TOUGH DAY LIKE A DINNER OF FLOWING SOMEN NOODLES!
Hm... Had they mentioned that before?
I THOUGHT WE COULD HAVE SOME FUN TODAY!
SHOOP
SHOOP
I WANTED US TO ENJOY IT TOGETHER. JUST THE TWO OF US!
HURRY UP NOW. I'VE BEEN WAITING ALL EVENING!
MASTER IS RELAXED AND ENJOYING HIMSELF.
WHEN HE IS HAPPY, I FEEL HAPPY.
I LOVE EVERYTHING ABOUT JAPAN.

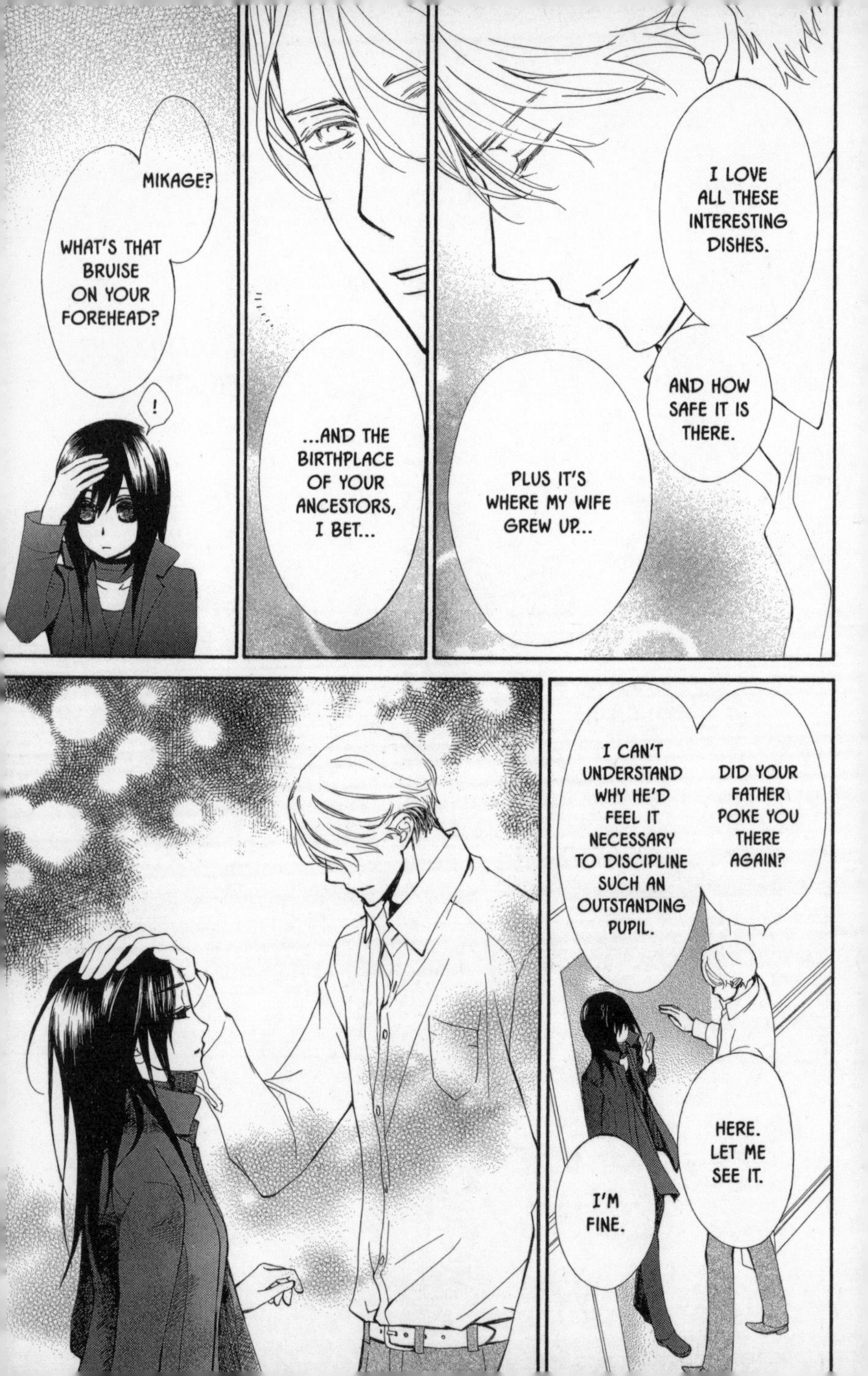
I LOVE ALL THESE INTERESTING DISHES.
AND HOW SAFE IT IS THERE.
PLUS IT'S WHERE MY WIFE GREW UP...
...AND THE BIRTHPLACE OF YOUR ANCESTORS, I BET...
MIKAGE?
WHAT'S THAT BRUISE ON YOUR FOREHEAD?
!
DID YOUR FATHER POKE YOU THERE AGAIN?
I CAN'T UNDERSTAND WHY HE'D FEEL IT NECESSARY TO DISCIPLINE SUCH AN OUTSTANDING PUPIL.
HERE. LET ME SEE IT.
I'M FINE.

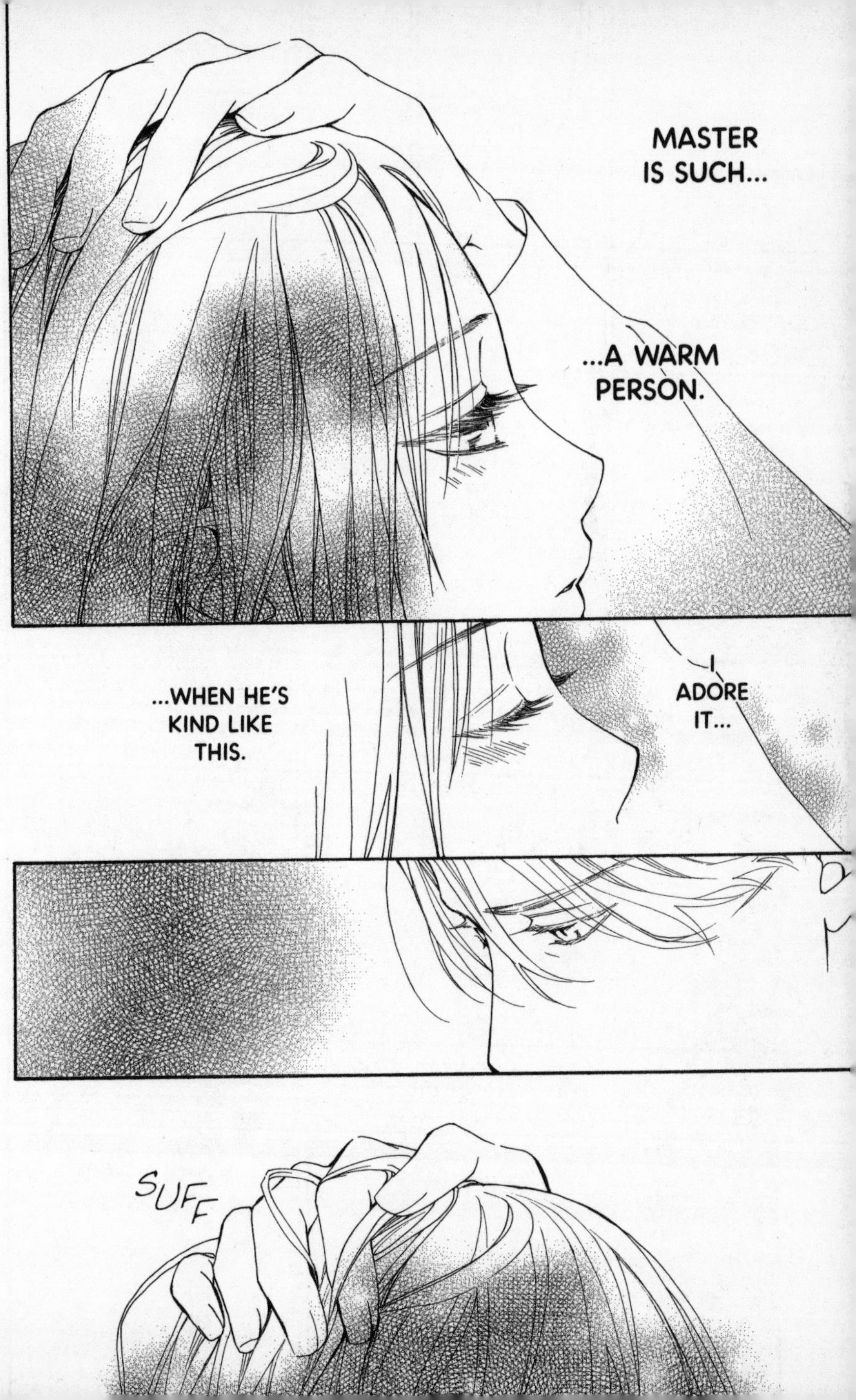
MASTER IS SUCH...
...A WARM PERSON.
I ADORE IT...
...WHEN HE'S KIND LIKE THIS.
SUFF

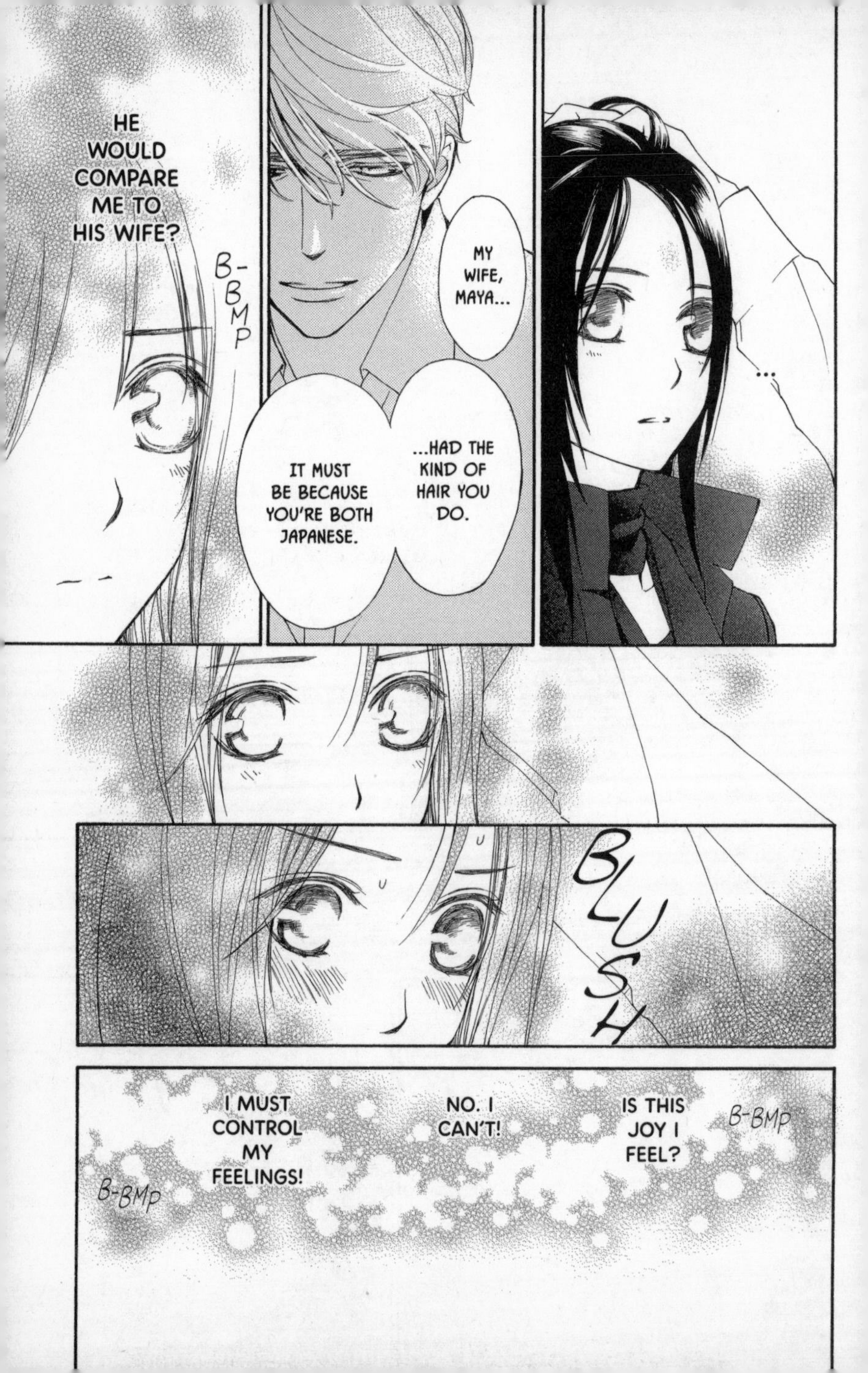
...
MY WIFE, MAYA...
...HAD THE KIND OF HAIR YOU DO.
IT MUST BE BECAUSE YOU'RE BOTH JAPANESE.
HE WOULD COMPARE ME TO HIS WIFE?
B-BMP
BLUSH
B-BMP
IS THIS JOY I FEEL?
NO. I CAN'T!
I MUST CONTROL MY FEELINGS!
B-BMP

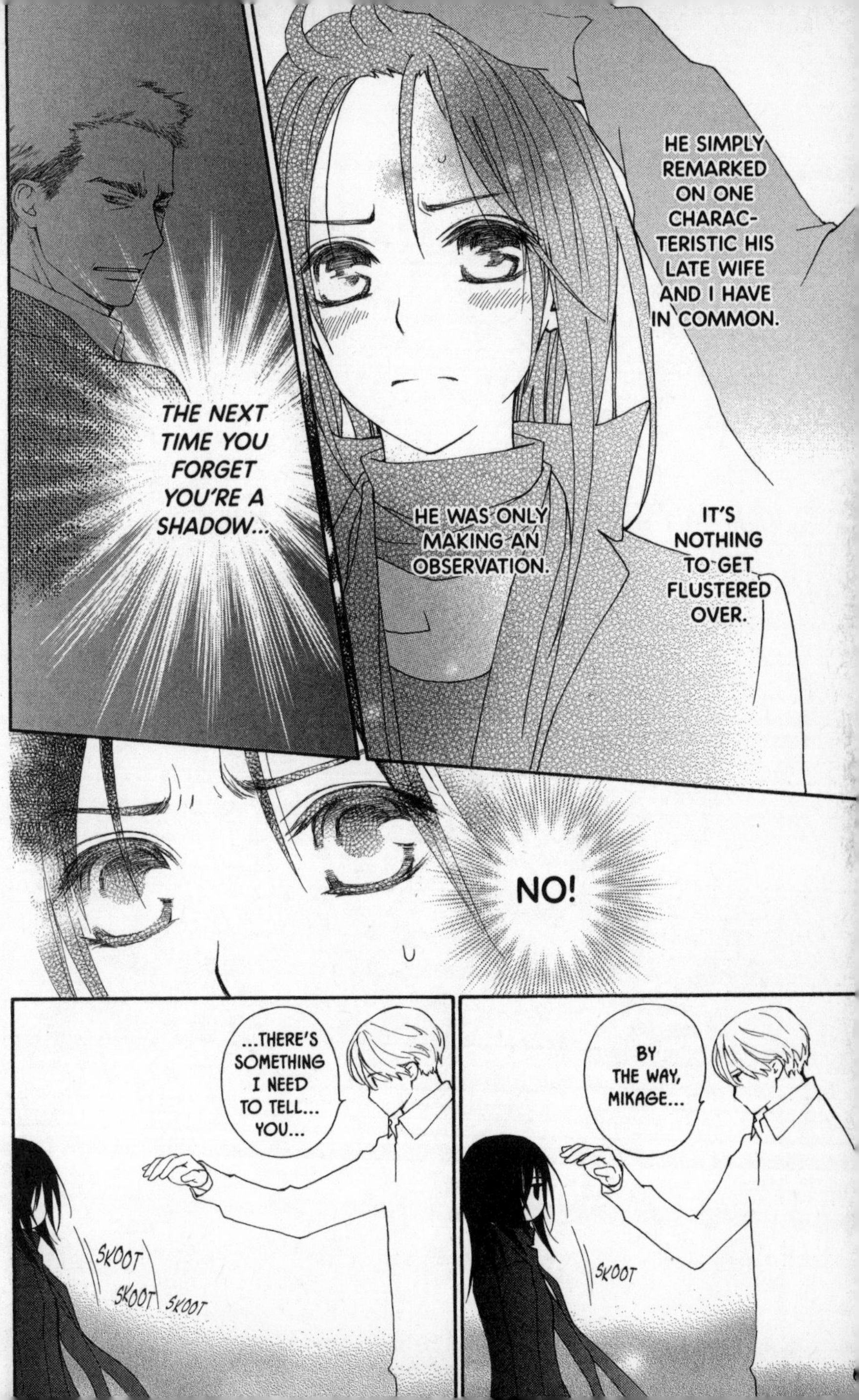
HE SIMPLY REMARKED ON ONE CHARAC-TERISTIC HIS LATE WIFE AND I HAVE IN COMMON.
IT'S NOTHING TO GET FLUSTERED OVER.
HE WAS ONLY MAKING AN OBSERVATION.
THE NEXT TIME YOU FORGET YOU'RE A SHADOW...
NO!
BY THE WAY, MIKAGE...
SKOOT
...THERE'S SOMETHING I NEED TO TELL... YOU...
SKOOT
SKOOT
SKOOT

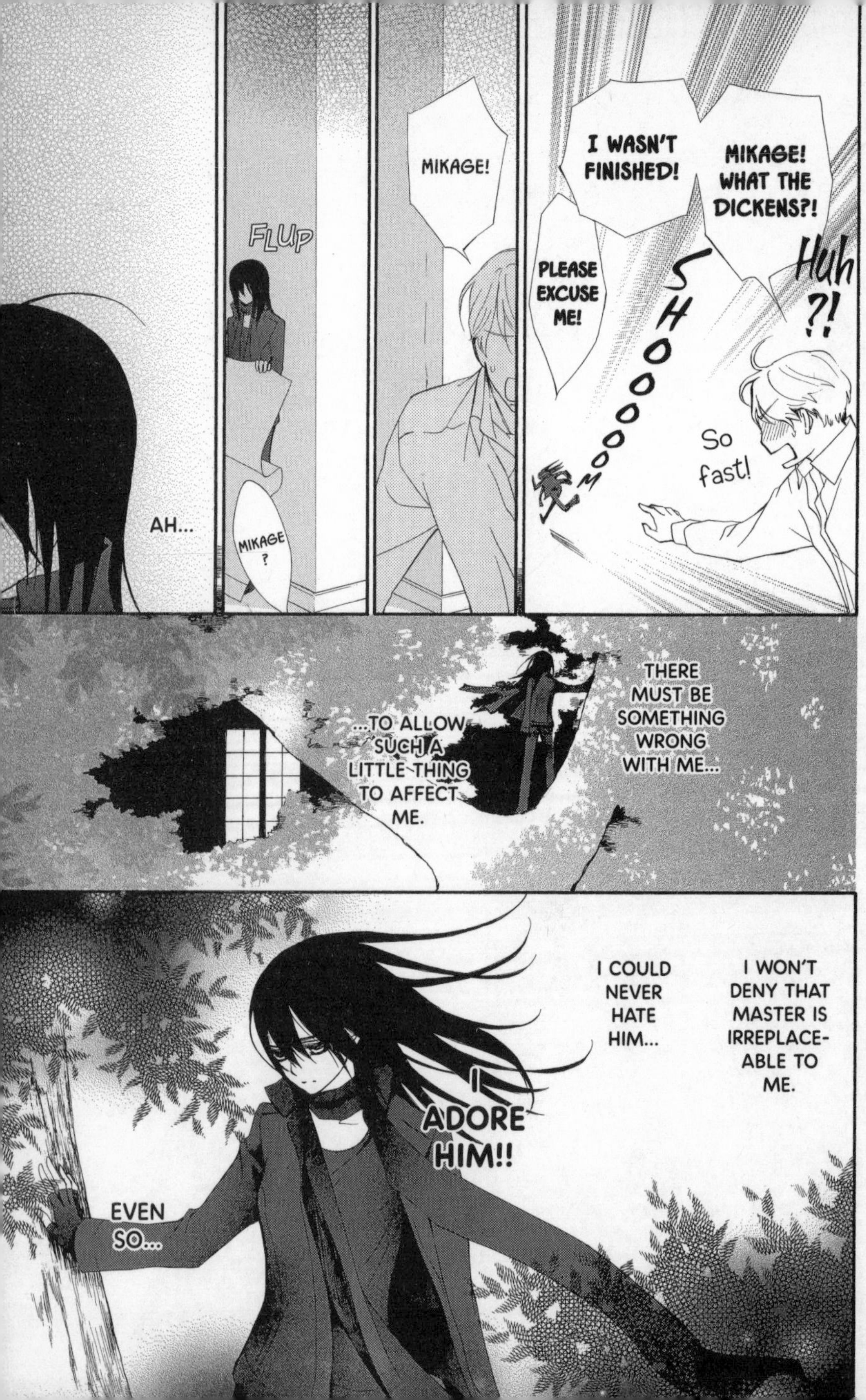
MIKAGE! WHAT THE DICKENS?!
I WASN'T FINISHED!
Huh ?!
PLEASE EXCUSE ME!
SHOOOOOOM
So fast!
MIKAGE!
FLUP
MIKAGE ?
AH...
THERE MUST BE SOMETHING WRONG WITH ME...
...TO ALLOW SUCH A LITTLE THING TO AFFECT ME.
I WON'T DENY THAT MASTER IS IRREPLACE-ABLE TO ME.
I COULD NEVER HATE HIM...
I ADORE HIM!!
EVEN SO...

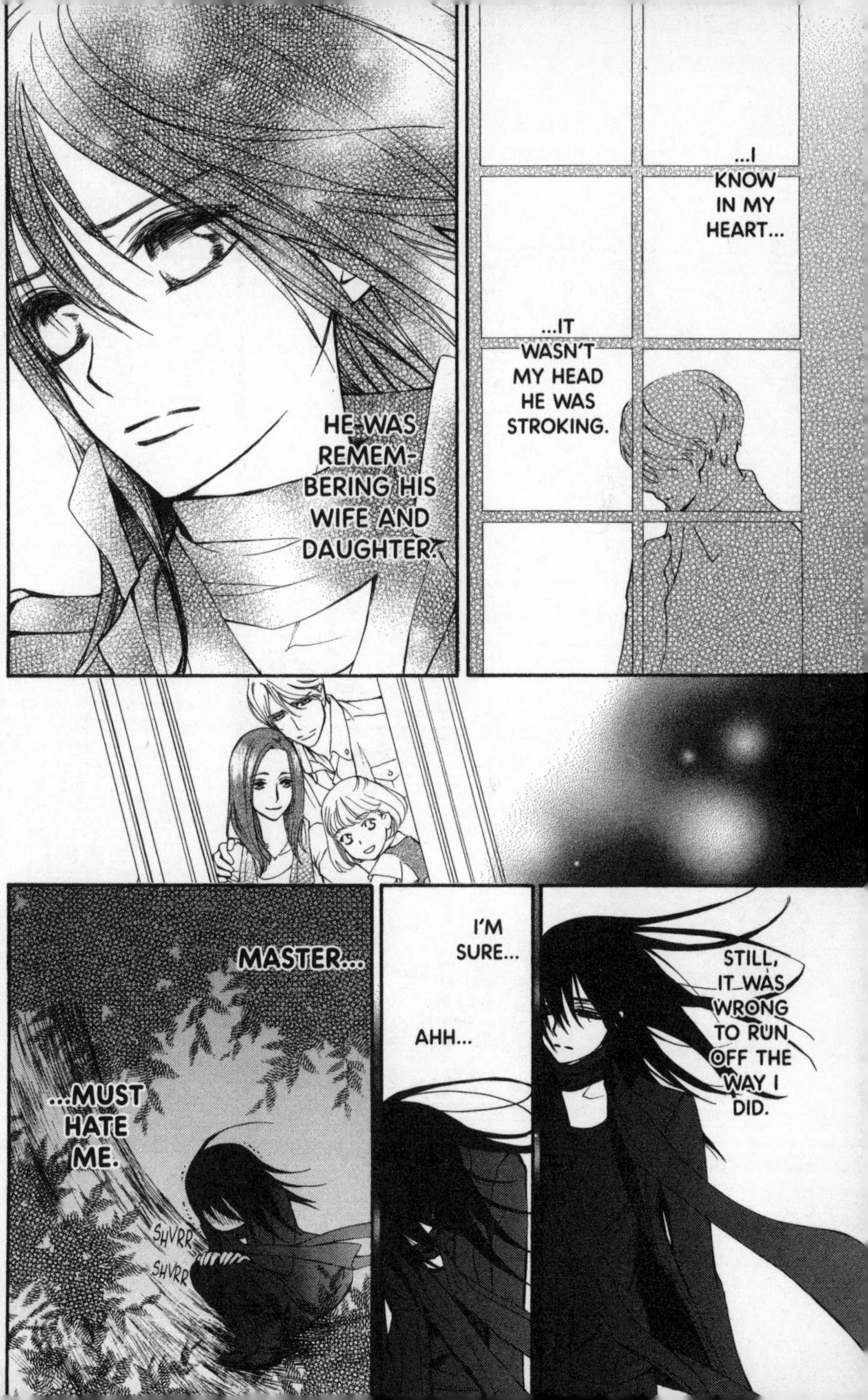
...I KNOW IN MY HEART...
...IT WASN'T MY HEAD HE WAS STROKING.
HE WAS REMEMBERING HIS WIFE AND DAUGHTER.
STILL, IT WAS WRONG TO RUN OFF THE WAY I DID.
I'M SURE...
AHH...
MASTER...
...MUST HATE ME.
SHVRR
SHVRR

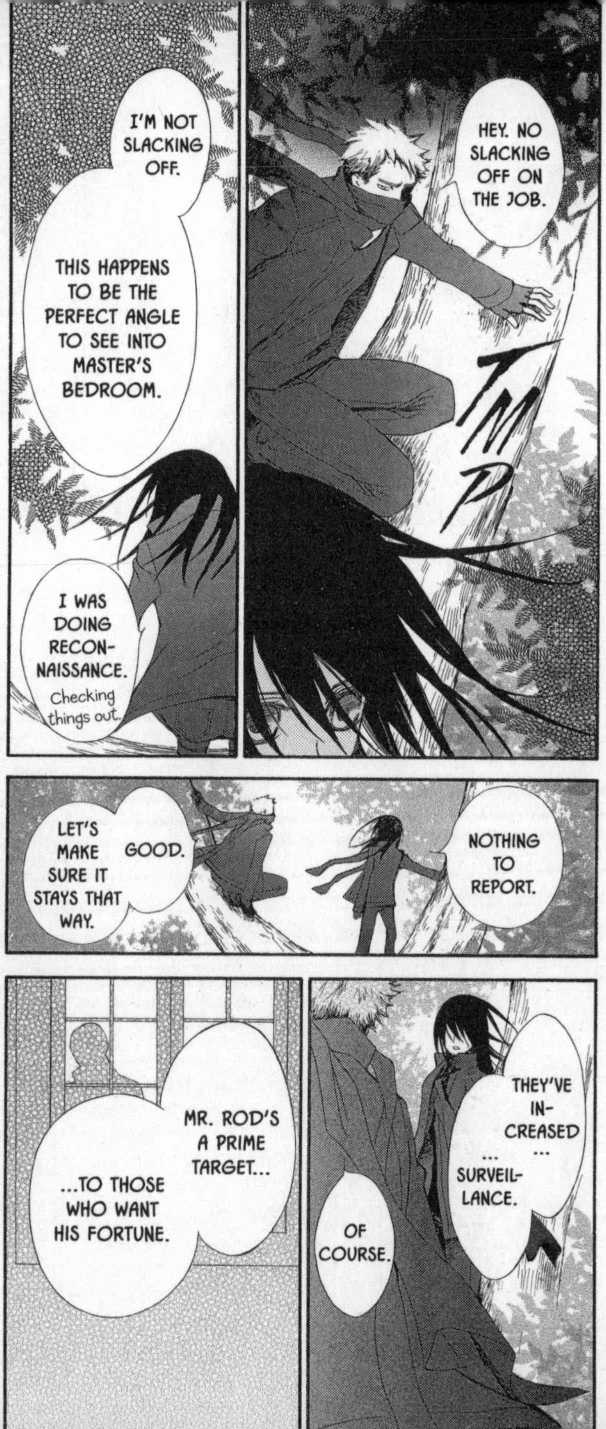
HEY. NO SLACKING OFF ON THE JOB.
TMP
I'M NOT SLACKING OFF.
THIS HAPPENS TO BE THE PERFECT ANGLE TO SEE INTO MASTER'S BEDROOM.
I WAS DOING RECONNAISSANCE. Checking things out.
NOTHING TO REPORT.
GOOD.
LET'S MAKE SURE IT STAYS THAT WAY.
THEY'VE INCREASED... ...SURVEILLANCE.
OF COURSE.
MR. ROD'S A PRIME TARGET...
...TO THOSE WHO WANT HIS FORTUNE.

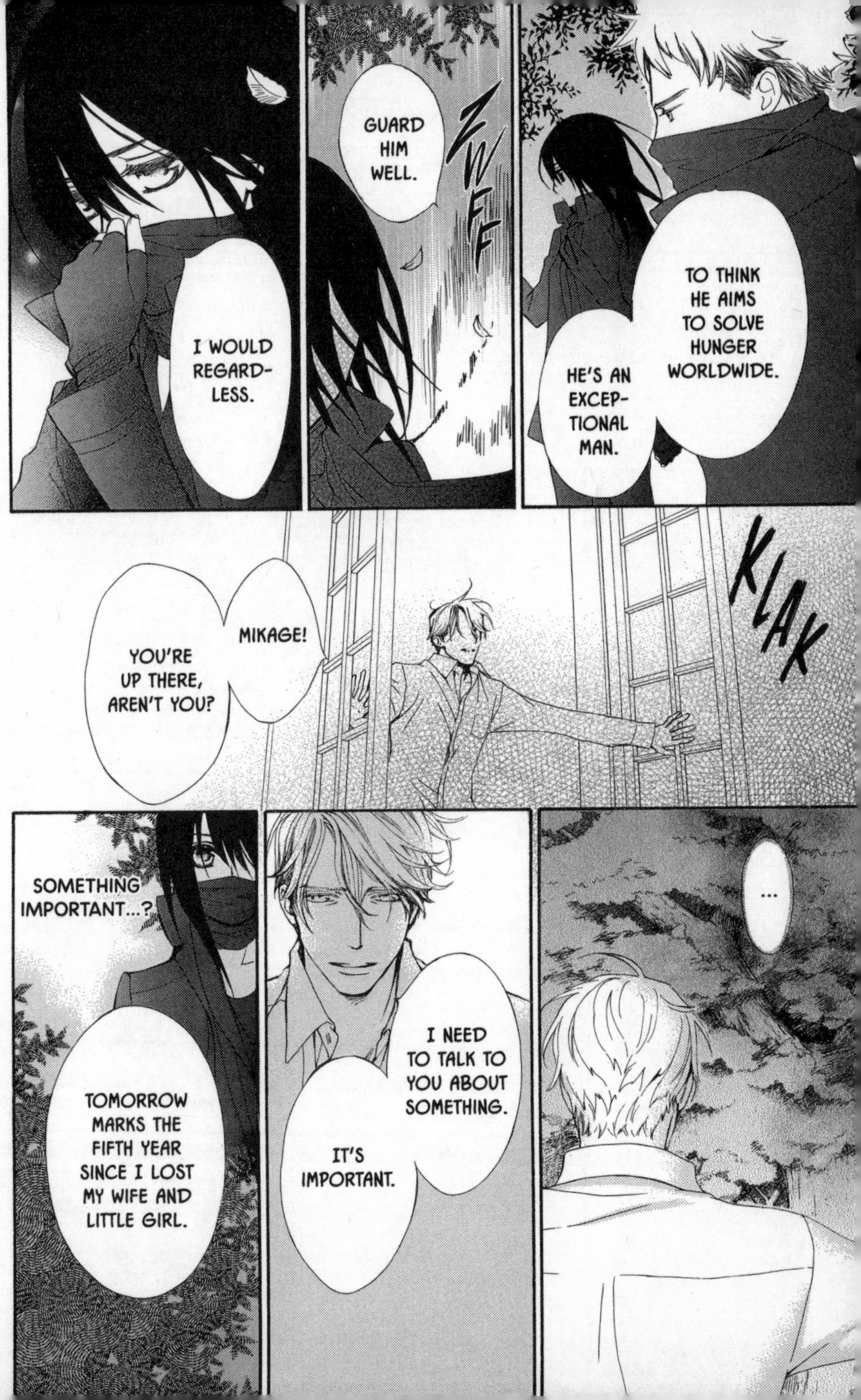
TO THINK HE AIMS TO SOLVE HUNGER WORLDWIDE.
HE'S AN EXCEPTIONAL MAN.
GUARD HIM WELL.
ZWFF
I WOULD REGARDLESS.
KLAK
MIKAGE!
YOU'RE UP THERE, AREN'T YOU?
...
I NEED TO TALK TO YOU ABOUT SOMETHING.
IT'S IMPORTANT.
SOMETHING IMPORTANT...?
TOMORROW MARKS THE FIFTH YEAR SINCE I LOST MY WIFE AND LITTLE GIRL.

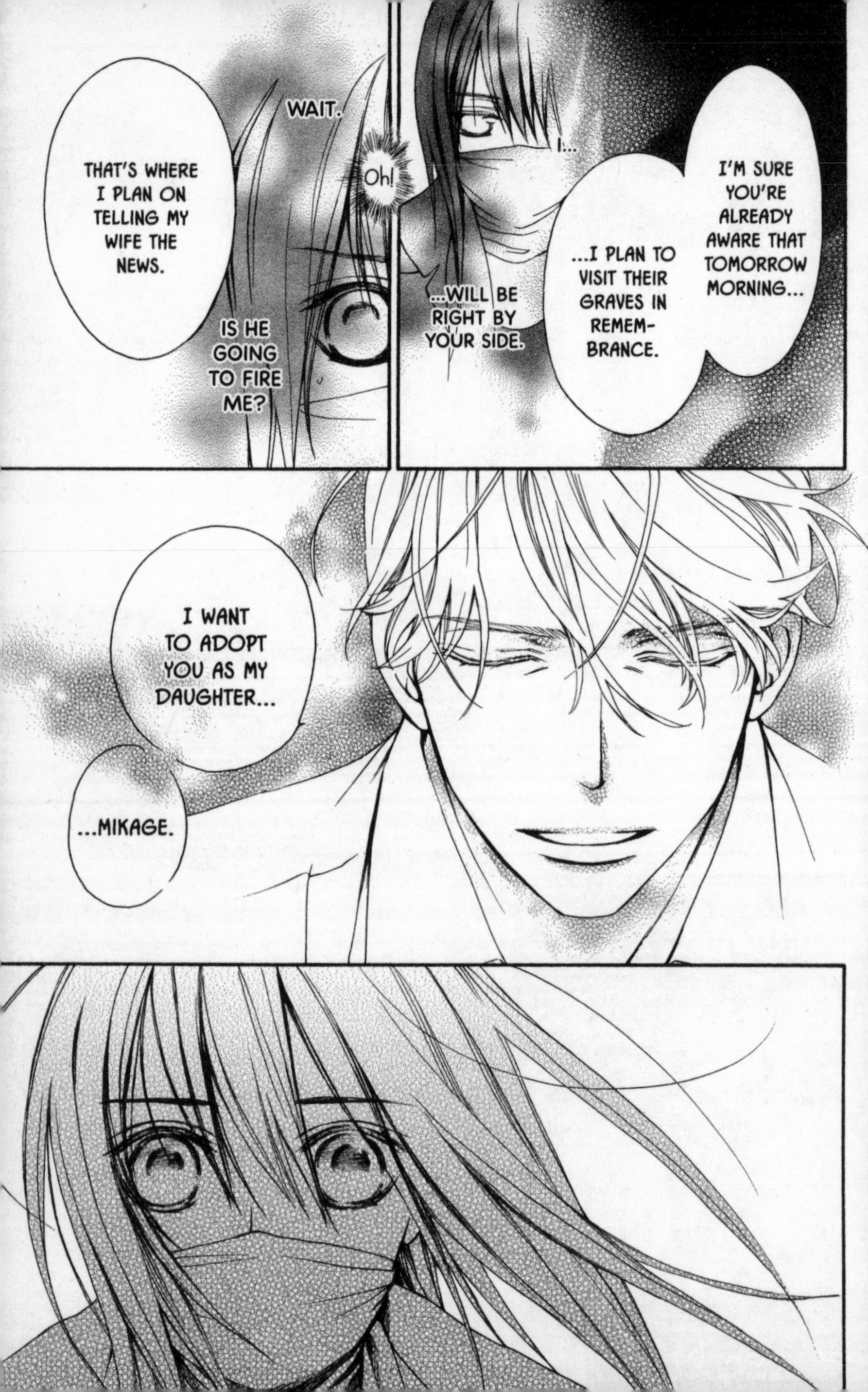
I'M SURE YOU'RE ALREADY AWARE THAT TOMORROW MORNING...
...I PLAN TO VISIT THEIR GRAVES IN REMEM-BRANCE.
I...
...WILL BE RIGHT BY YOUR SIDE.
THAT'S WHERE I PLAN ON TELLING MY WIFE THE NEWS.
WAIT.
Oh!
IS HE GOING TO FIRE ME?
I WANT TO ADOPT YOU AS MY DAUGHTER...
...MIKAGE.

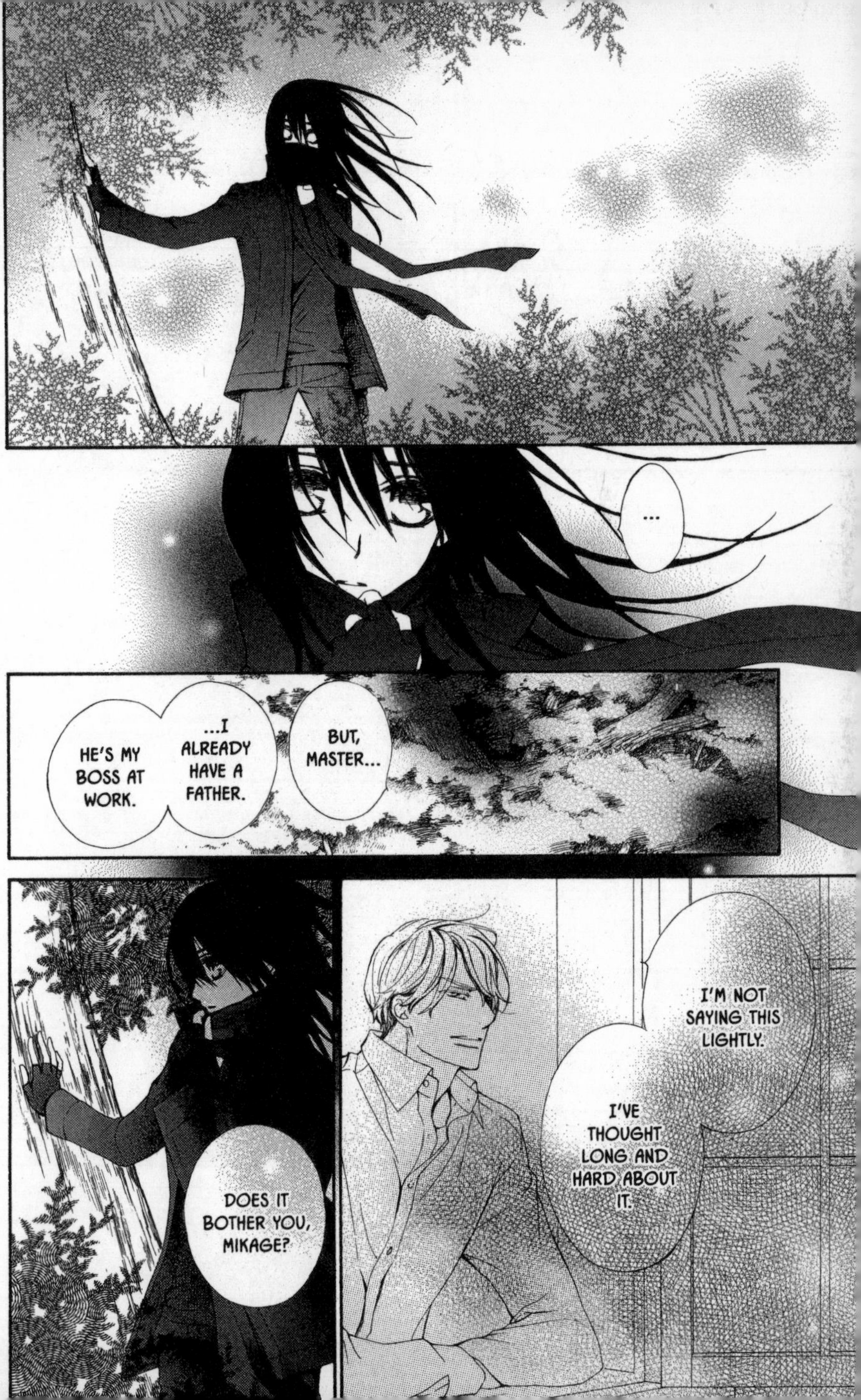
...
BUT, MASTER...
...I ALREADY HAVE A FATHER.
HE'S MY BOSS AT WORK.
I'M NOT SAYING THIS LIGHTLY.
I'VE THOUGHT LONG AND HARD ABOUT IT.
DOES IT BOTHER YOU, MIKAGE?

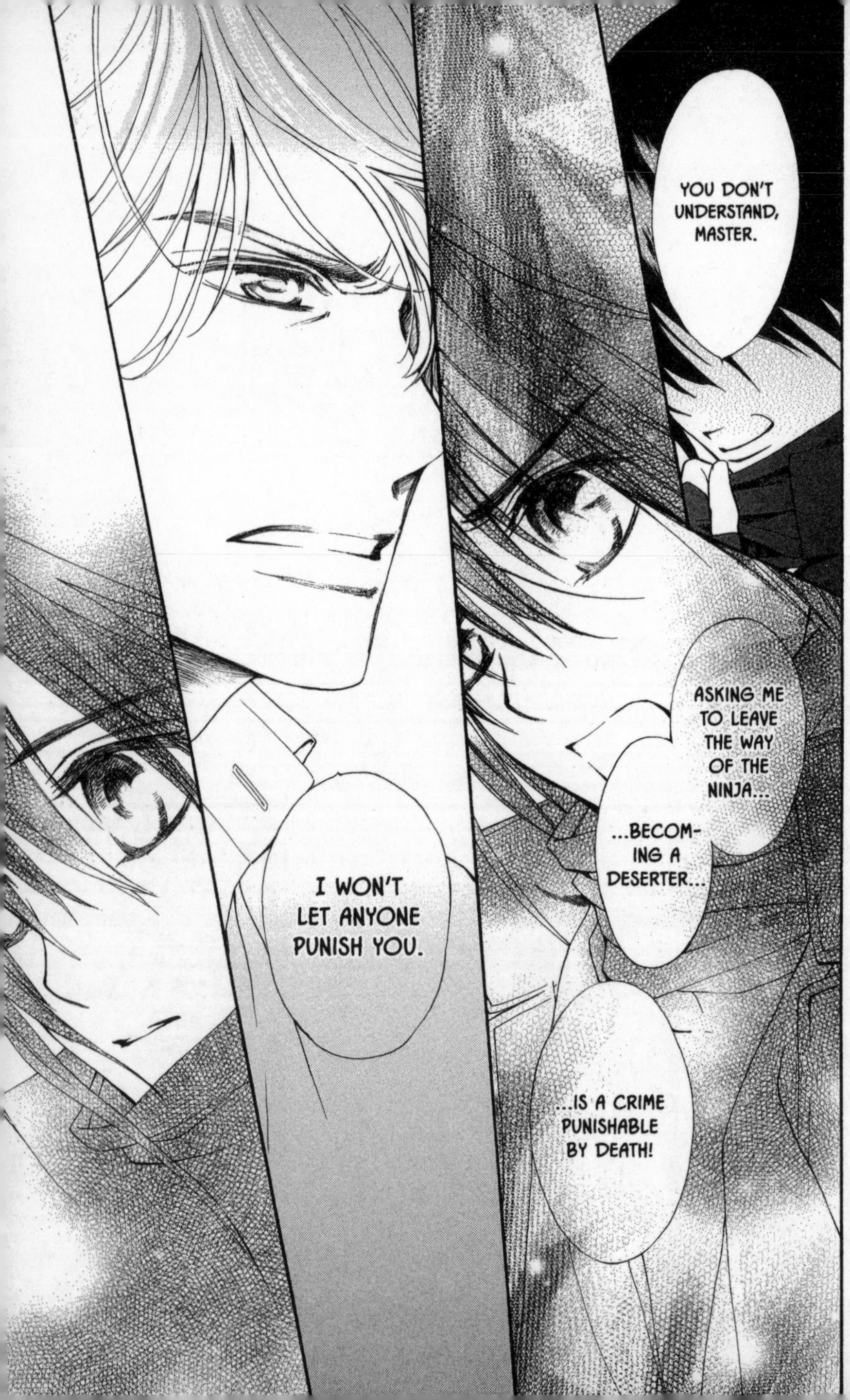
YOU DON'T UNDERSTAND, MASTER.
ASKING ME TO LEAVE THE WAY OF THE NINJA...
...BECOM-ING A DESERTER...
...IS A CRIME PUNISHABLE BY DEATH!
I WON'T LET ANYONE PUNISH YOU.

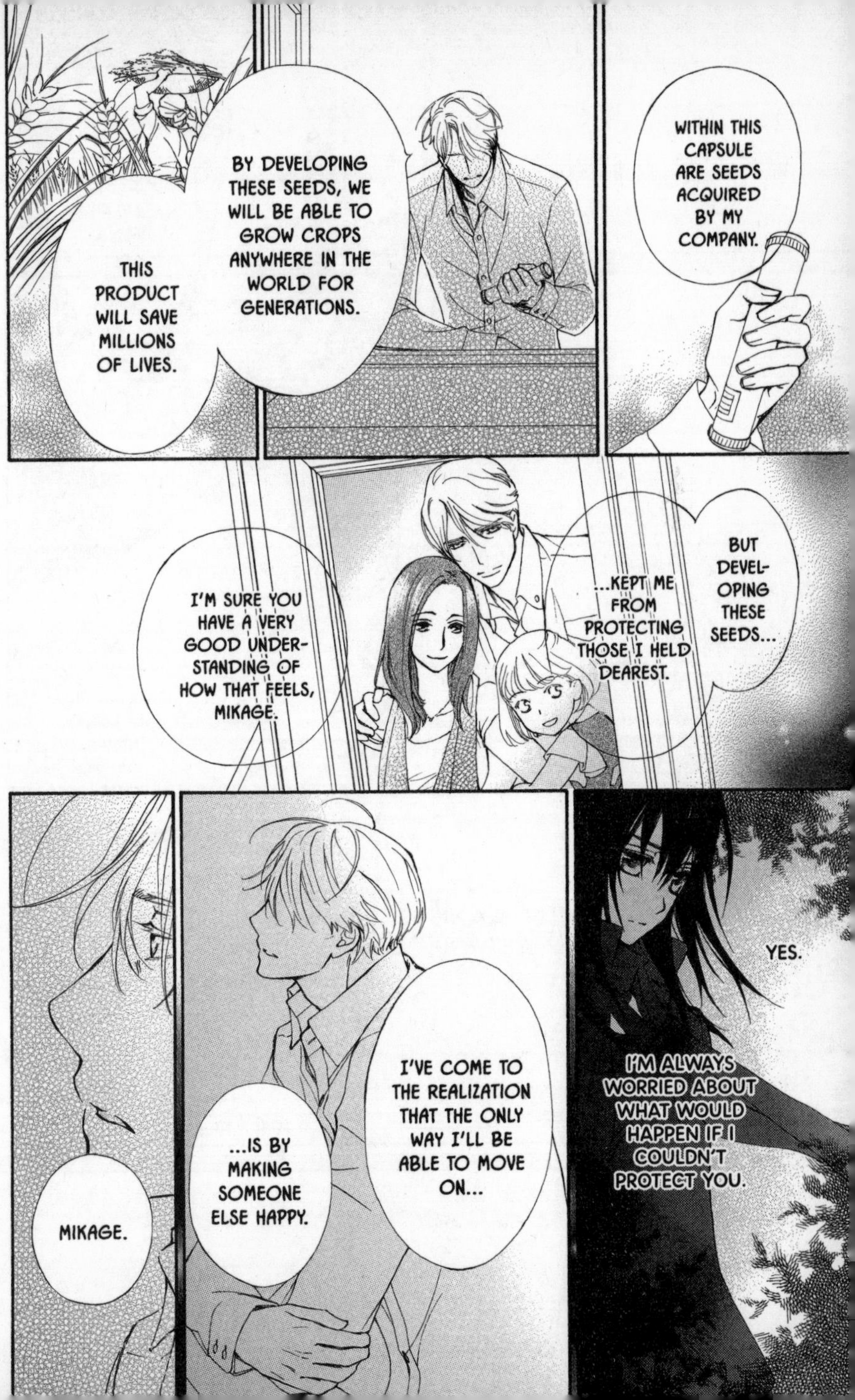
WITHIN THIS CAPSULE ARE SEEDS ACQUIRED BY MY COMPANY.
BY DEVELOPING THESE SEEDS, WE WILL BE ABLE TO GROW CROPS ANYWHERE IN THE WORLD FOR GENERATIONS.
THIS PRODUCT WILL SAVE MILLIONS OF LIVES.
BUT DEVELOPING THESE SEEDS...
...KEPT ME FROM PROTECTING THOSE I HELD DEAREST.
I'M SURE YOU HAVE A VERY GOOD UNDERSTANDING OF HOW THAT FEELS, MIKAGE.
YES.
I'M ALWAYS WORRIED ABOUT WHAT WOULD HAPPEN IF I COULDN'T PROTECT YOU.
I'VE COME TO THE REALIZATION THAT THE ONLY WAY I'LL BE ABLE TO MOVE ON...
...IS BY MAKING SOMEONE ELSE HAPPY.
MIKAGE.

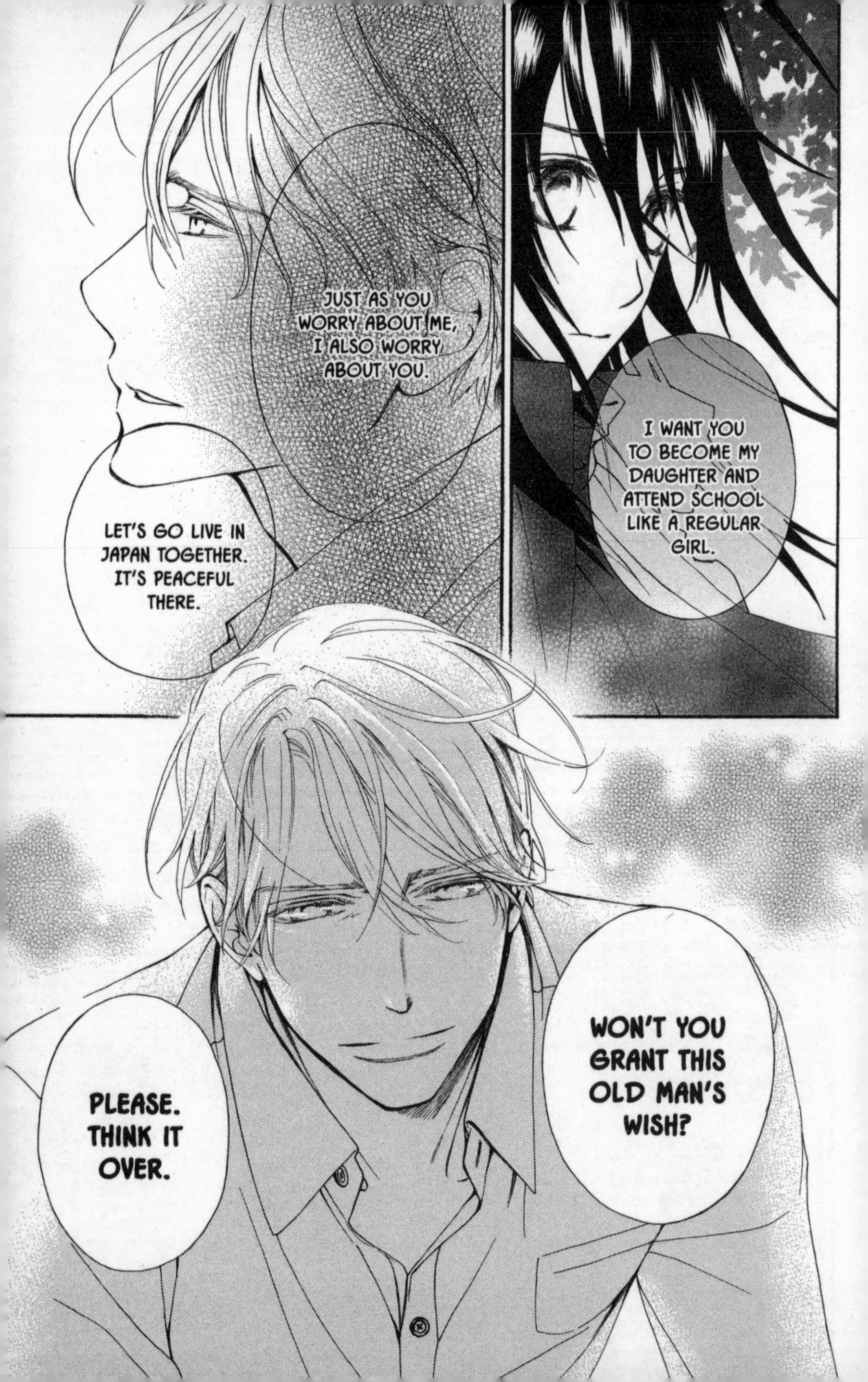
I WANT YOU TO BECOME MY DAUGHTER AND ATTEND SCHOOL LIKE A REGULAR GIRL.
JUST AS YOU WORRY ABOUT ME, I ALSO WORRY ABOUT YOU.
LET'S GO LIVE IN JAPAN TOGETHER. IT'S PEACEFUL THERE.
WON'T YOU GRANT THIS OLD MAN'S WISH?
PLEASE. THINK IT OVER.

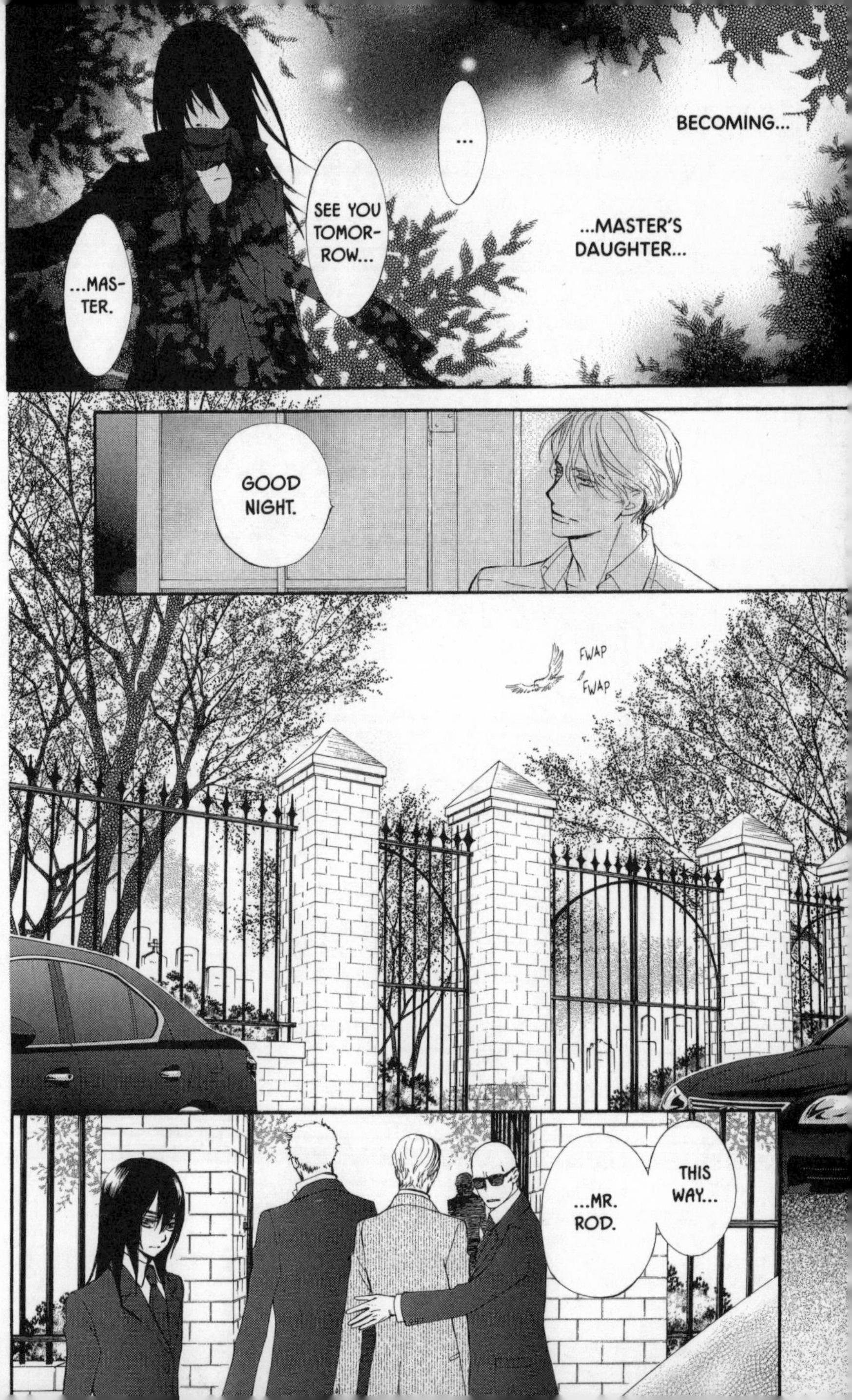
BECOMING...
...MASTER'S DAUGHTER...
...
SEE YOU TOMOR-ROW...
...MAS-TER.
GOOD NIGHT.
FWAP
FWAP
THIS WAY...
...MR. ROD.

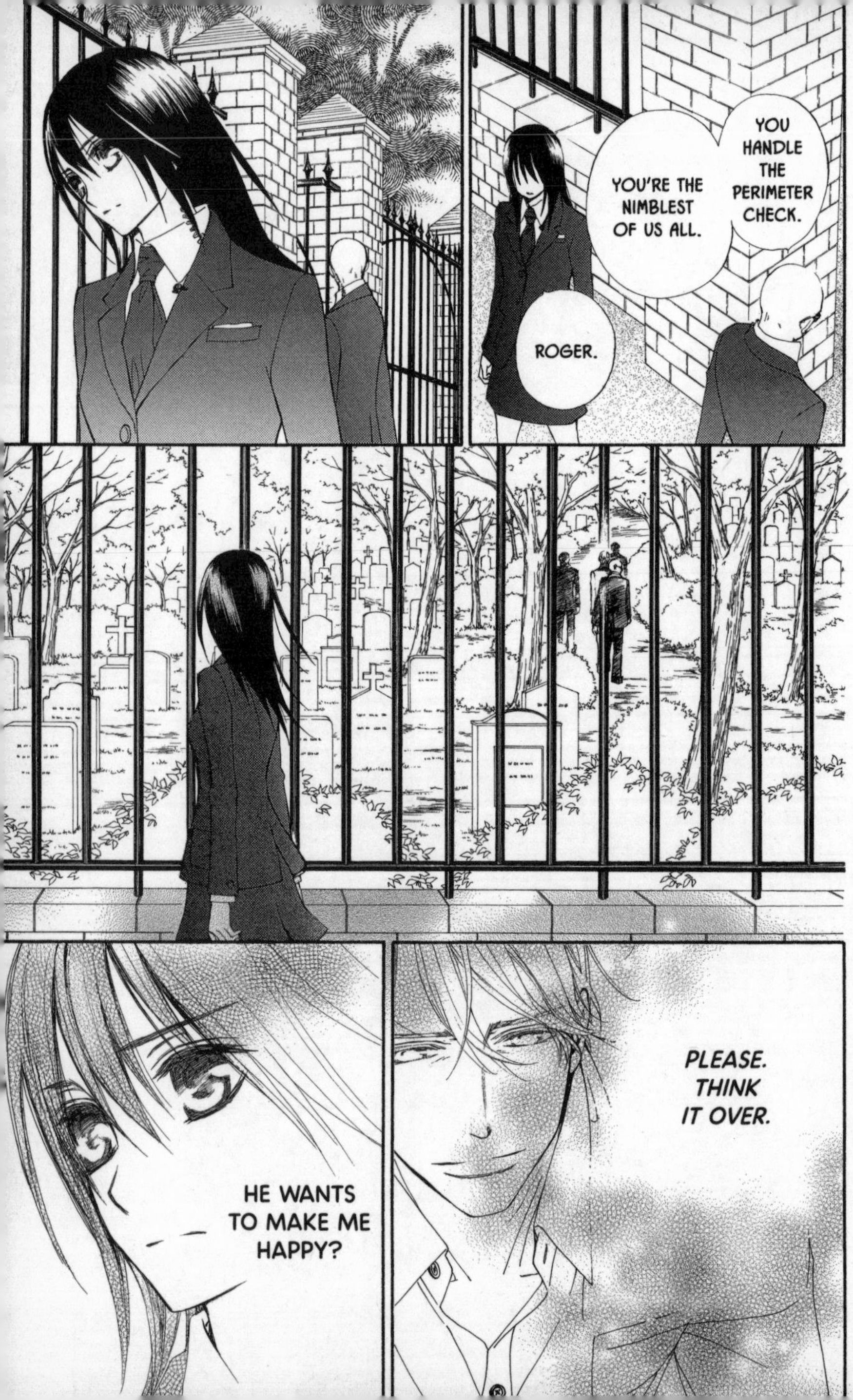
YOU HANDLE THE PERIMETER CHECK.
YOU'RE THE NIMBLEST OF US ALL.
ROGER.
PLEASE. THINK IT OVER.
HE WANTS TO MAKE ME HAPPY?

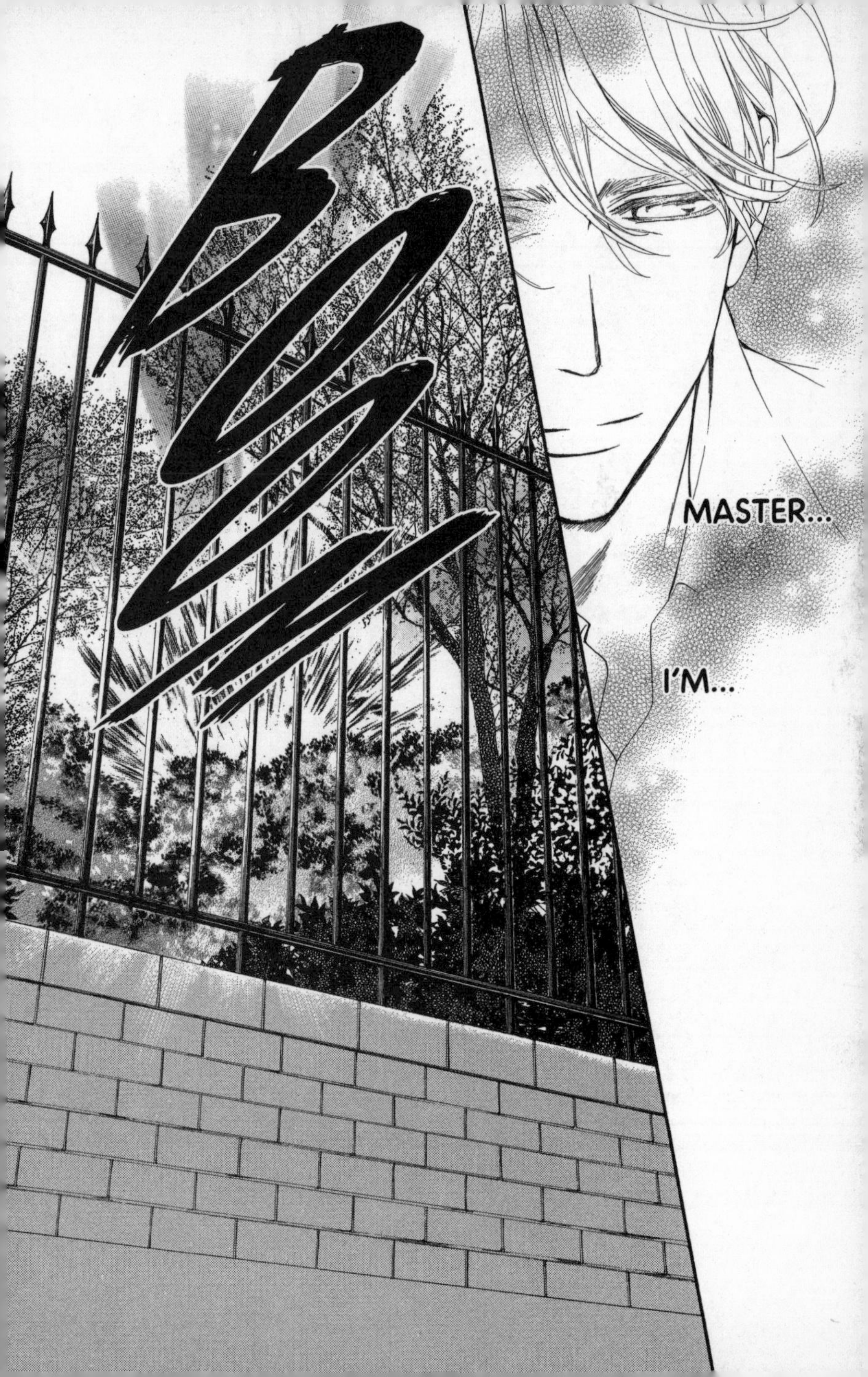
MASTER...
I'M...

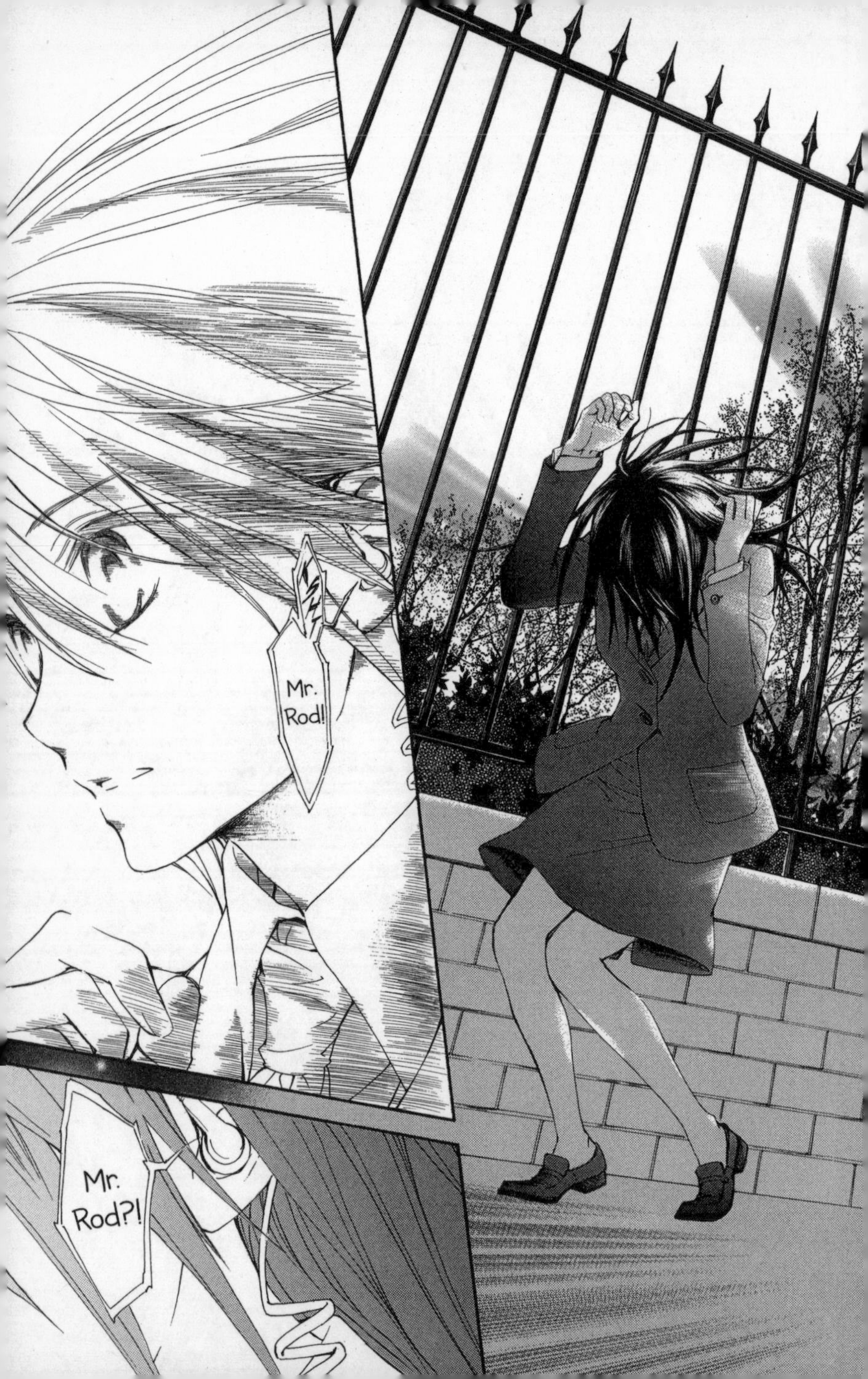
Mr. Rod!
Mr. Rod?!

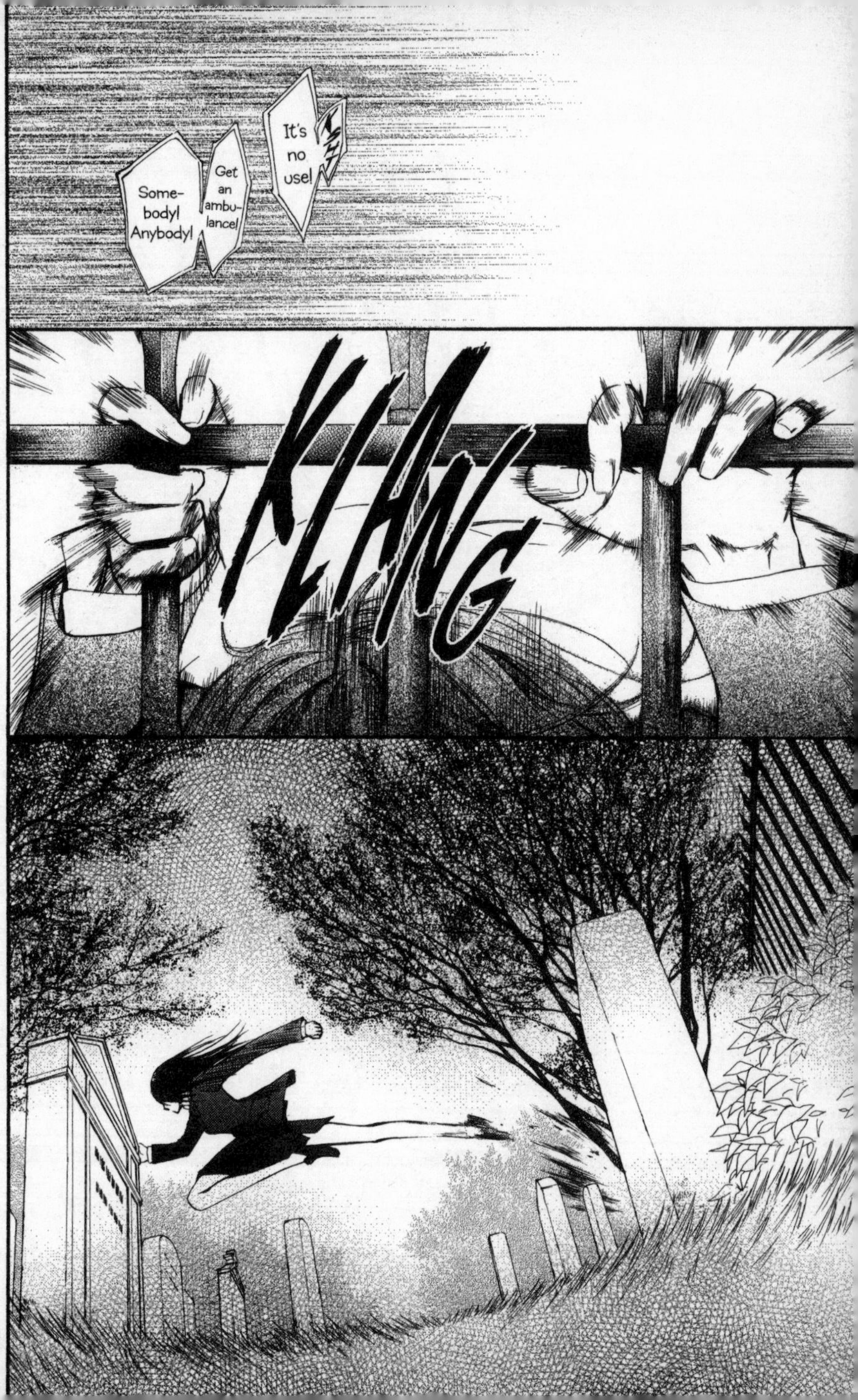
It's no use!
Get an ambulance!
Somebody! Anybody!
KLANG

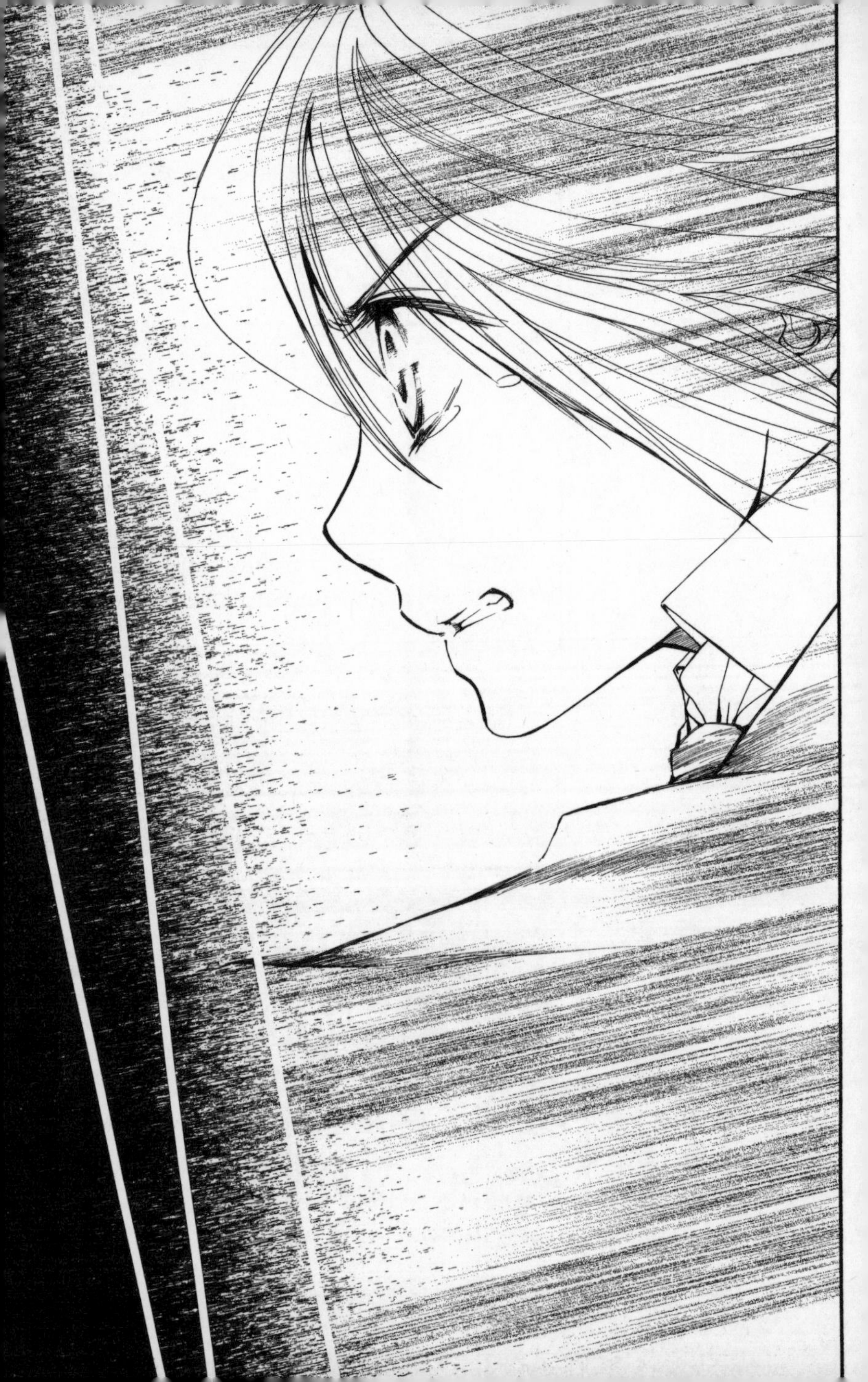

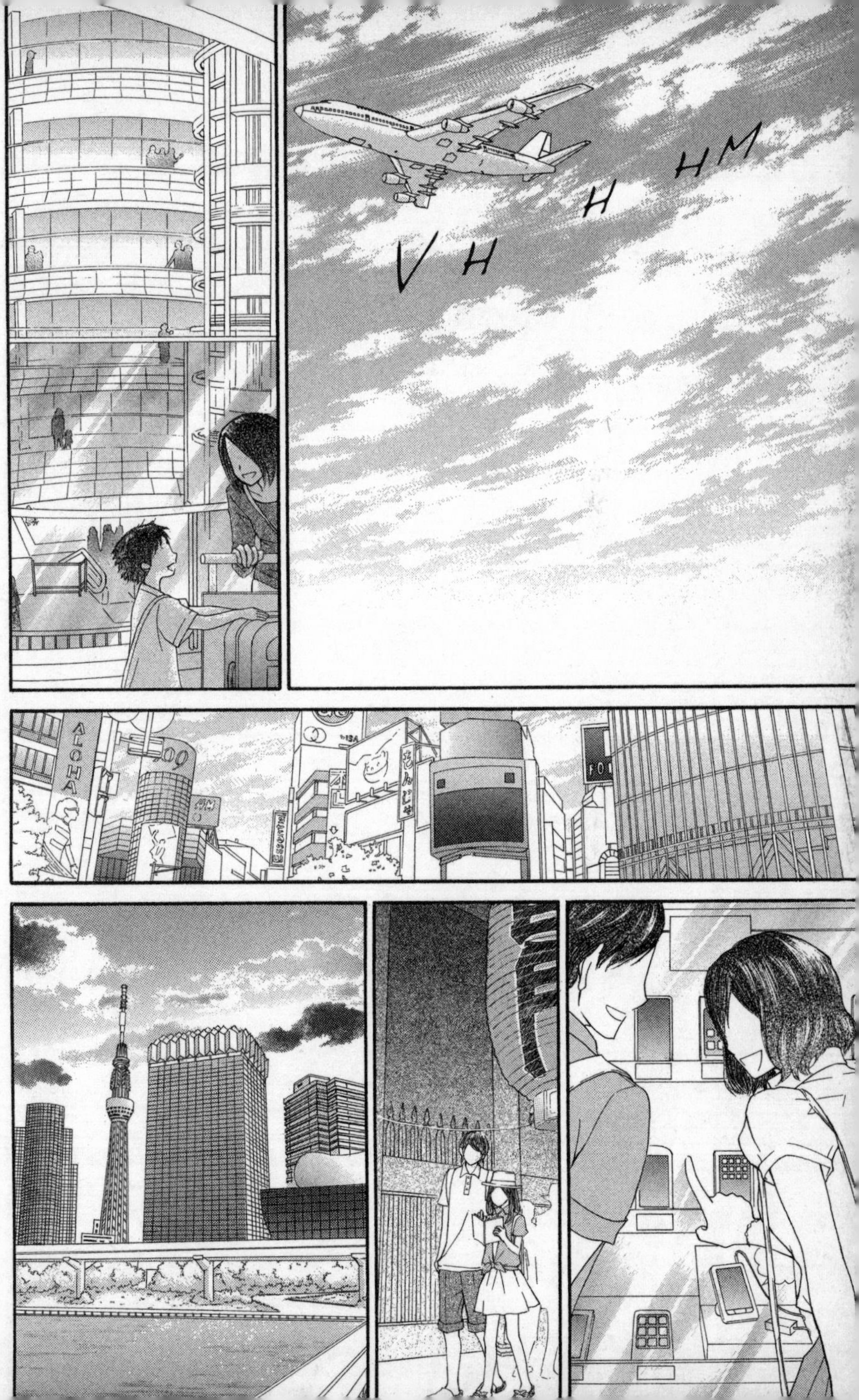
VHHHM
ALOHA
109

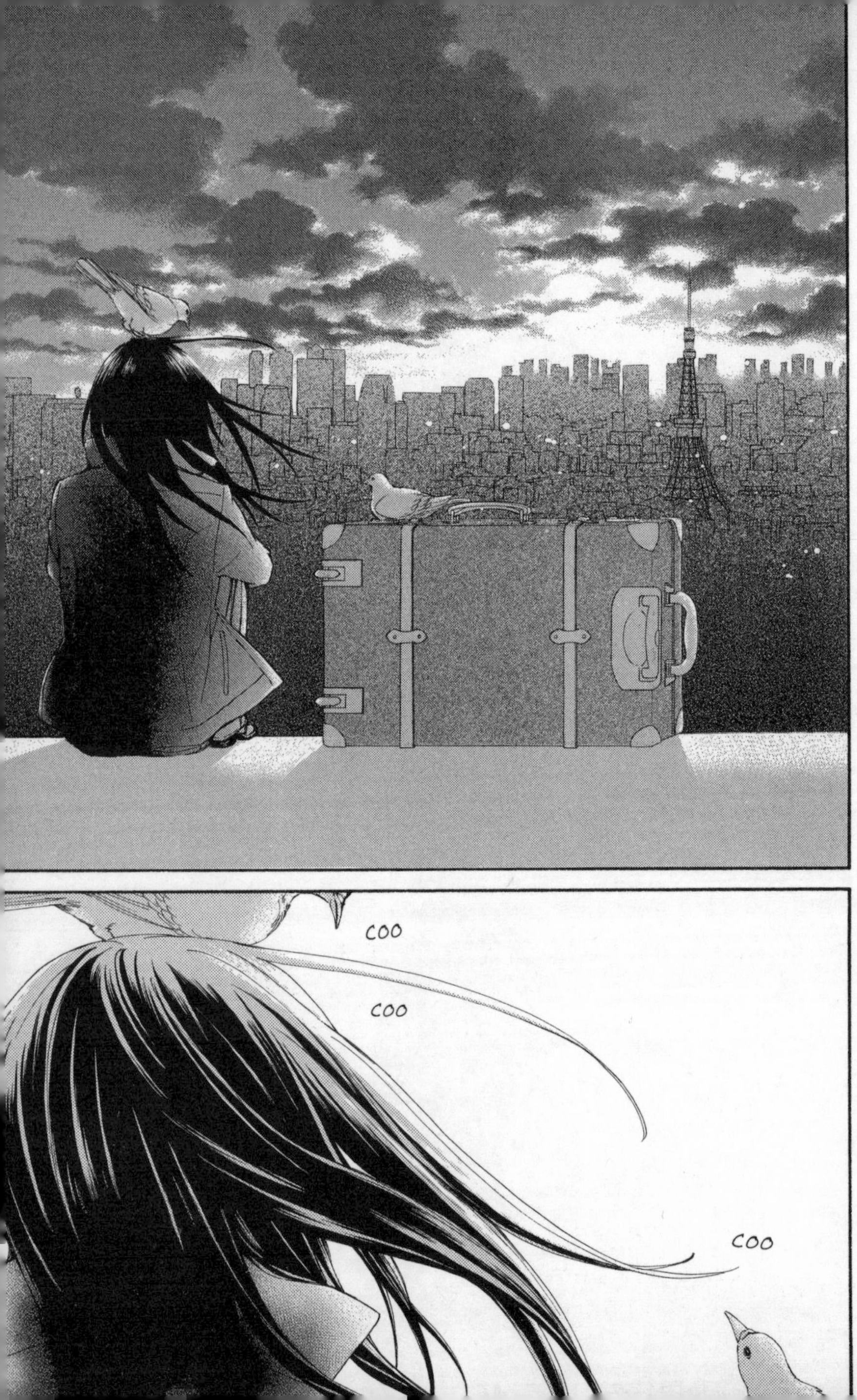
COO
COO
COO

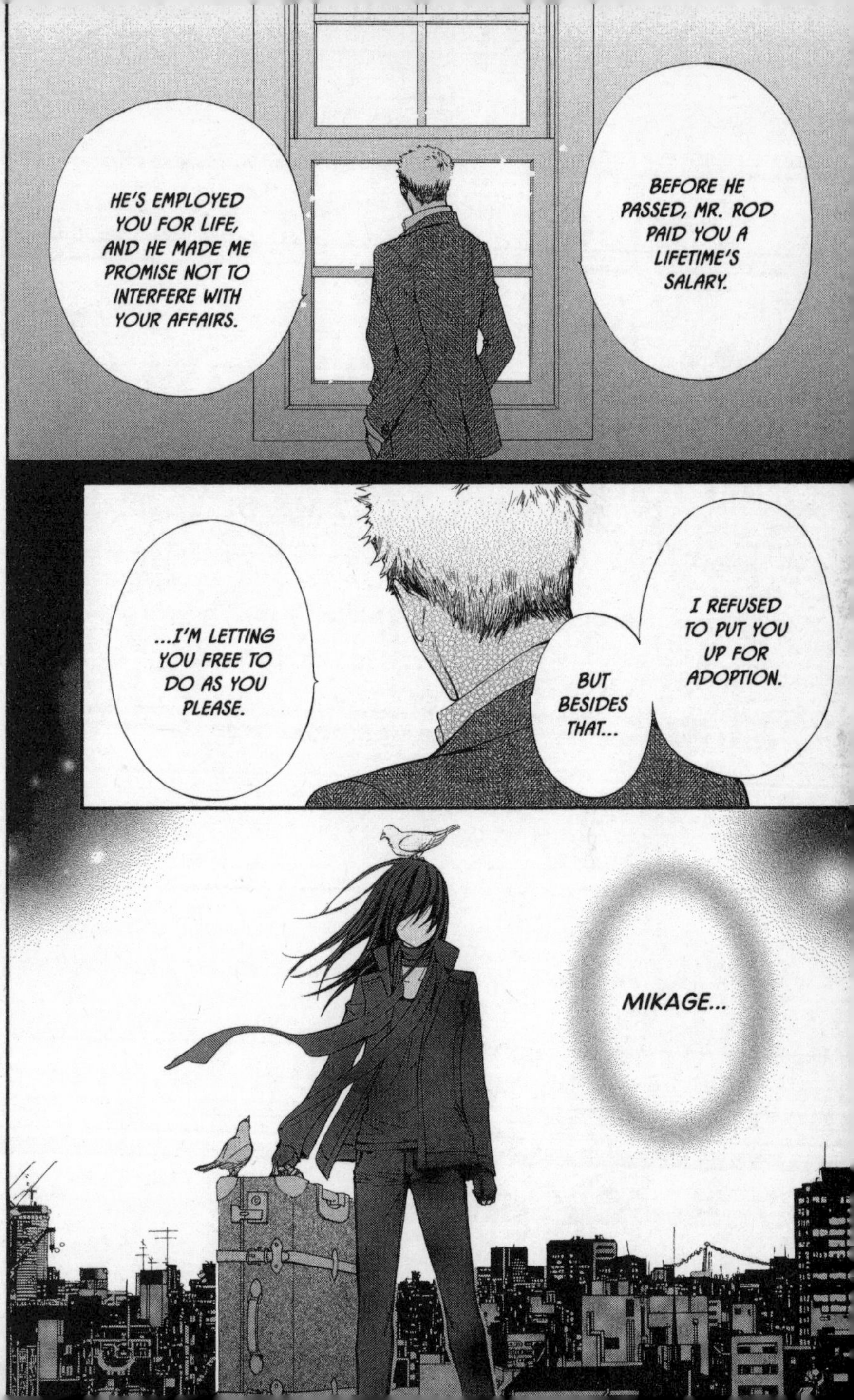
BEFORE HE PASSED, MR. ROD PAID YOU A LIFETIME'S SALARY.
HE'S EMPLOYED YOU FOR LIFE, AND HE MADE ME PROMISE NOT TO INTERFERE WITH YOUR AFFAIRS.
I REFUSED TO PUT YOU UP FOR ADOPTION.
BUT BESIDES THAT...
...I'M LETTING YOU FREE TO DO AS YOU PLEASE.
MIKAGE...

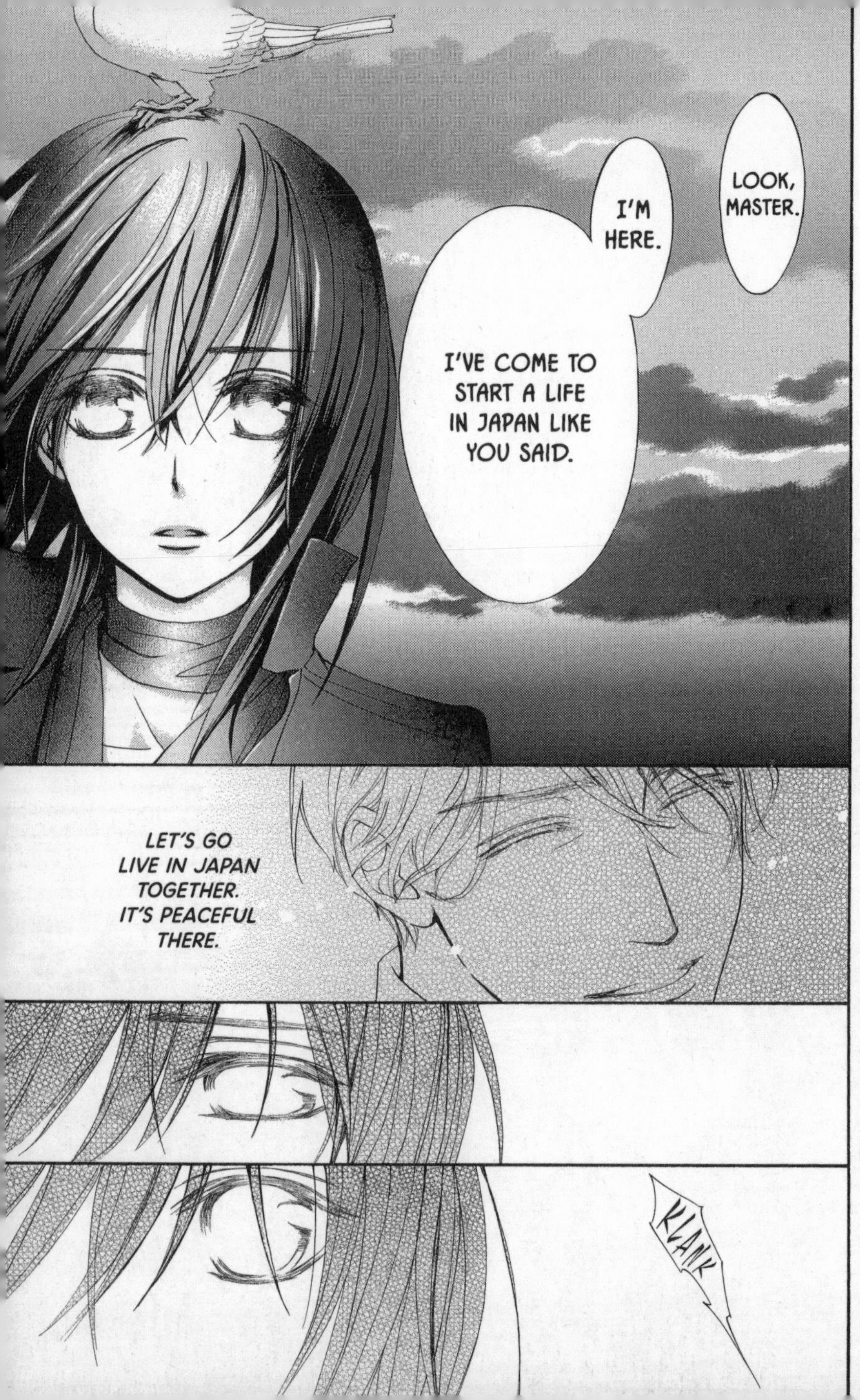
LOOK, MASTER.
I'M HERE.
I'VE COME TO START A LIFE IN JAPAN LIKE YOU SAID.
LET'S GO LIVE IN JAPAN TOGETHER. IT'S PEACEFUL THERE.
KLANK

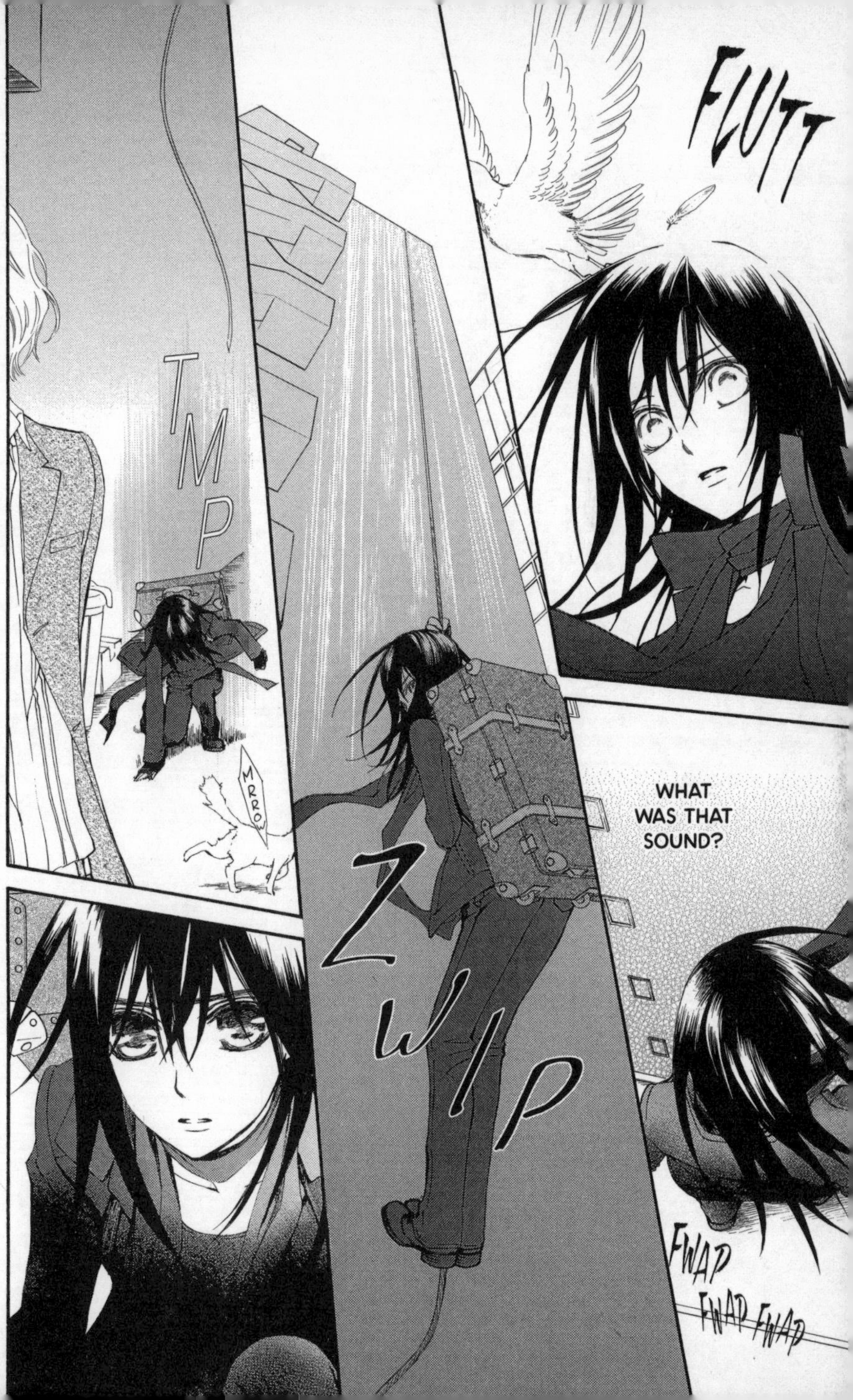
FLUTT
WHAT WAS THAT SOUND?
FWAP
FWAP FWAP
ZWIP
TMP
MRROW

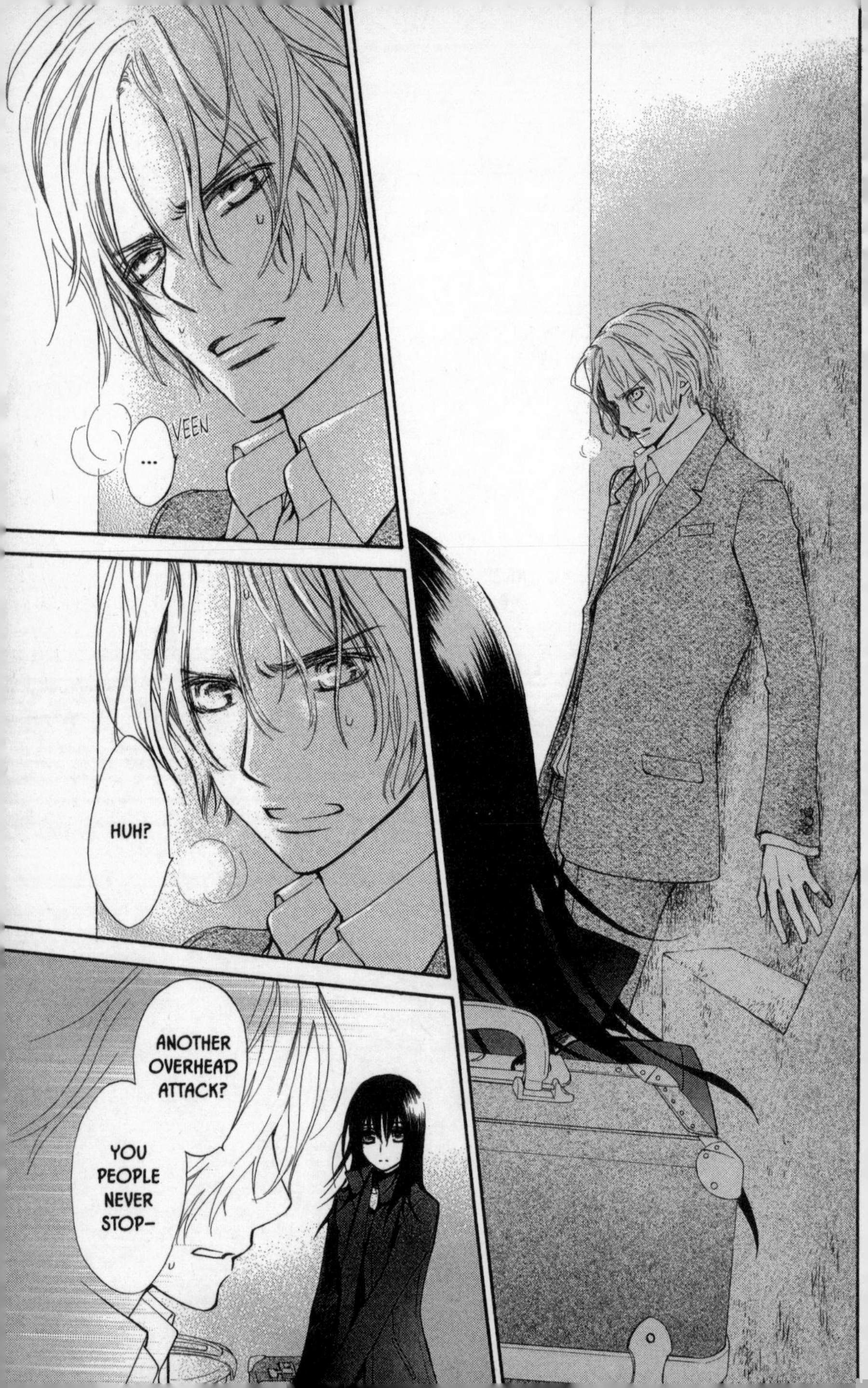
VEEN
...
HUH?
ANOTHER OVERHEAD ATTACK?
YOU PEOPLE NEVER STOP-

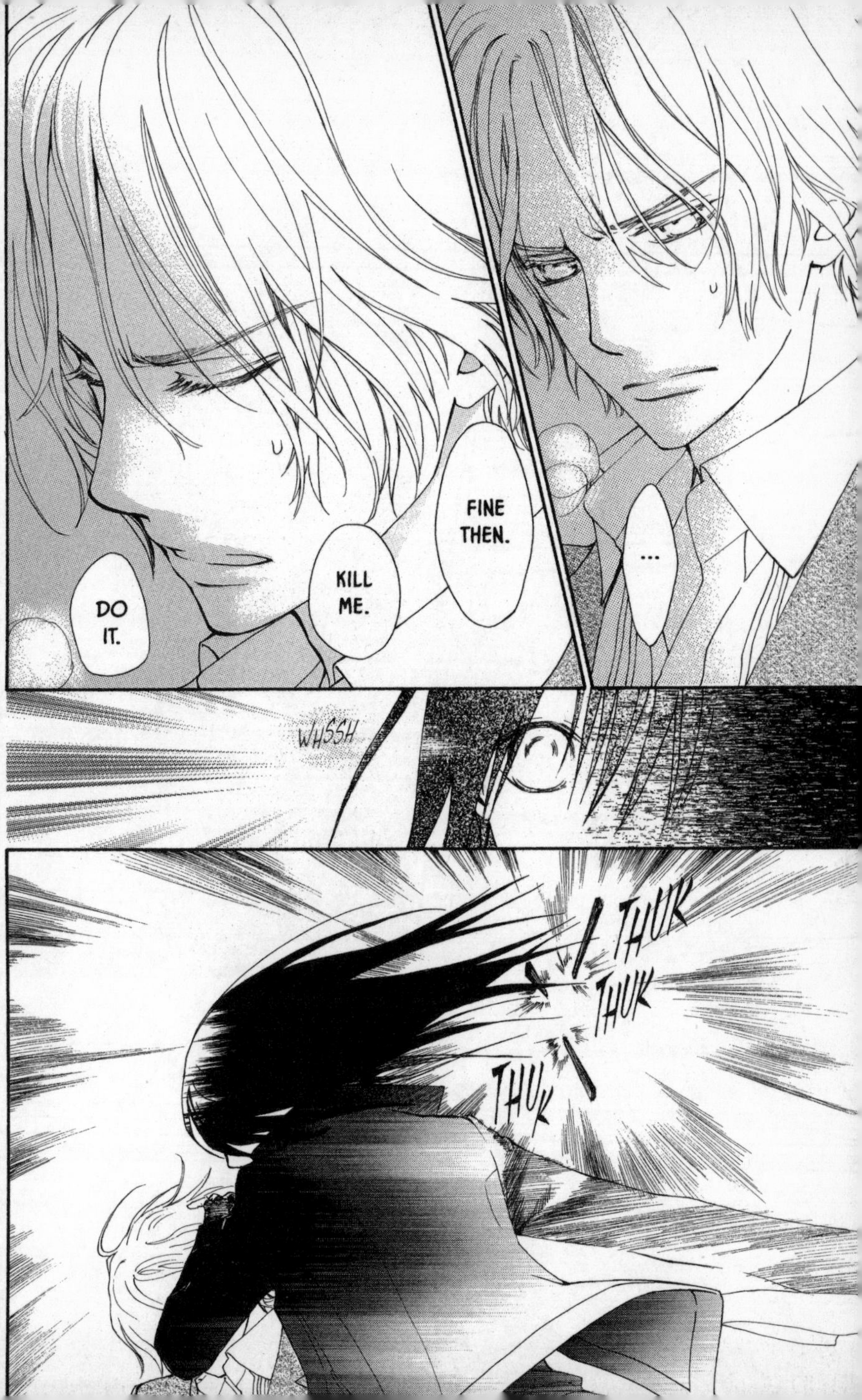
...
FINE THEN.
KILL ME.
DO IT.
WHSSH
THUK
THUK
THUK

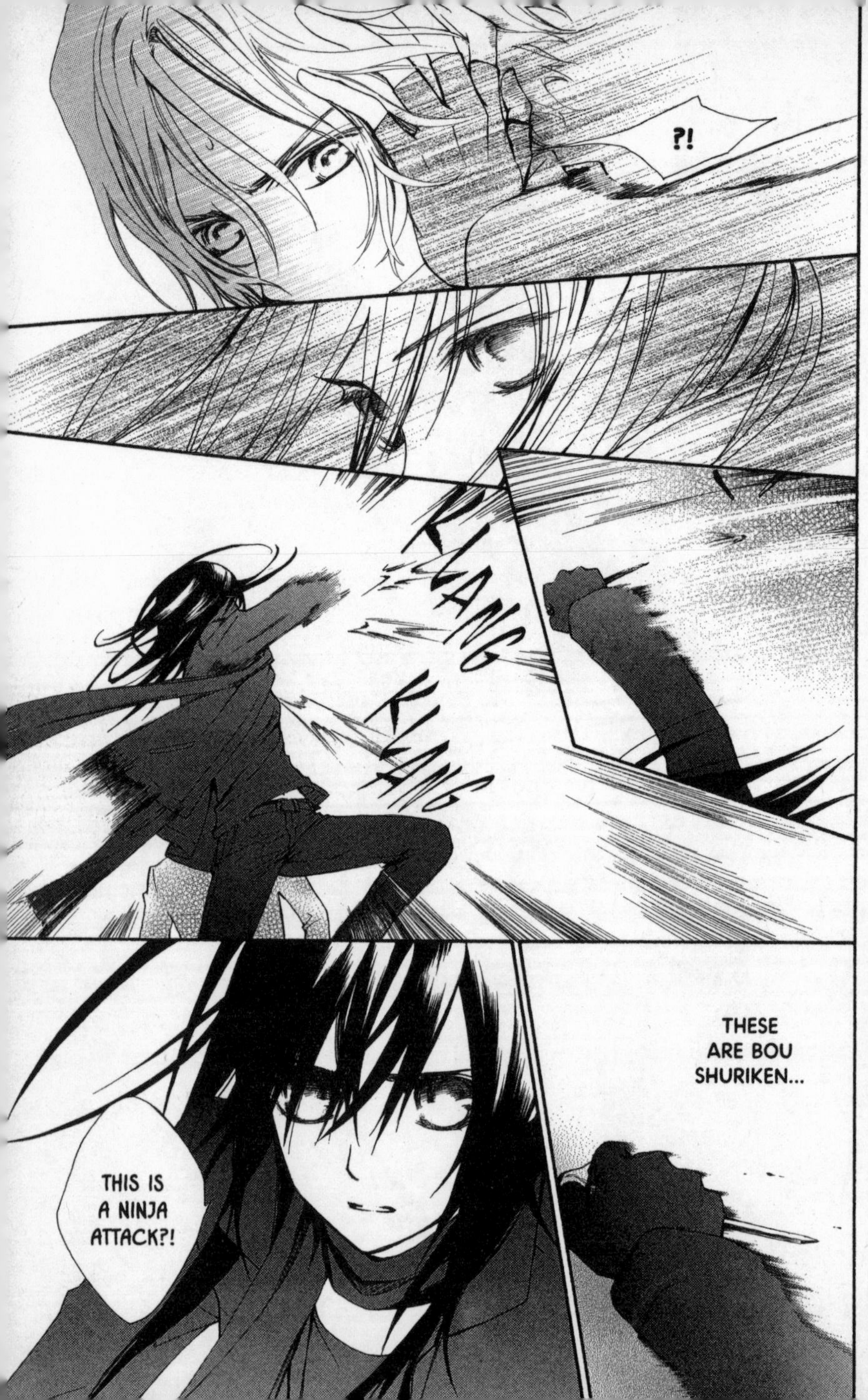
?!
KLANG
KLANG
THESE ARE BOU SHURIKEN...
THIS IS A NINJA ATTACK?!

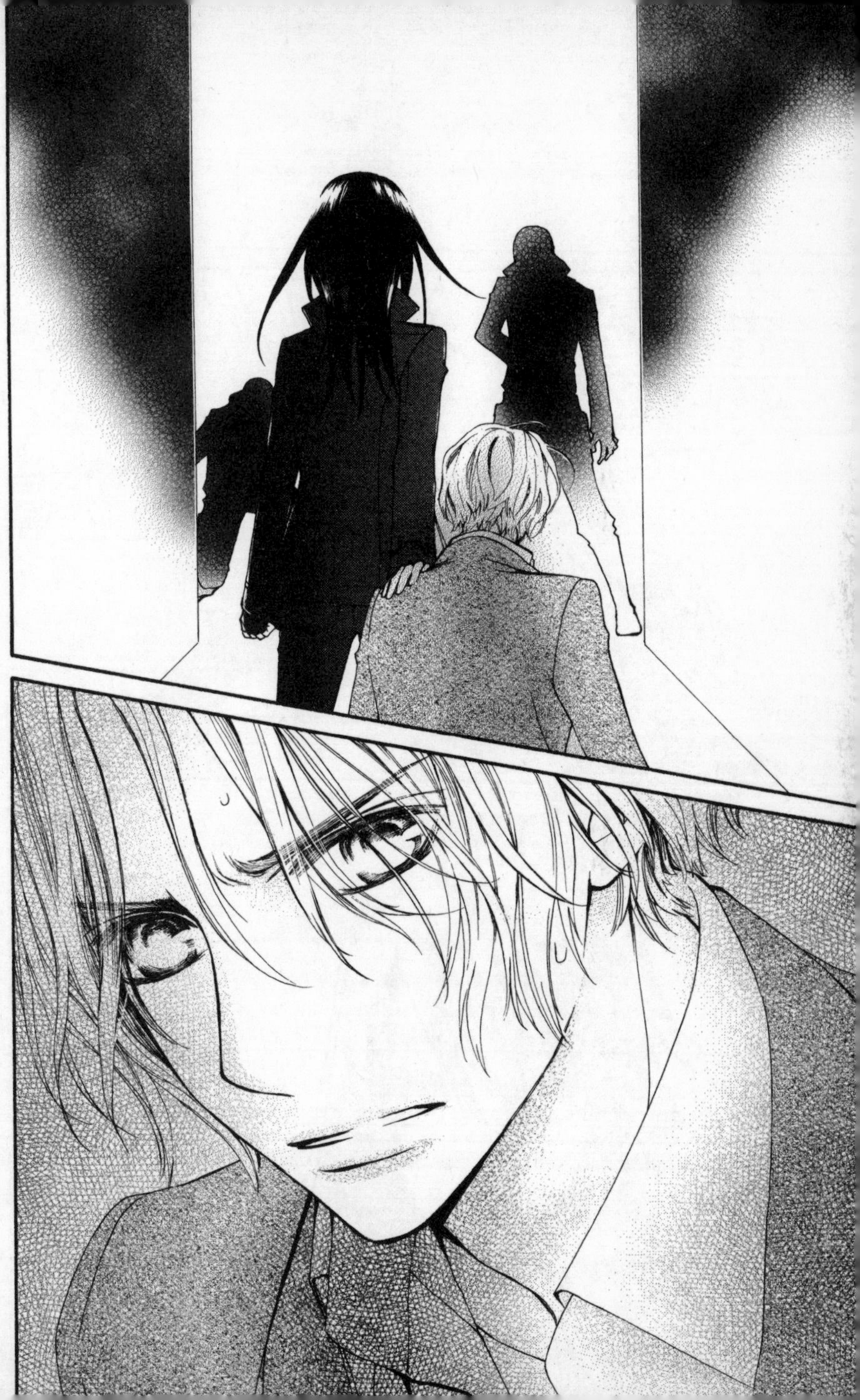

Chapter 2

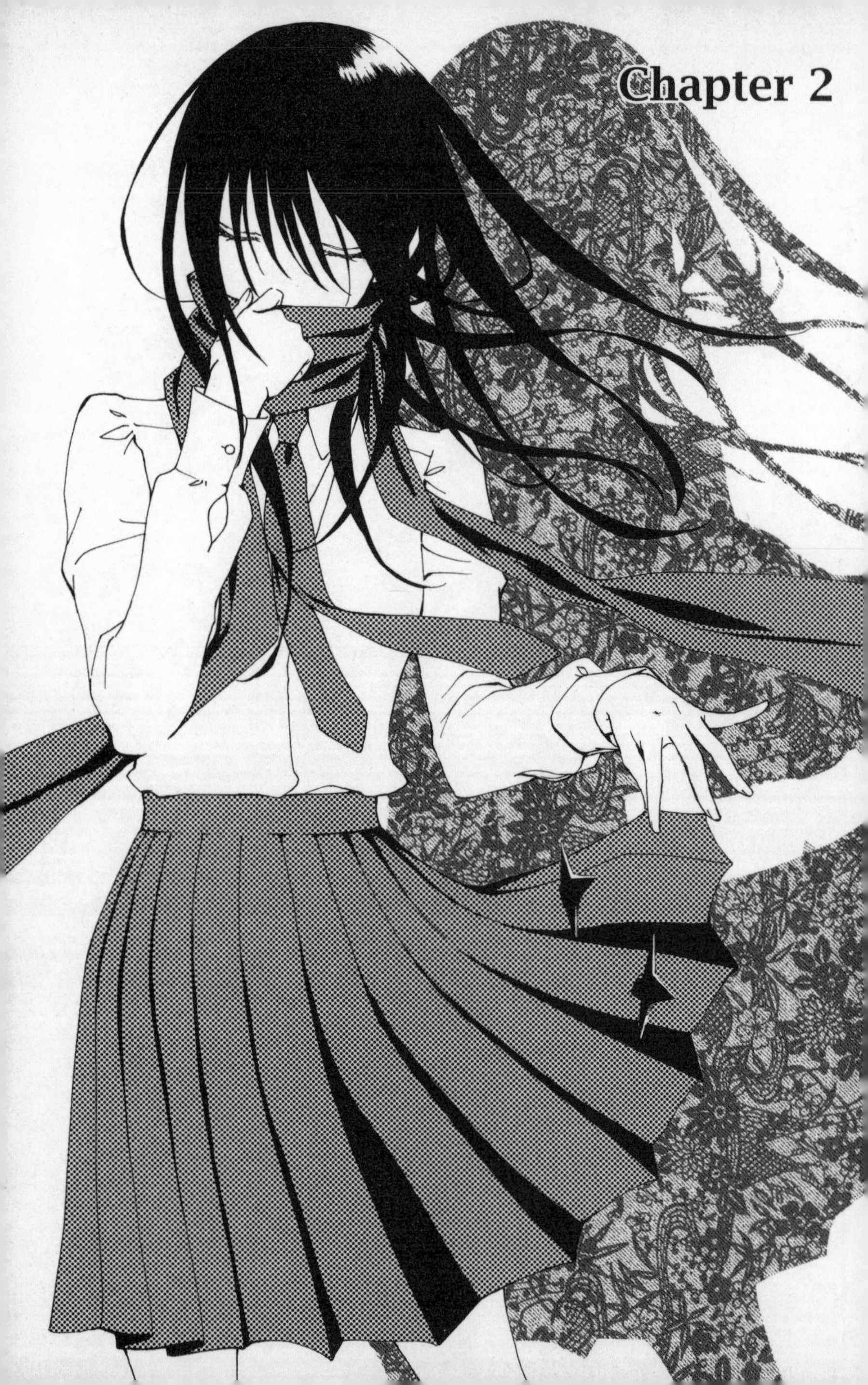

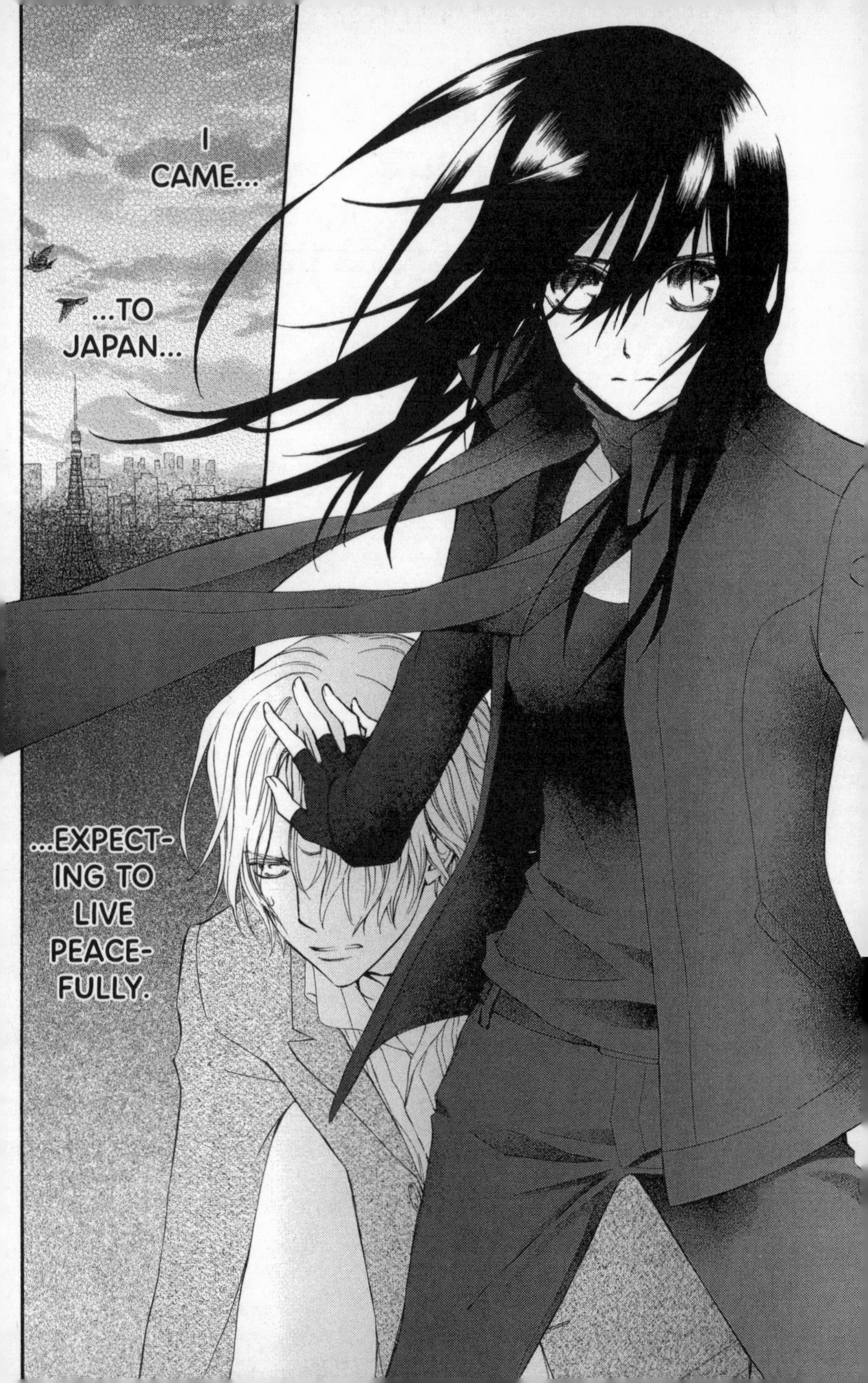
I CAME...
...TO JAPAN...
...EXPECTING TO LIVE PEACEFULLY.

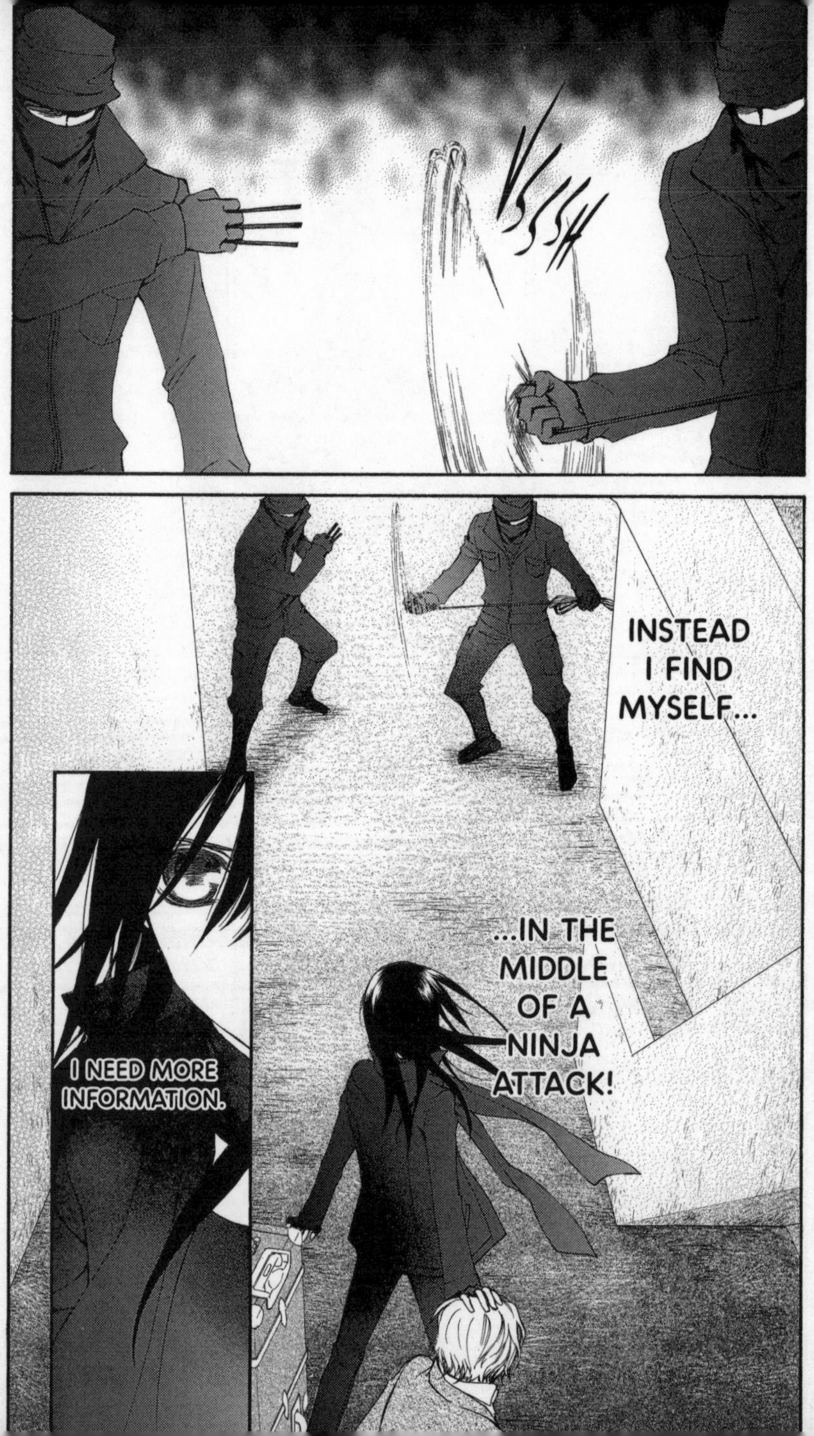
VSSH
INSTEAD I FIND MYSELF...
...IN THE MIDDLE OF A NINJA ATTACK!
I NEED MORE INFORMATION.

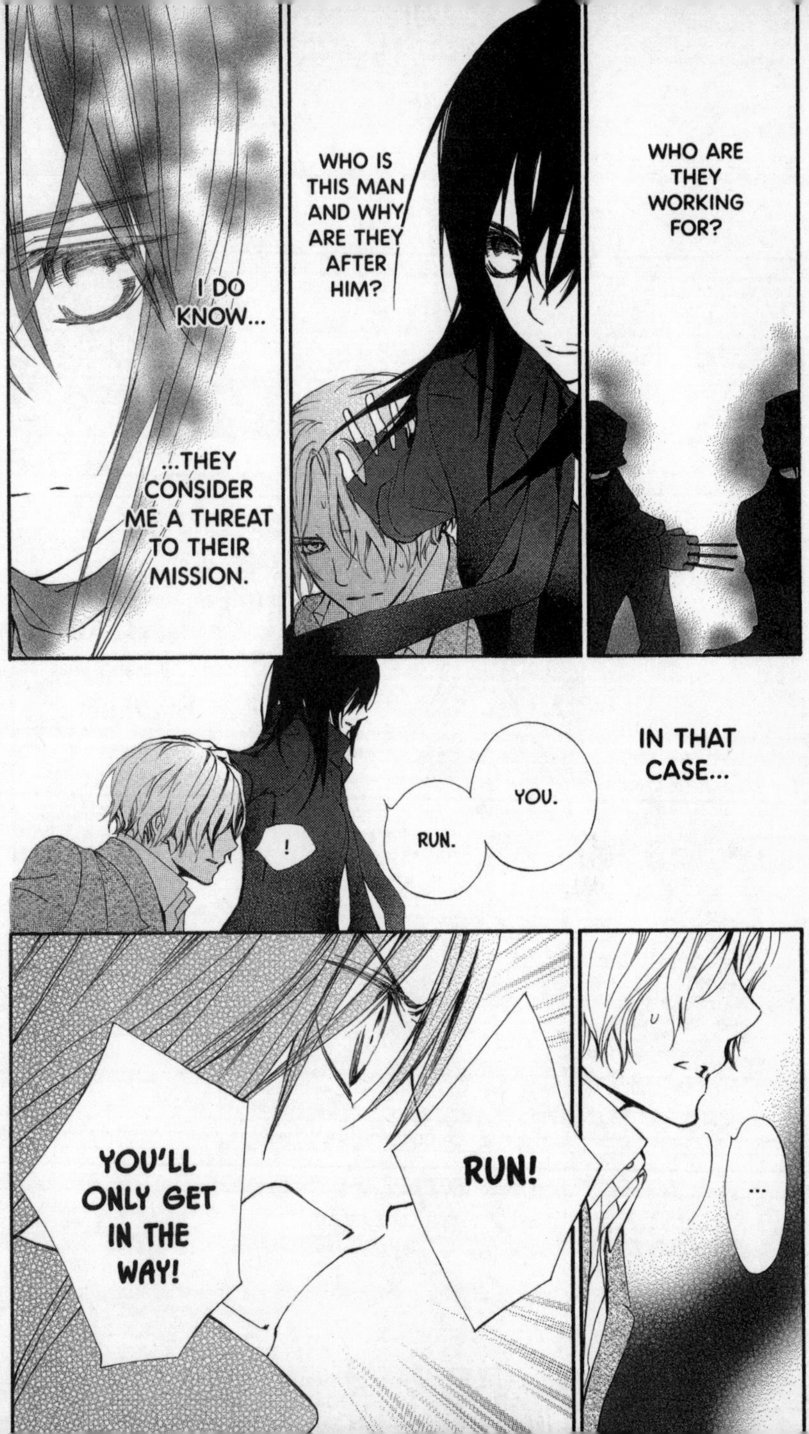
WHO ARE THEY WORKING FOR?
WHO IS THIS MAN AND WHY ARE THEY AFTER HIM?
I DO KNOW...
...THEY CONSIDER ME A THREAT TO THEIR MISSION.
IN THAT CASE...
YOU.
RUN.
!
...
RUN!
YOU'LL ONLY GET IN THE WAY!

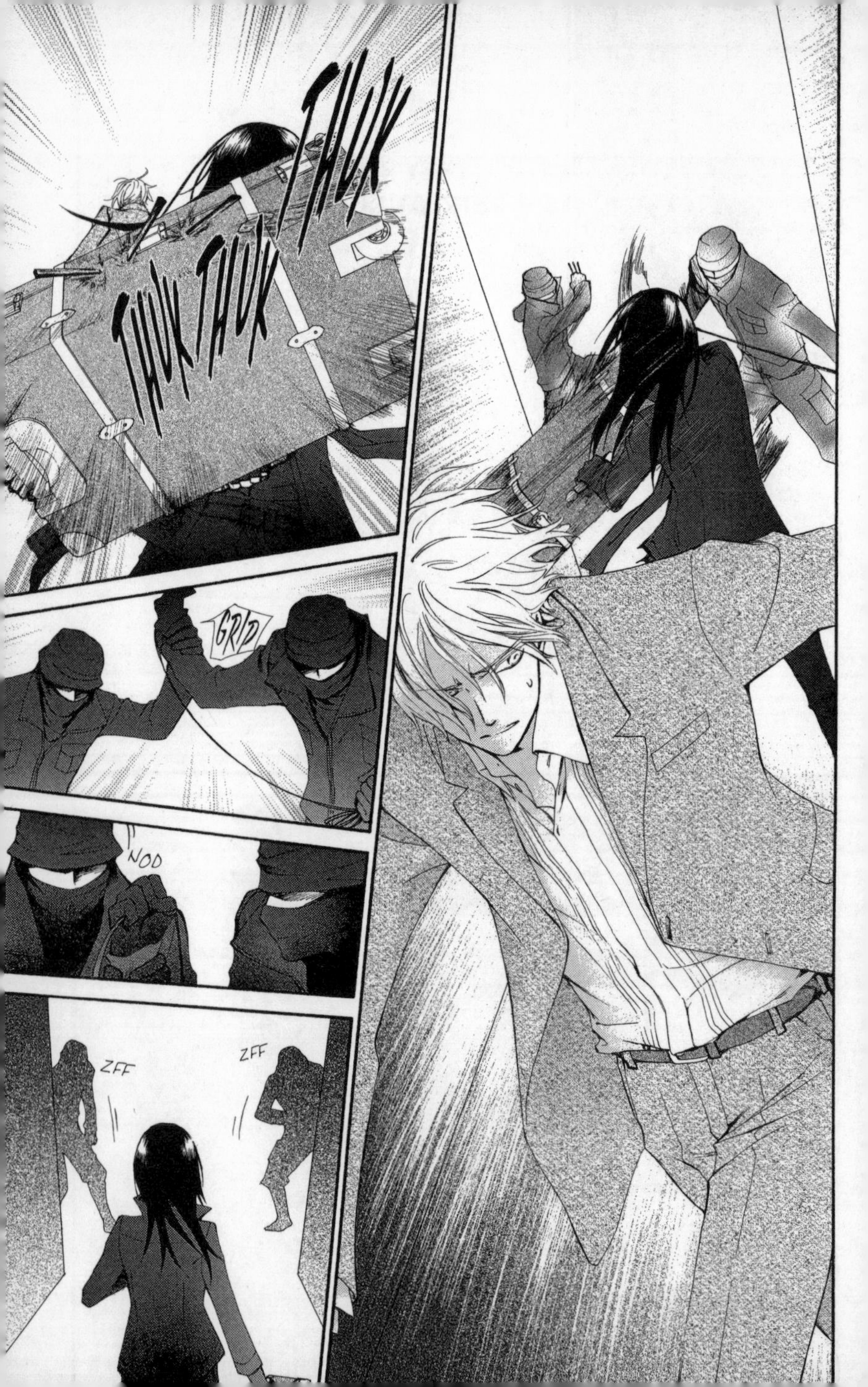
THUK THUK THUK
GRID
NOD
ZFF
ZFF

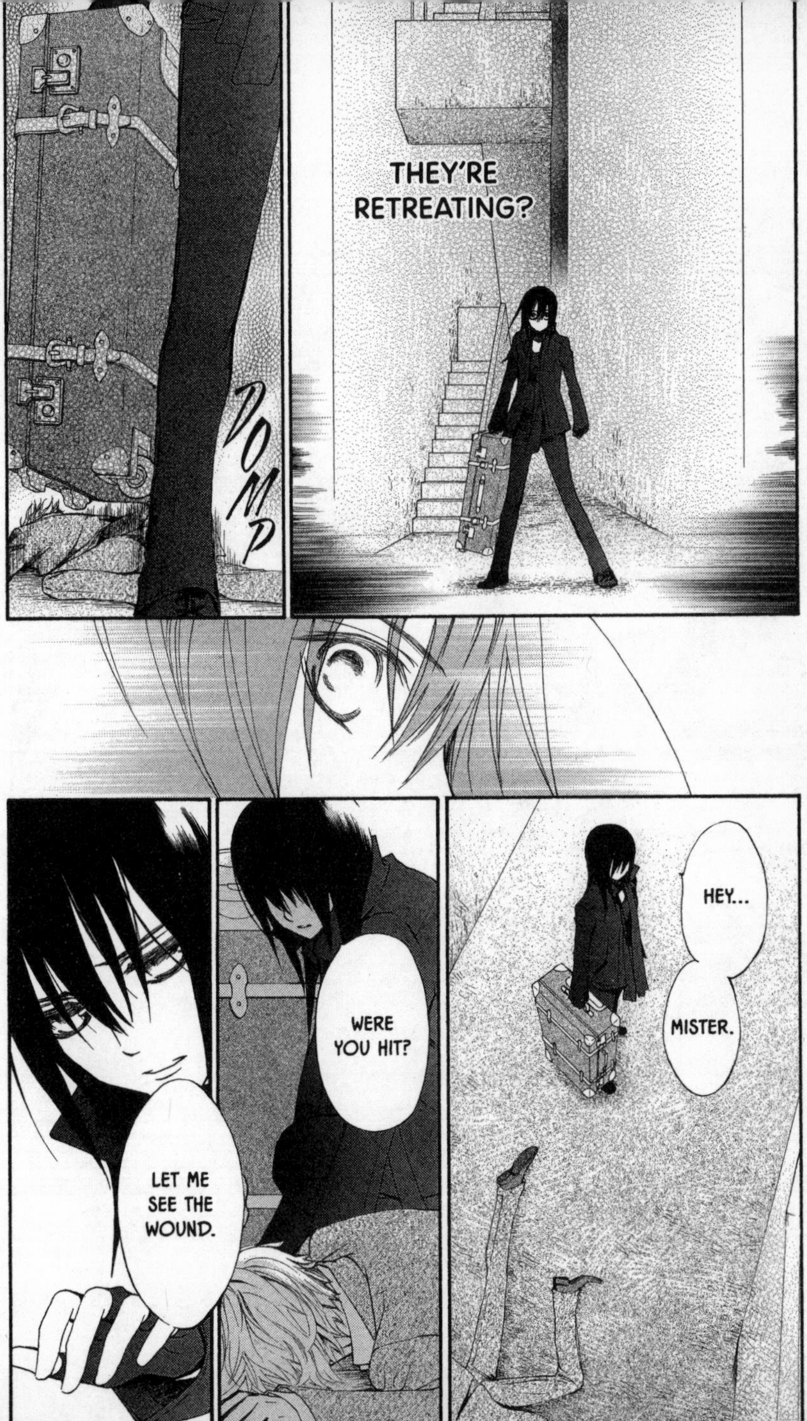
THEY'RE RETREATING?
DOMP
HEY...
MISTER.
WERE YOU HIT?
LET ME SEE THE WOUND.

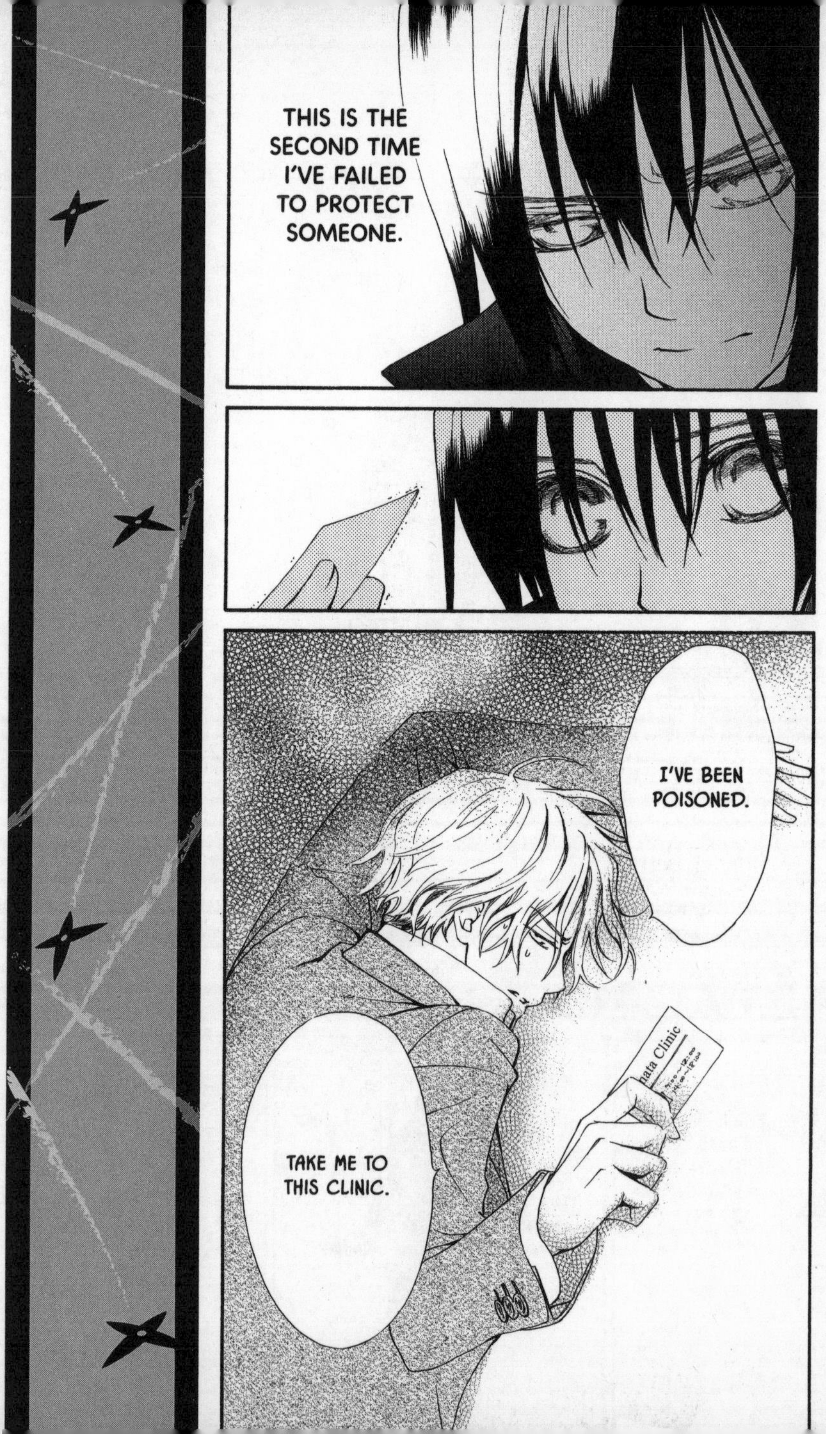
THIS IS THE SECOND TIME I'VE FAILED TO PROTECT SOMEONE.
I'VE BEEN POISONED.
TAKE ME TO THIS CLINIC.

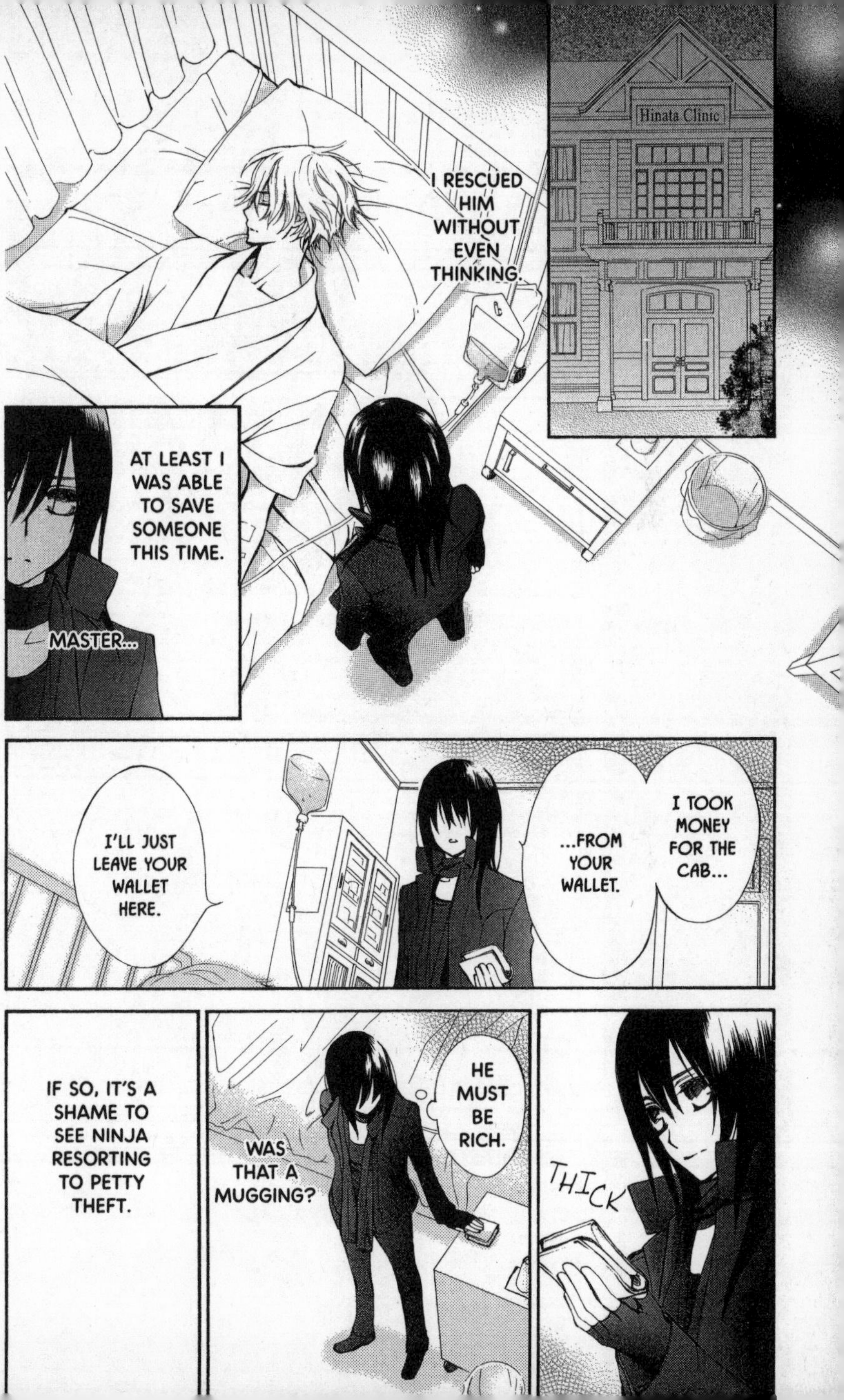
Hinata Clinic
I RESCUED HIM WITHOUT EVEN THINKING.
AT LEAST I WAS ABLE TO SAVE SOMEONE THIS TIME.
MASTER...
I TOOK MONEY FOR THE CAB...
...FROM YOUR WALLET.
I'LL JUST LEAVE YOUR WALLET HERE.
THICK
HE MUST BE RICH.
WAS THAT A MUGGING?
IF SO, IT'S A SHAME TO SEE NINJA RESORTING TO PETTY THEFT.

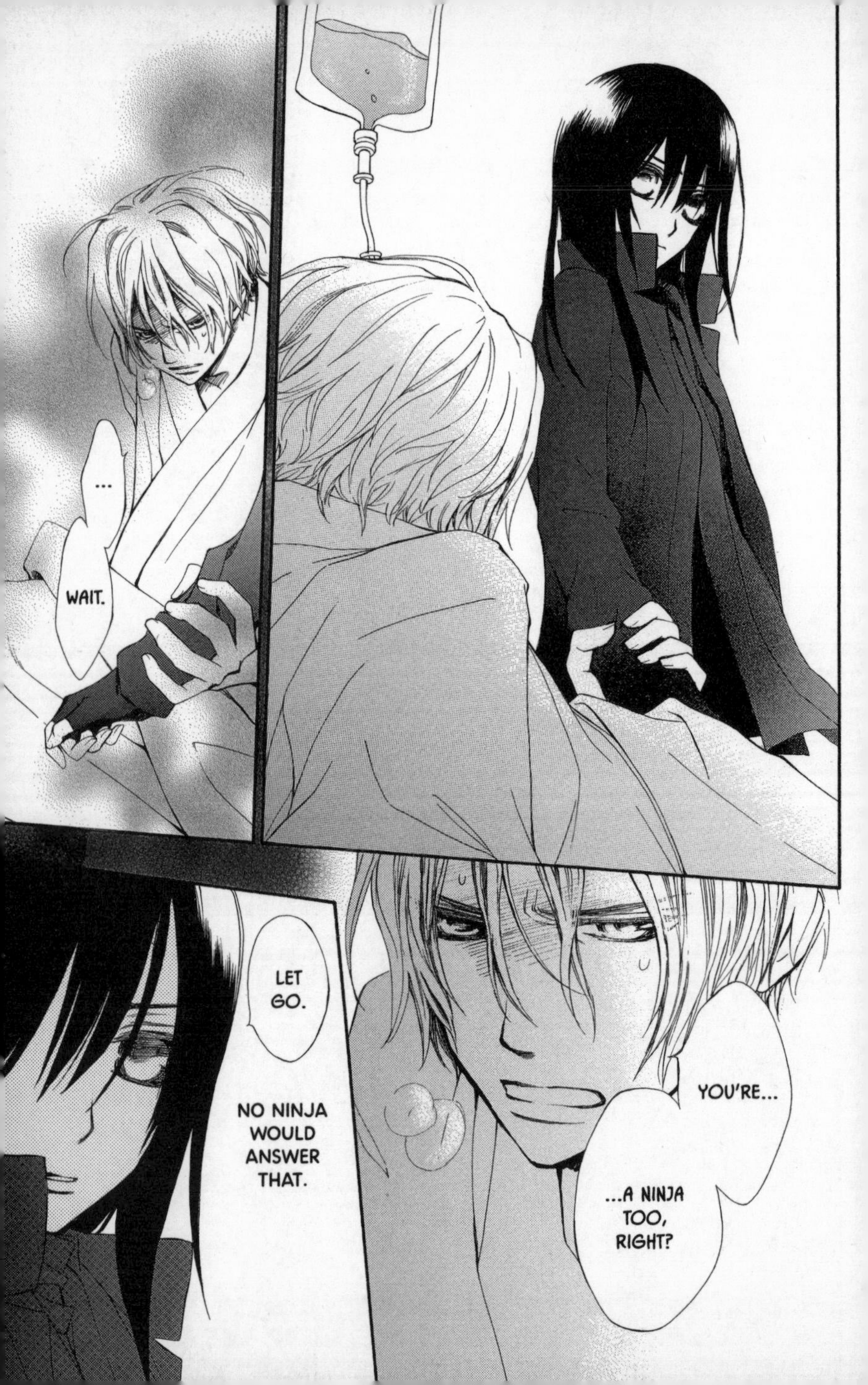
...
WAIT.
LET GO.
YOU'RE...
...A NINJA TOO, RIGHT?
NO NINJA WOULD ANSWER THAT.

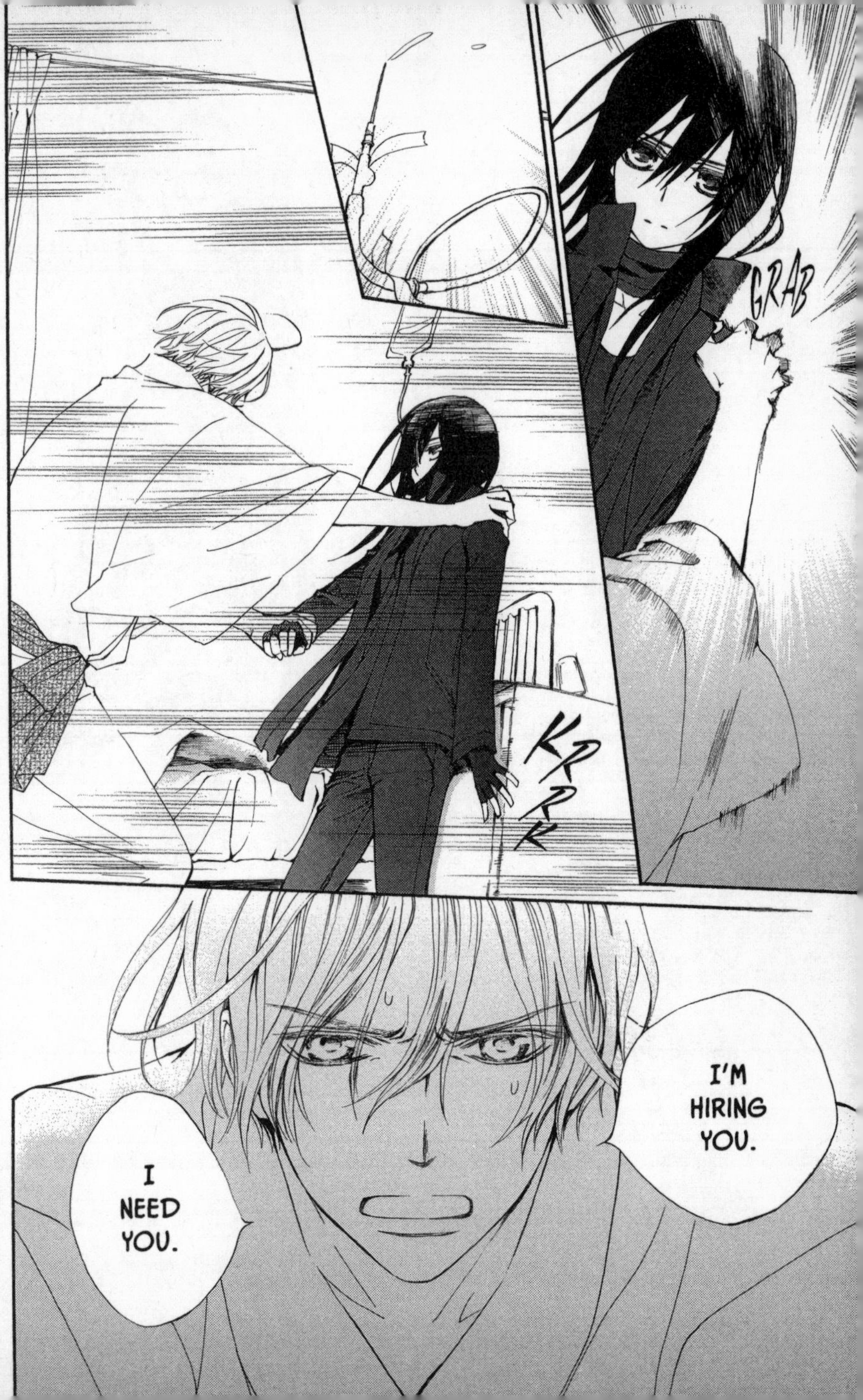
GRAB
KRRRK
I'M HIRING YOU.
I NEED YOU.

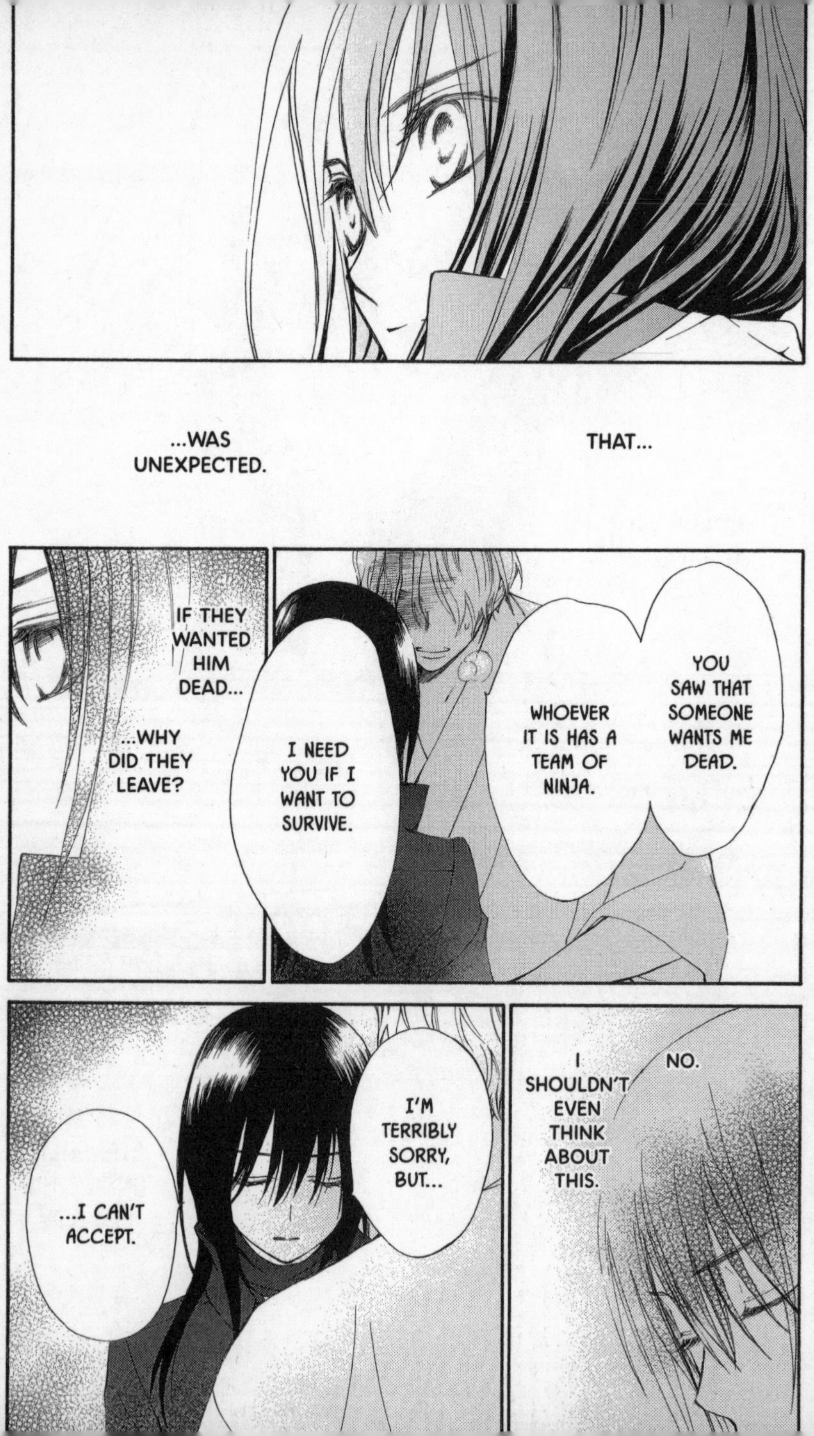
THAT...
...WAS UNEXPECTED.
YOU SAW THAT SOMEONE WANTS ME DEAD.
WHOEVER IT IS HAS A TEAM OF NINJA.
I NEED YOU IF I WANT TO SURVIVE.
IF THEY WANTED HIM DEAD...
...WHY DID THEY LEAVE?
NO.
I SHOULDN'T EVEN THINK ABOUT THIS.
I'M TERRIBLY SORRY, BUT...
...I CAN'T ACCEPT.

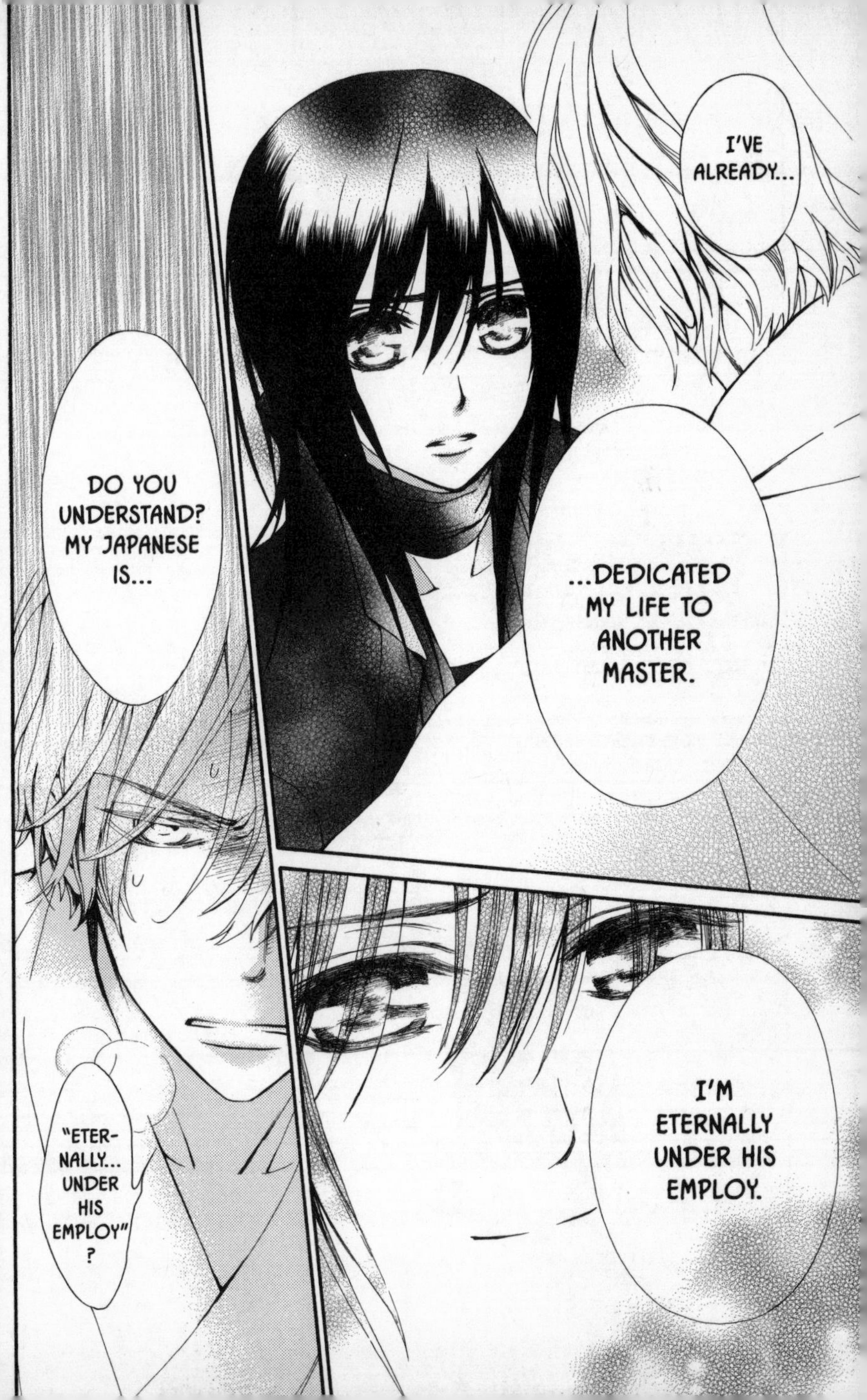
I'VE ALREADY...
...DEDICATED MY LIFE TO ANOTHER MASTER.
I'M ETERNALLY UNDER HIS EMPLOY.
DO YOU UNDERSTAND? MY JAPANESE IS...
"ETER-NALLY... UNDER HIS EMPLOY"?

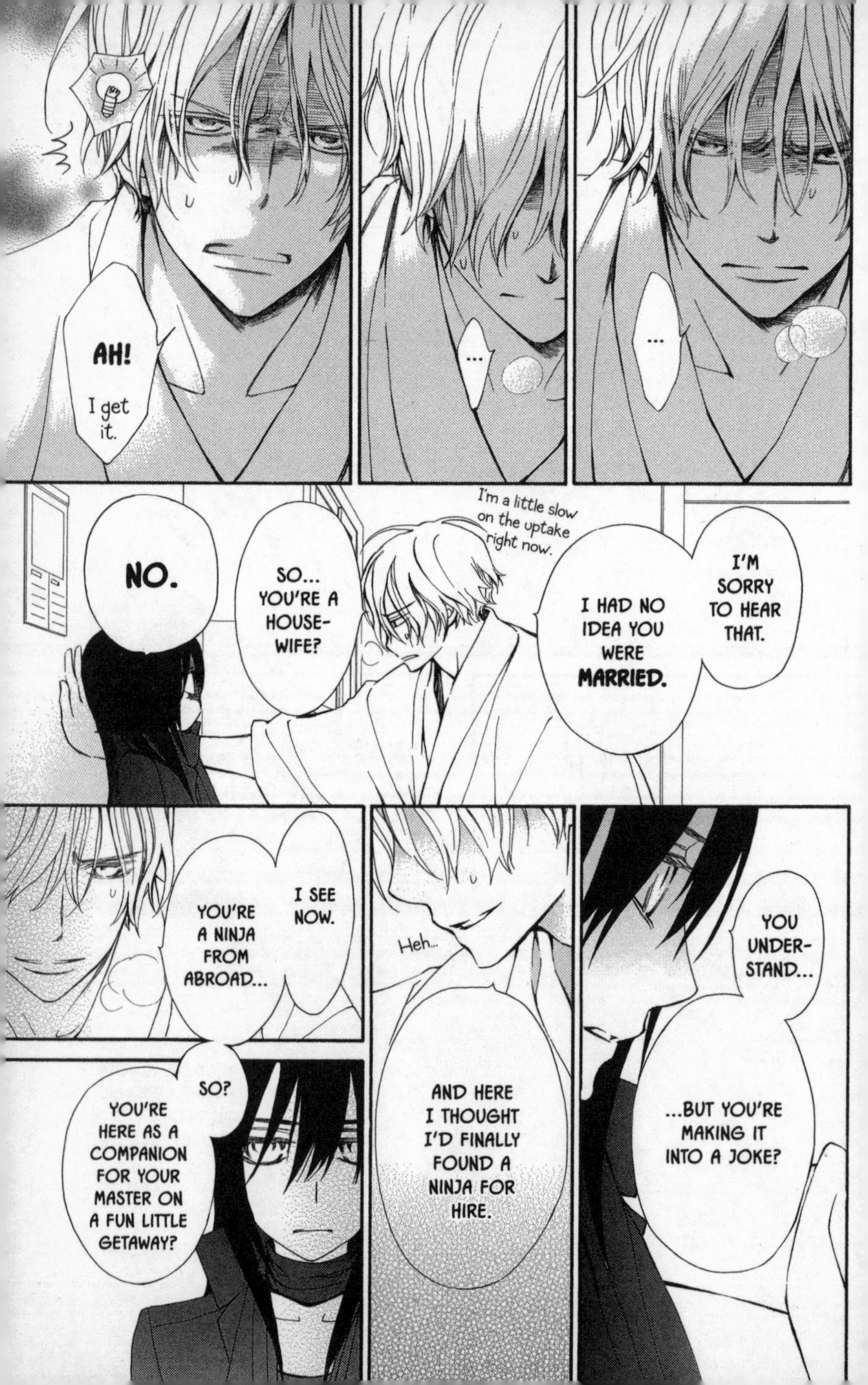
...
...
AH!
I get it.
I'M SORRY TO HEAR THAT.
I HAD NO IDEA YOU WERE MARRIED.
I'm a little slow on the uptake right now.
SO... YOU'RE A HOUSE-WIFE?
NO.
YOU UNDER-STAND...
...BUT YOU'RE MAKING IT INTO A JOKE?
Heh...
AND HERE I THOUGHT I'D FINALLY FOUND A NINJA FOR HIRE.
I SEE NOW.
YOU'RE A NINJA FROM ABROAD...
SO?
YOU'RE HERE AS A COMPANION FOR YOUR MASTER ON A FUN LITTLE GETAWAY?

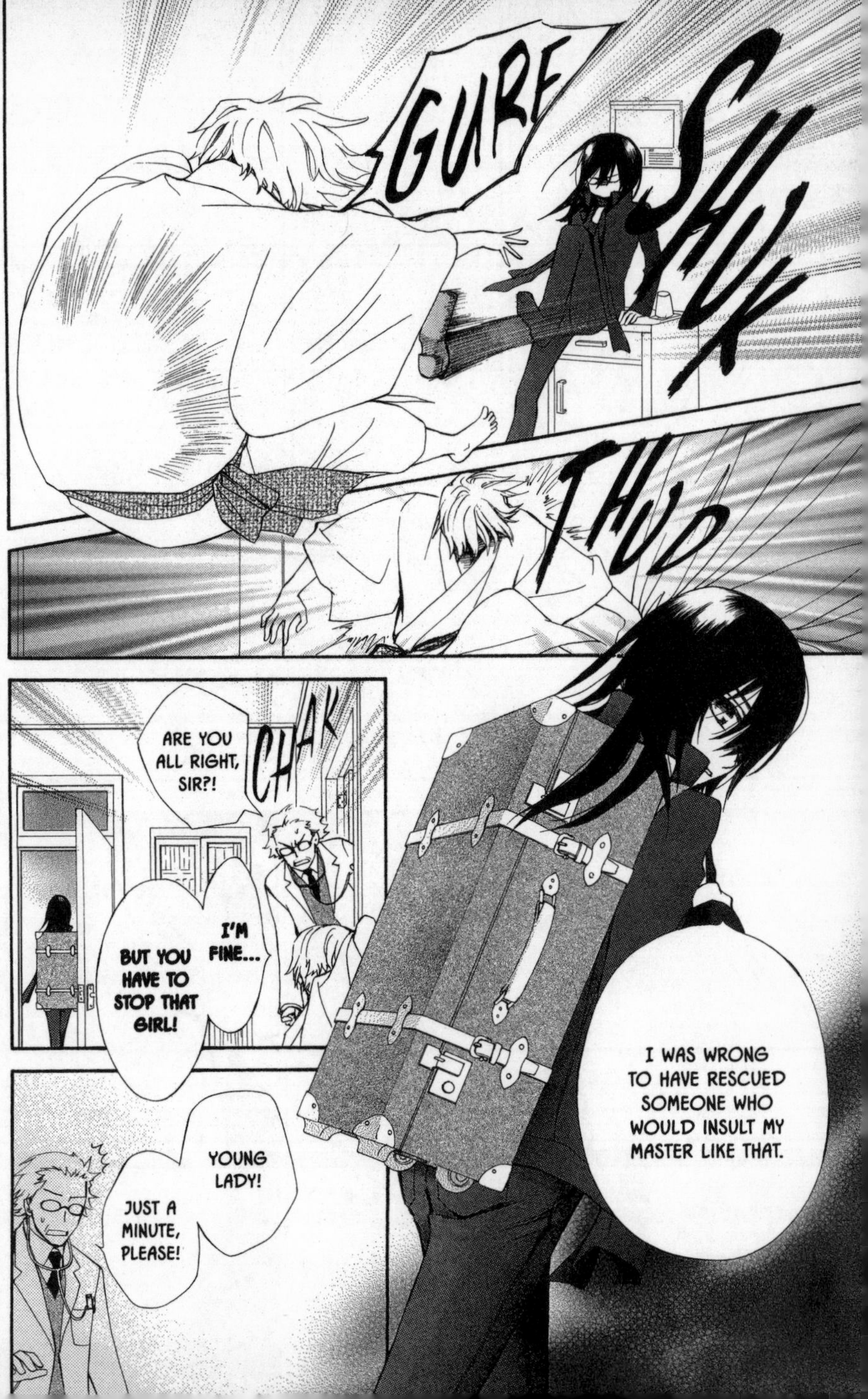
SHUK
GURE
THUD
I WAS WRONG TO HAVE RESCUED SOMEONE WHO WOULD INSULT MY MASTER LIKE THAT.
CHAK
ARE YOU ALL RIGHT, SIR?!
I'M FINE...
BUT YOU HAVE TO STOP THAT GIRL!
YOUNG LADY!
JUST A MINUTE, PLEASE!

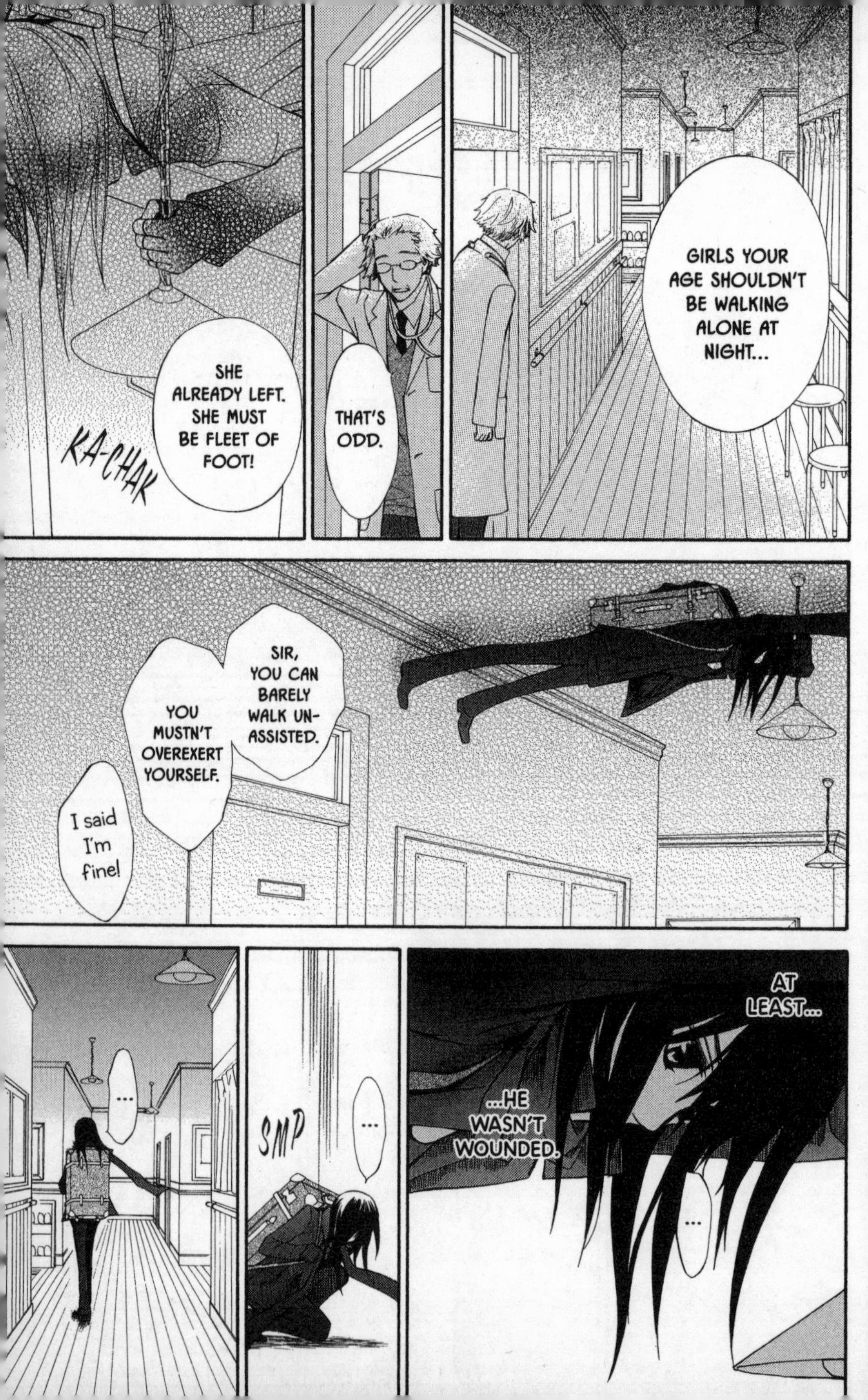
GIRLS YOUR AGE SHOULDN'T BE WALKING ALONE AT NIGHT...
THAT'S ODD.
SHE ALREADY LEFT. SHE MUST BE FLEET OF FOOT!
KA-CHAK
SIR, YOU CAN BARELY WALK UN-ASSISTED.
YOU MUSTN'T OVEREXERT YOURSELF.
I said I'm fine!
AT LEAST...
...HE WASN'T WOUNDED.
...
SMP
...
...

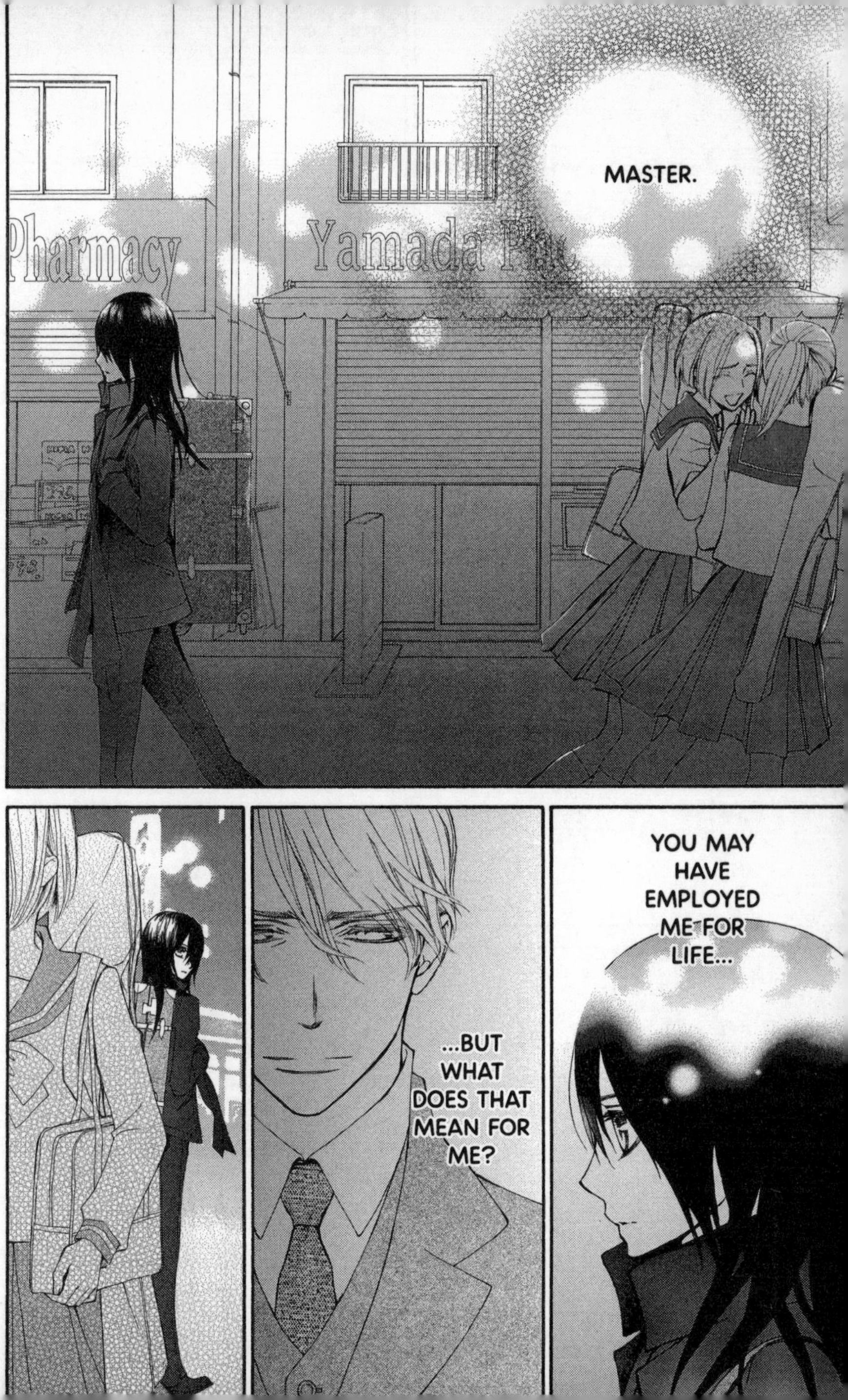
Pharmacy
Yamada
MASTER.
YOU MAY HAVE EMPLOYED ME FOR LIFE...
...BUT WHAT DOES THAT MEAN FOR ME?

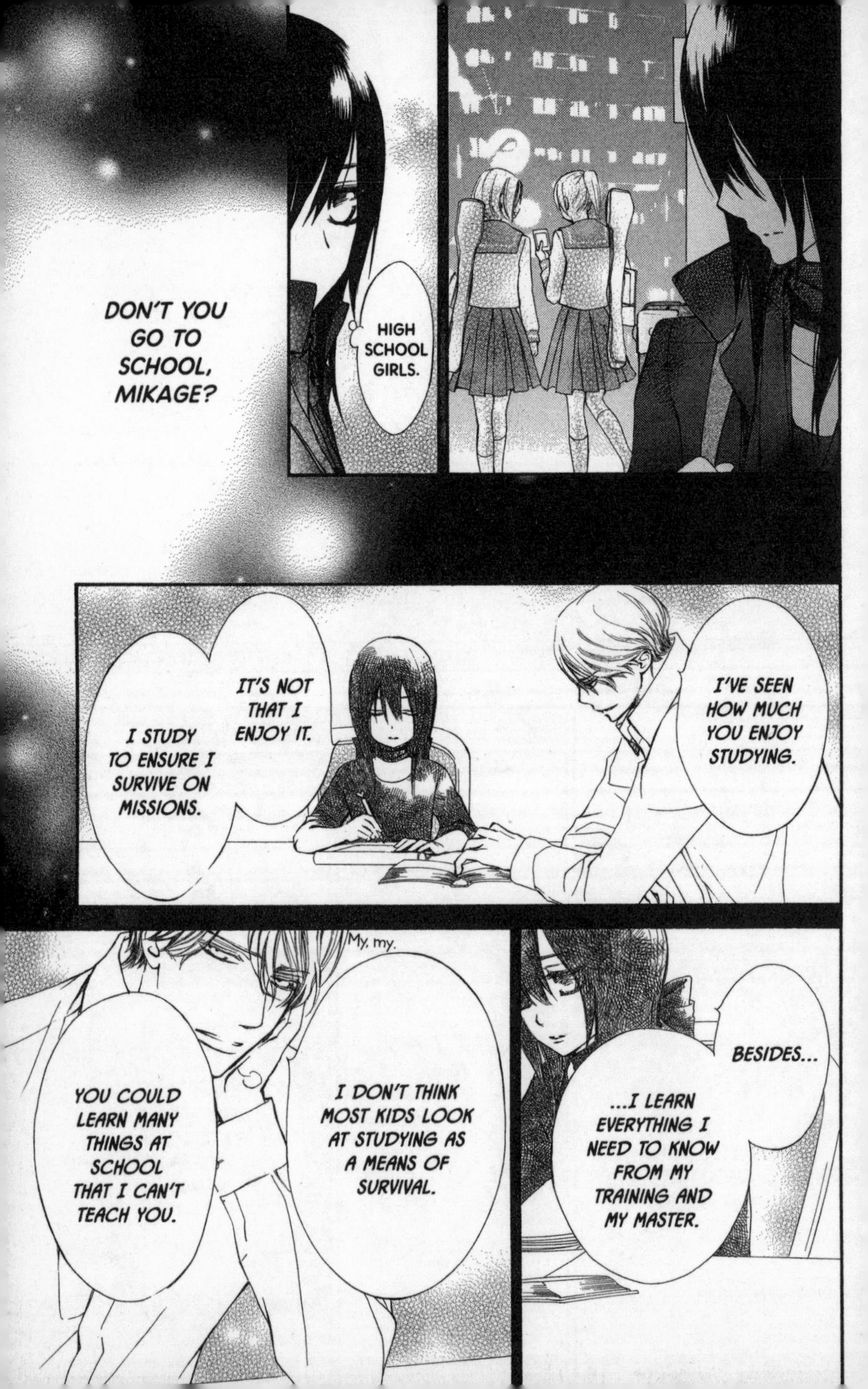
HIGH SCHOOL GIRLS.
DON'T YOU GO TO SCHOOL, MIKAGE?
I'VE SEEN HOW MUCH YOU ENJOY STUDYING.
IT'S NOT THAT I ENJOY IT.
I STUDY TO ENSURE I SURVIVE ON MISSIONS.
BESIDES...
...I LEARN EVERYTHING I NEED TO KNOW FROM MY TRAINING AND MY MASTER.
My, my.
I DON'T THINK MOST KIDS LOOK AT STUDYING AS A MEANS OF SURVIVAL.
YOU COULD LEARN MANY THINGS AT SCHOOL THAT I CAN'T TEACH YOU.

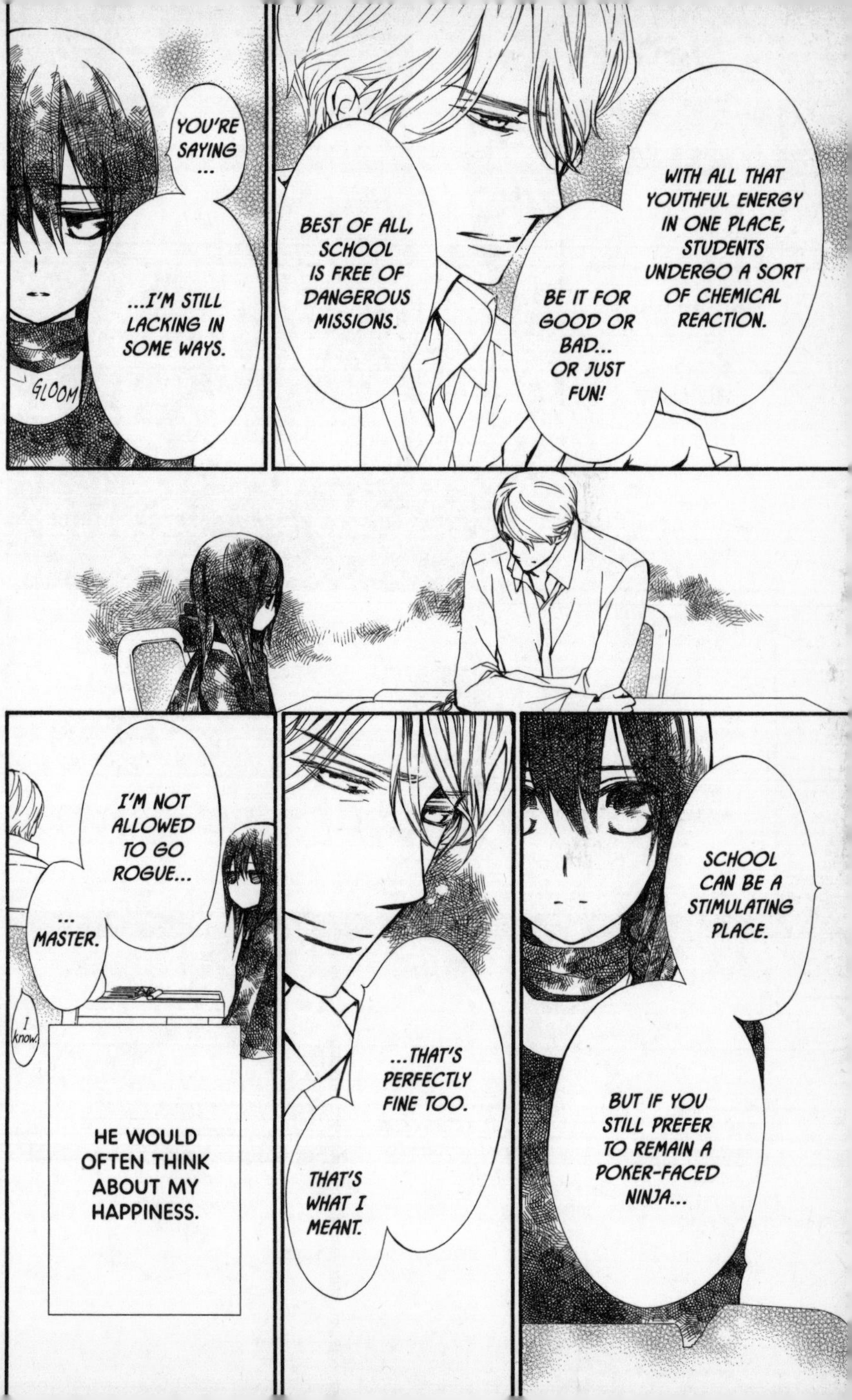
WITH ALL THAT YOUTHFUL ENERGY IN ONE PLACE, STUDENTS UNDERGO A SORT OF CHEMICAL REACTION.
BE IT FOR GOOD OR BAD... OR JUST FUN!
BEST OF ALL, SCHOOL IS FREE OF DANGEROUS MISSIONS.
YOU'RE SAYING...
...I'M STILL LACKING IN SOME WAYS.
GLOOM
SCHOOL CAN BE A STIMULATING PLACE.
BUT IF YOU STILL PREFER TO REMAIN A POKER-FACED NINJA...
...THAT'S PERFECTLY FINE TOO.
THAT'S WHAT I MEANT.
I'M NOT ALLOWED TO GO ROGUE...
...MASTER.
I know.
HE WOULD OFTEN THINK ABOUT MY HAPPINESS.

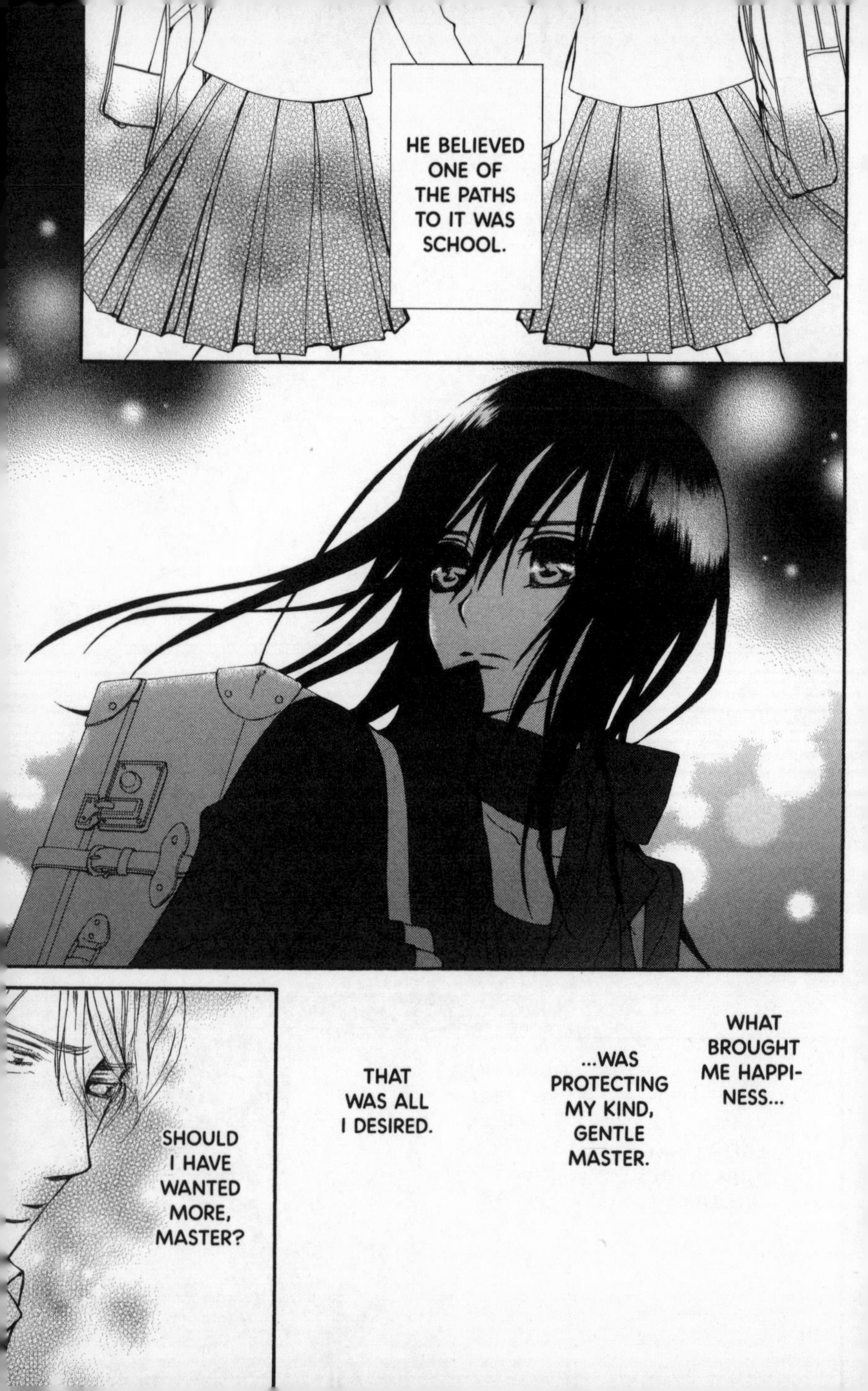
HE BELIEVED ONE OF THE PATHS TO IT WAS SCHOOL.
WHAT BROUGHT ME HAPPI-NESS...
...WAS PROTECTING MY KIND, GENTLE MASTER.
THAT WAS ALL I DESIRED.
SHOULD I HAVE WANTED MORE, MASTER?

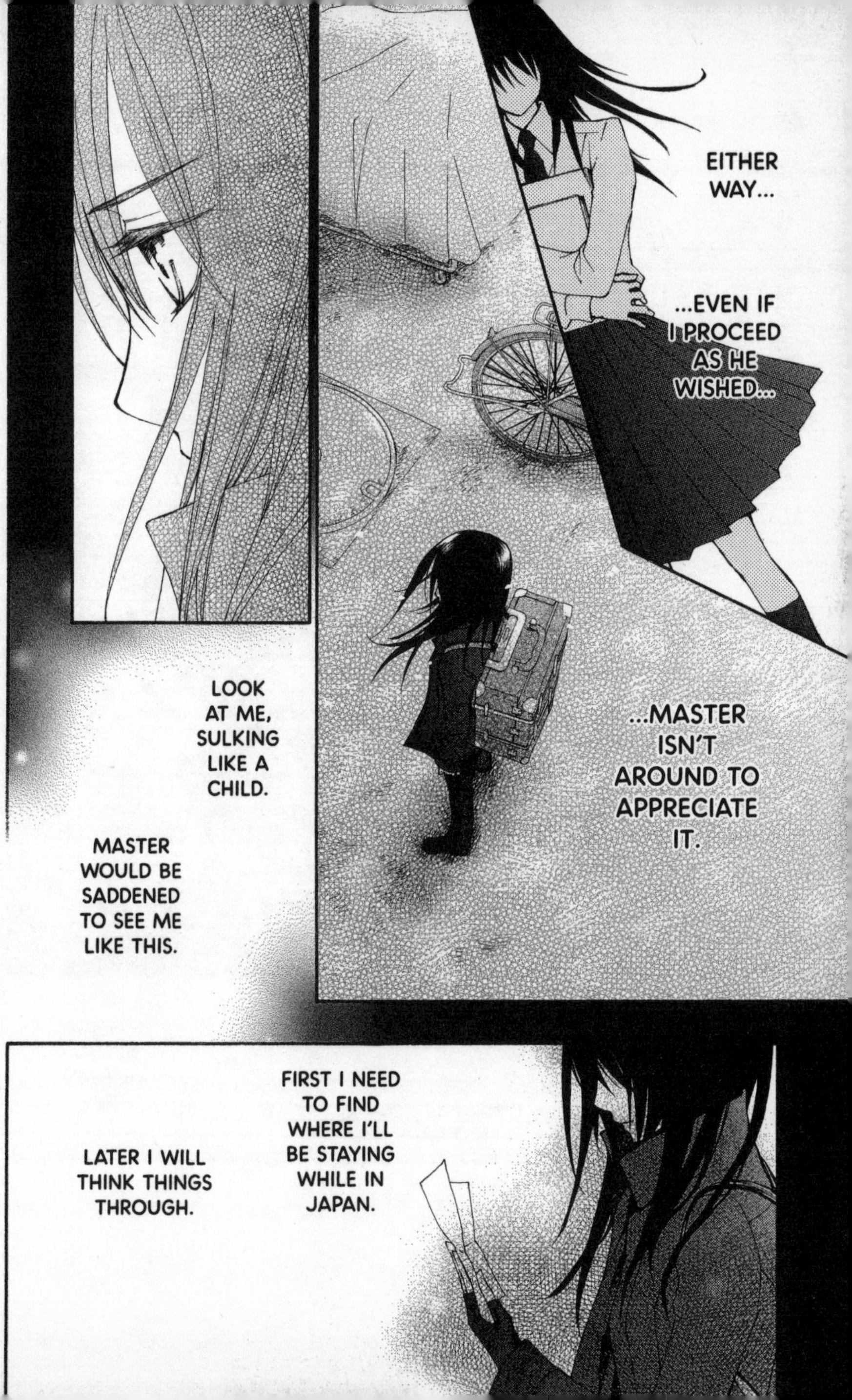
EITHER WAY...
...EVEN IF I PROCEED AS HE WISHED...
...MASTER ISN'T AROUND TO APPRECIATE IT.
LOOK AT ME, SULKING LIKE A CHILD.
MASTER WOULD BE SADDENED TO SEE ME LIKE THIS.
FIRST I NEED TO FIND WHERE I'LL BE STAYING WHILE IN JAPAN.
LATER I WILL THINK THINGS THROUGH.

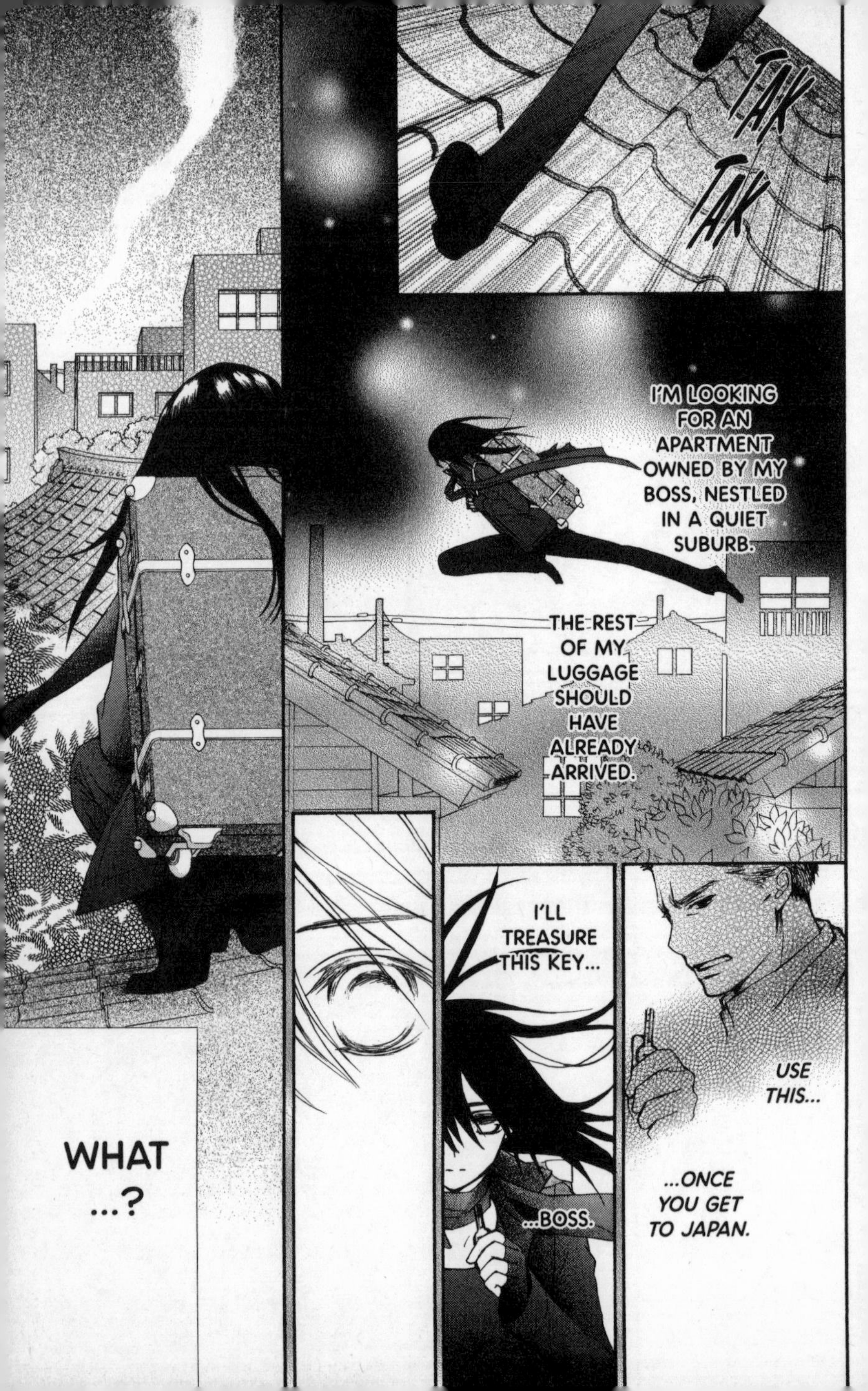
TAK TAK
I'M LOOKING FOR AN APARTMENT OWNED BY MY BOSS, NESTLED IN A QUIET SUBURB.
THE REST OF MY LUGGAGE SHOULD HAVE ALREADY ARRIVED.
USE THIS...
...ONCE YOU GET TO JAPAN.
I'LL TREASURE THIS KEY...
...BOSS.
WHAT ...?

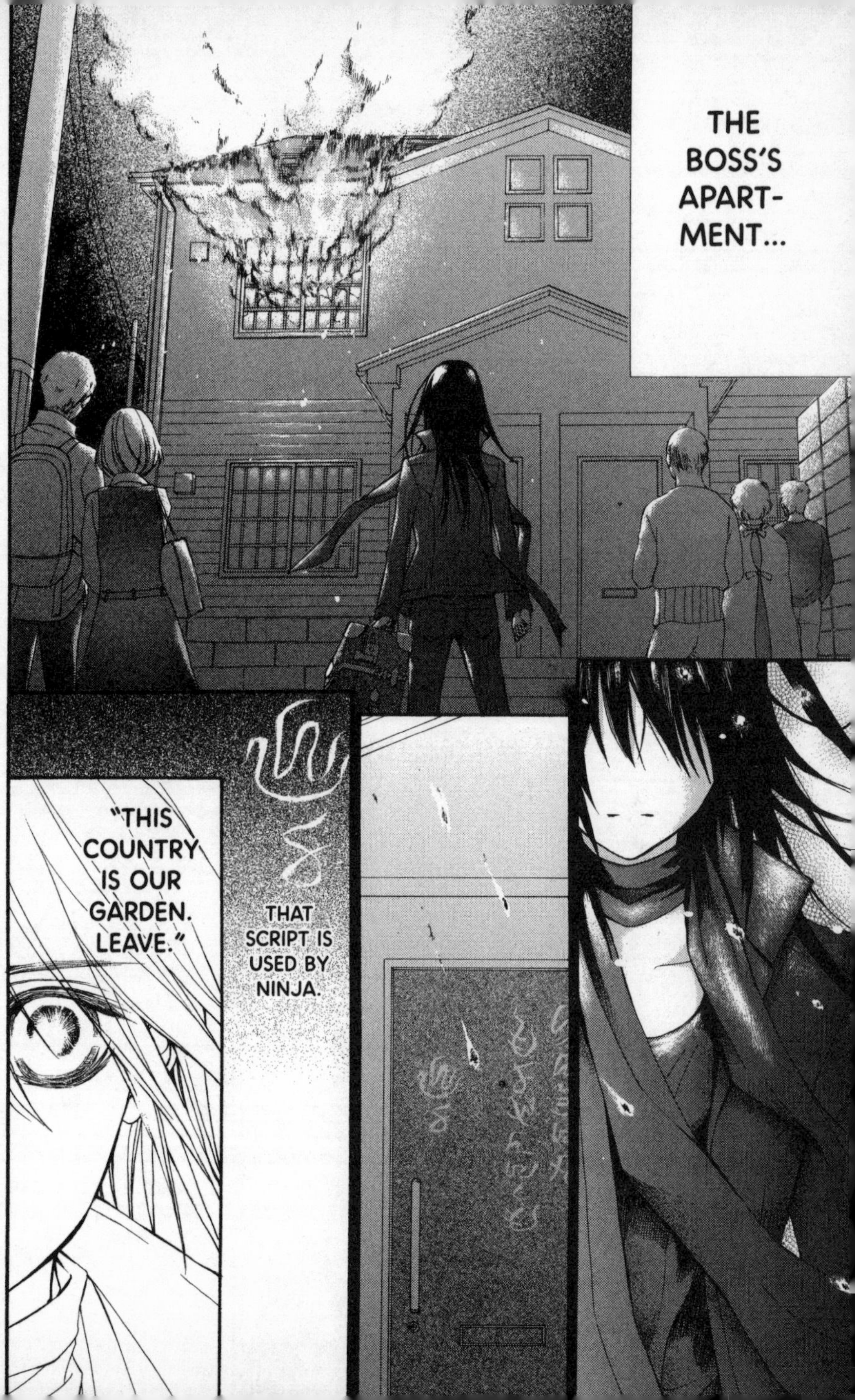
THE BOSS'S APARTMENT...
"THIS COUNTRY IS OUR GARDEN. LEAVE."
THAT SCRIPT IS USED BY NINJA.

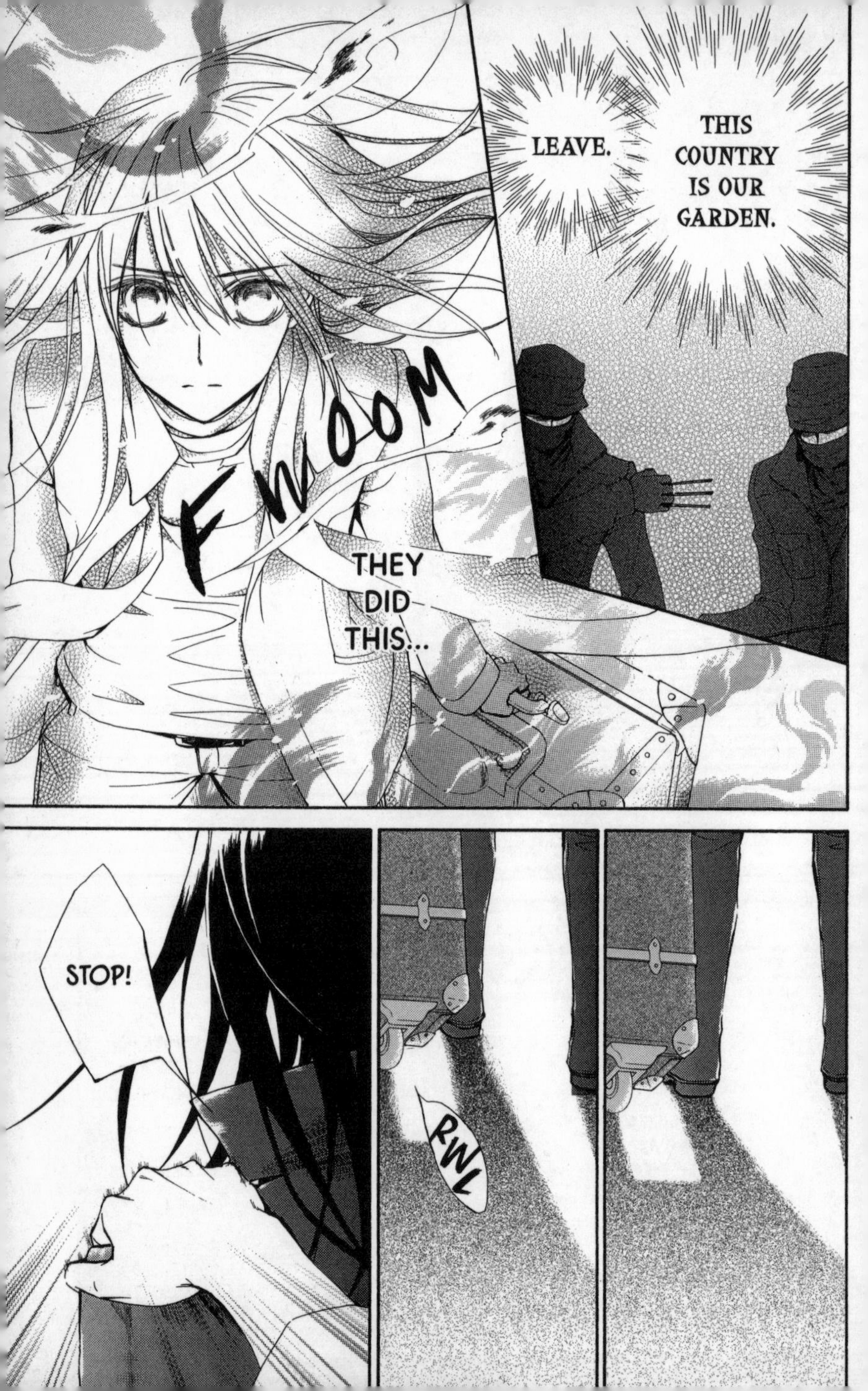
THIS COUNTRY IS OUR GARDEN.
LEAVE.
FWOOM
THEY DID THIS...
RWL
STOP!

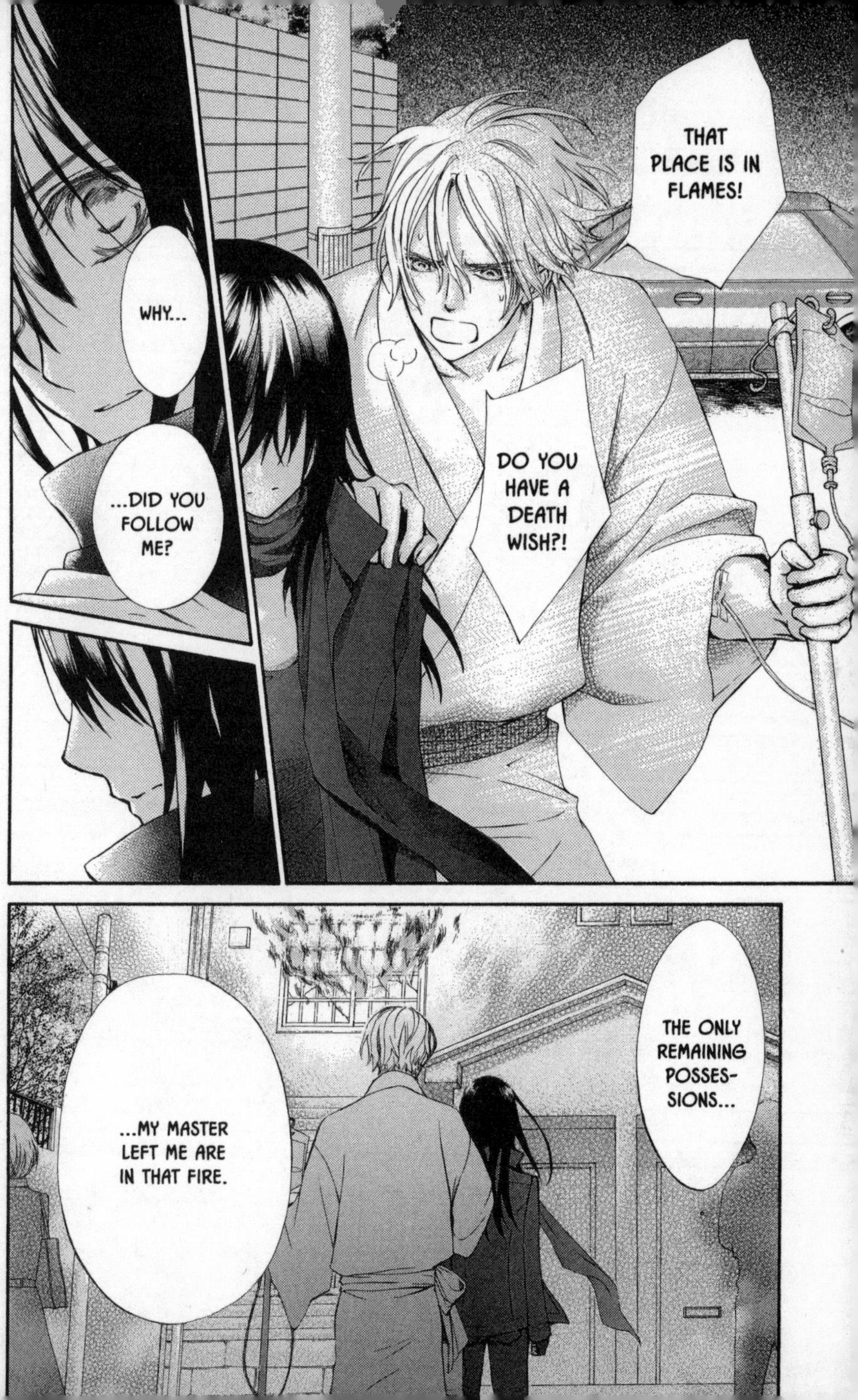
THAT PLACE IS IN FLAMES!
DO YOU HAVE A DEATH WISH?!
WHY...
...DID YOU FOLLOW ME?
THE ONLY REMAINING POSSES-SIONS...
...MY MASTER LEFT ME ARE IN THAT FIRE.

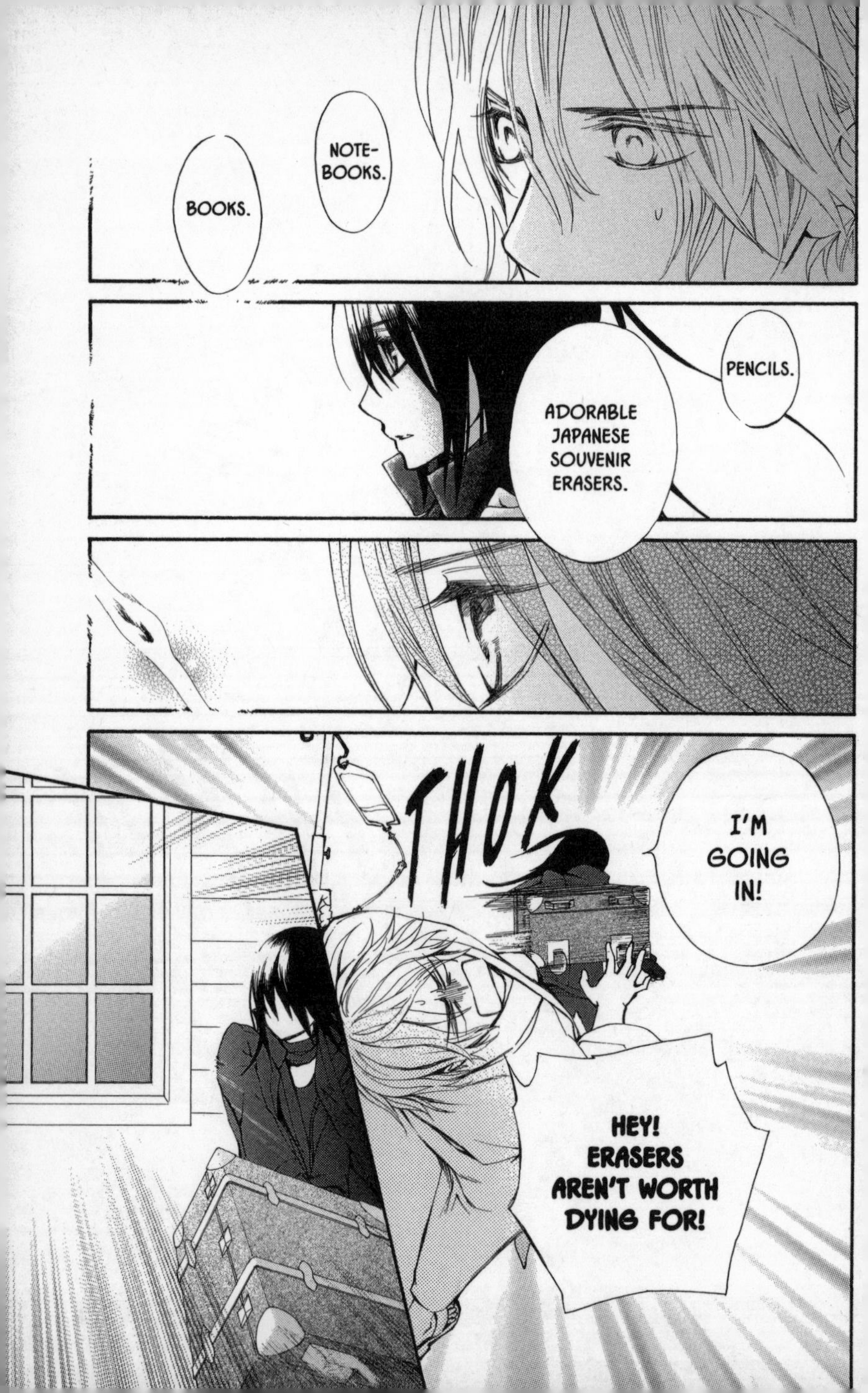
NOTE-BOOKS.
BOOKS.
PENCILS.
ADORABLE JAPANESE SOUVENIR ERASERS.
THOK
I'M GOING IN!
HEY! ERASERS AREN'T WORTH DYING FOR!

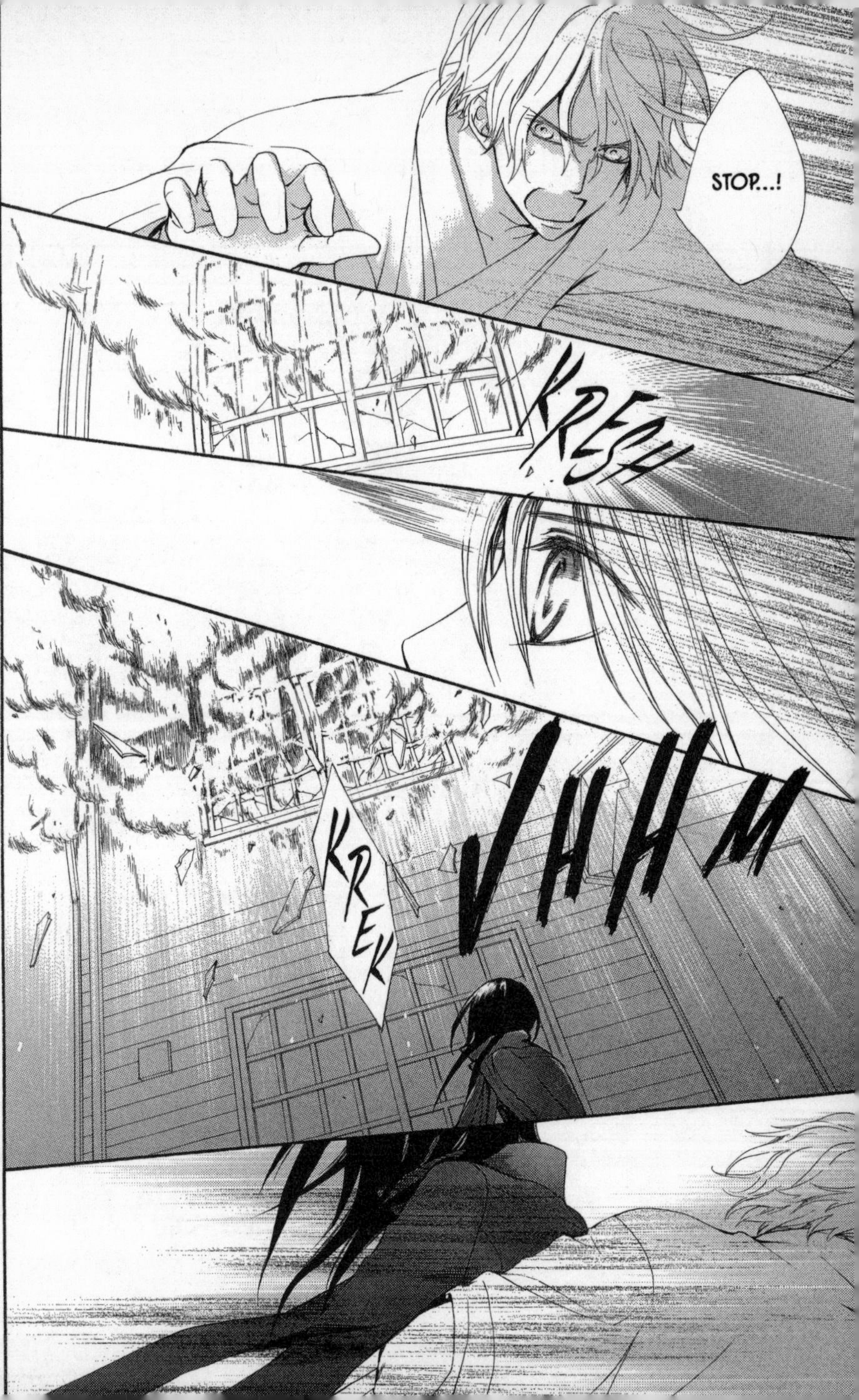
STOP...!
KRESH
VHHM
KREK

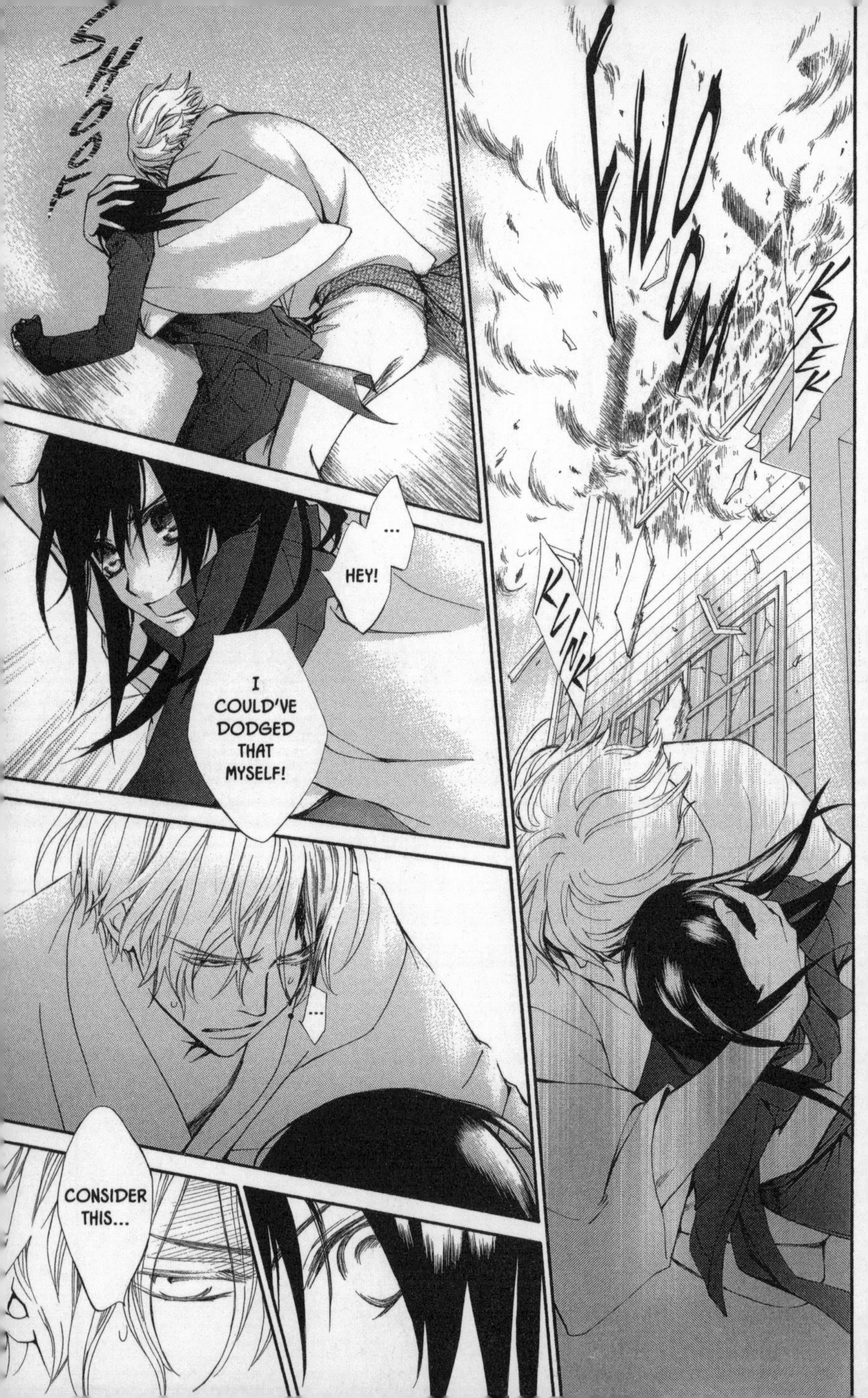
WHOOM
KREK
KLINK
SHOOF
...
HEY!
I COULD'VE DODGED THAT MYSELF!
...
CONSIDER THIS...

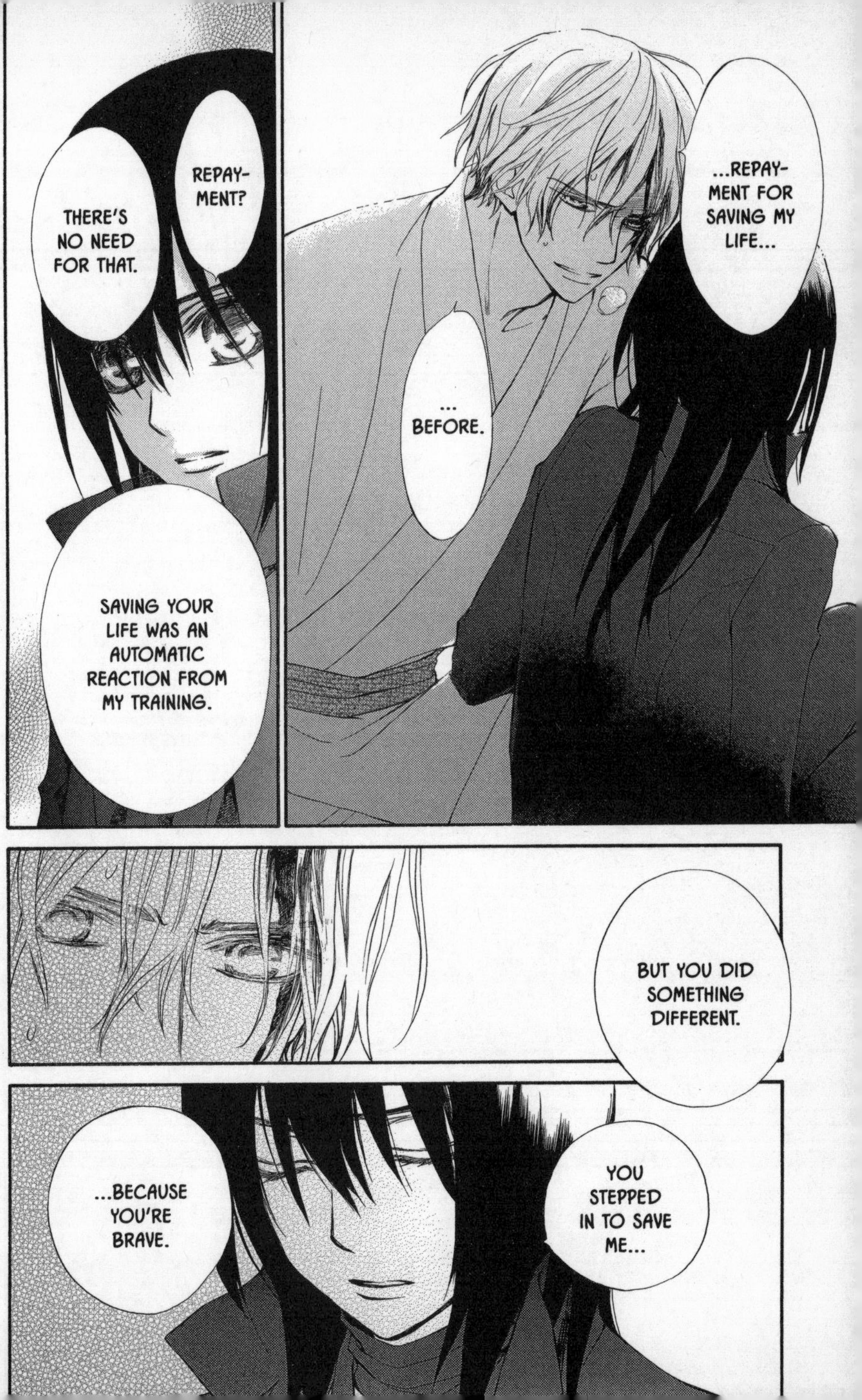
...REPAY-MENT FOR SAVING MY LIFE...
... BEFORE.
REPAY-MENT?
THERE'S NO NEED FOR THAT.
SAVING YOUR LIFE WAS AN AUTOMATIC REACTION FROM MY TRAINING.
BUT YOU DID SOMETHING DIFFERENT.
YOU STEPPED IN TO SAVE ME...
...BECAUSE YOU'RE BRAVE.

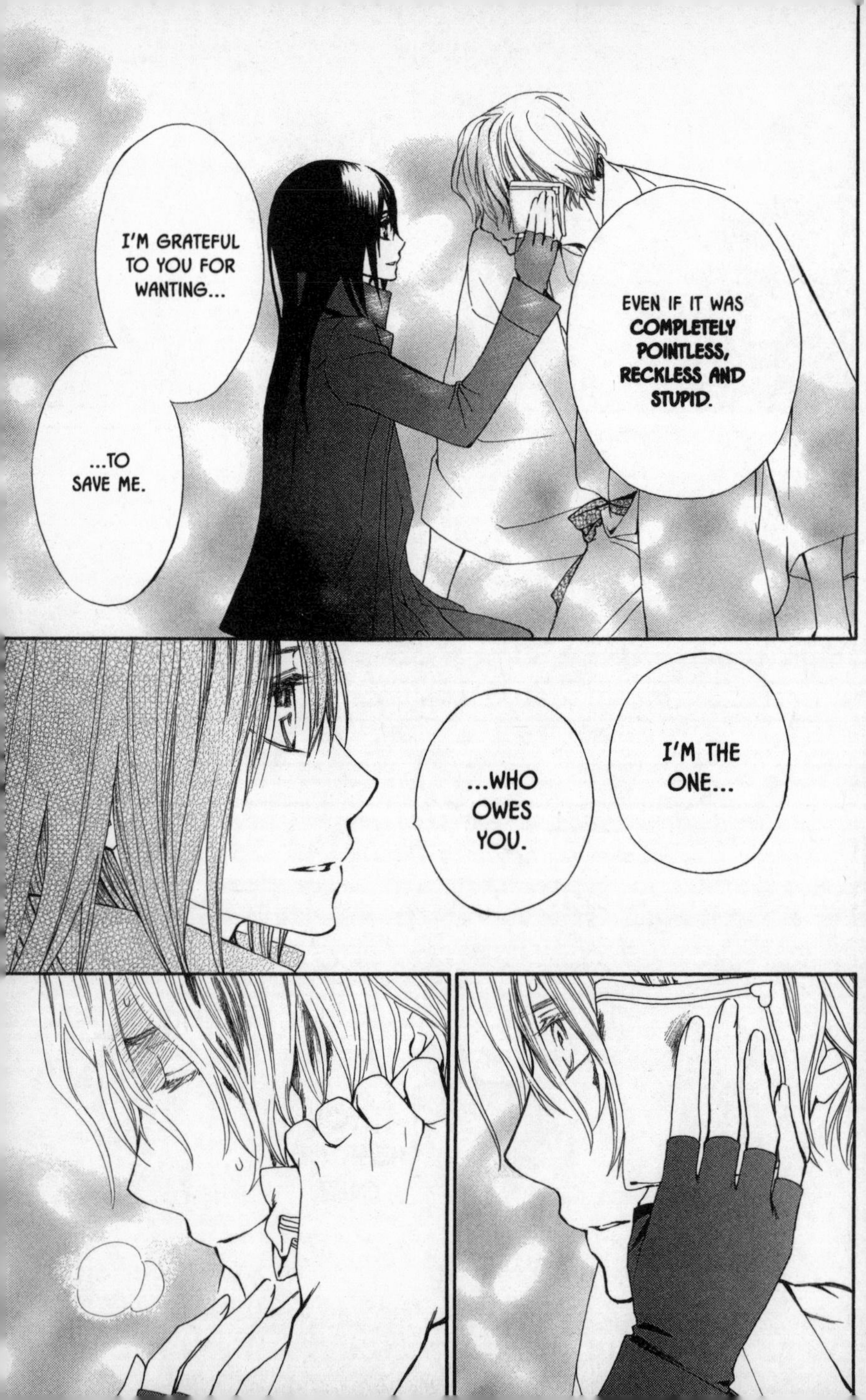
I'M GRATEFUL TO YOU FOR WANTING...
...TO SAVE ME.
EVEN IF IT WAS COMPLETELY POINTLESS, RECKLESS AND STUPID.
I'M THE ONE...
...WHO OWES YOU.

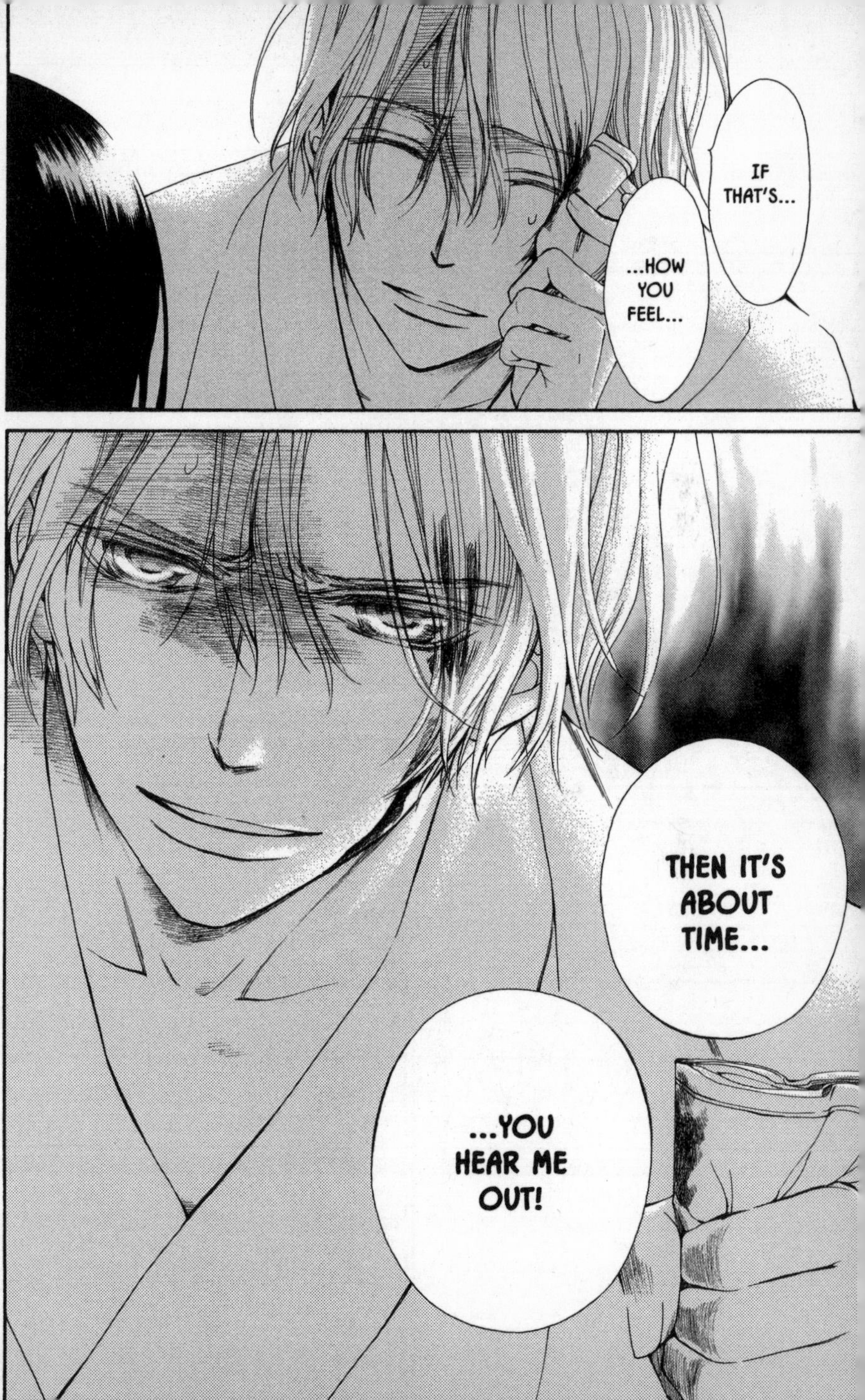
IF THAT'S...
...HOW YOU FEEL...
THEN IT'S ABOUT TIME...
...YOU HEAR ME OUT!

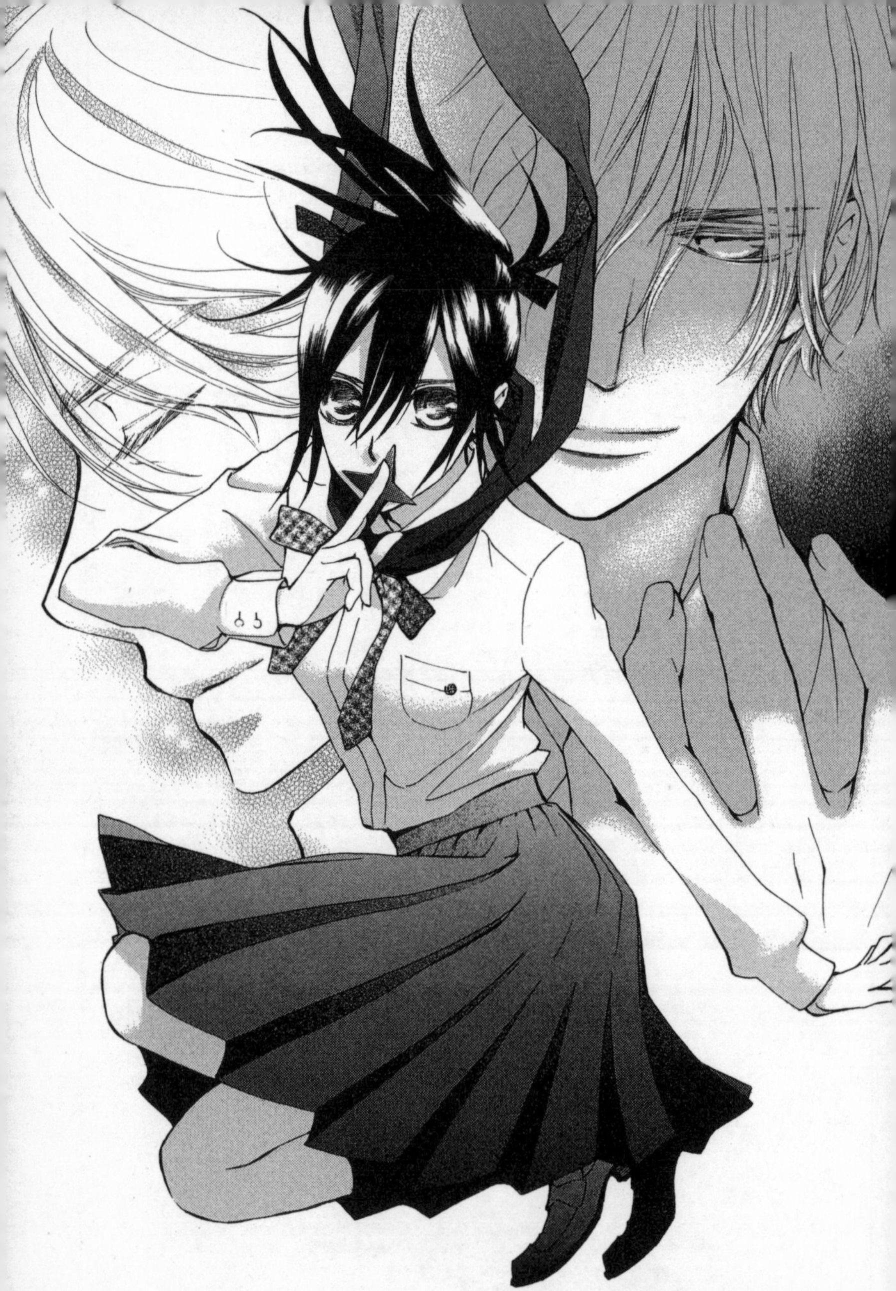

Chapter 3

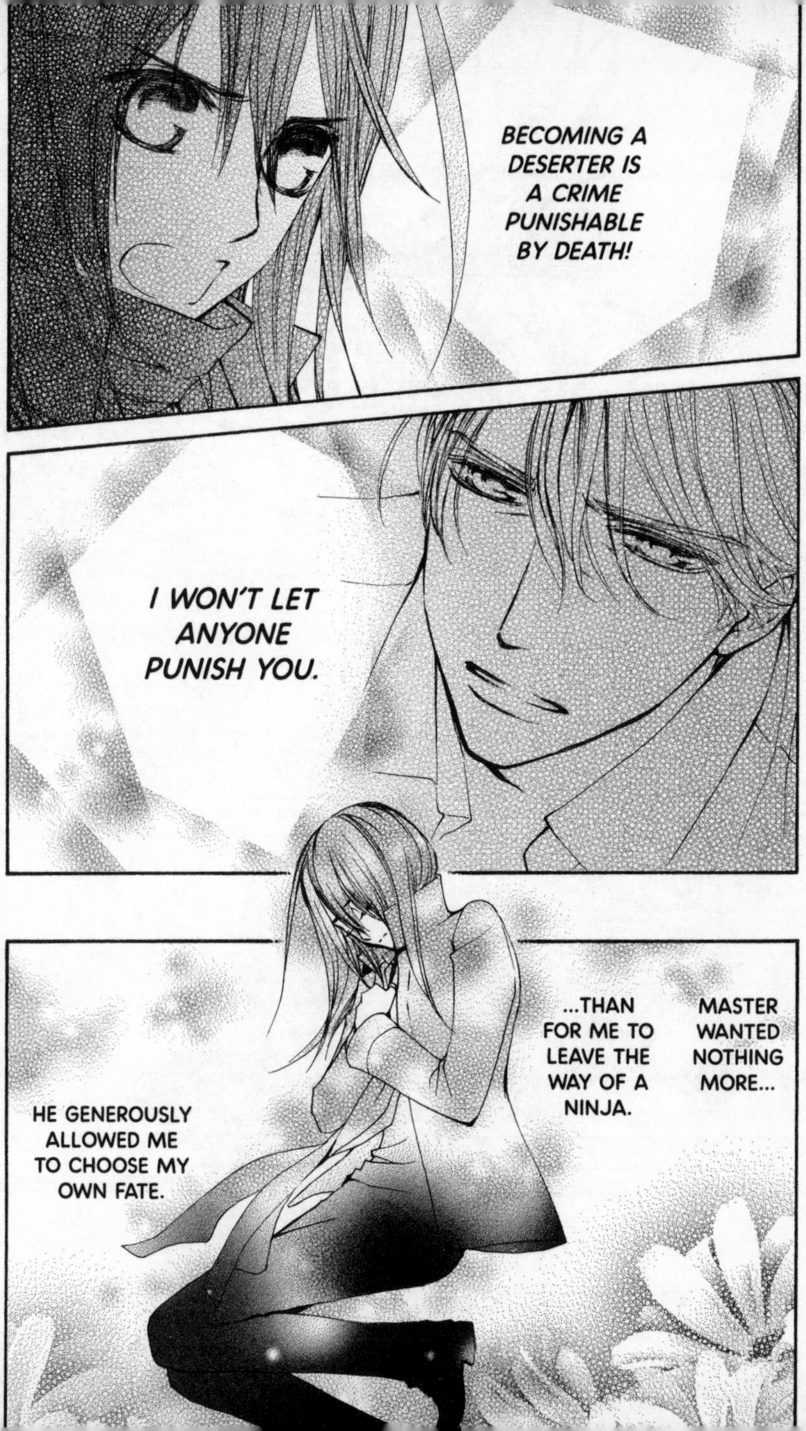
BECOMING A DESERTER IS A CRIME PUNISHABLE BY DEATH!
I WON'T LET ANYONE PUNISH YOU.
MASTER WANTED NOTHING MORE...
...THAN FOR ME TO LEAVE THE WAY OF A NINJA.
HE GENEROUSLY ALLOWED ME TO CHOOSE MY OWN FATE.

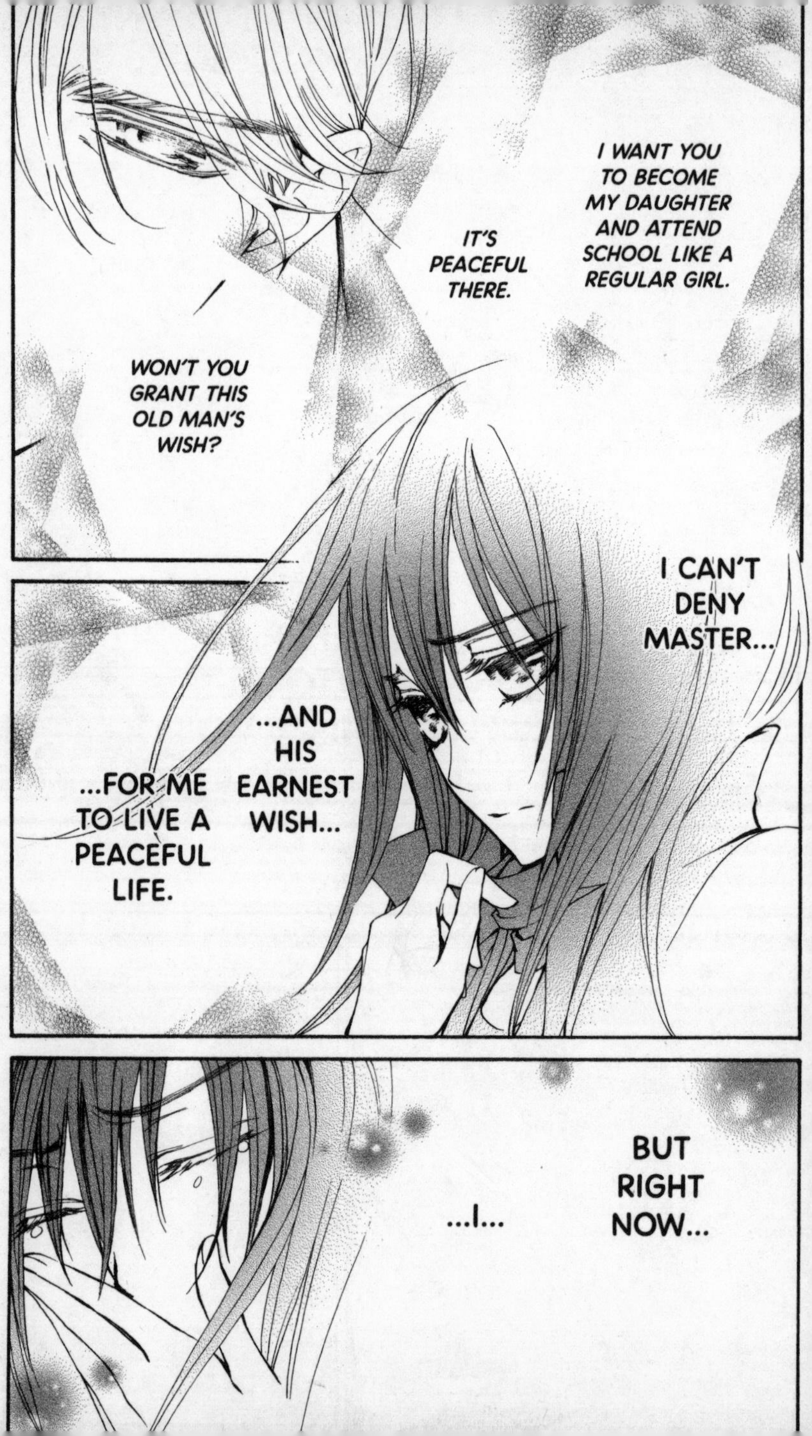
I WANT YOU TO BECOME MY DAUGHTER AND ATTEND SCHOOL LIKE A REGULAR GIRL.
IT'S PEACEFUL THERE.
WON'T YOU GRANT THIS OLD MAN'S WISH?
I CAN'T DENY MASTER...
...AND HIS EARNEST WISH...
...FOR ME TO LIVE A PEACEFUL LIFE.
BUT RIGHT NOW...
...I...

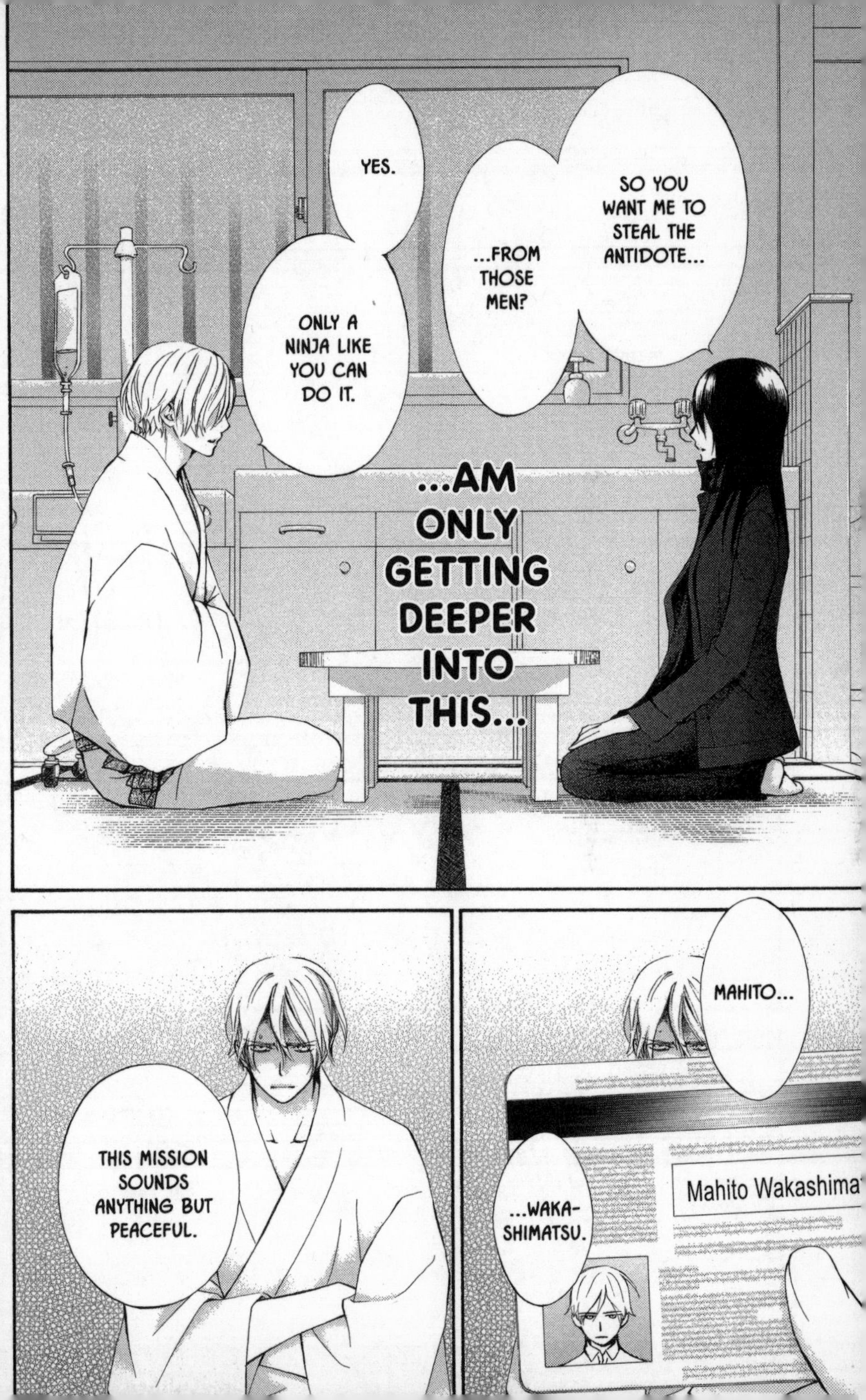
SO YOU WANT ME TO STEAL THE ANTIDOTE...
...FROM THOSE MEN?
YES.
ONLY A NINJA LIKE YOU CAN DO IT.
...AM ONLY GETTING DEEPER INTO THIS...
MAHITO...
...WAKA-SHIMATSU.
Mahito Wakashima
THIS MISSION SOUNDS ANYTHING BUT PEACEFUL.

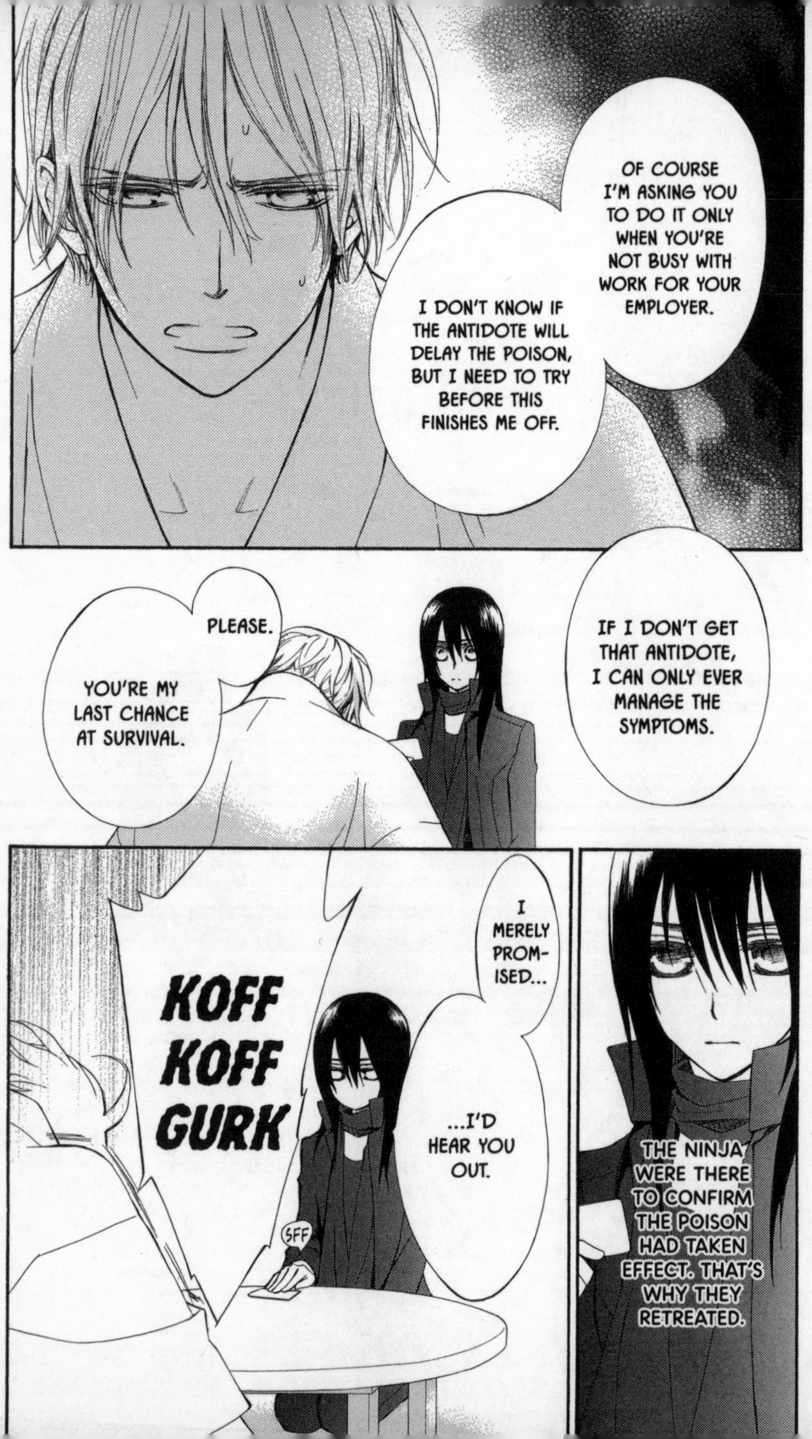
OF COURSE I'M ASKING YOU TO DO IT ONLY WHEN YOU'RE NOT BUSY WITH WORK FOR YOUR EMPLOYER.
I DON'T KNOW IF THE ANTIDOTE WILL DELAY THE POISON, BUT I NEED TO TRY BEFORE THIS FINISHES ME OFF.
IF I DON'T GET THAT ANTIDOTE, I CAN ONLY EVER MANAGE THE SYMPTOMS.
PLEASE.
YOU'RE MY LAST CHANCE AT SURVIVAL.
THE NINJA WERE THERE TO CONFIRM THE POISON HAD TAKEN EFFECT. THAT'S WHY THEY RETREATED.
I MERELY PROM-ISED...
...I'D HEAR YOU OUT.
KOFF KOFF GURK
SFF

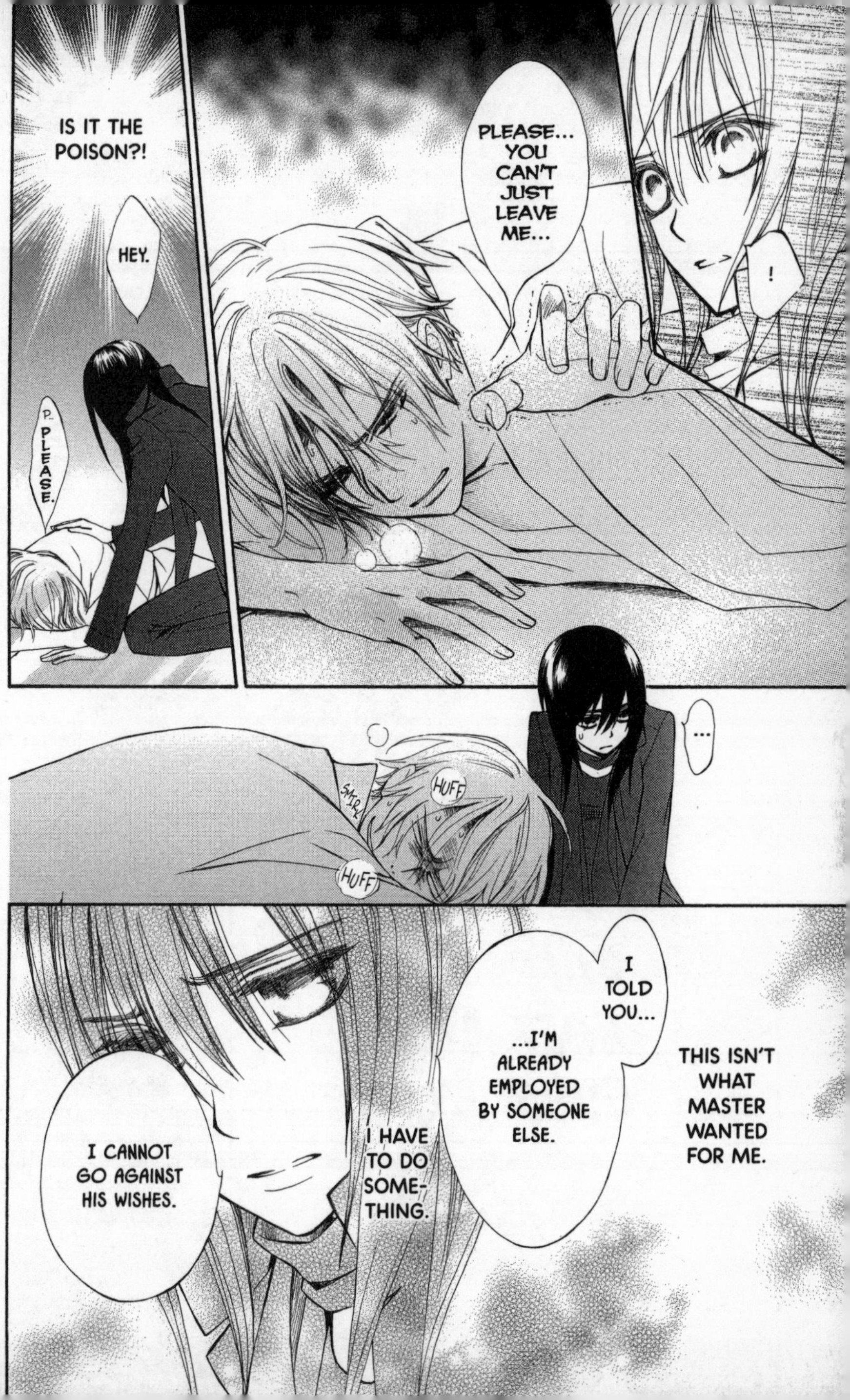
!
PLEASE... YOU CAN'T JUST LEAVE ME...
IS IT THE POISON?!
HEY.
P-PLEASE.
...
SMIRK
HUFF
HUFF
I TOLD YOU... ...I'M ALREADY EMPLOYED BY SOMEONE ELSE.
THIS ISN'T WHAT MASTER WANTED FOR ME.
I HAVE TO DO SOMETHING.
I CANNOT GO AGAINST HIS WISHES.

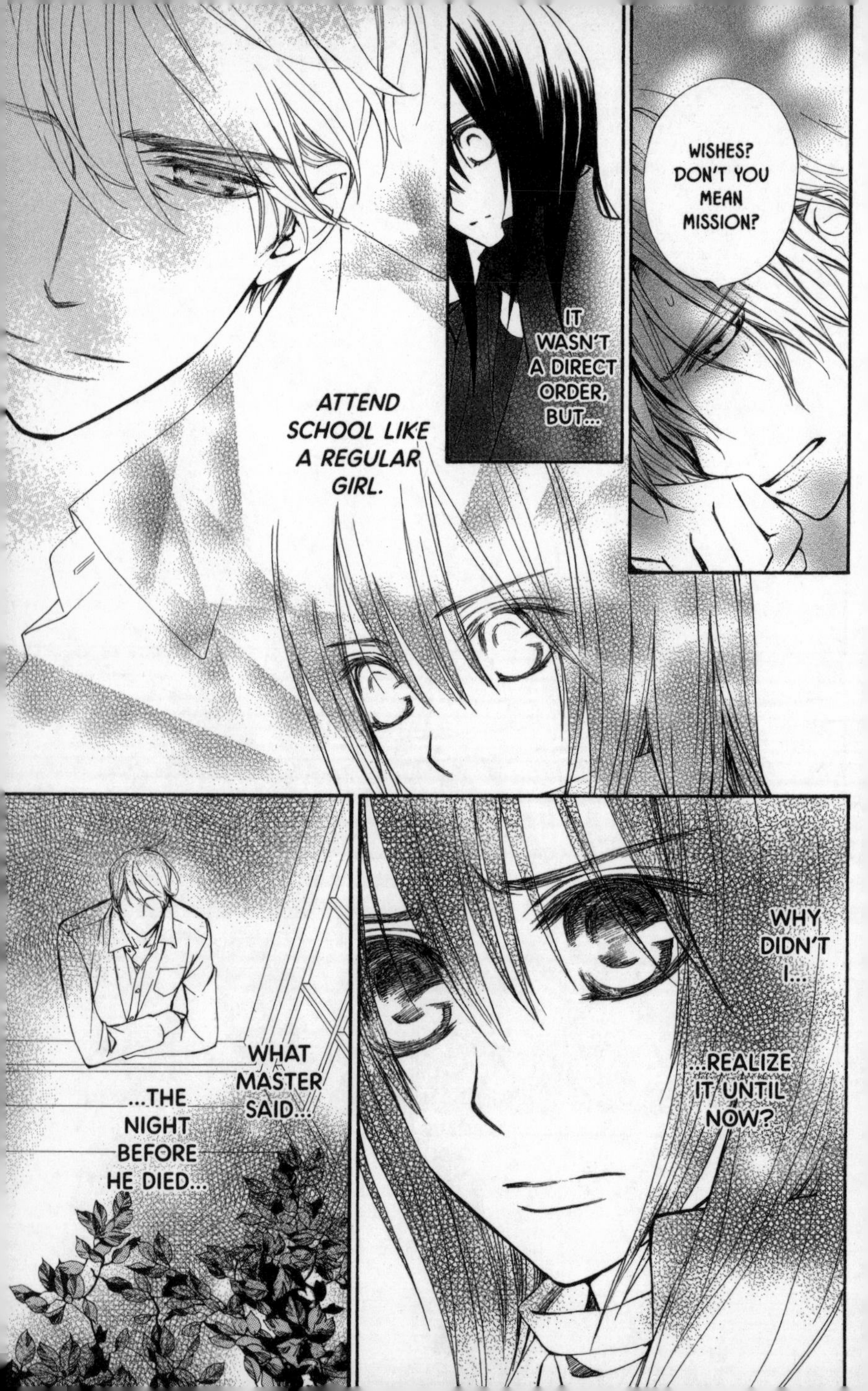
WISHES? DON'T YOU MEAN MISSION?
IT WASN'T A DIRECT ORDER, BUT...
ATTEND SCHOOL LIKE A REGULAR GIRL.
WHY DIDN'T I...
...REALIZE IT UNTIL NOW?
WHAT MASTER SAID...
...THE NIGHT BEFORE HE DIED...

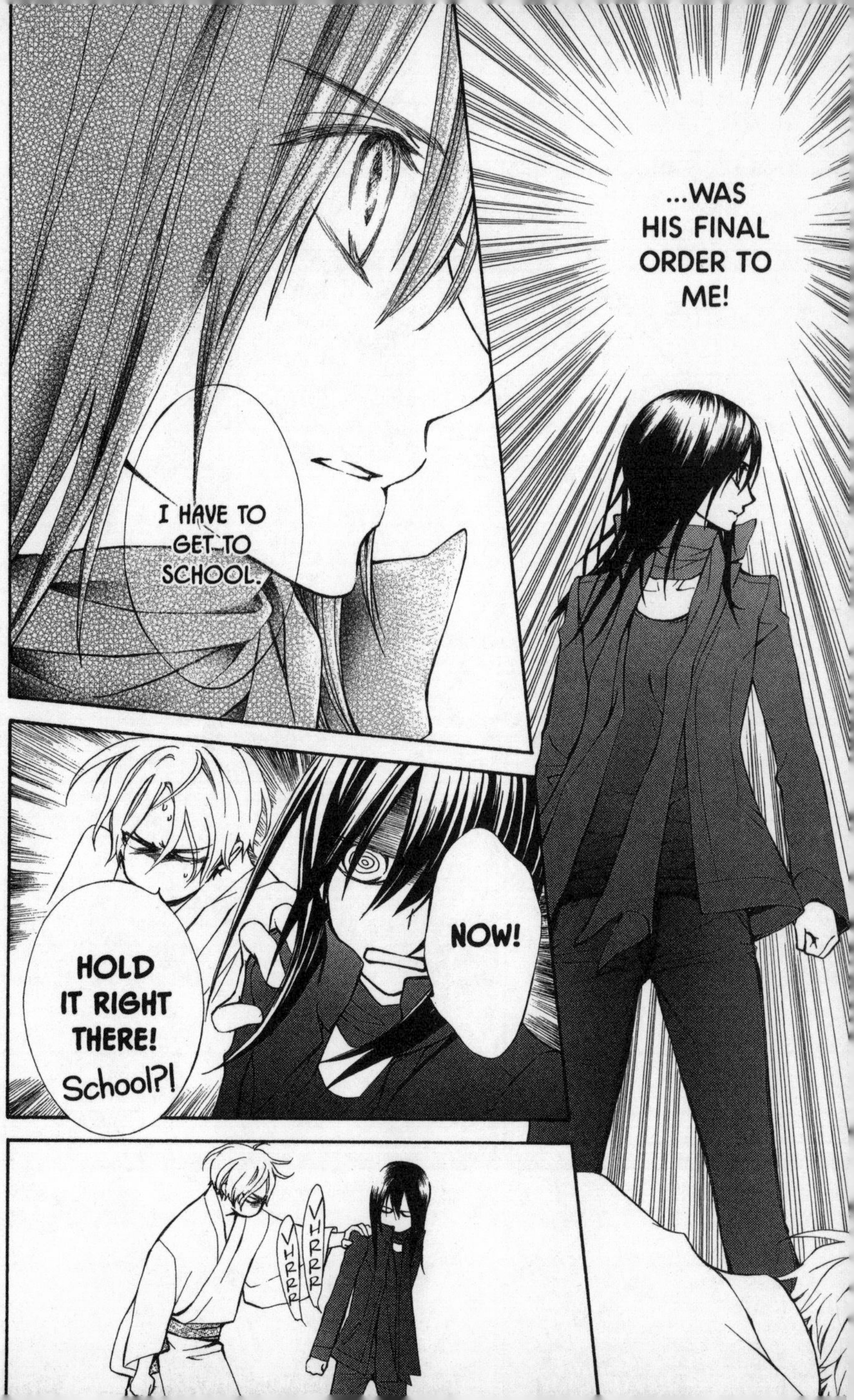
...WAS HIS FINAL ORDER TO ME!
I HAVE TO GET TO SCHOOL.
NOW!
HOLD IT RIGHT THERE! School?!
VHRRR
VHRRR

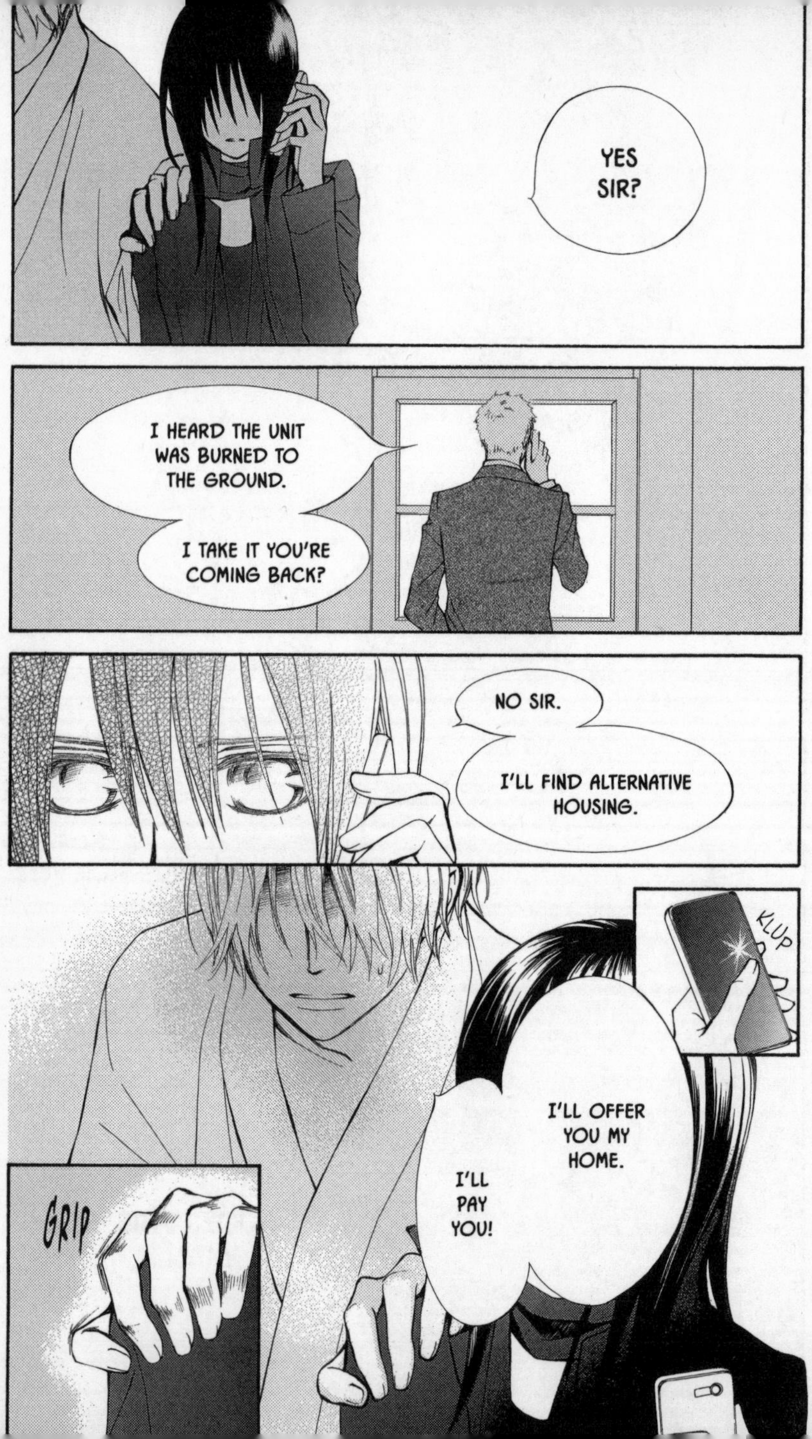
YES SIR?
I HEARD THE UNIT WAS BURNED TO THE GROUND.
I TAKE IT YOU'RE COMING BACK?
NO SIR.
I'LL FIND ALTERNATIVE HOUSING.
KLUP
I'LL OFFER YOU MY HOME.
I'LL PAY YOU!
GRIP

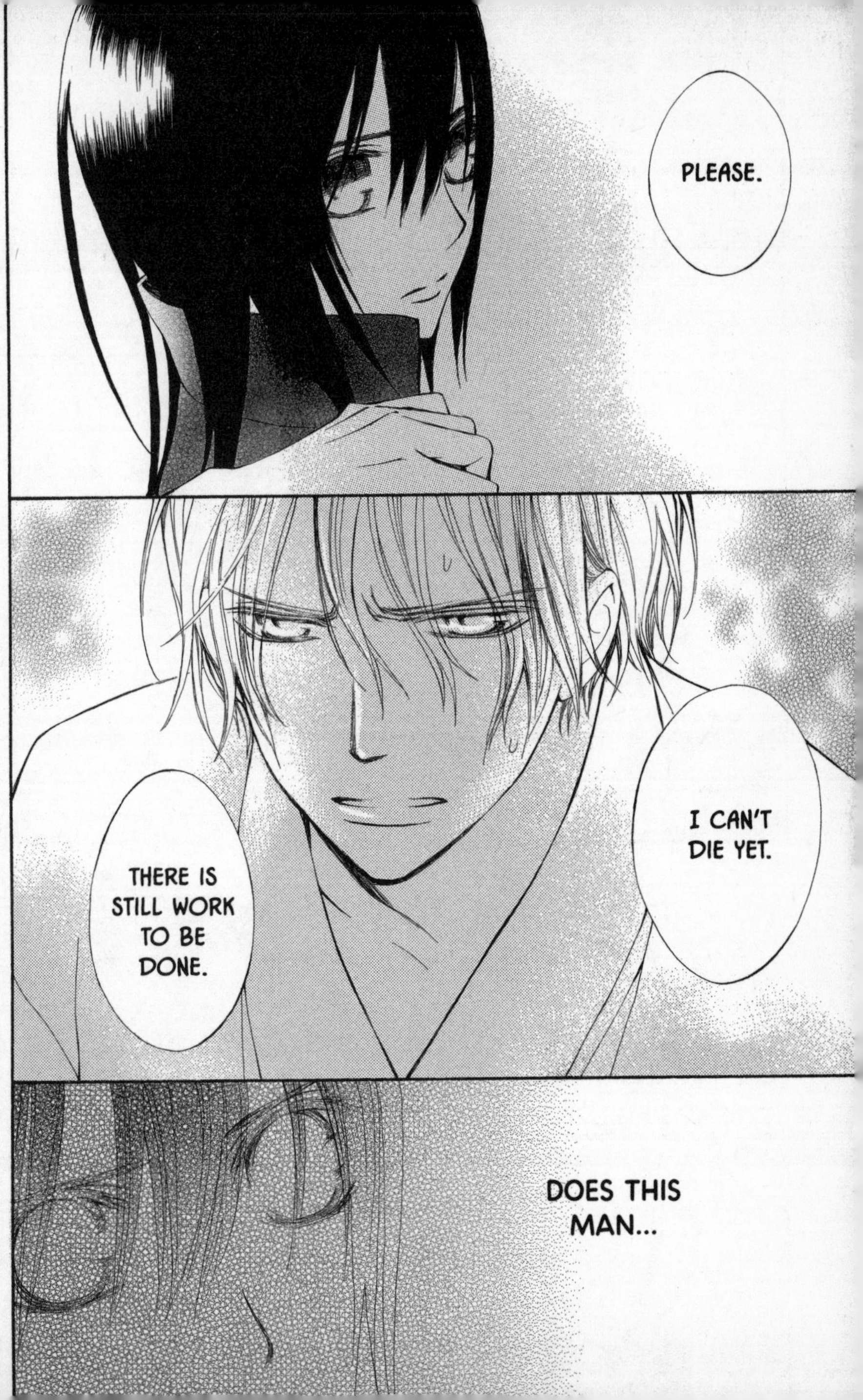
PLEASE.
I CAN'T DIE YET.
THERE IS STILL WORK TO BE DONE.
DOES THIS MAN...

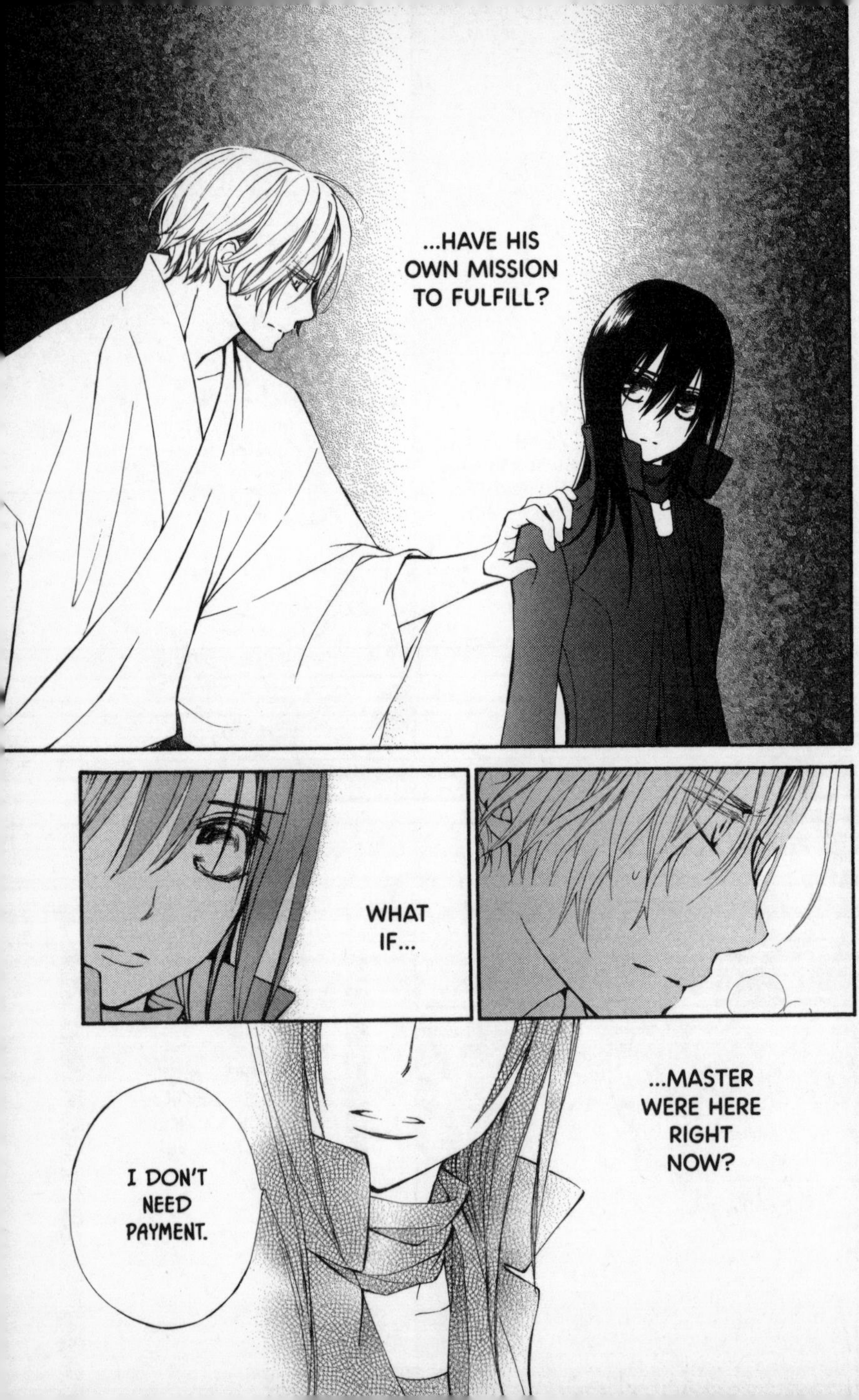
...HAVE HIS OWN MISSION TO FULFILL?
WHAT IF...
...MASTER WERE HERE RIGHT NOW?
I DON'T NEED PAYMENT.

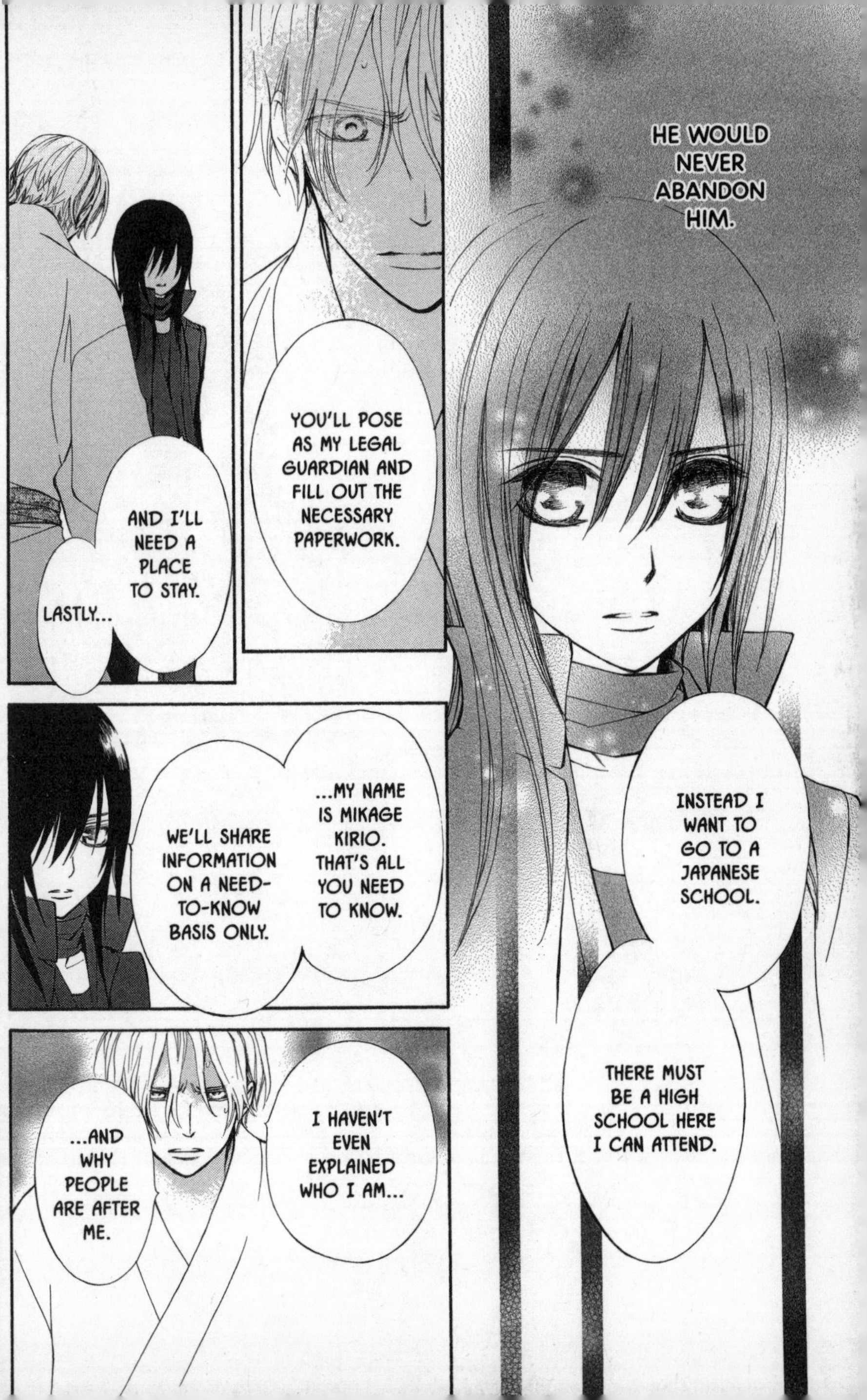

HE WOULD NEVER ABANDON HIM.
INSTEAD I WANT TO GO TO A JAPANESE SCHOOL.
THERE MUST BE A HIGH SCHOOL HERE I CAN ATTEND.
YOU'LL POSE AS MY LEGAL GUARDIAN AND FILL OUT THE NECESSARY PAPERWORK.
AND I'LL NEED A PLACE TO STAY.
LASTLY...
...MY NAME IS MIKAGE KIRIO. THAT'S ALL YOU NEED TO KNOW.
WE'LL SHARE INFORMATION ON A NEED-TO-KNOW BASIS ONLY.
I HAVEN'T EVEN EXPLAINED WHO I AM...
...AND WHY PEOPLE ARE AFTER ME.

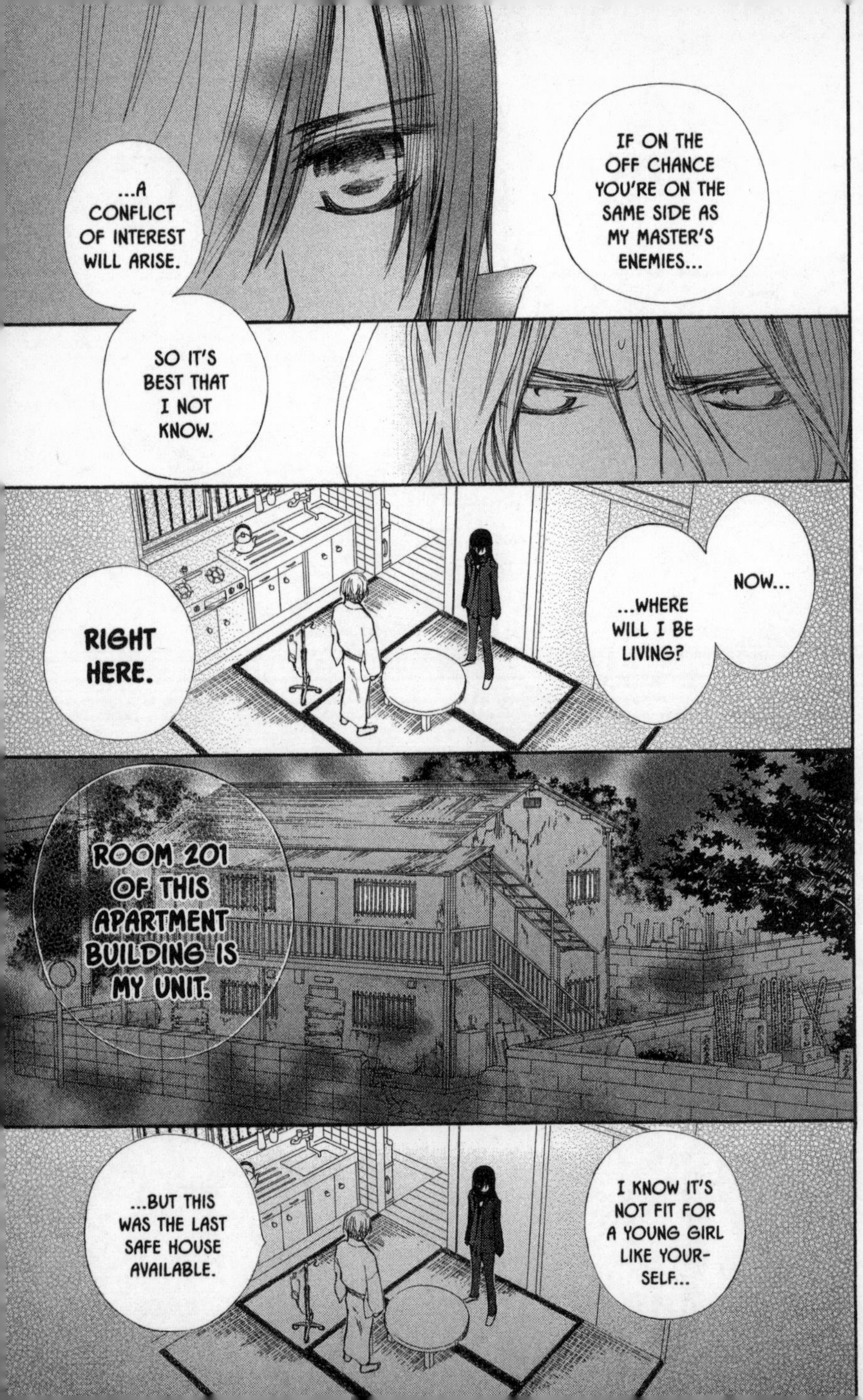
IF ON THE OFF CHANCE YOU'RE ON THE SAME SIDE AS MY MASTER'S ENEMIES...
...A CONFLICT OF INTEREST WILL ARISE.
SO IT'S BEST THAT I NOT KNOW.
NOW...
...WHERE WILL I BE LIVING?
RIGHT HERE.
ROOM 201 OF THIS APARTMENT BUILDING IS MY UNIT.
I KNOW IT'S NOT FIT FOR A YOUNG GIRL LIKE YOUR-SELF...
...BUT THIS WAS THE LAST SAFE HOUSE AVAILABLE.

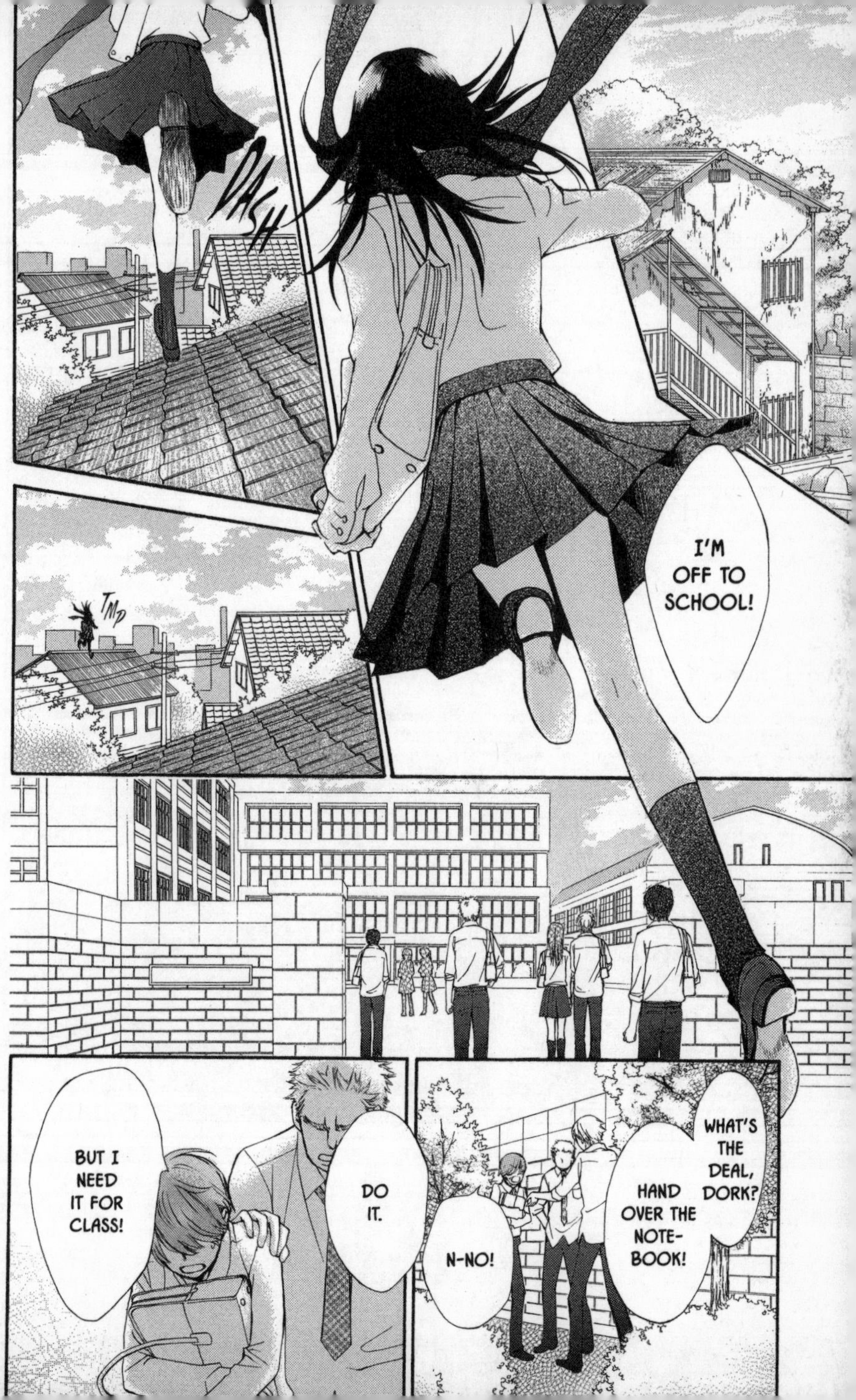
I'M OFF TO SCHOOL!
DASH
TMP
WHAT'S THE DEAL, DORK?
HAND OVER THE NOTE-BOOK!
N-NO!
DO IT.
BUT I NEED IT FOR CLASS!

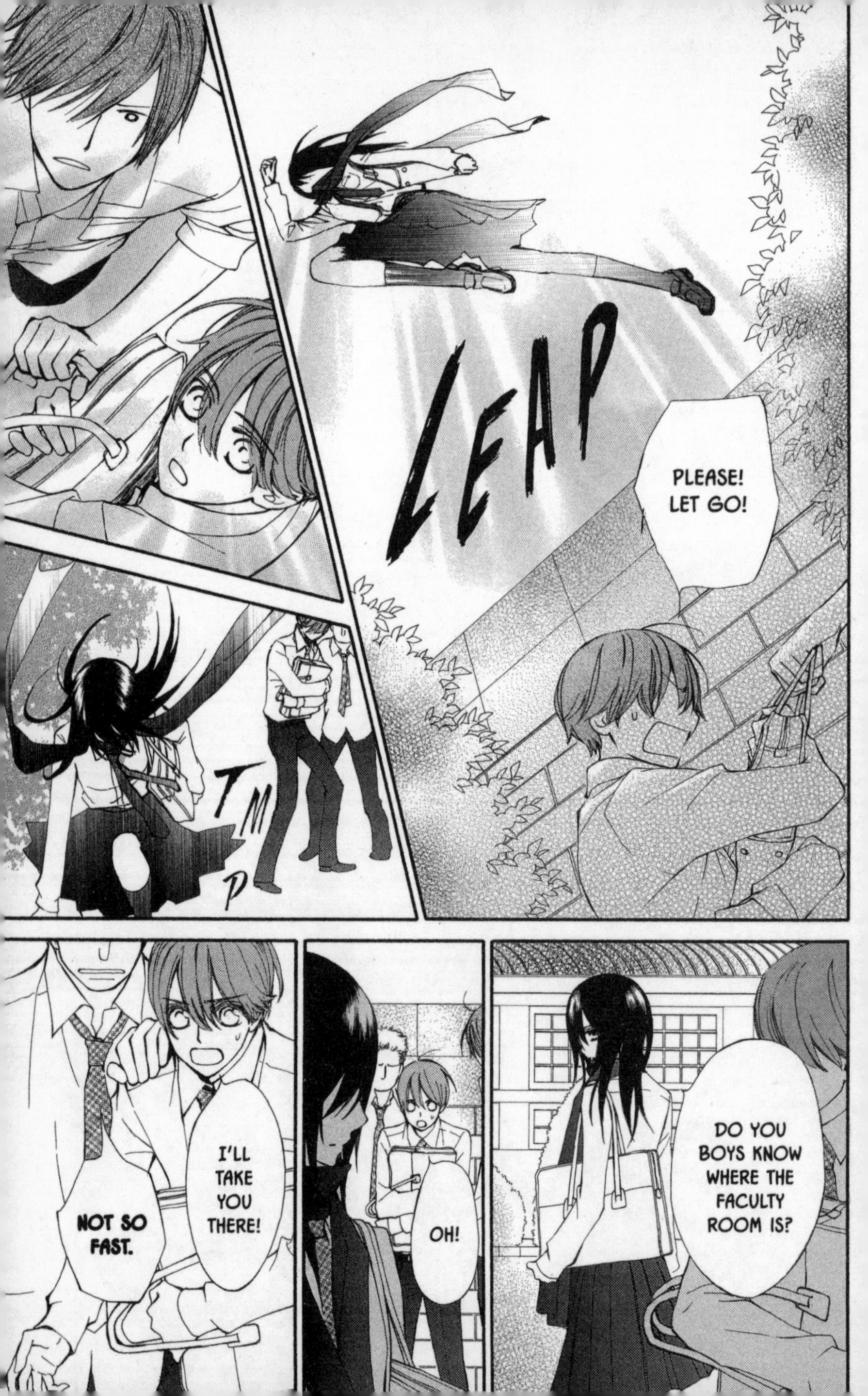
PLEASE! LET GO!
LEAP
TMP
DO YOU BOYS KNOW WHERE THE FACULTY ROOM IS?
OH!
I'LL TAKE YOU THERE!
NOT SO FAST.

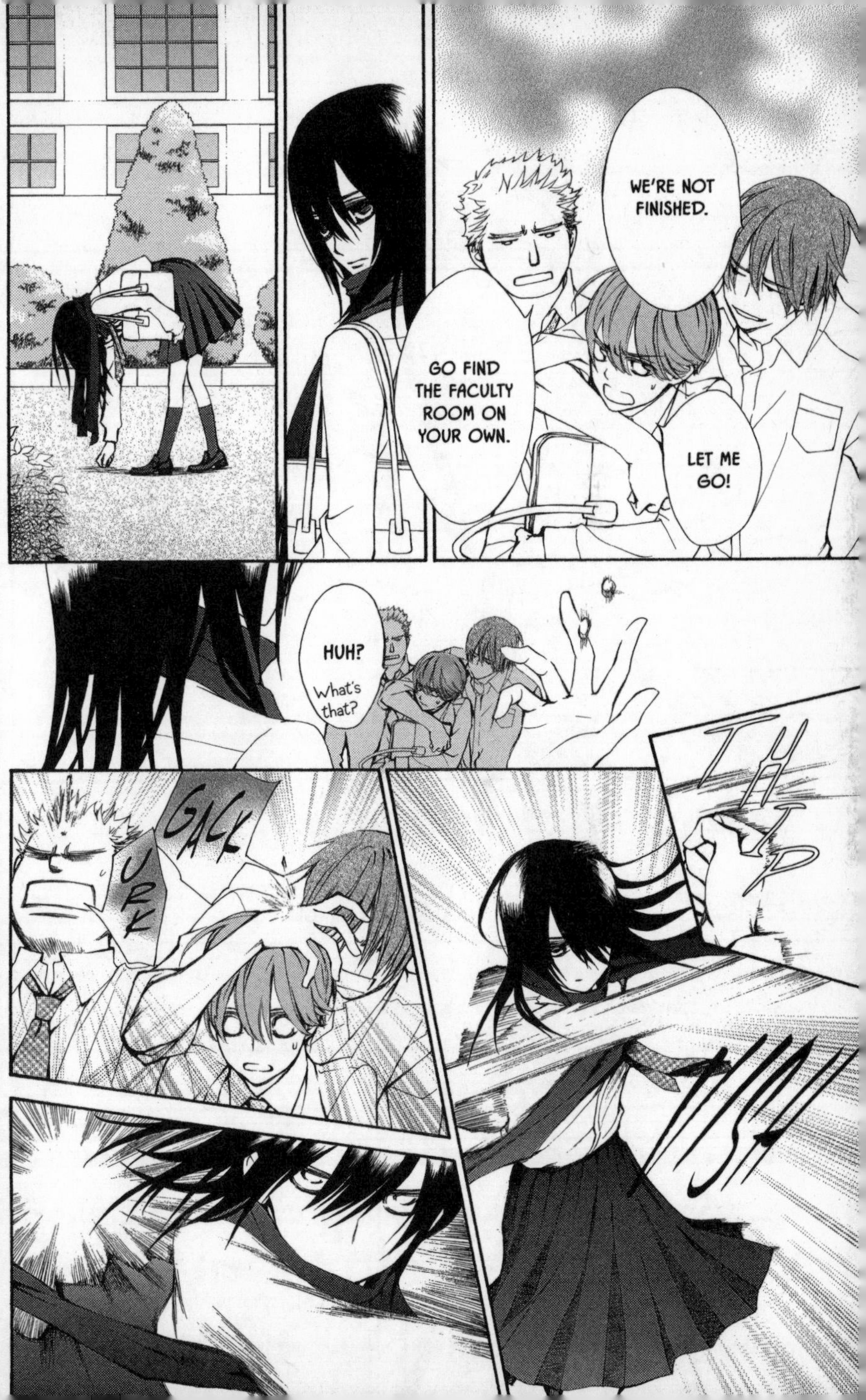
WE'RE NOT FINISHED.
GO FIND THE FACULTY ROOM ON YOUR OWN.
LET ME GO!
HUH?
What's that?
THIP
GACK
URK

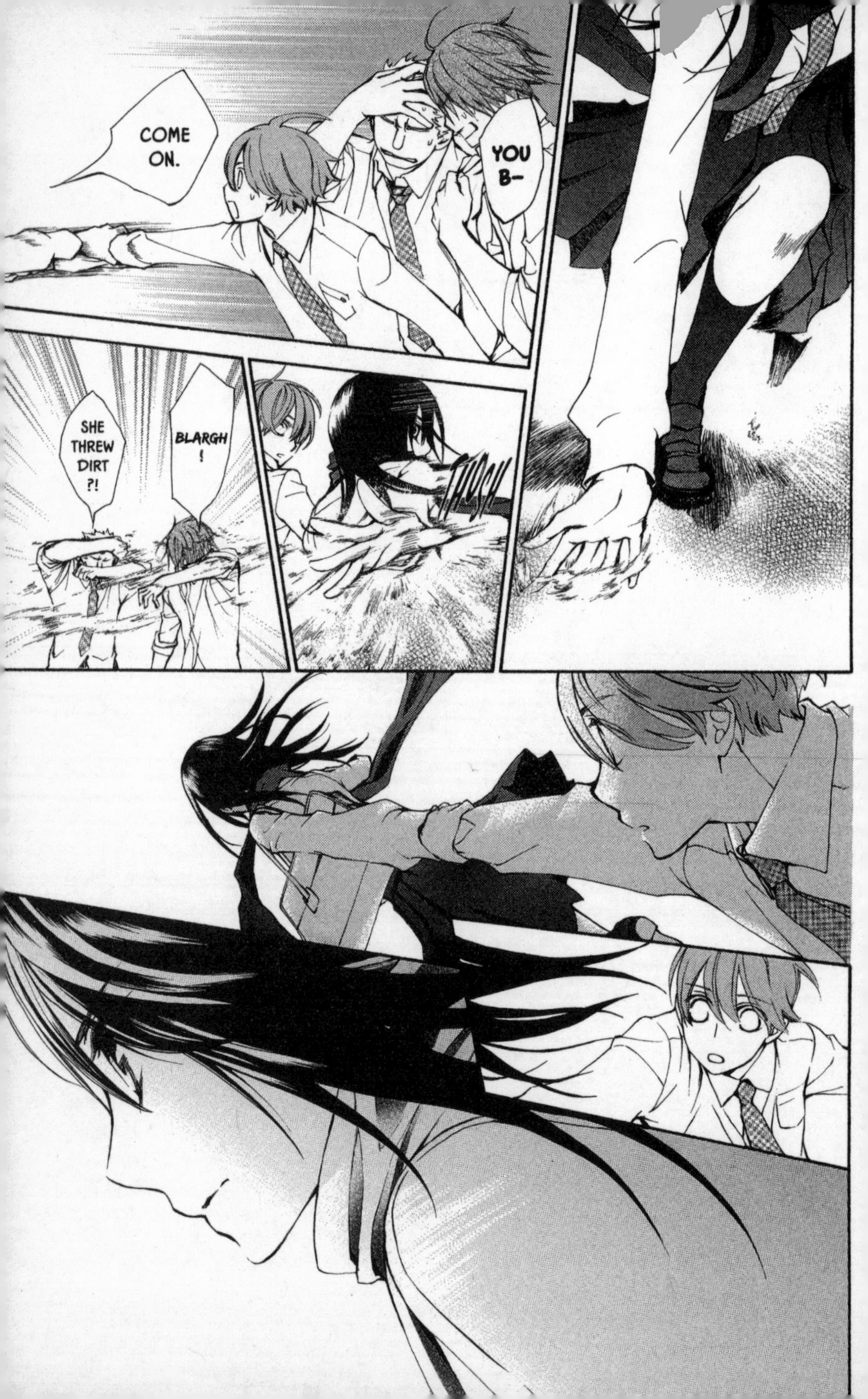
YOU B-
COME ON.
BLARGH!
SHE THREW DIRT?!

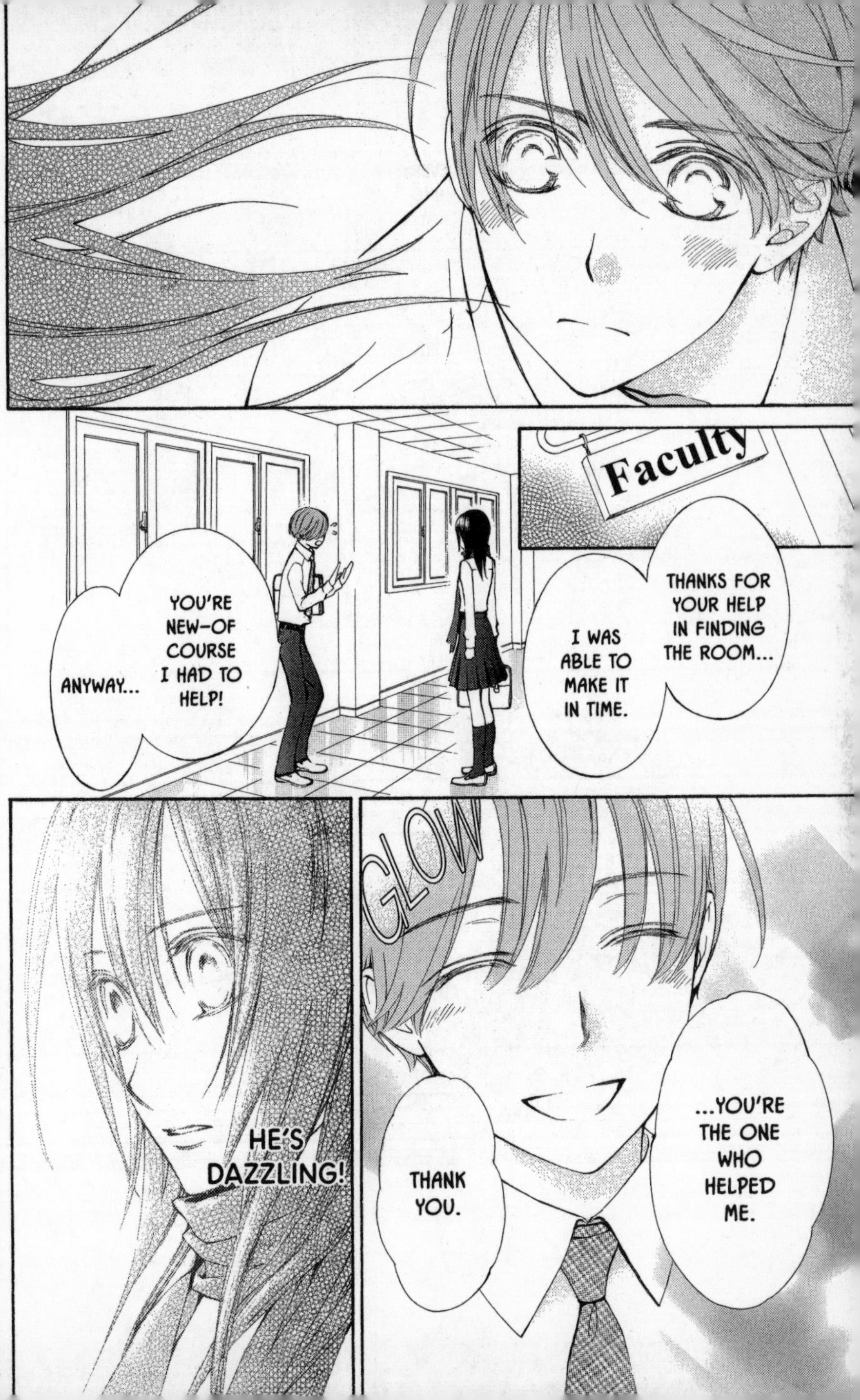
Faculty
THANKS FOR YOUR HELP IN FINDING THE ROOM...
I WAS ABLE TO MAKE IT IN TIME.
YOU'RE NEW—OF COURSE I HAD TO HELP!
ANYWAY...
GLOW
...YOU'RE THE ONE WHO HELPED ME.
THANK YOU.
HE'S DAZZLING!

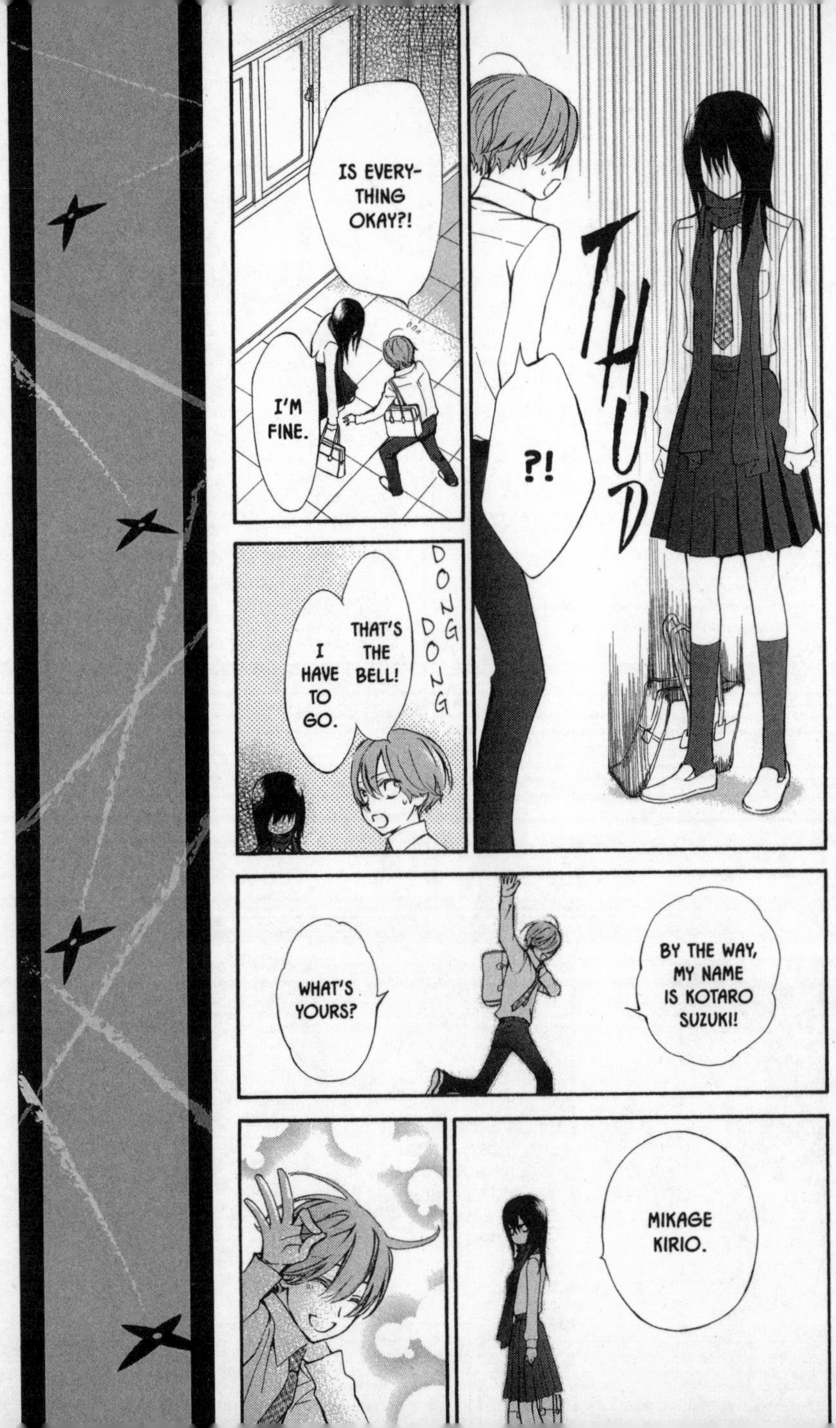
THUD
?!
IS EVERY-THING OKAY?!
I'M FINE.
DONG DONG
THAT'S THE BELL!
I HAVE TO GO.
BY THE WAY, MY NAME IS KOTARO SUZUKI!
WHAT'S YOURS?
MIKAGE KIRIO.

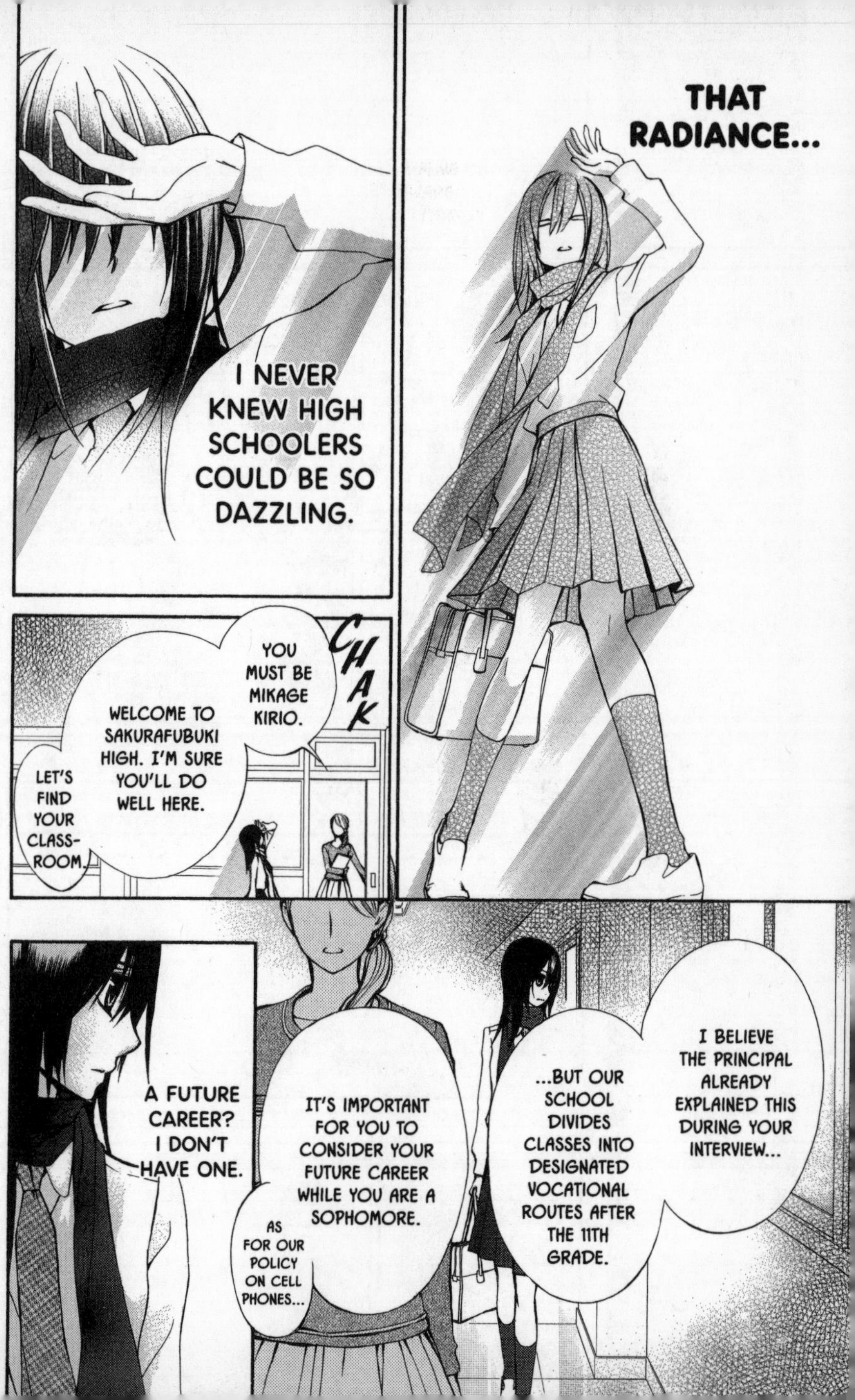
THAT RADIANCE...
I NEVER KNEW HIGH SCHOOLERS COULD BE SO DAZZLING.
CHAK
YOU MUST BE MIKAGE KIRIO.
WELCOME TO SAKURAFUBUKI HIGH. I'M SURE YOU'LL DO WELL HERE.
LET'S FIND YOUR CLASS-ROOM.
I BELIEVE THE PRINCIPAL ALREADY EXPLAINED THIS DURING YOUR INTERVIEW...
...BUT OUR SCHOOL DIVIDES CLASSES INTO DESIGNATED VOCATIONAL ROUTES AFTER THE 11TH GRADE.
IT'S IMPORTANT FOR YOU TO CONSIDER YOUR FUTURE CAREER WHILE YOU ARE A SOPHOMORE.
AS FOR OUR POLICY ON CELL PHONES...
A FUTURE CAREER? I DON'T HAVE ONE.

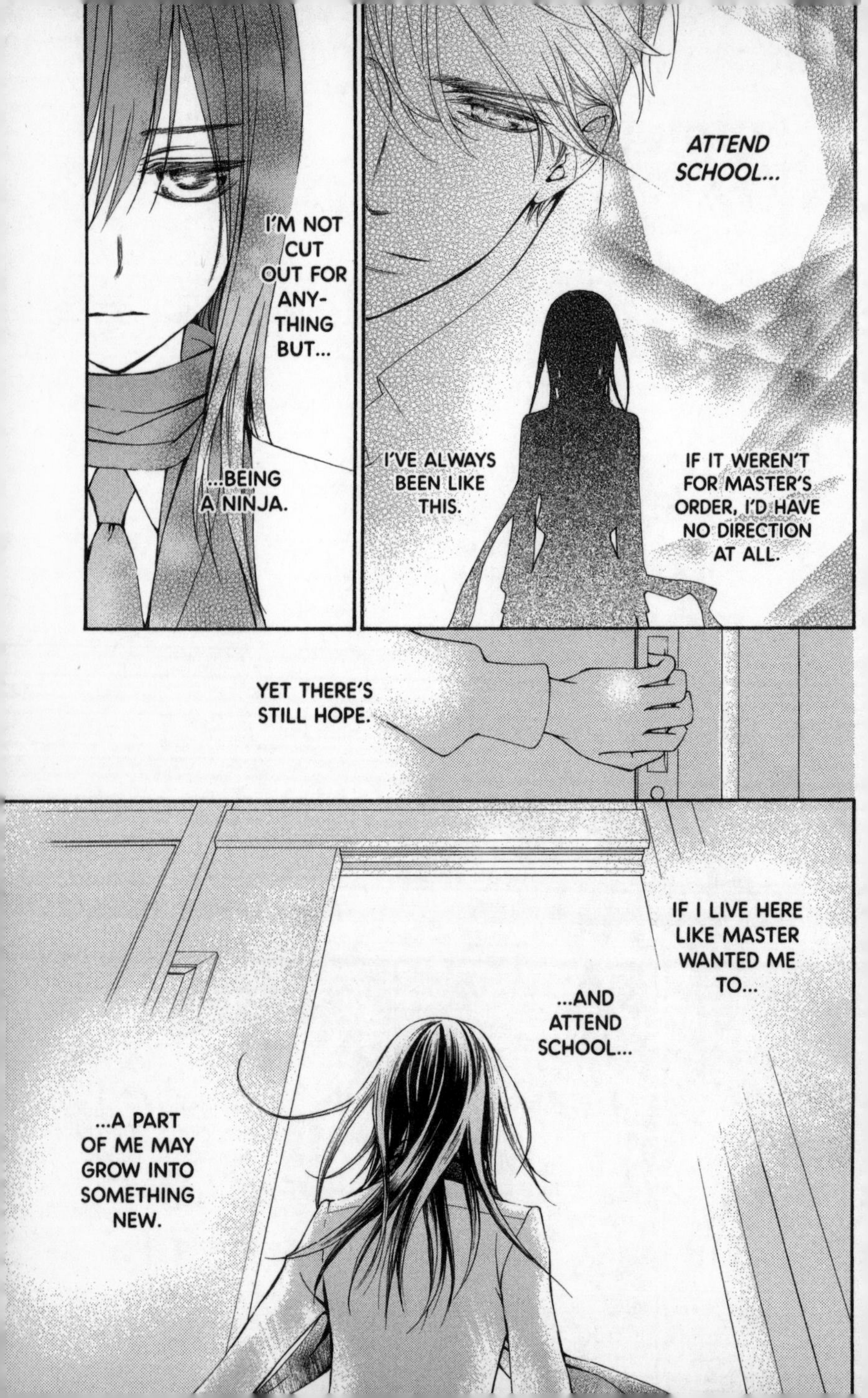
ATTEND SCHOOL...
IF IT WEREN'T FOR MASTER'S ORDER, I'D HAVE NO DIRECTION AT ALL.
I'VE ALWAYS BEEN LIKE THIS.
I'M NOT CUT OUT FOR ANY-THING BUT...
...BEING A NINJA.
YET THERE'S STILL HOPE.
IF I LIVE HERE LIKE MASTER WANTED ME TO...
...AND ATTEND SCHOOL...
...A PART OF ME MAY GROW INTO SOMETHING NEW.

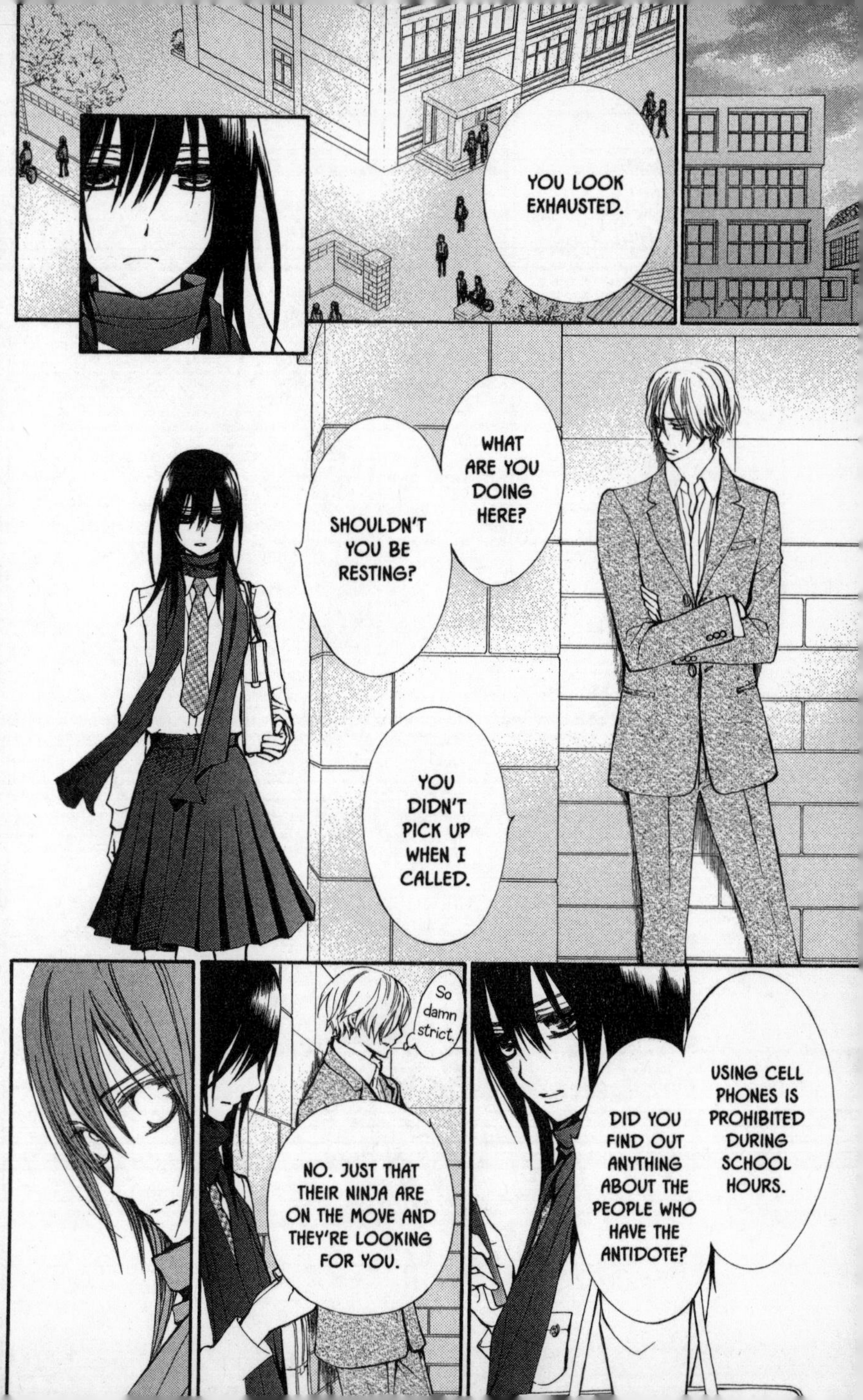
YOU LOOK EXHAUSTED.
WHAT ARE YOU DOING HERE?
SHOULDN'T YOU BE RESTING?
YOU DIDN'T PICK UP WHEN I CALLED.
USING CELL PHONES IS PROHIBITED DURING SCHOOL HOURS.
DID YOU FIND OUT ANYTHING ABOUT THE PEOPLE WHO HAVE THE ANTIDOTE?
So damn strict.
NO. JUST THAT THEIR NINJA ARE ON THE MOVE AND THEY'RE LOOKING FOR YOU.

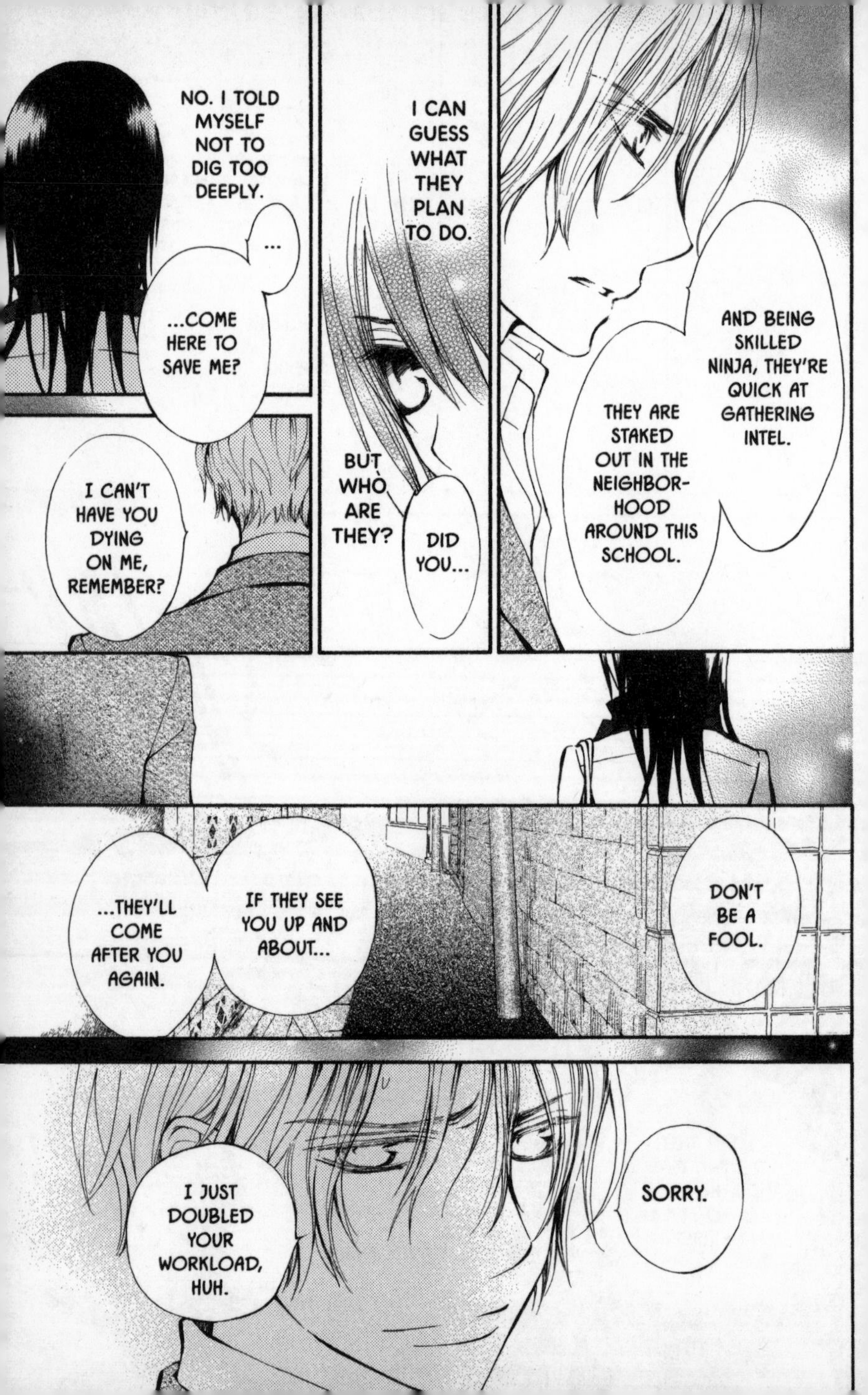
AND BEING SKILLED NINJA, THEY'RE QUICK AT GATHERING INTEL.
THEY ARE STAKED OUT IN THE NEIGHBOR-HOOD AROUND THIS SCHOOL.
I CAN GUESS WHAT THEY PLAN TO DO.
BUT WHO ARE THEY?
DID YOU...
NO. I TOLD MYSELF NOT TO DIG TOO DEEPLY.
...
...COME HERE TO SAVE ME?
I CAN'T HAVE YOU DYING ON ME, REMEMBER?
DON'T BE A FOOL.
IF THEY SEE YOU UP AND ABOUT...
...THEY'LL COME AFTER YOU AGAIN.
SORRY.
I JUST DOUBLED YOUR WORKLOAD, HUH.

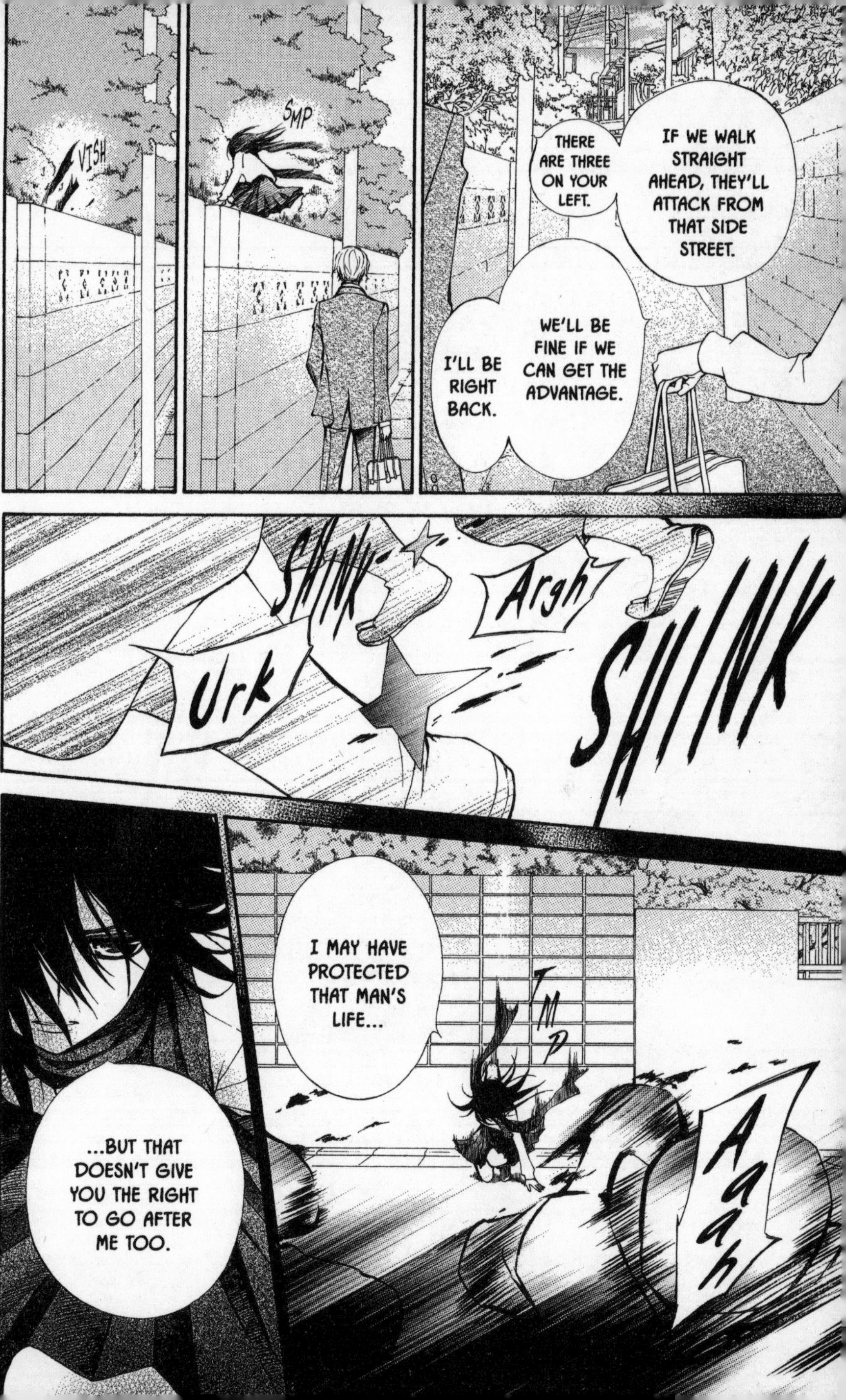
IF WE WALK STRAIGHT AHEAD, THEY'LL ATTACK FROM THAT SIDE STREET.
THERE ARE THREE ON YOUR LEFT.
WE'LL BE FINE IF WE CAN GET THE ADVANTAGE.
I'LL BE RIGHT BACK.
SMP
VISH
SHINK
Argh
SHINK
Urk
I MAY HAVE PROTECTED THAT MAN'S LIFE...
TMP
Aaah
...BUT THAT DOESN'T GIVE YOU THE RIGHT TO GO AFTER ME TOO.

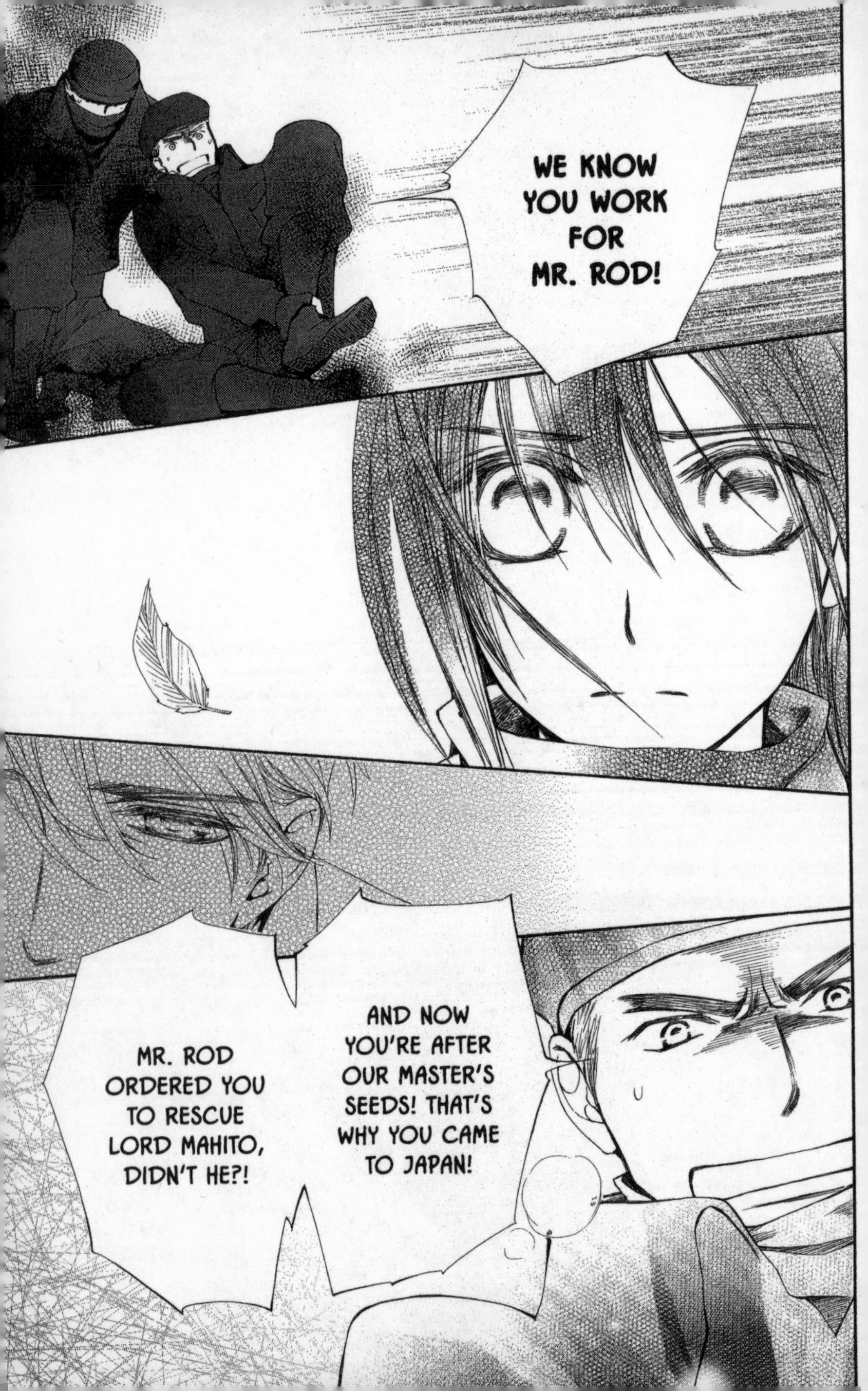
WE KNOW YOU WORK FOR MR. ROD!
AND NOW YOU'RE AFTER OUR MASTER'S SEEDS! THAT'S WHY YOU CAME TO JAPAN!
MR. ROD ORDERED YOU TO RESCUE LORD MAHITO, DIDN'T HE?!

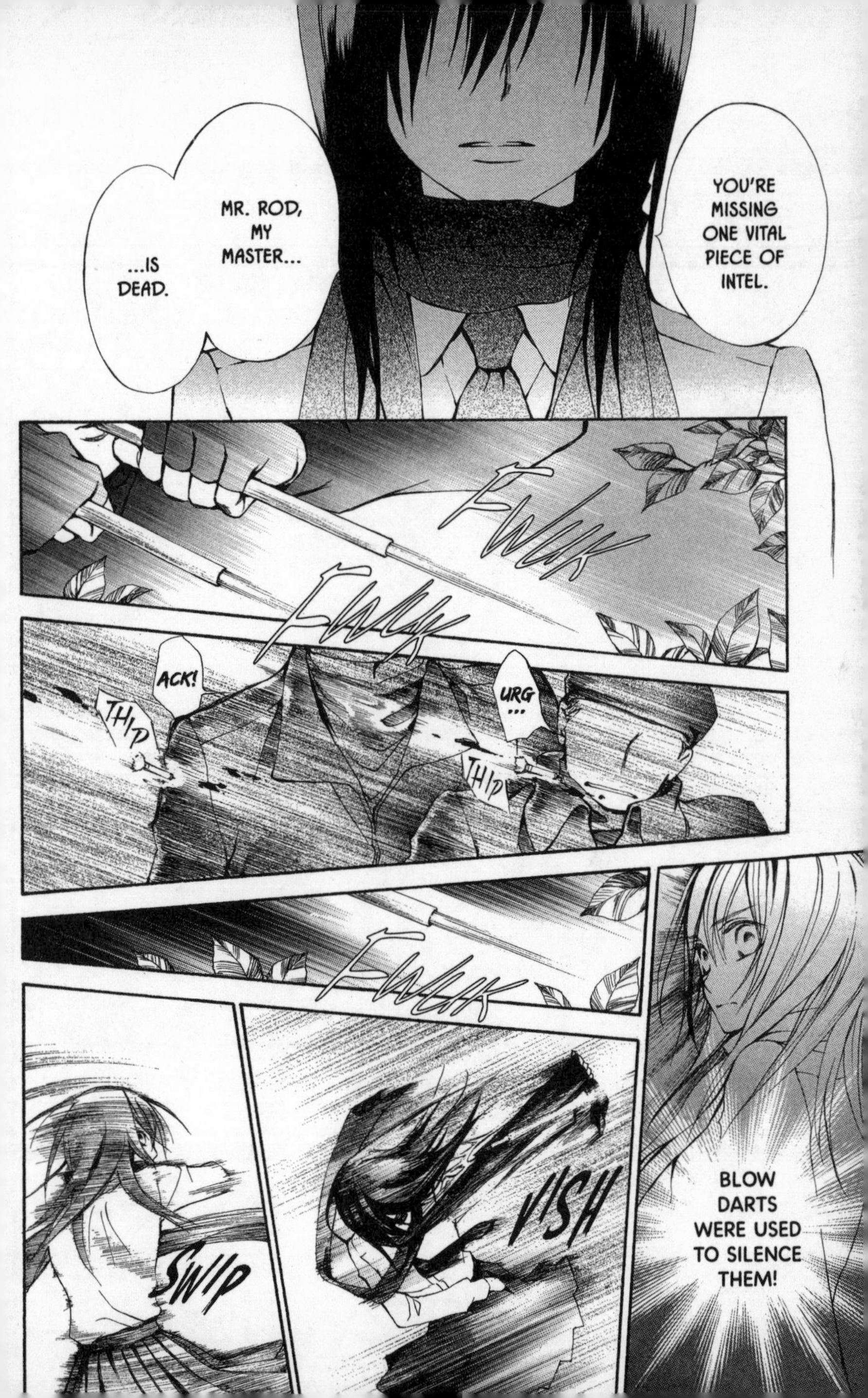
YOU'RE MISSING ONE VITAL PIECE OF INTEL.
MR. ROD, MY MASTER...
...IS DEAD.
FWIK
FWIK
URG...
THIP
ACK!
THIP
BLOW DARTS WERE USED TO SILENCE THEM!
FWIK
VISH
SWIP

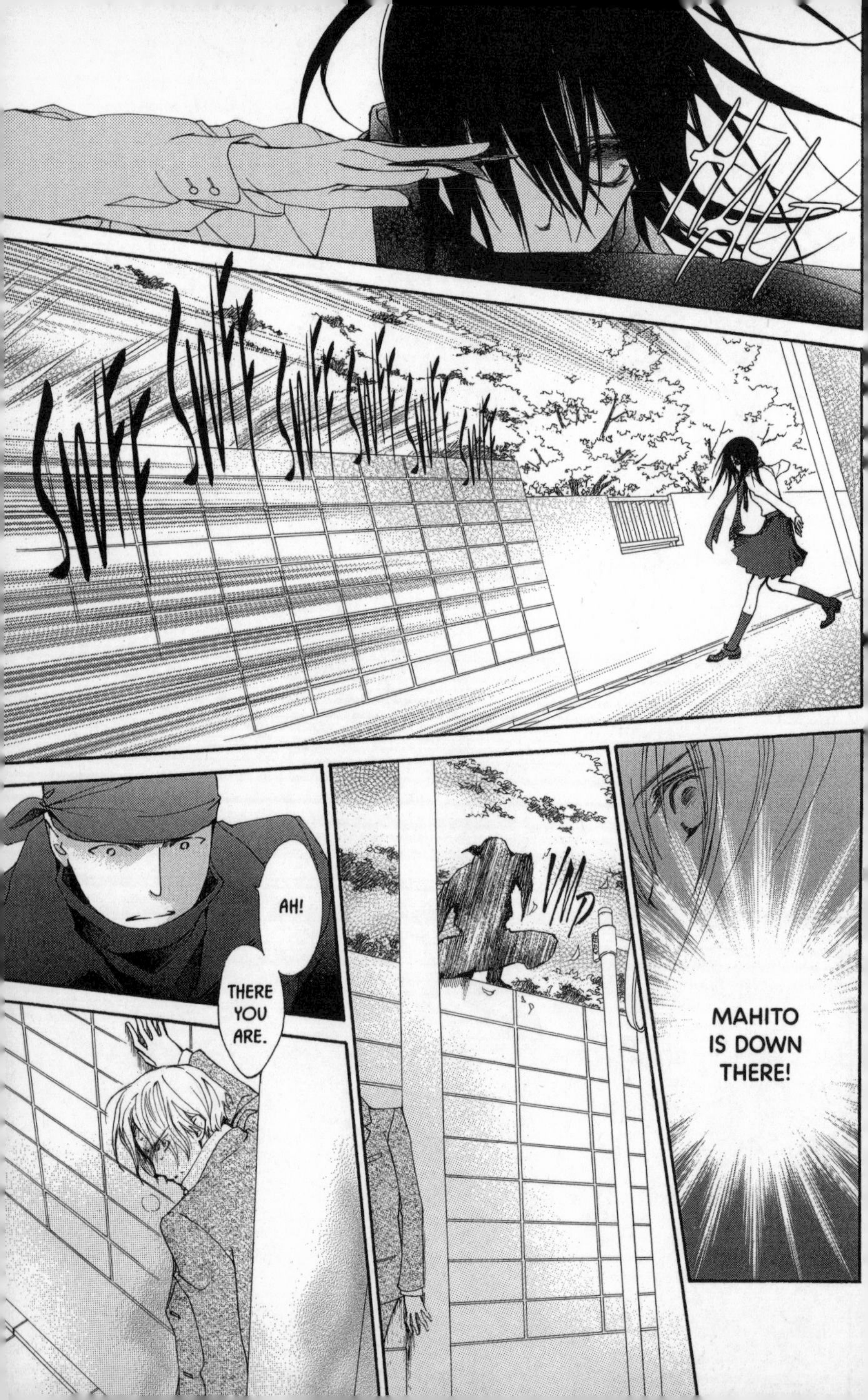
HALT
MAHITO IS DOWN THERE!
AH!
THERE YOU ARE.

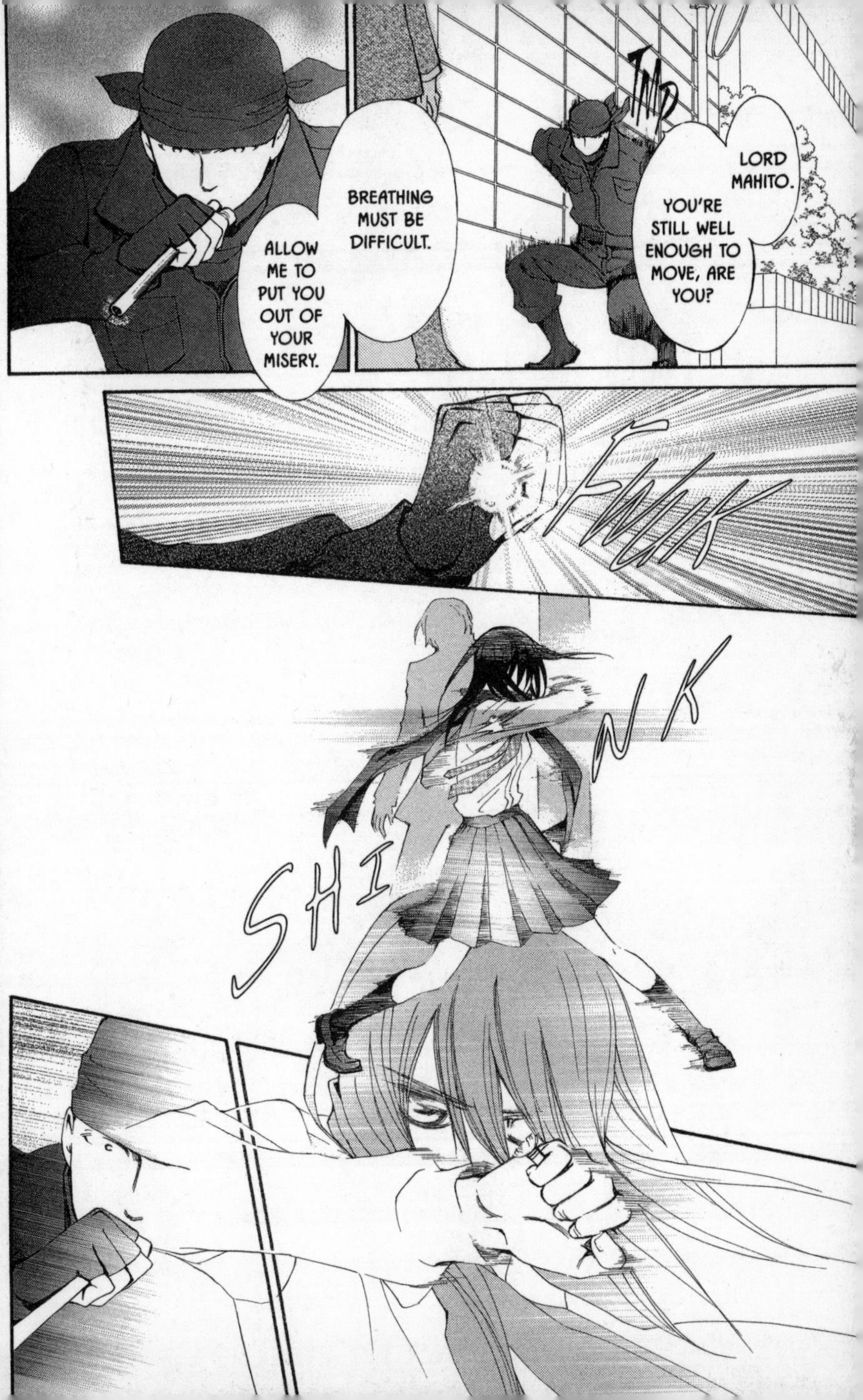
TMP
LORD MAHITO. YOU'RE STILL WELL ENOUGH TO MOVE, ARE YOU?
BREATHING MUST BE DIFFICULT.
ALLOW ME TO PUT YOU OUT OF YOUR MISERY.
FWUK
SHINK

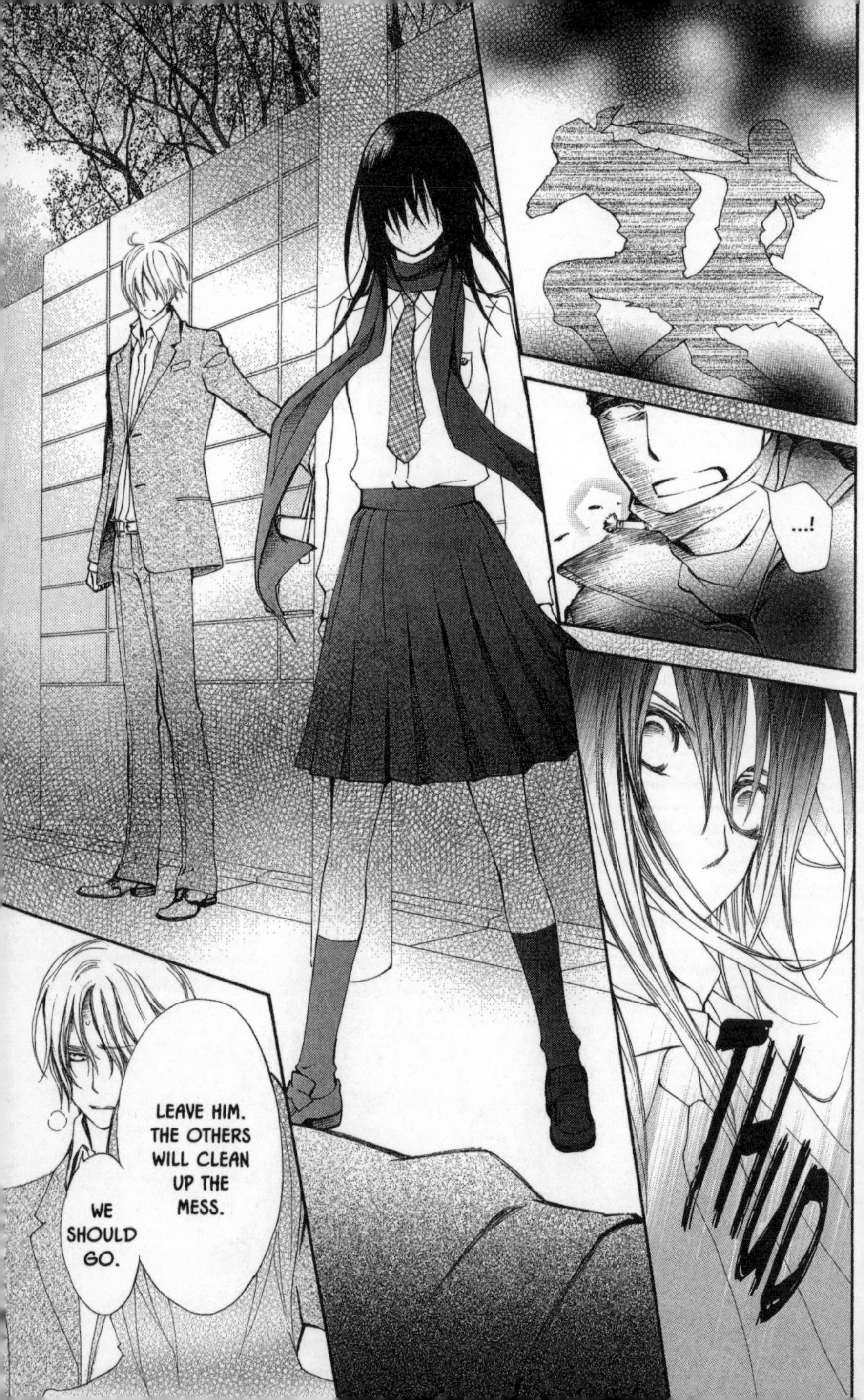
...!
THUD
LEAVE HIM. THE OTHERS WILL CLEAN UP THE MESS.
WE SHOULD GO.

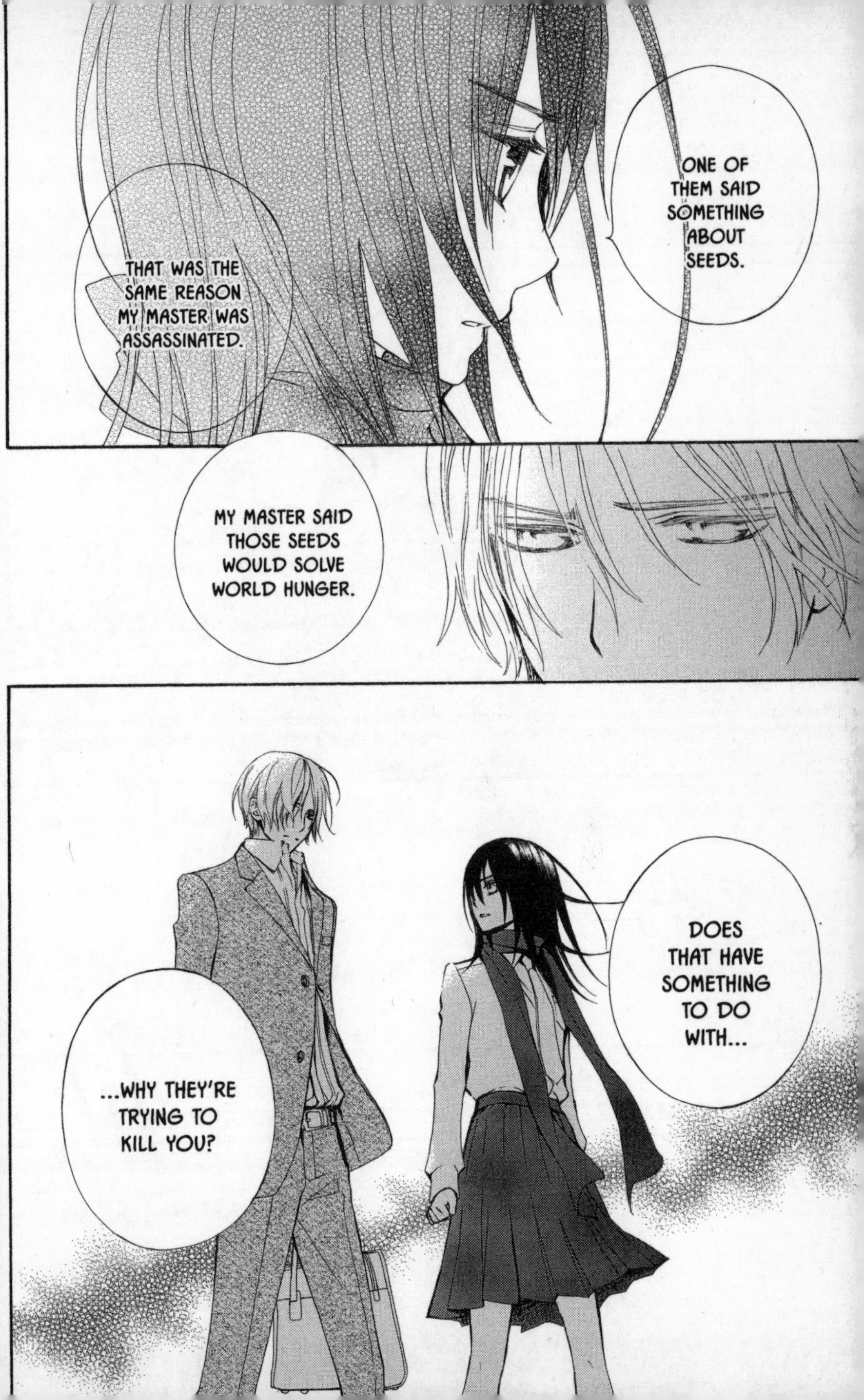
ONE OF THEM SAID SOMETHING ABOUT SEEDS.
THAT WAS THE SAME REASON MY MASTER WAS ASSASSINATED.
MY MASTER SAID THOSE SEEDS WOULD SOLVE WORLD HUNGER.
DOES THAT HAVE SOMETHING TO DO WITH...
...WHY THEY'RE TRYING TO KILL YOU?

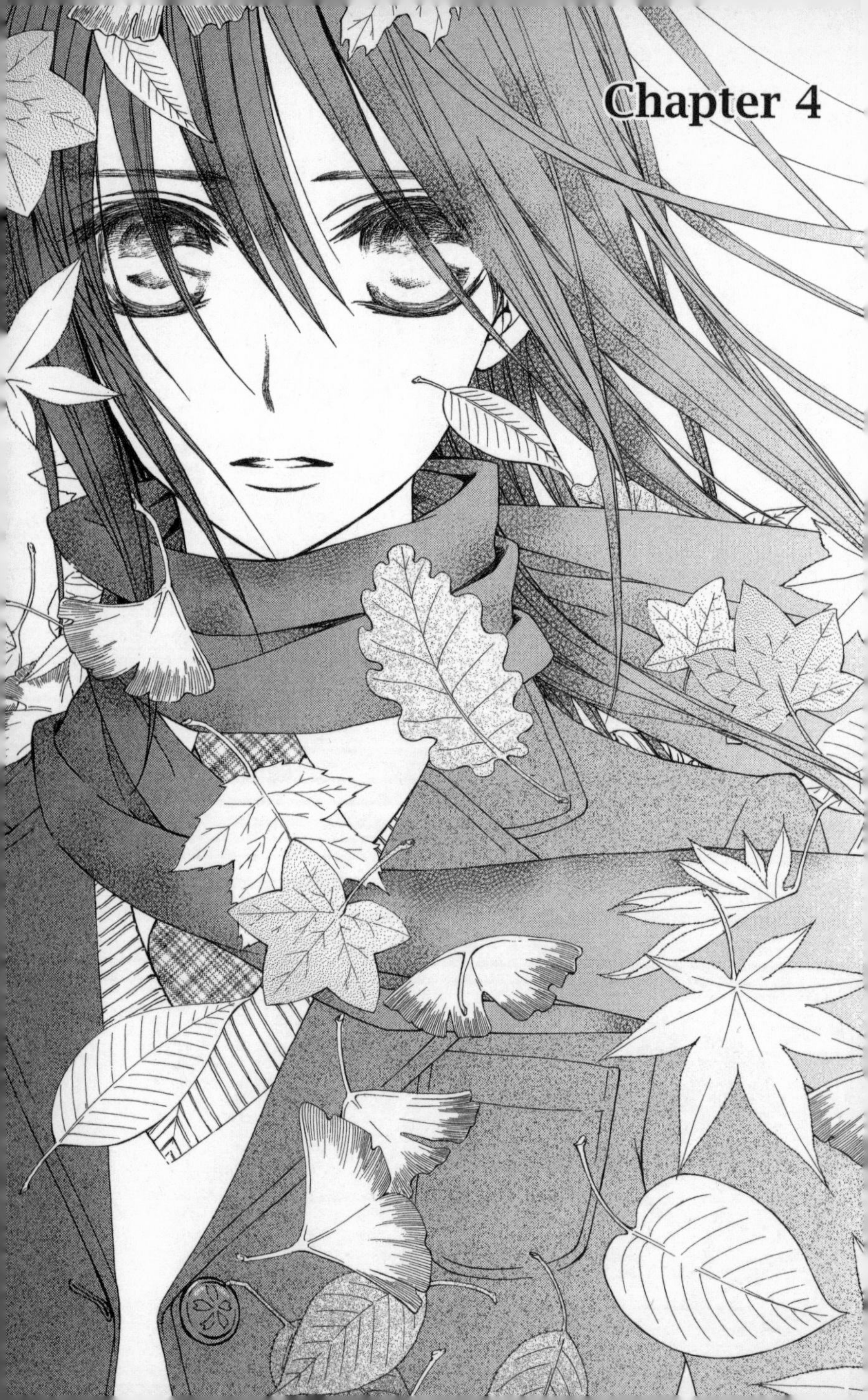
Chapter 4

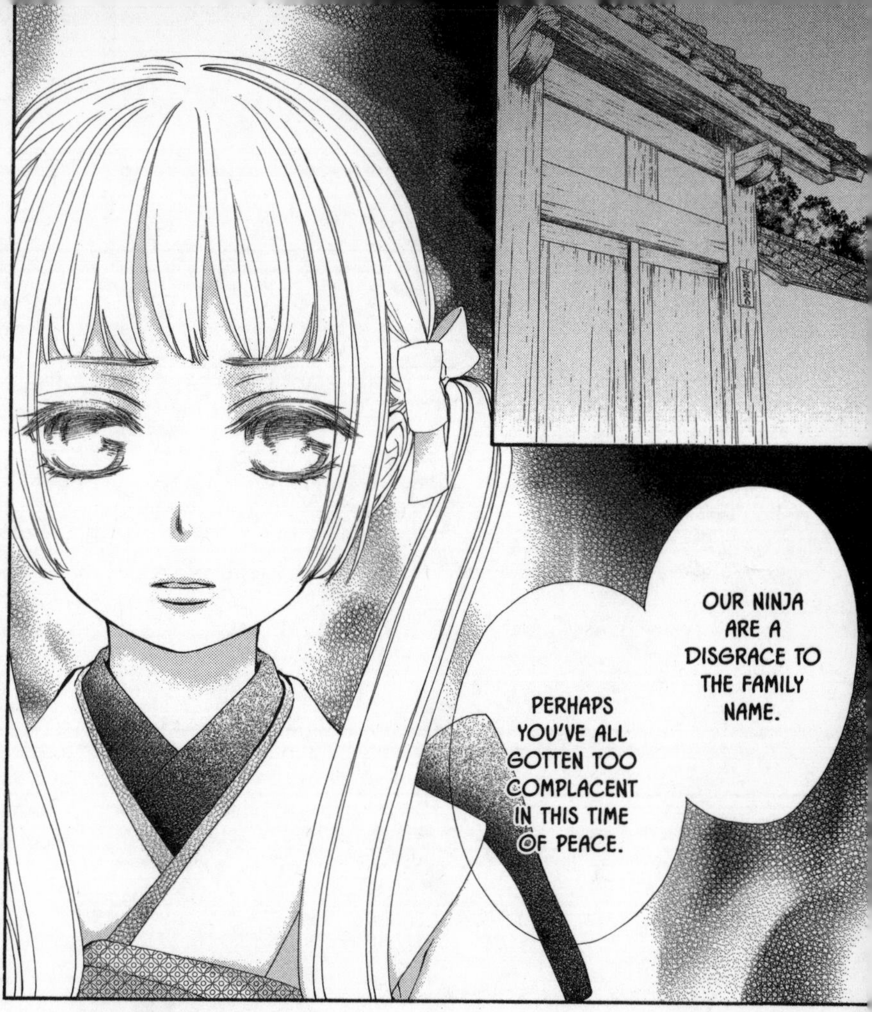
OUR NINJA ARE A DISGRACE TO THE FAMILY NAME.
PERHAPS YOU'VE ALL GOTTEN TOO COMPLACENT IN THIS TIME OF PEACE.

Shuriken and Pleats

MATSURI HINO

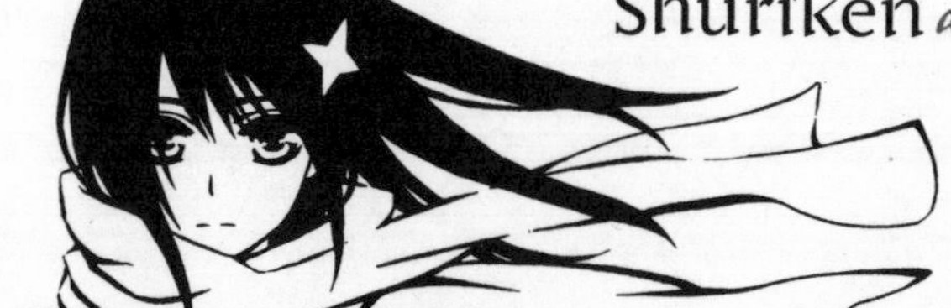

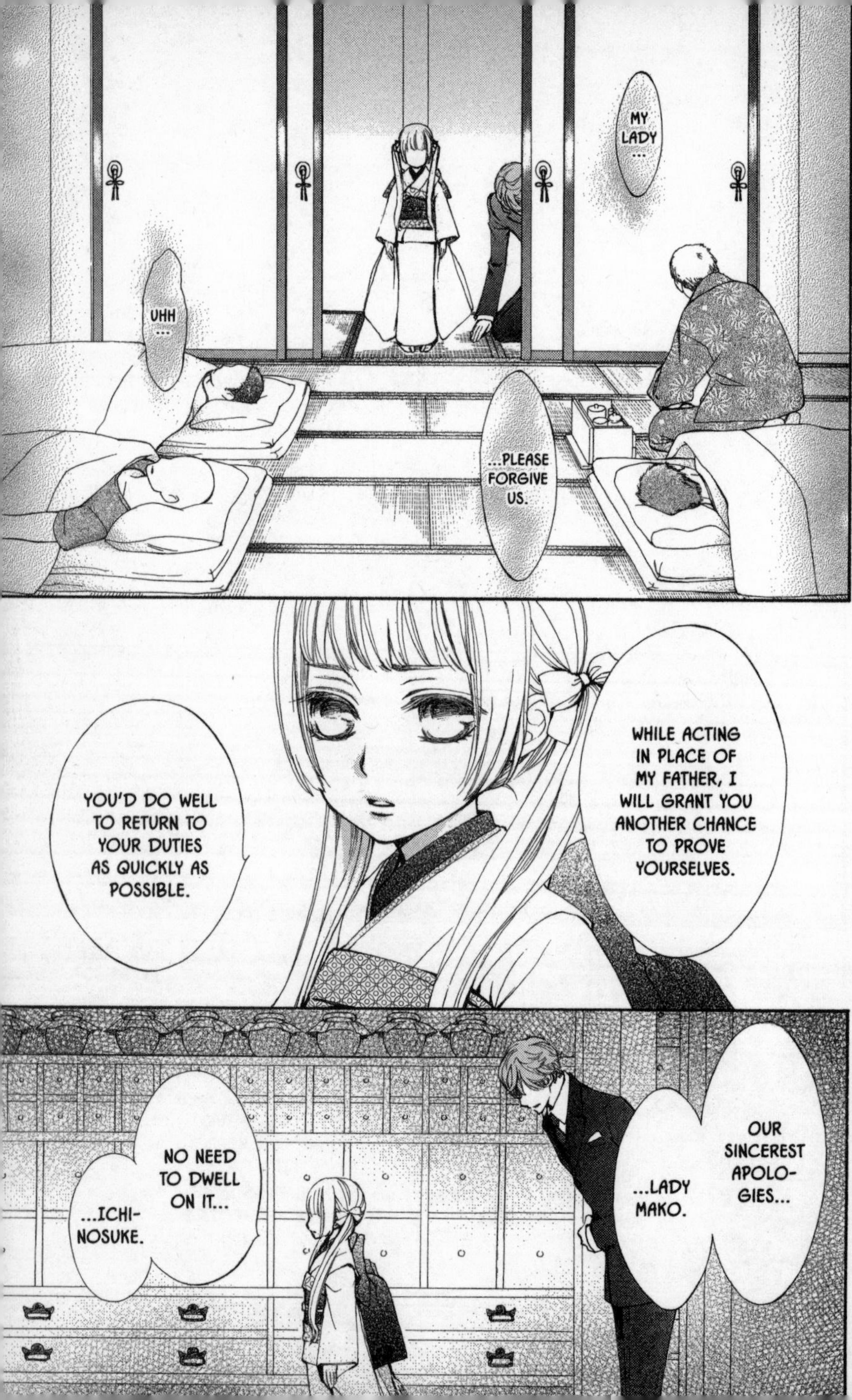
MY LADY...
...PLEASE FORGIVE US.
UHH...
WHILE ACTING IN PLACE OF MY FATHER, I WILL GRANT YOU ANOTHER CHANCE TO PROVE YOURSELVES.
YOU'D DO WELL TO RETURN TO YOUR DUTIES AS QUICKLY AS POSSIBLE.
OUR SINCEREST APOLOGIES...
...LADY MAKO.
NO NEED TO DWELL ON IT...
...ICHINOSUKE.

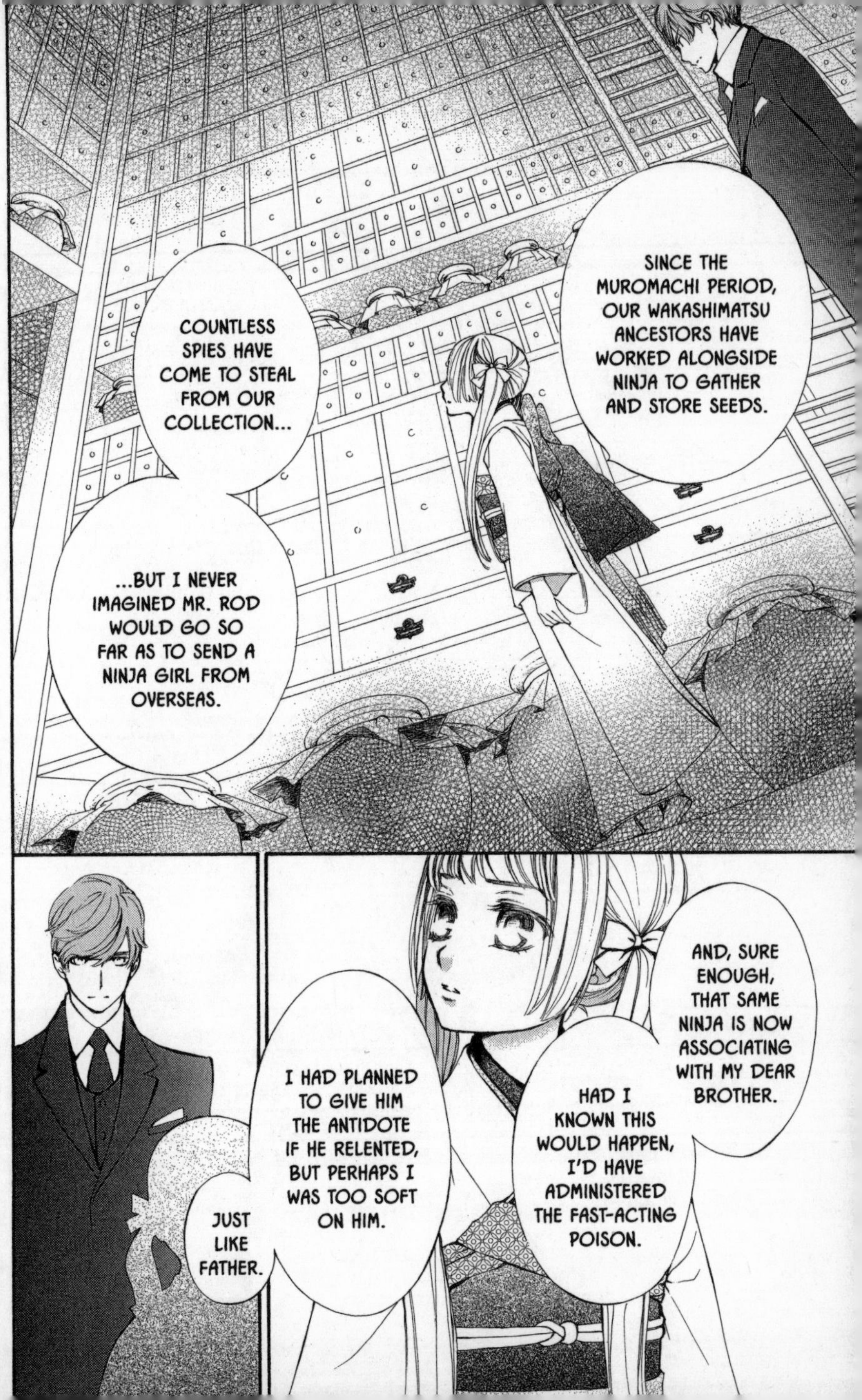
SINCE THE MUROMACHI PERIOD, OUR WAKASHIMATSU ANCESTORS HAVE WORKED ALONGSIDE NINJA TO GATHER AND STORE SEEDS.
COUNTLESS SPIES HAVE COME TO STEAL FROM OUR COLLECTION...
...BUT I NEVER IMAGINED MR. ROD WOULD GO SO FAR AS TO SEND A NINJA GIRL FROM OVERSEAS.
AND, SURE ENOUGH, THAT SAME NINJA IS NOW ASSOCIATING WITH MY DEAR BROTHER.
HAD I KNOWN THIS WOULD HAPPEN, I'D HAVE ADMINISTERED THE FAST-ACTING POISON.
I HAD PLANNED TO GIVE HIM THE ANTIDOTE IF HE RELENTED, BUT PERHAPS I WAS TOO SOFT ON HIM.
JUST LIKE FATHER.

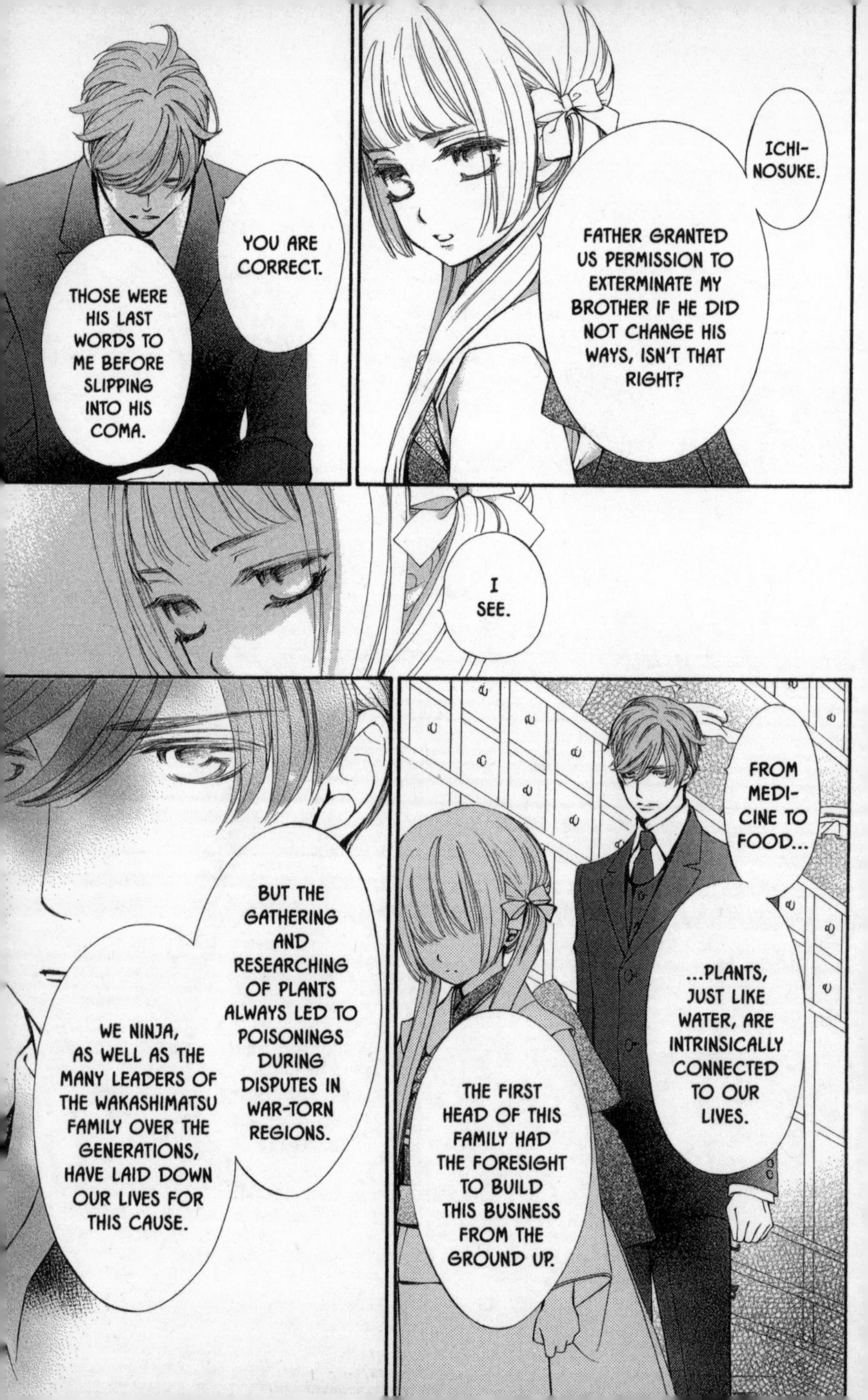
ICHINOSUKE.
FATHER GRANTED US PERMISSION TO EXTERMINATE MY BROTHER IF HE DID NOT CHANGE HIS WAYS, ISN'T THAT RIGHT?
YOU ARE CORRECT.
THOSE WERE HIS LAST WORDS TO ME BEFORE SLIPPING INTO HIS COMA.
I SEE.
FROM MEDICINE TO FOOD...
...PLANTS, JUST LIKE WATER, ARE INTRINSICALLY CONNECTED TO OUR LIVES.
THE FIRST HEAD OF THIS FAMILY HAD THE FORESIGHT TO BUILD THIS BUSINESS FROM THE GROUND UP.
BUT THE GATHERING AND RESEARCHING OF PLANTS ALWAYS LED TO POISONINGS DURING DISPUTES IN WAR-TORN REGIONS.
WE NINJA, AS WELL AS THE MANY LEADERS OF THE WAKASHIMATSU FAMILY OVER THE GENERATIONS, HAVE LAID DOWN OUR LIVES FOR THIS CAUSE.

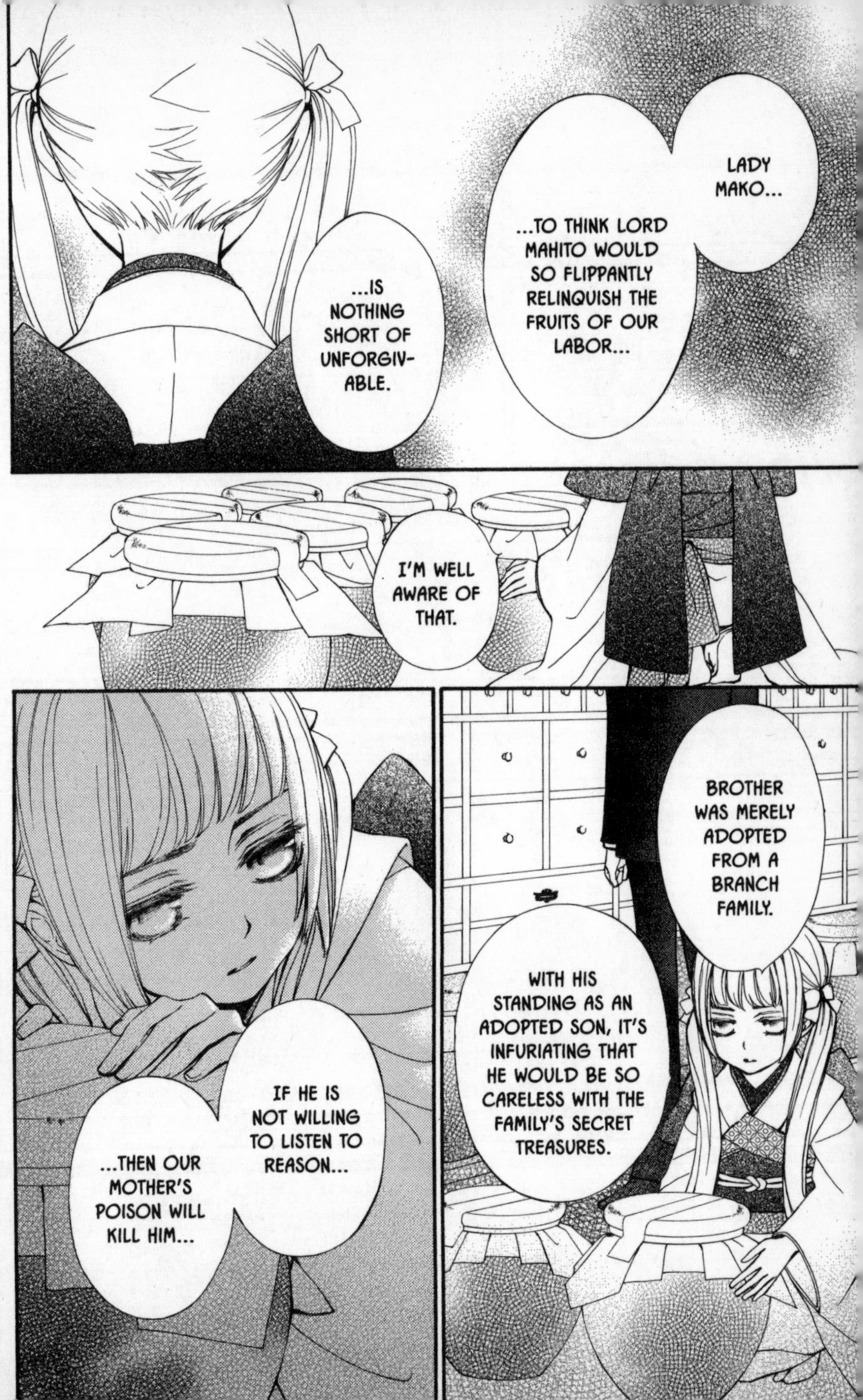
LADY MAKO...
...TO THINK LORD MAHITO WOULD SO FLIPPANTLY RELINQUISH THE FRUITS OF OUR LABOR...
...IS NOTHING SHORT OF UNFORGIVABLE.
I'M WELL AWARE OF THAT.
BROTHER WAS MERELY ADOPTED FROM A BRANCH FAMILY.
WITH HIS STANDING AS AN ADOPTED SON, IT'S INFURIATING THAT HE WOULD BE SO CARELESS WITH THE FAMILY'S SECRET TREASURES.
IF HE IS NOT WILLING TO LISTEN TO REASON...
...THEN OUR MOTHER'S POISON WILL KILL HIM...

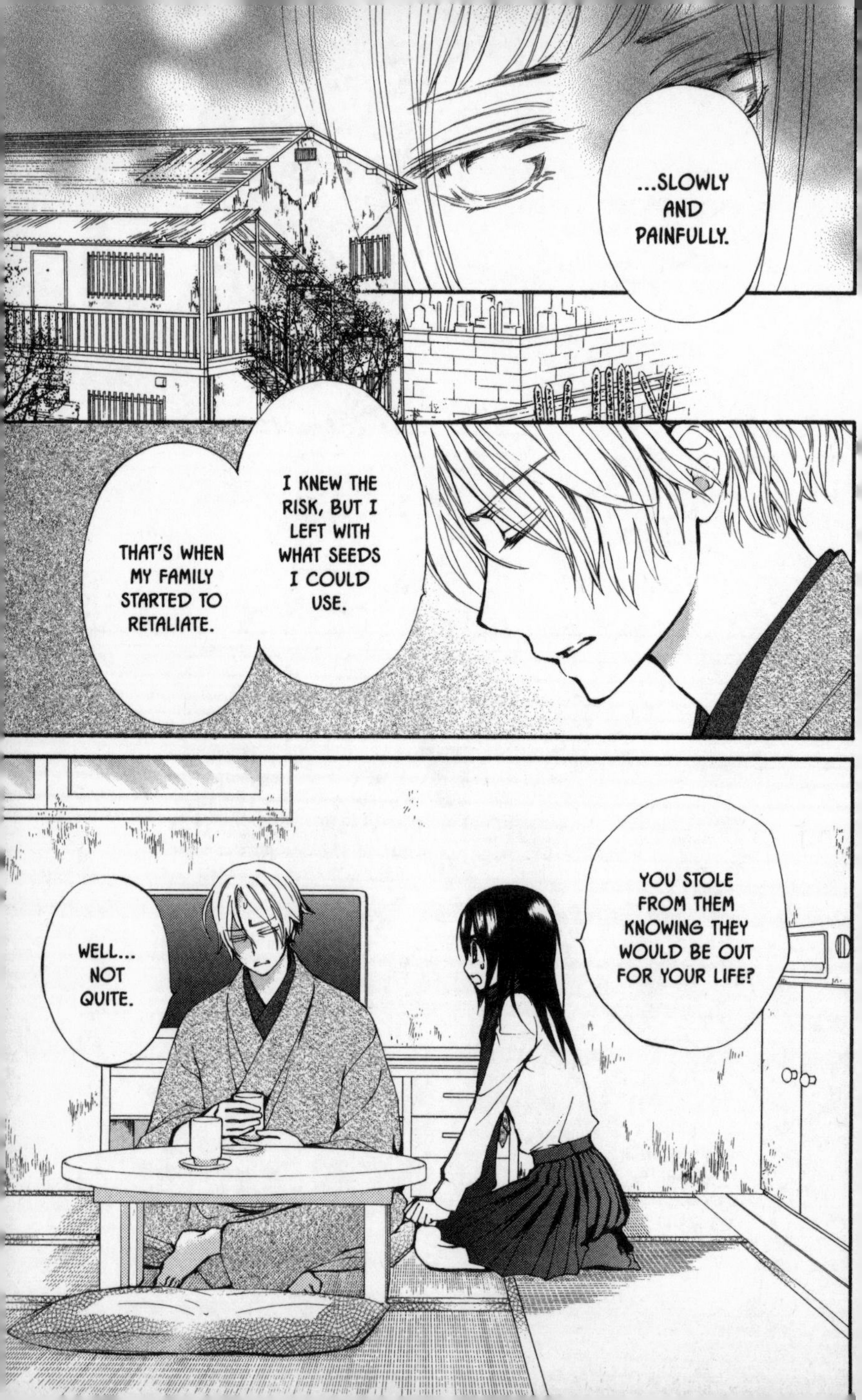
...SLOWLY AND PAINFULLY.
I KNEW THE RISK, BUT I LEFT WITH WHAT SEEDS I COULD USE.
THAT'S WHEN MY FAMILY STARTED TO RETALIATE.
YOU STOLE FROM THEM KNOWING THEY WOULD BE OUT FOR YOUR LIFE?
WELL... NOT QUITE.

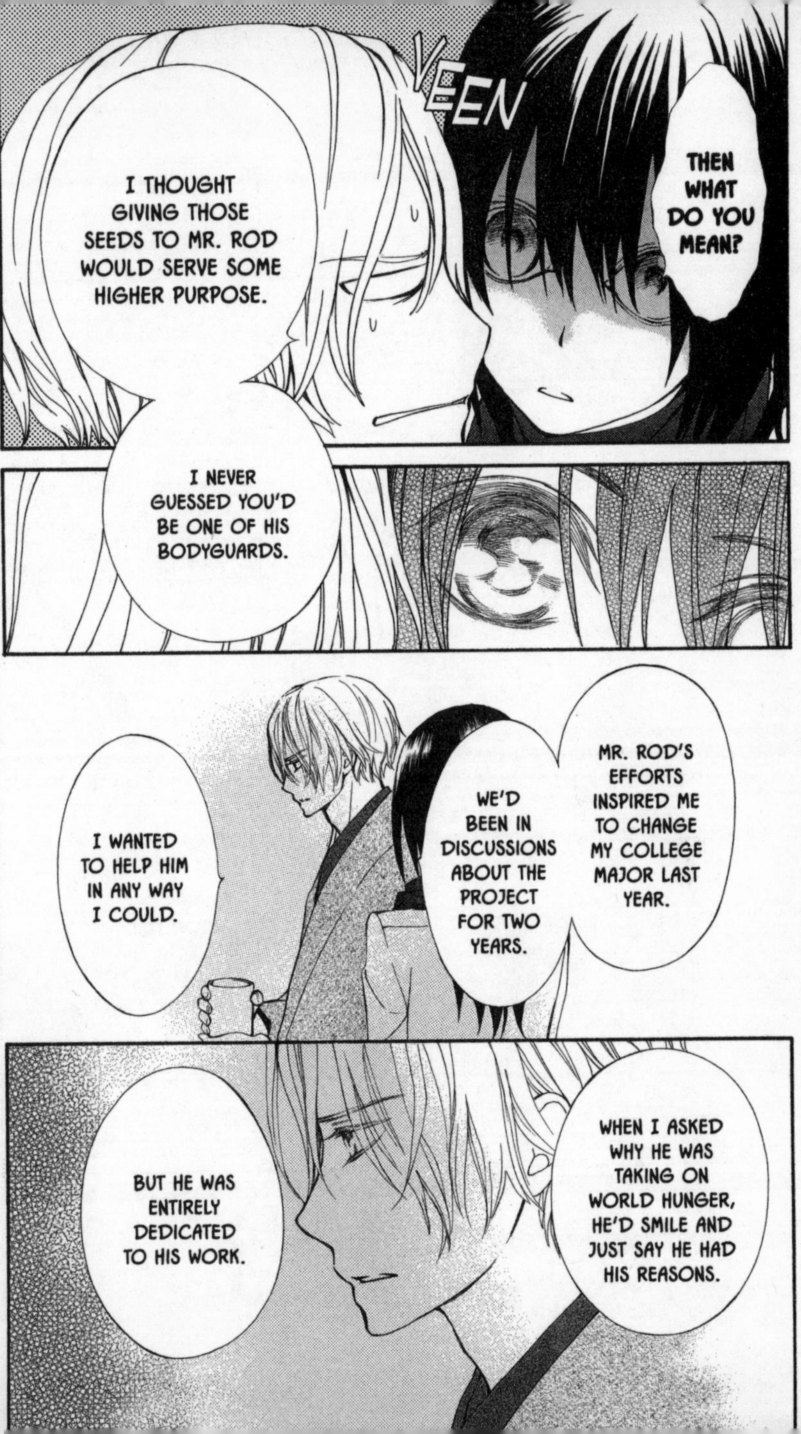
VEEN
THEN WHAT DO YOU MEAN?
I THOUGHT GIVING THOSE SEEDS TO MR. ROD WOULD SERVE SOME HIGHER PURPOSE.
I NEVER GUESSED YOU'D BE ONE OF HIS BODYGUARDS.
MR. ROD'S EFFORTS INSPIRED ME TO CHANGE MY COLLEGE MAJOR LAST YEAR.
WE'D BEEN IN DISCUSSIONS ABOUT THE PROJECT FOR TWO YEARS.
I WANTED TO HELP HIM IN ANY WAY I COULD.
WHEN I ASKED WHY HE WAS TAKING ON WORLD HUNGER, HE'D SMILE AND JUST SAY HE HAD HIS REASONS.
BUT HE WAS ENTIRELY DEDICATED TO HIS WORK.

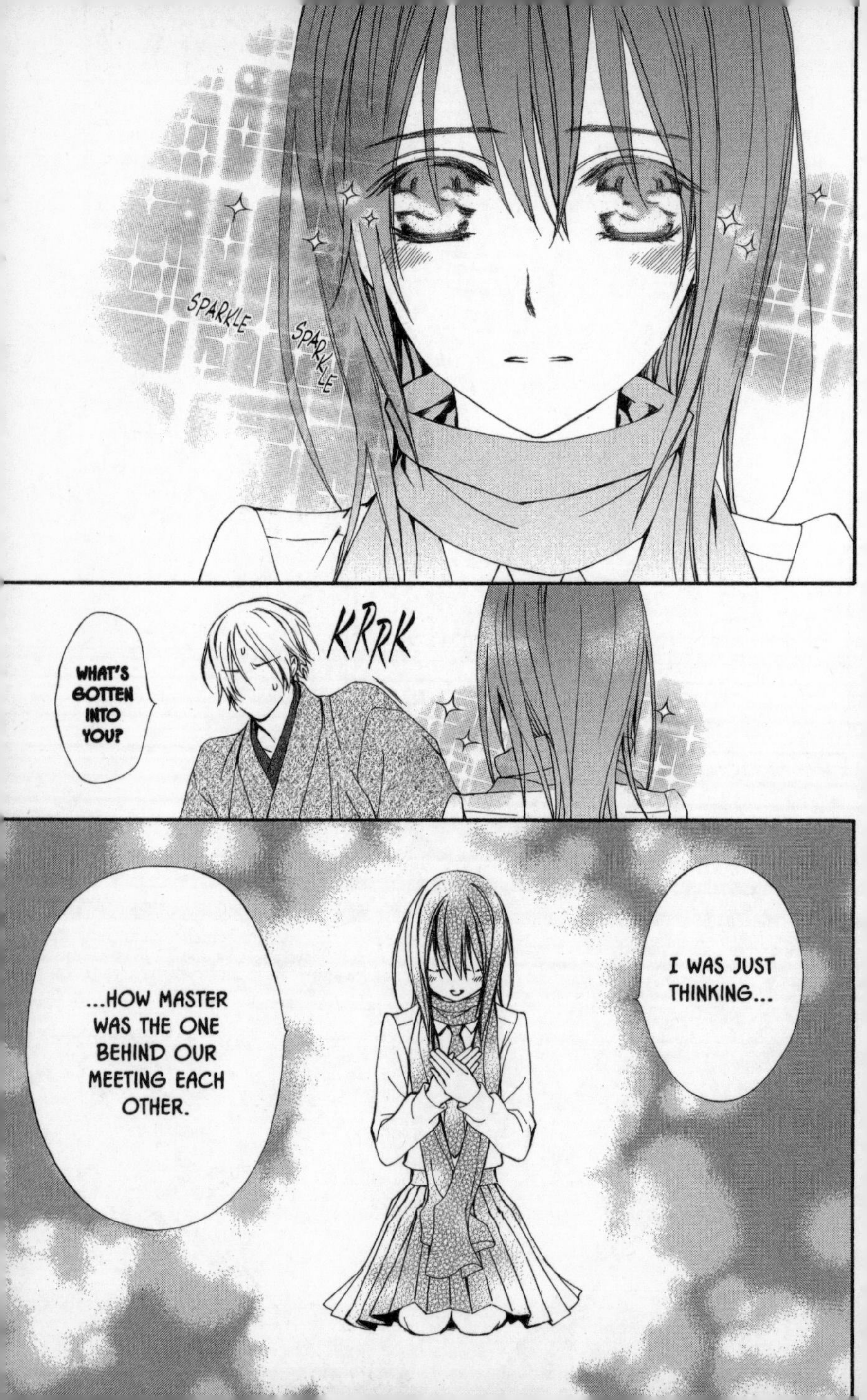
SPARKLE
SPARKLE
KRRK
WHAT'S GOTTEN INTO YOU?
I WAS JUST THINKING...
...HOW MASTER WAS THE ONE BEHIND OUR MEETING EACH OTHER.

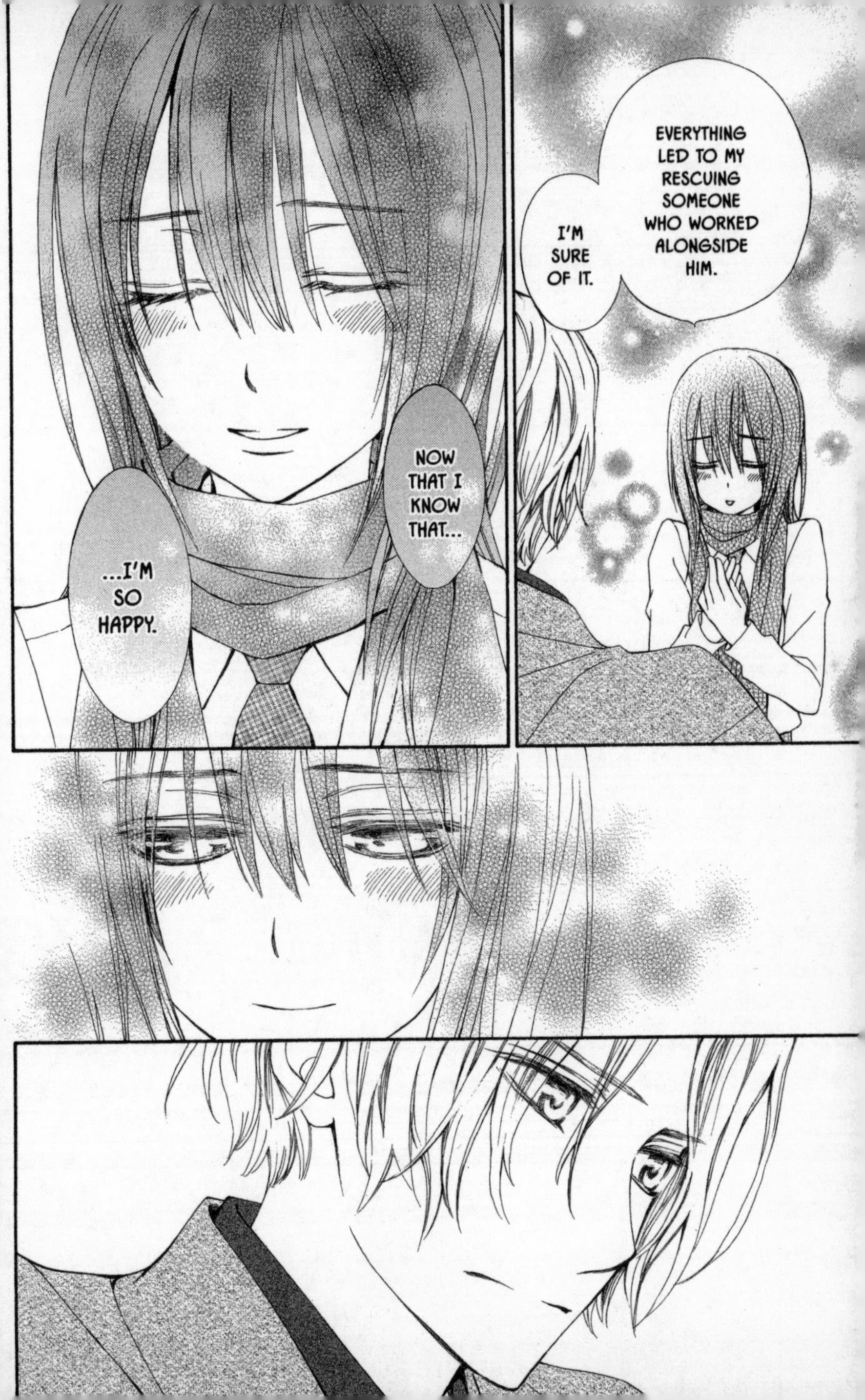
EVERYTHING LED TO MY RESCUING SOMEONE WHO WORKED ALONGSIDE HIM.
I'M SURE OF IT.
NOW THAT I KNOW THAT...
...I'M SO HAPPY.

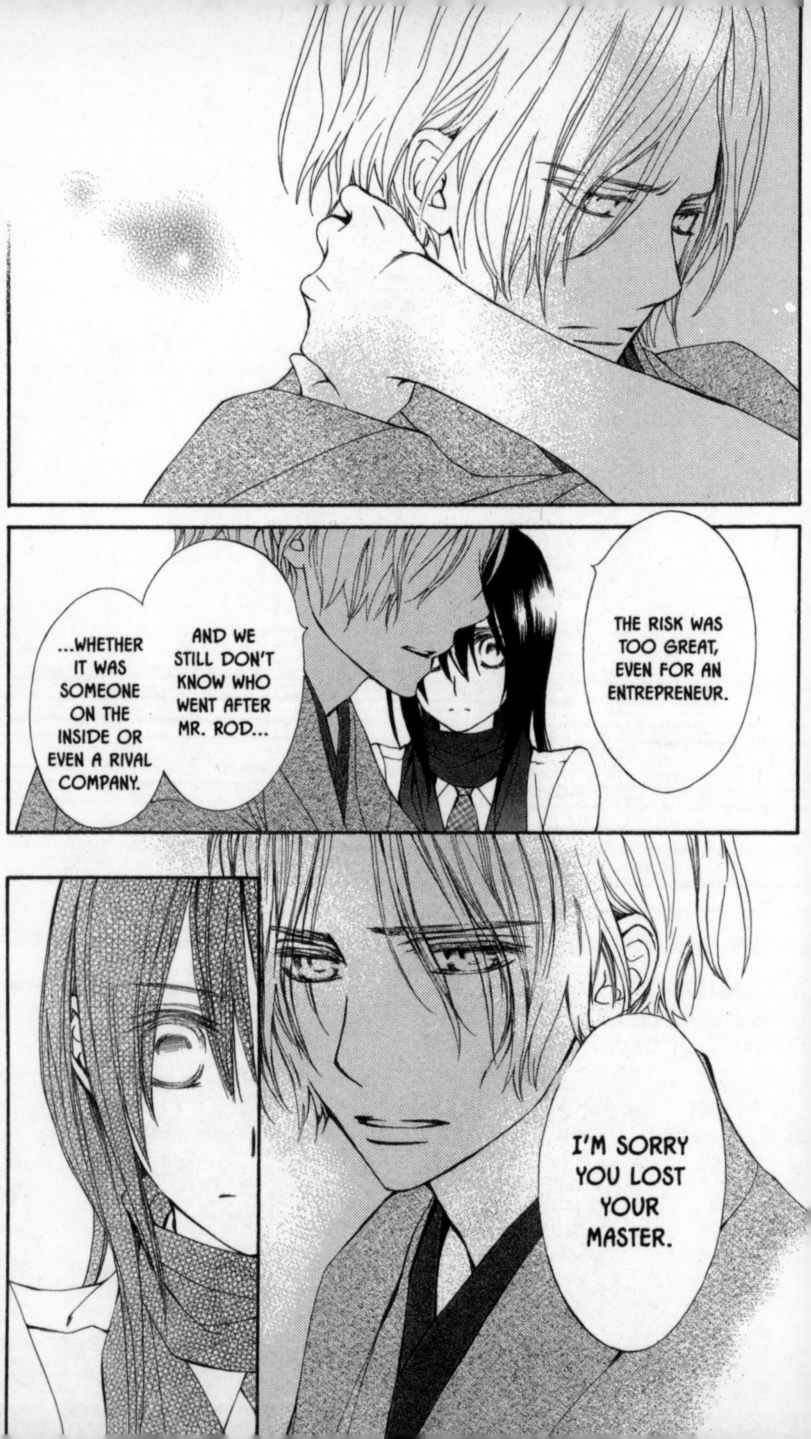
THE RISK WAS TOO GREAT, EVEN FOR AN ENTREPRENEUR.
AND WE STILL DON'T KNOW WHO WENT AFTER MR. ROD...
...WHETHER IT WAS SOMEONE ON THE INSIDE OR EVEN A RIVAL COMPANY.
I'M SORRY YOU LOST YOUR MASTER.

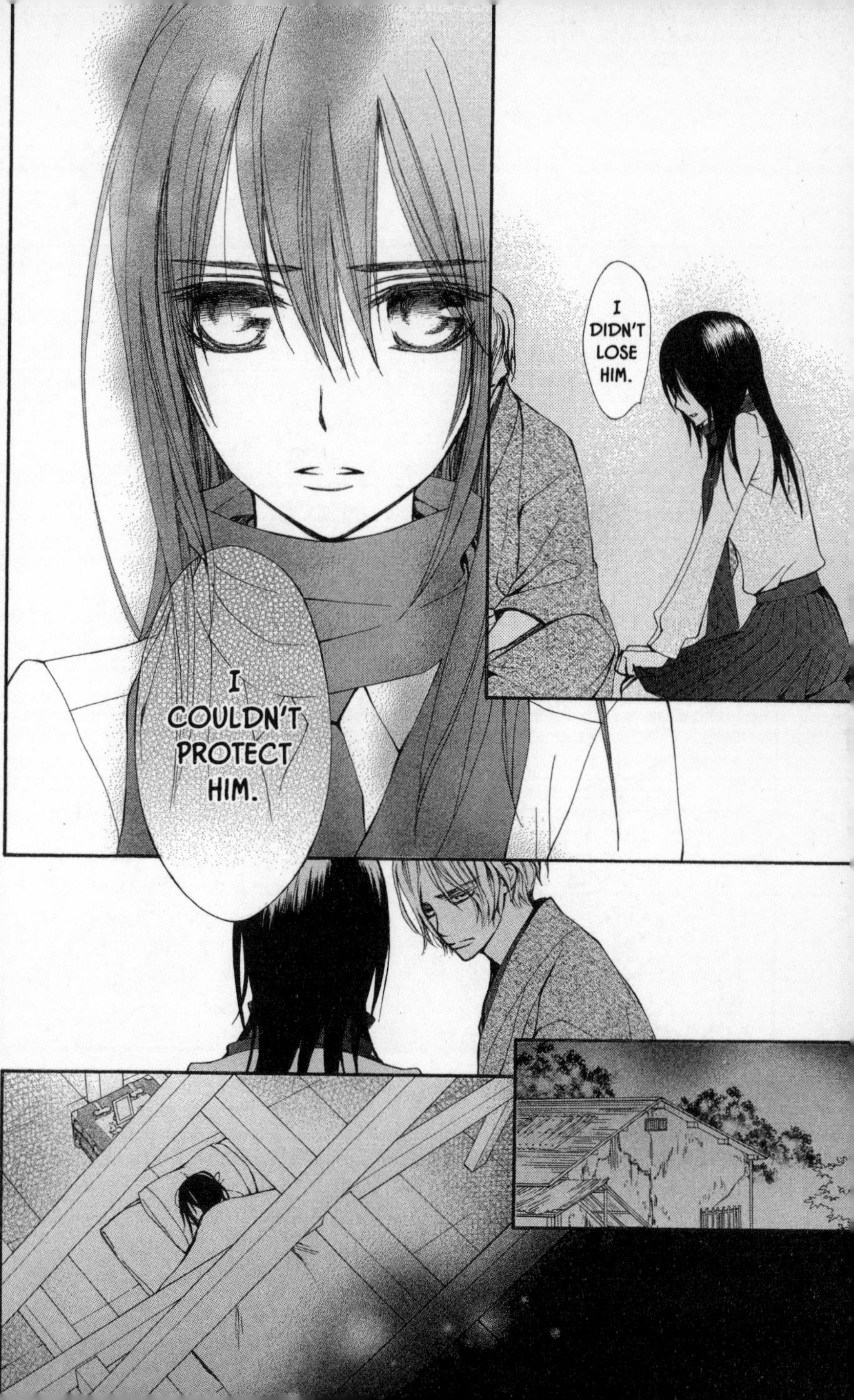
I DIDN'T LOSE HIM.
I COULDN'T PROTECT HIM.

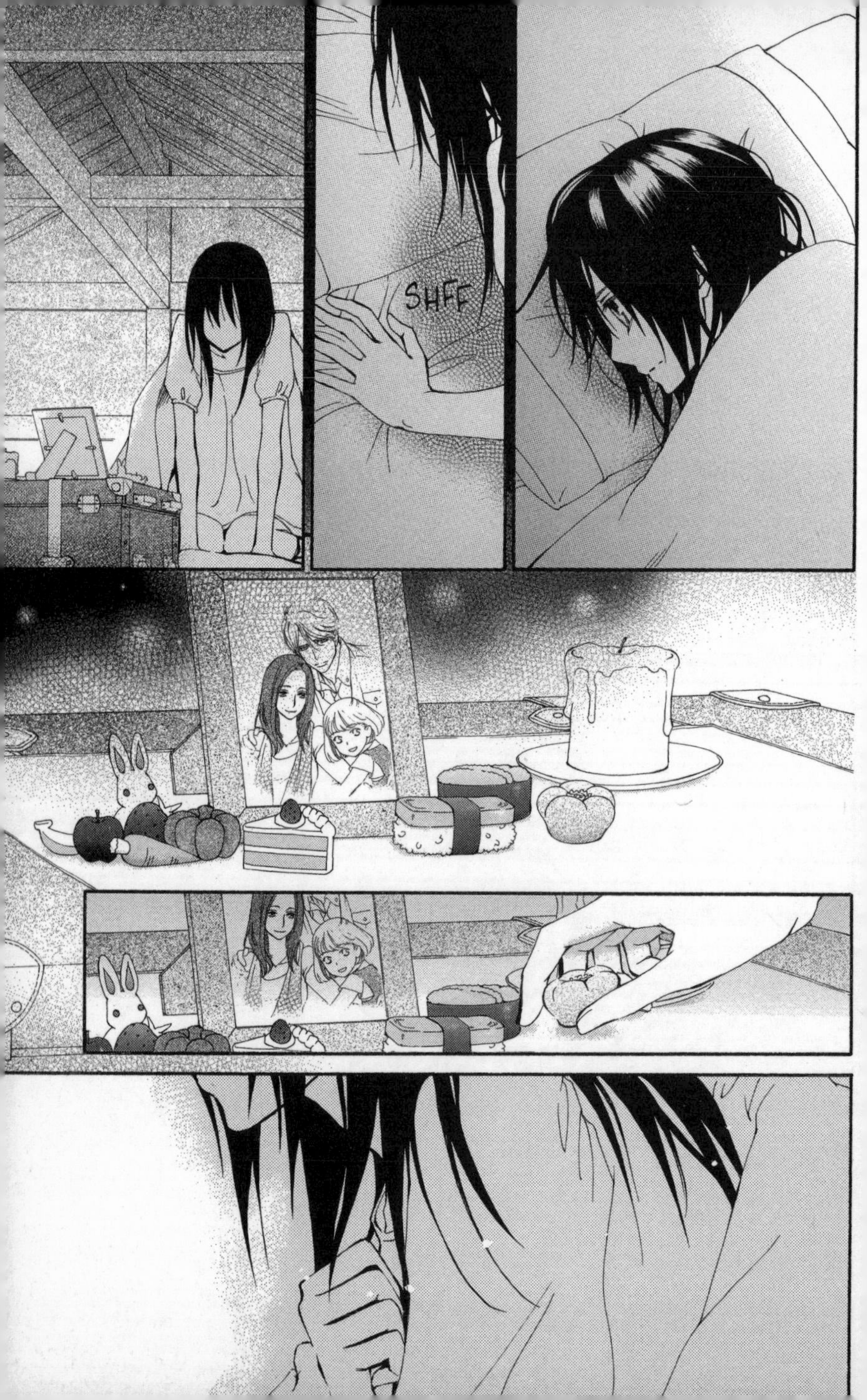
SHFF

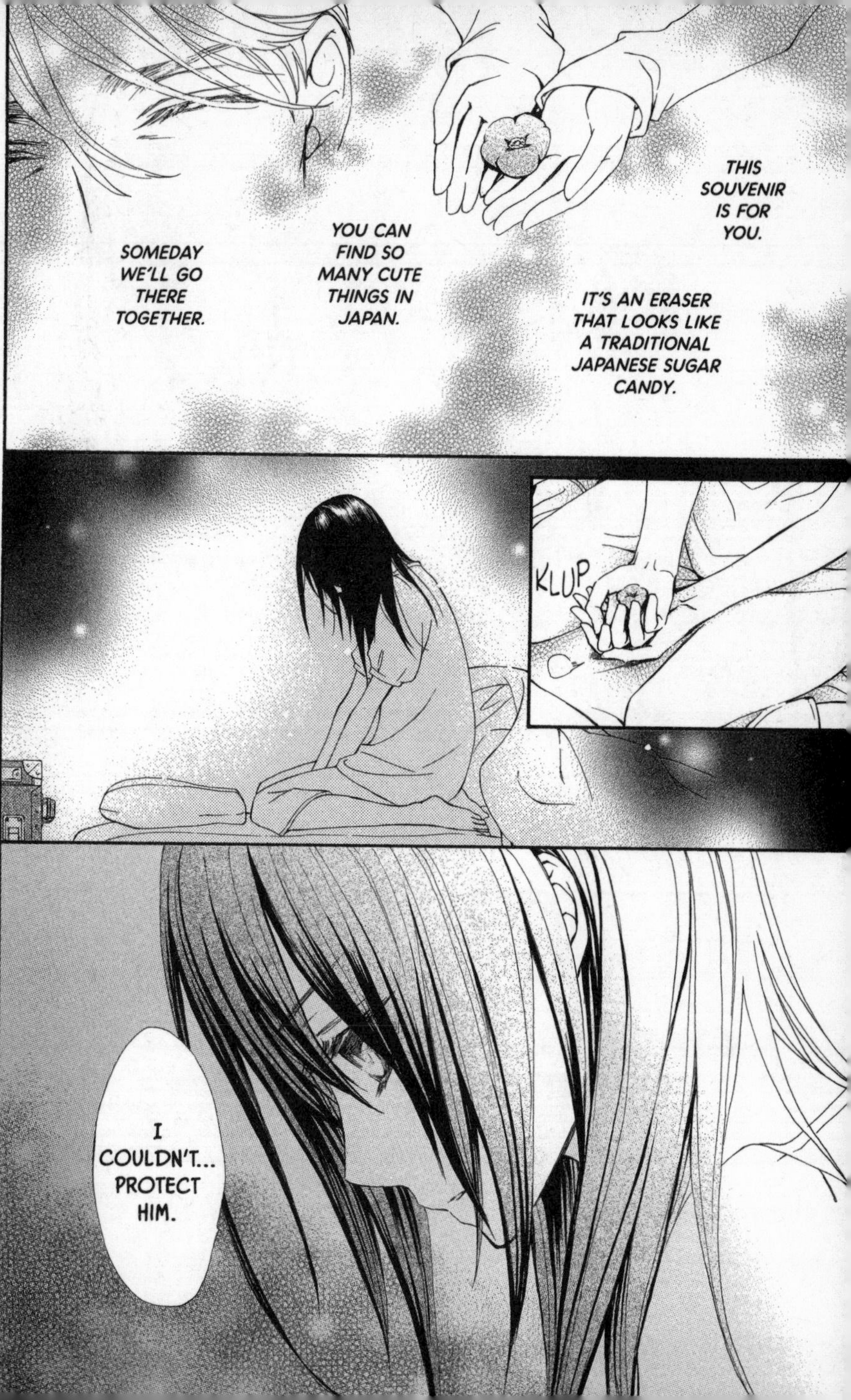
THIS SOUVENIR IS FOR YOU.
IT'S AN ERASER THAT LOOKS LIKE A TRADITIONAL JAPANESE SUGAR CANDY.
YOU CAN FIND SO MANY CUTE THINGS IN JAPAN.
SOMEDAY WE'LL GO THERE TOGETHER.
KLUP
I COULDN'T... PROTECT HIM.

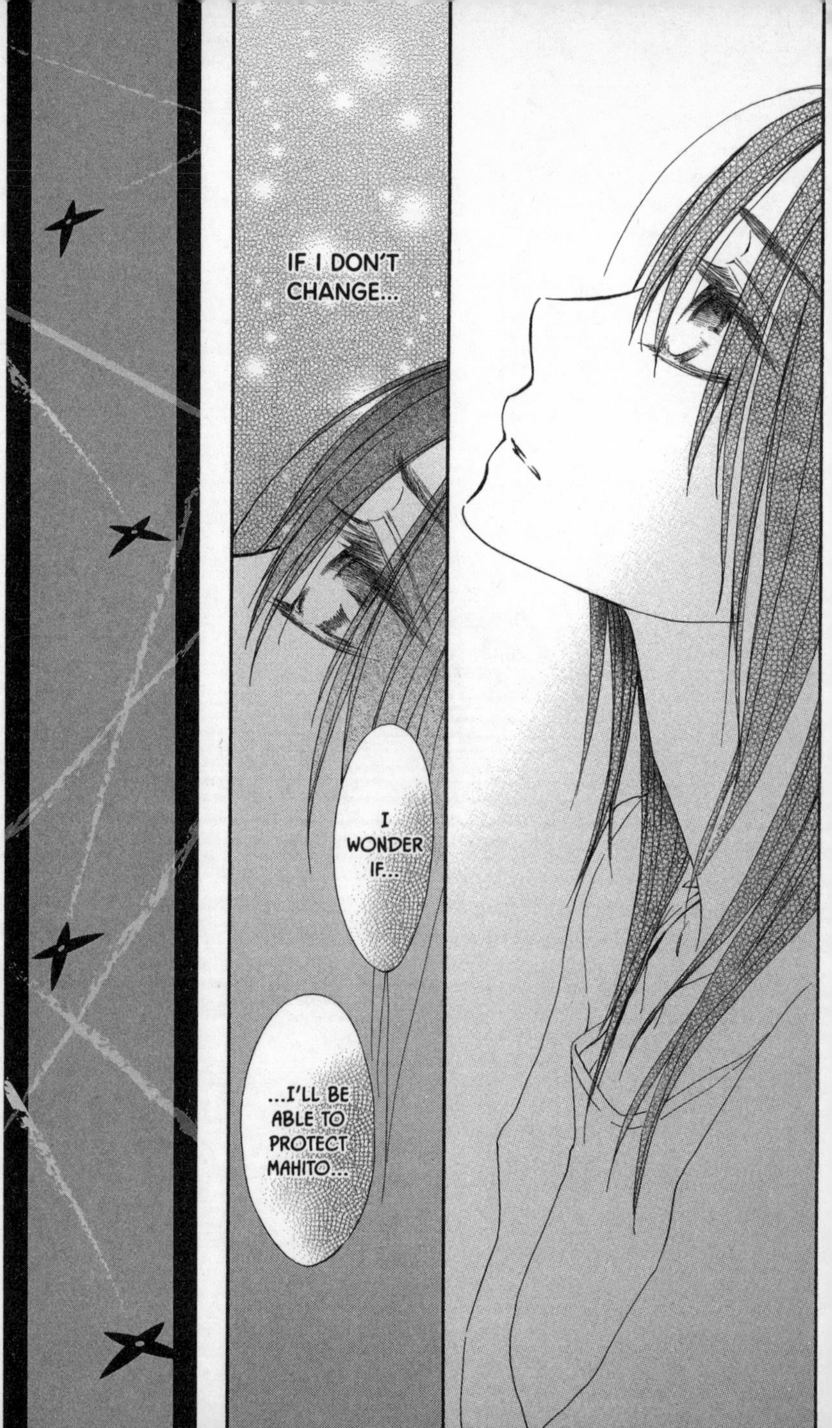
IF I DON'T CHANGE...
I WONDER IF...
...I'LL BE ABLE TO PROTECT MAHITO...

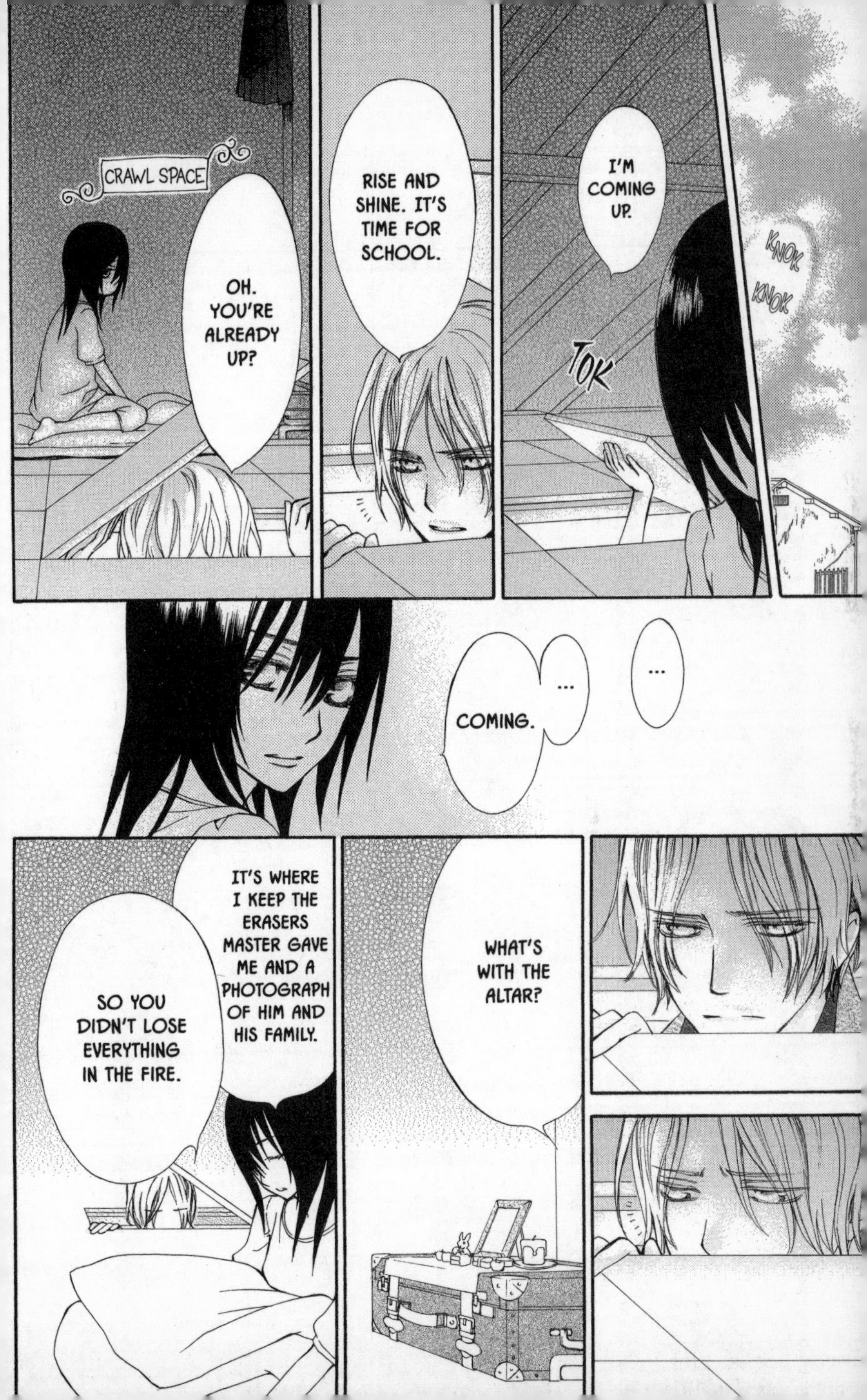
KNOK KNOK
I'M COMING UP.
TOK
RISE AND SHINE. IT'S TIME FOR SCHOOL.
CRAWL SPACE
OH. YOU'RE ALREADY UP?
...
...
COMING.
WHAT'S WITH THE ALTAR?
IT'S WHERE I KEEP THE ERASERS MASTER GAVE ME AND A PHOTOGRAPH OF HIM AND HIS FAMILY.
SO YOU DIDN'T LOSE EVERYTHING IN THE FIRE.

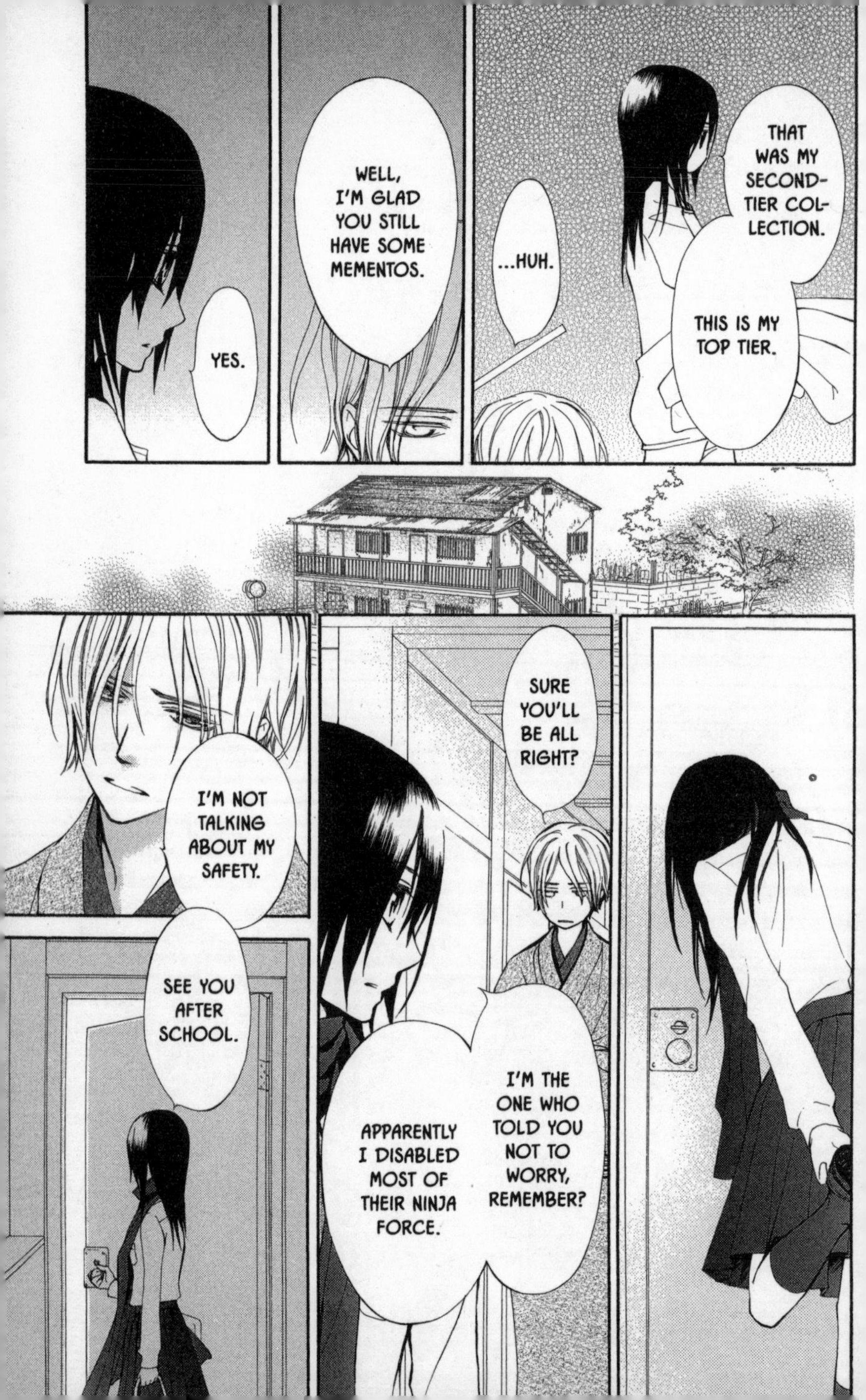
THAT WAS MY SECOND-TIER COLLECTION.
THIS IS MY TOP TIER.
...HUH.
WELL, I'M GLAD YOU STILL HAVE SOME MEMENTOS.
YES.
SURE YOU'LL BE ALL RIGHT?
I'M THE ONE WHO TOLD YOU NOT TO WORRY, REMEMBER?
APPARENTLY I DISABLED MOST OF THEIR NINJA FORCE.
I'M NOT TALKING ABOUT MY SAFETY.
SEE YOU AFTER SCHOOL.

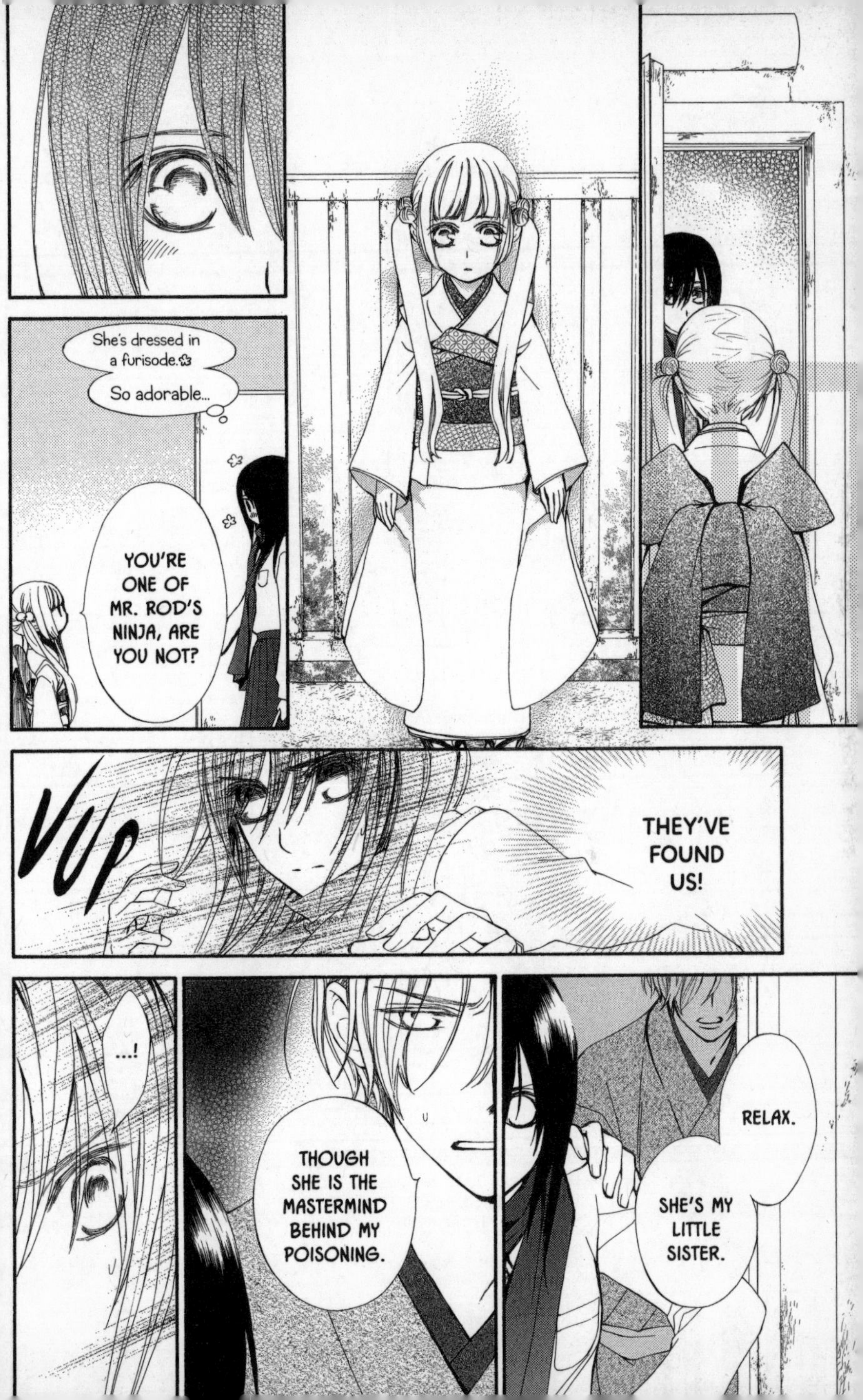
She's dressed in a furisode.
So adorable...
YOU'RE ONE OF MR. ROD'S NINJA, ARE YOU NOT?
THEY'VE FOUND US!
VUP
RELAX.
SHE'S MY LITTLE SISTER.
THOUGH SHE IS THE MASTERMIND BEHIND MY POISONING.
...!

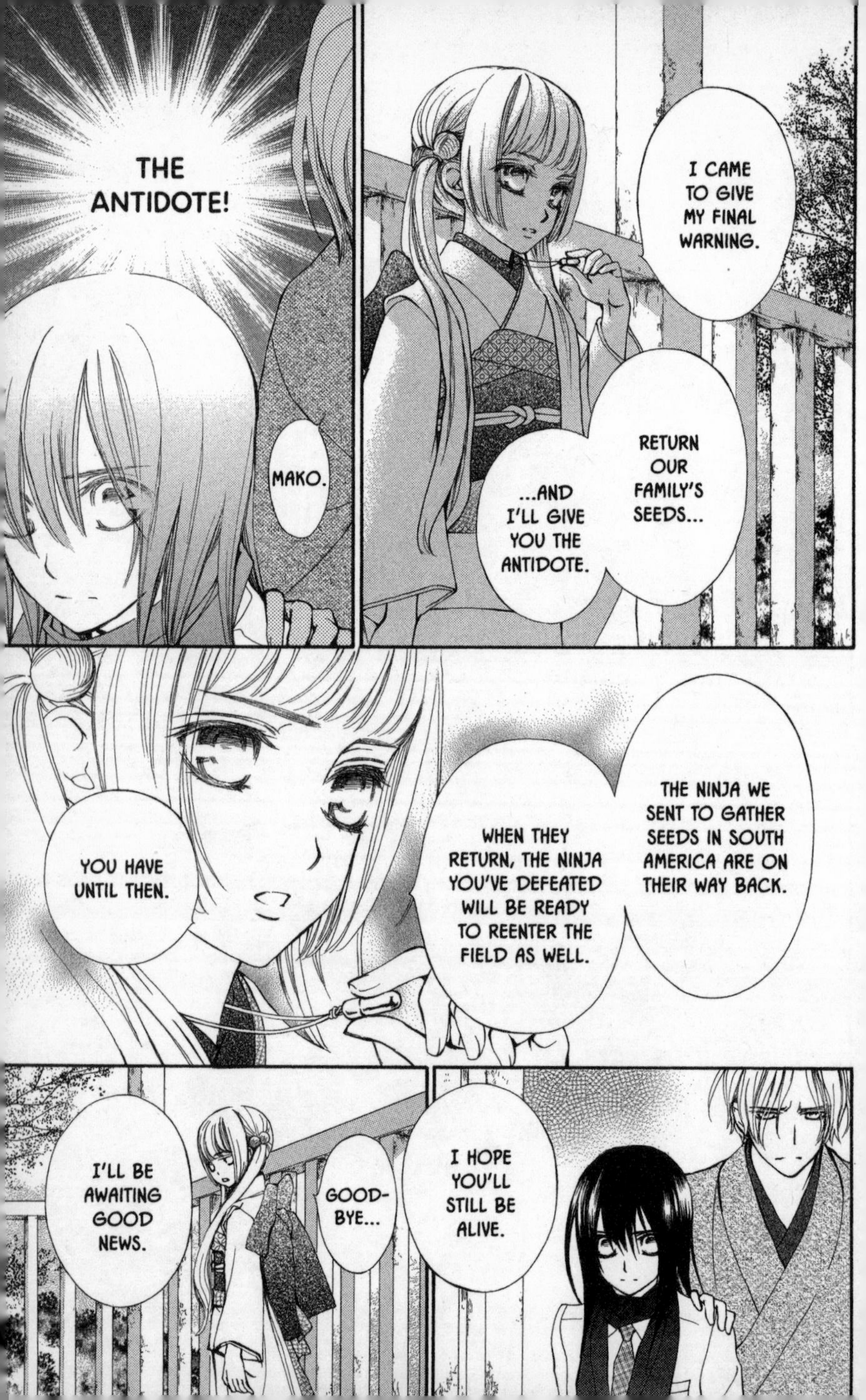
I CAME TO GIVE MY FINAL WARNING.
RETURN OUR FAMILY'S SEEDS...
...AND I'LL GIVE YOU THE ANTIDOTE.
THE ANTIDOTE!
MAKO.
THE NINJA WE SENT TO GATHER SEEDS IN SOUTH AMERICA ARE ON THEIR WAY BACK.
WHEN THEY RETURN, THE NINJA YOU'VE DEFEATED WILL BE READY TO REENTER THE FIELD AS WELL.
YOU HAVE UNTIL THEN.
I HOPE YOU'LL STILL BE ALIVE.
GOOD-BYE...
I'LL BE AWAITING GOOD NEWS.

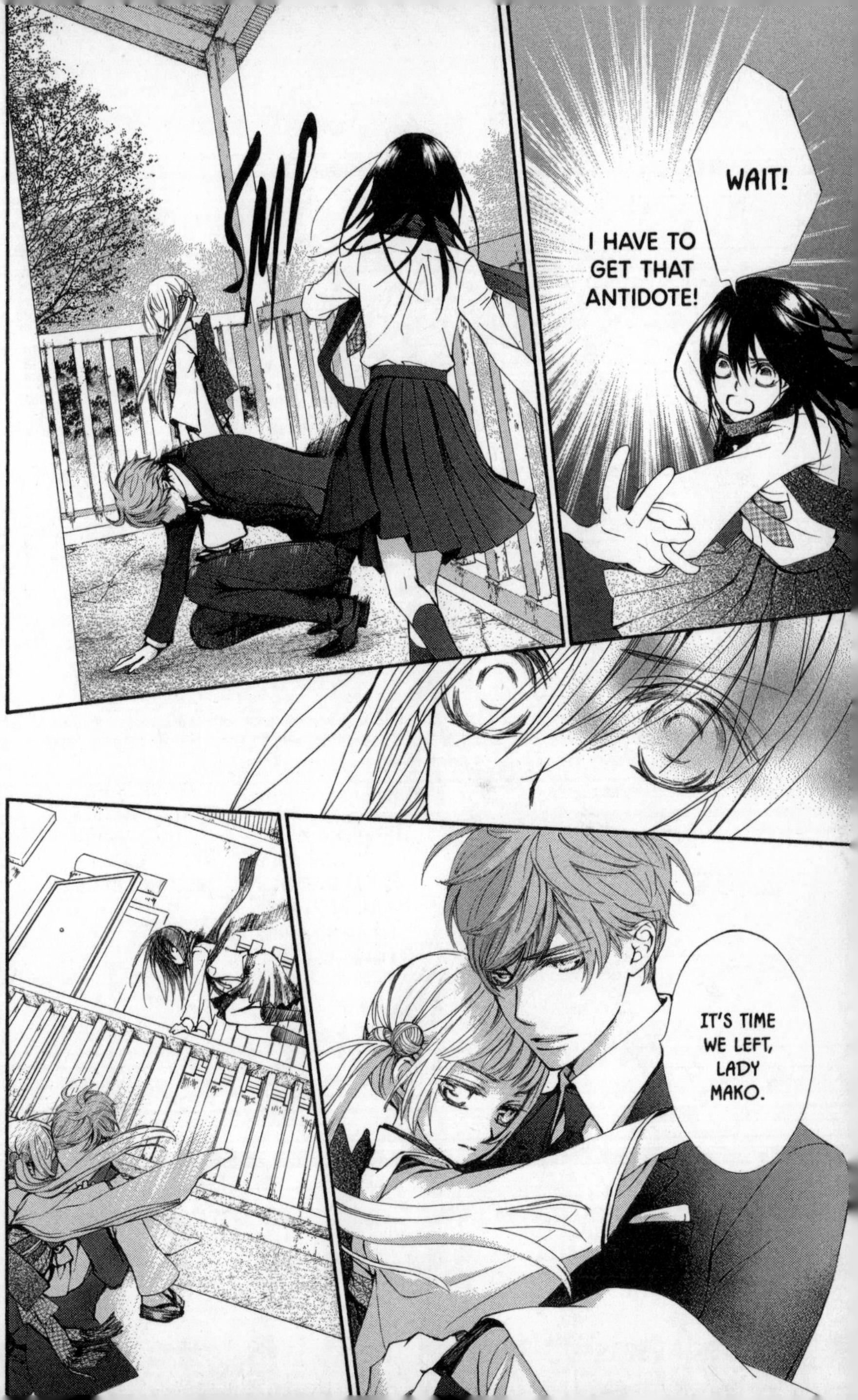
WAIT!
I HAVE TO GET THAT ANTIDOTE!
SMP
IT'S TIME WE LEFT, LADY MAKO.

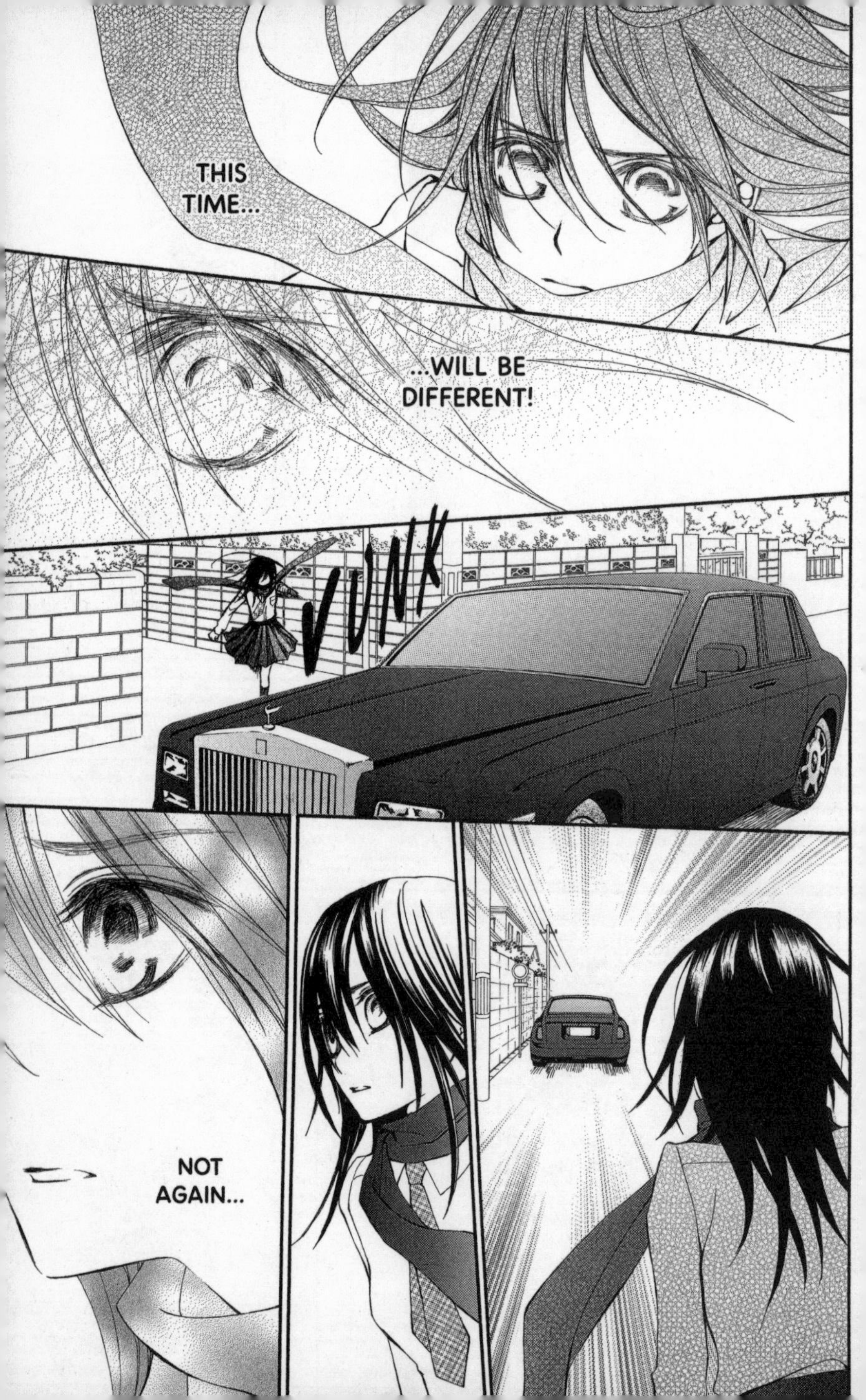
THIS TIME...
...WILL BE DIFFERENT!
VUNK
NOT AGAIN...

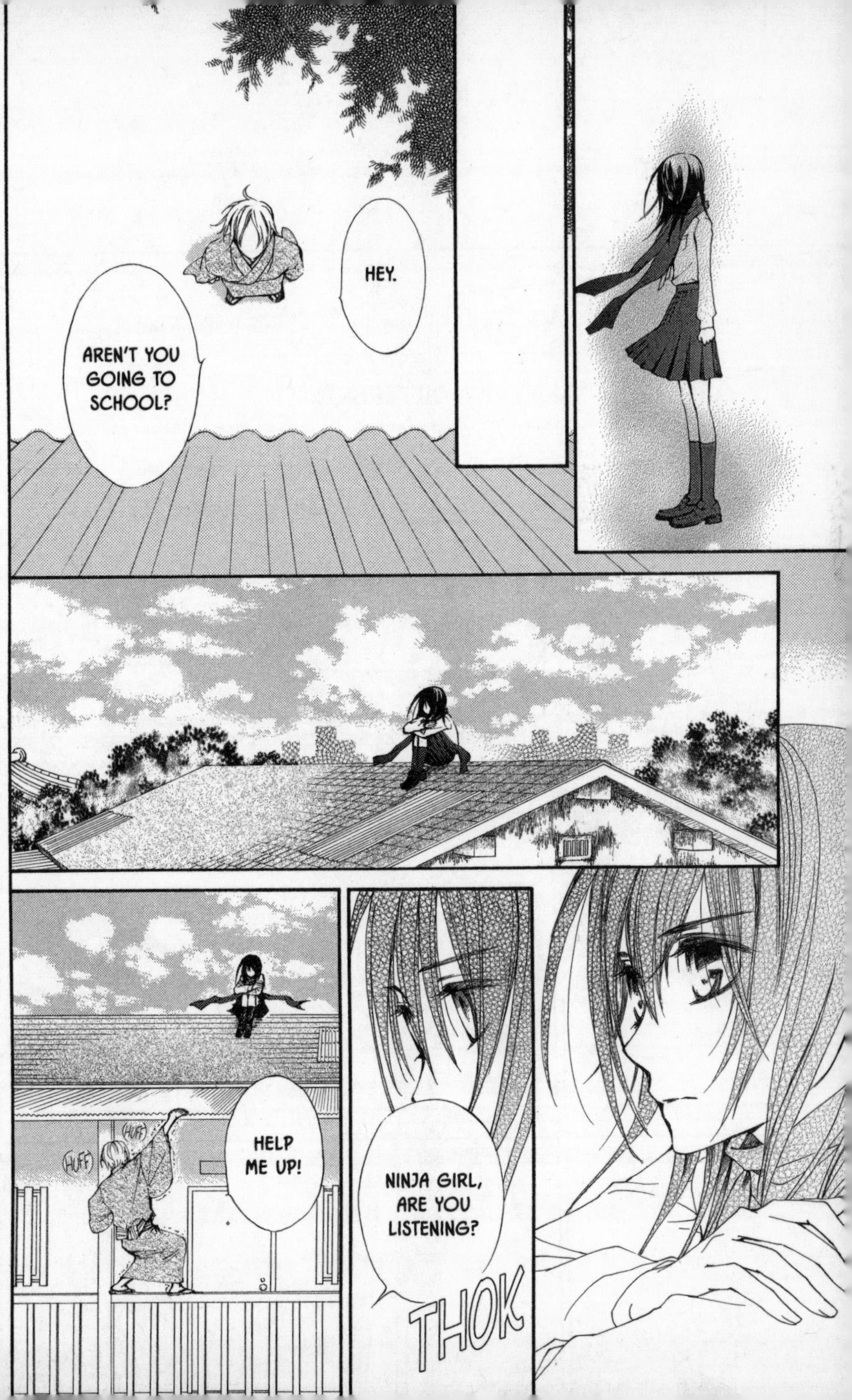
HEY.
AREN'T YOU GOING TO SCHOOL?
NINJA GIRL, ARE YOU LISTENING?
THOK
HELP ME UP!
HUFF
HUFF

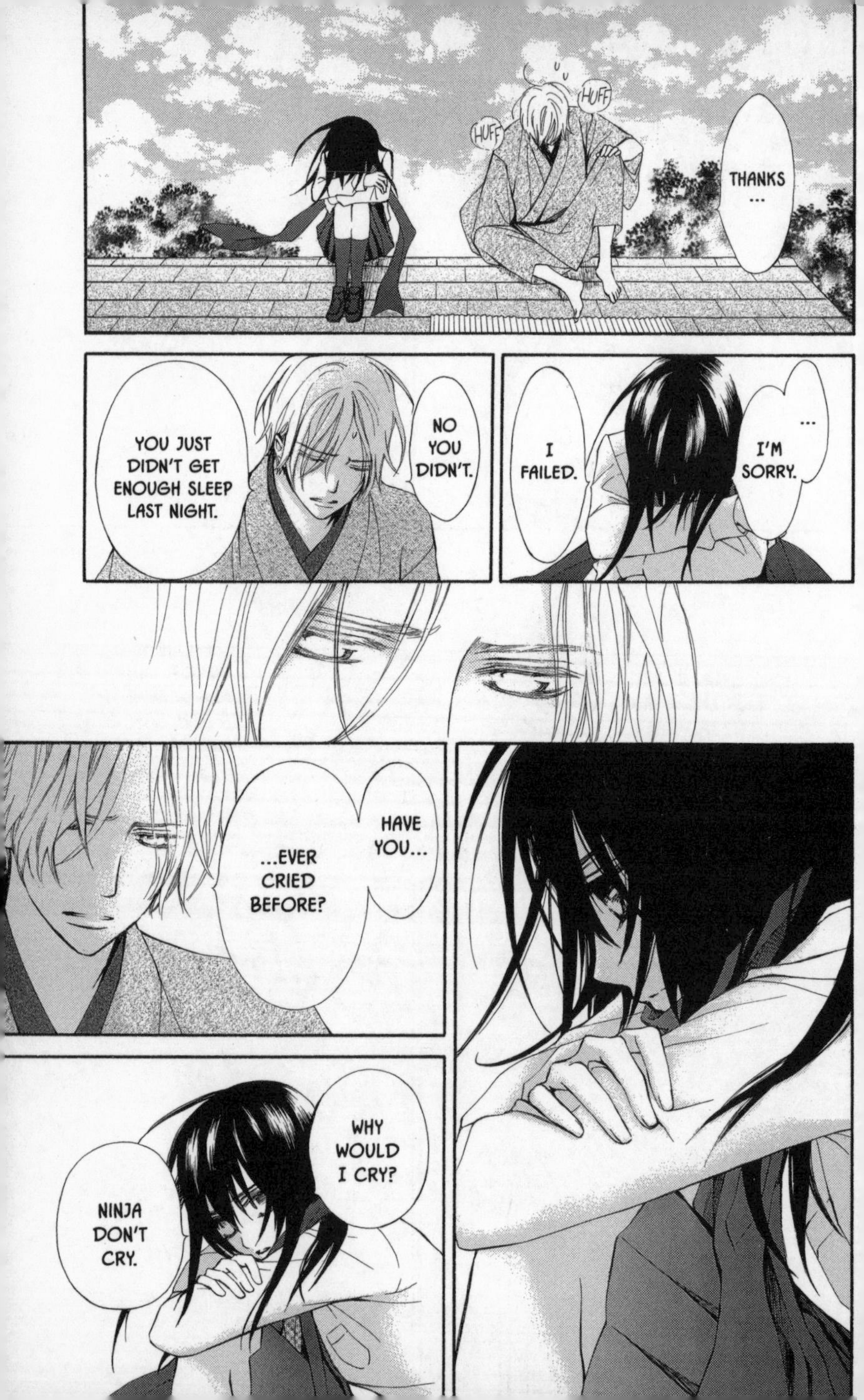
THANKS...
HUFF
HUFF
... I'M SORRY.
I FAILED.
NO YOU DIDN'T.
YOU JUST DIDN'T GET ENOUGH SLEEP LAST NIGHT.
HAVE YOU...
...EVER CRIED BEFORE?
WHY WOULD I CRY?
NINJA DON'T CRY.

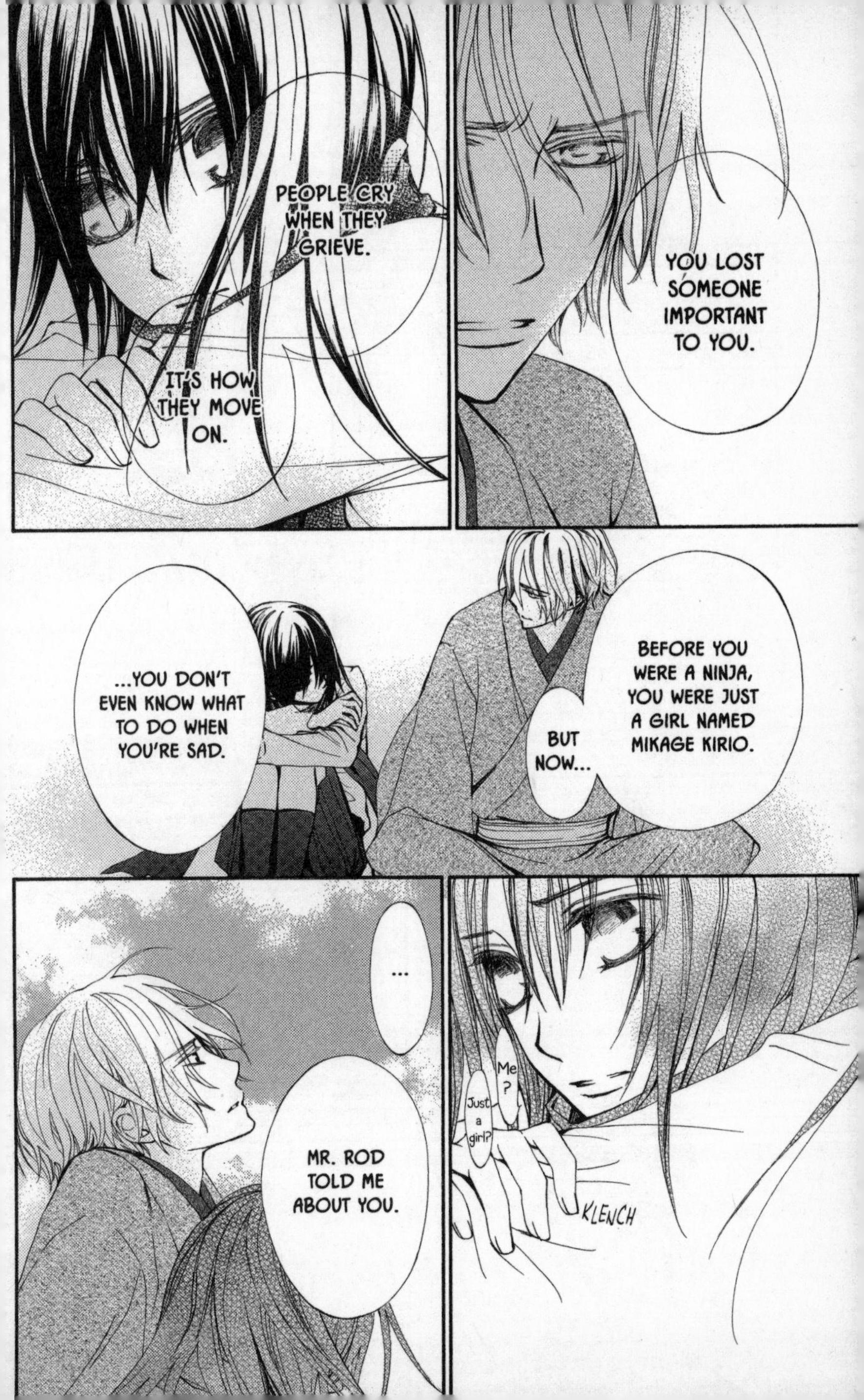
YOU LOST SOMEONE IMPORTANT TO YOU.
PEOPLE CRY WHEN THEY GRIEVE.
IT'S HOW THEY MOVE ON.
BEFORE YOU WERE A NINJA, YOU WERE JUST A GIRL NAMED MIKAGE KIRIO.
BUT NOW...
...YOU DON'T EVEN KNOW WHAT TO DO WHEN YOU'RE SAD.
Me?
Just a girl?
KLENCH
...
MR. ROD TOLD ME ABOUT YOU.

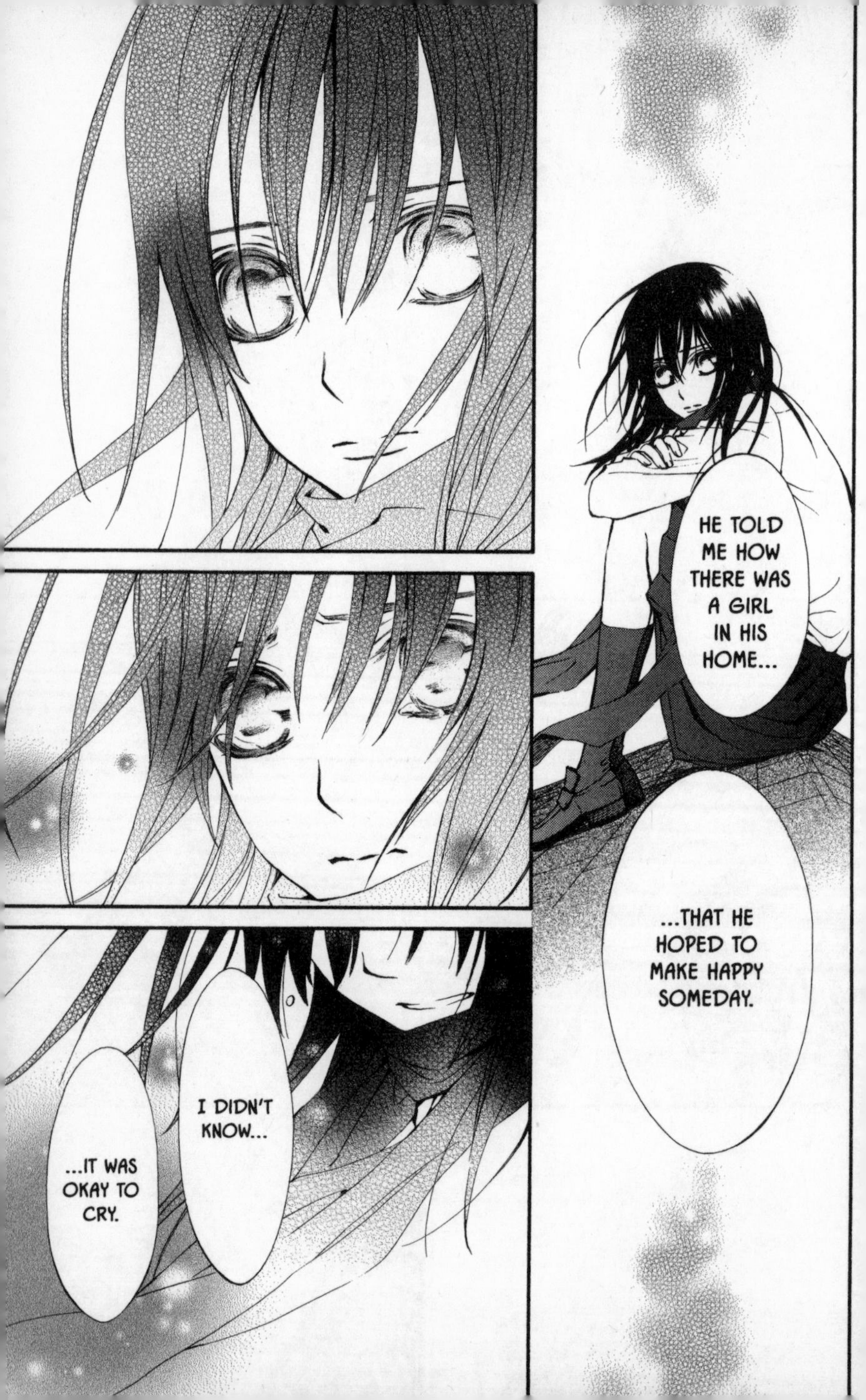
HE TOLD ME HOW THERE WAS A GIRL IN HIS HOME...
...THAT HE HOPED TO MAKE HAPPY SOMEDAY.
I DIDN'T KNOW...
...IT WAS OKAY TO CRY.

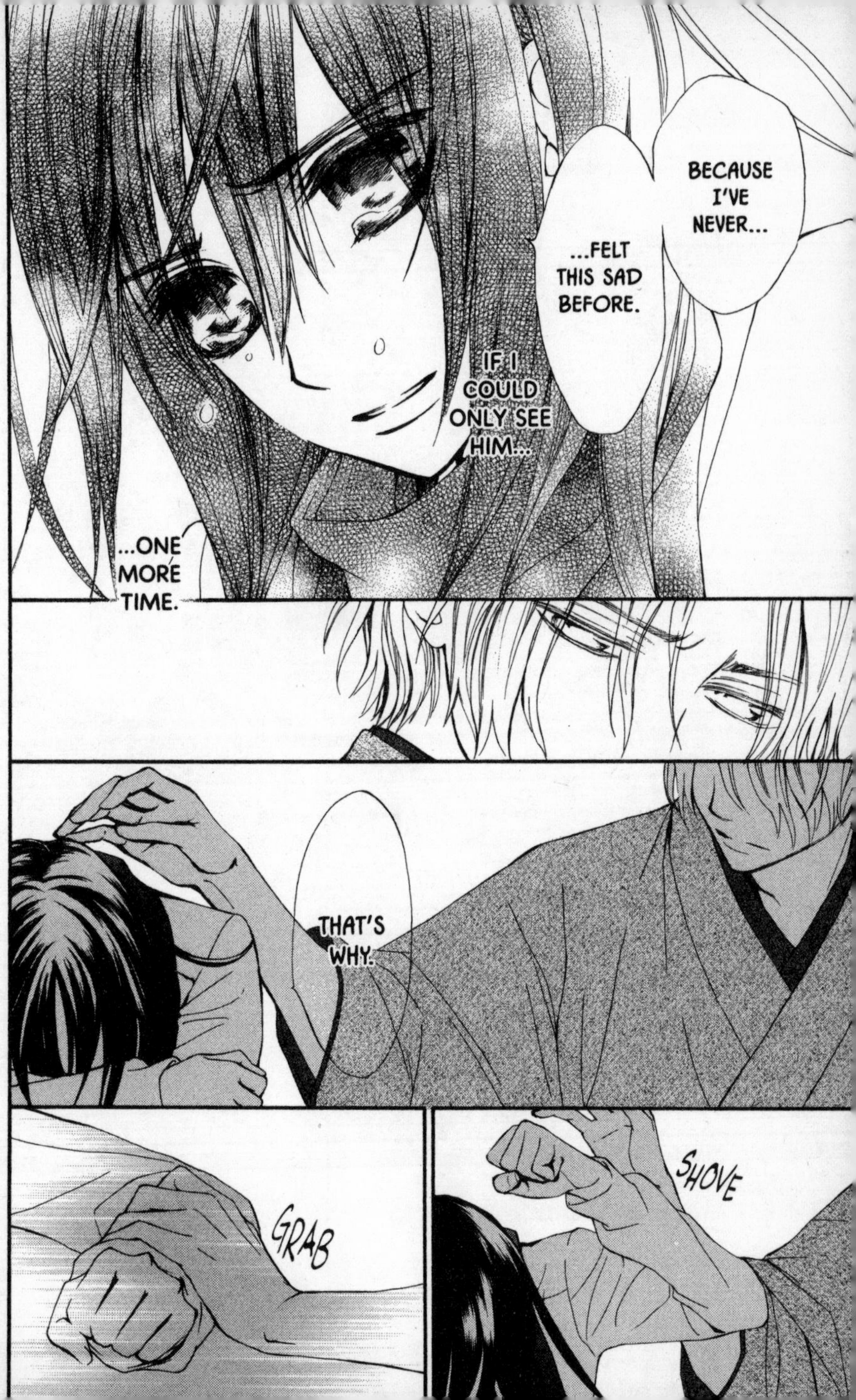
BECAUSE I'VE NEVER...
...FELT THIS SAD BEFORE.
IF I COULD ONLY SEE HIM...
...ONE MORE TIME.
THAT'S WHY.
SHOVE
GRAB

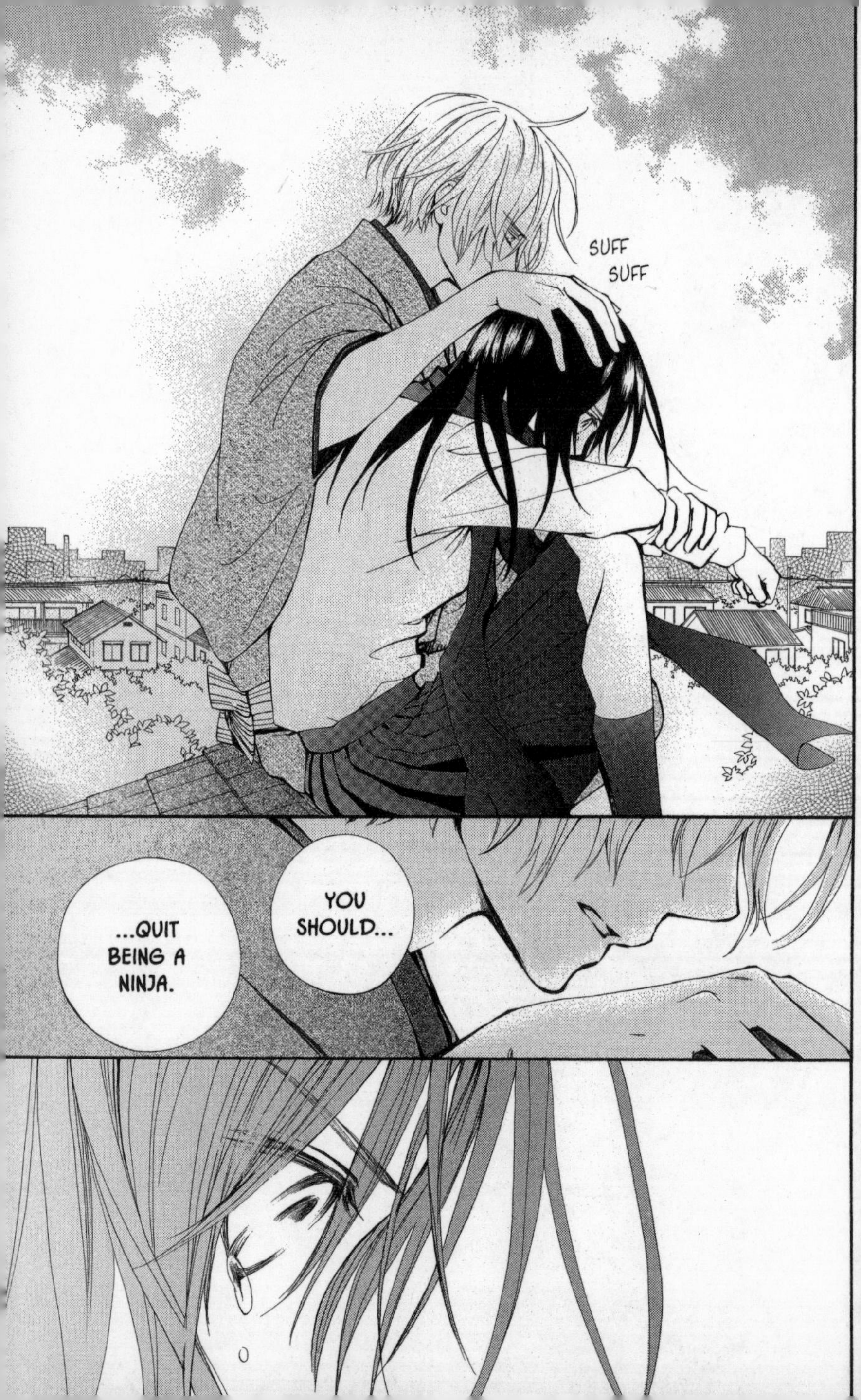
SUFF
SUFF
YOU SHOULD...
...QUIT BEING A NINJA.

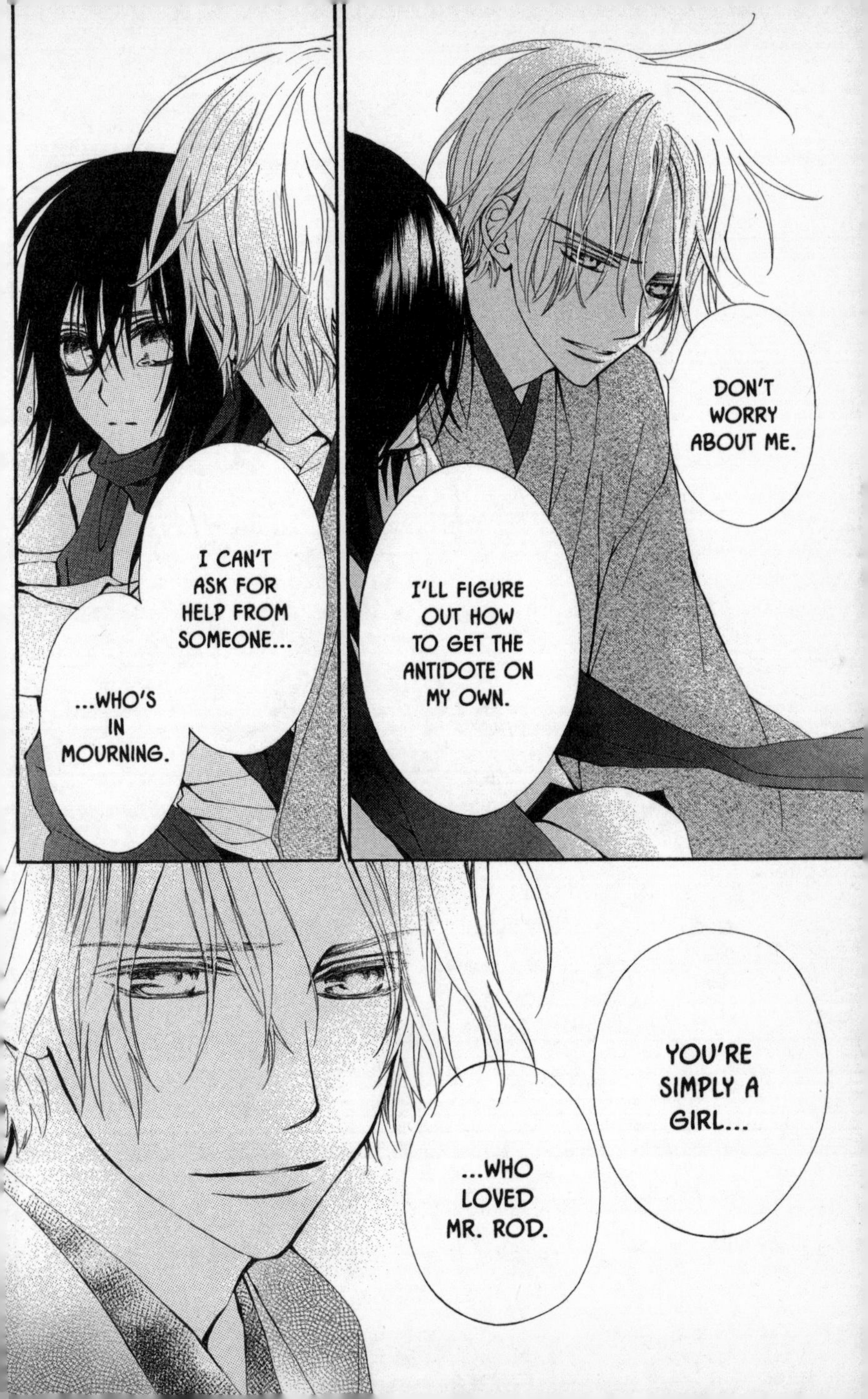
DON'T WORRY ABOUT ME.
I'LL FIGURE OUT HOW TO GET THE ANTIDOTE ON MY OWN.
I CAN'T ASK FOR HELP FROM SOMEONE...
...WHO'S IN MOURNING.
YOU'RE SIMPLY A GIRL...
...WHO LOVED MR. ROD.

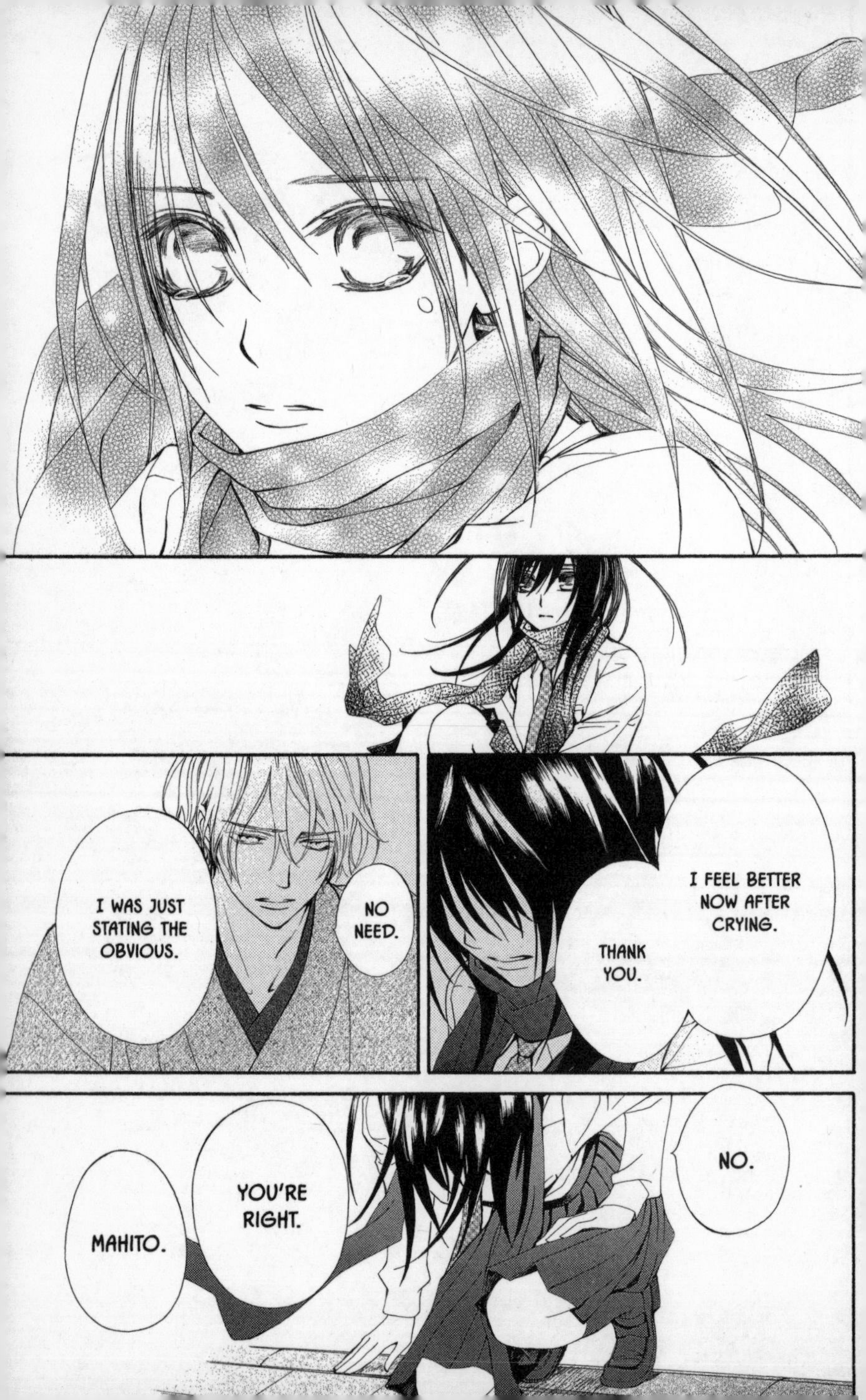
I FEEL BETTER NOW AFTER CRYING.
THANK YOU.
NO NEED.
I WAS JUST STATING THE OBVIOUS.
NO.
YOU'RE RIGHT.
MAHITO.

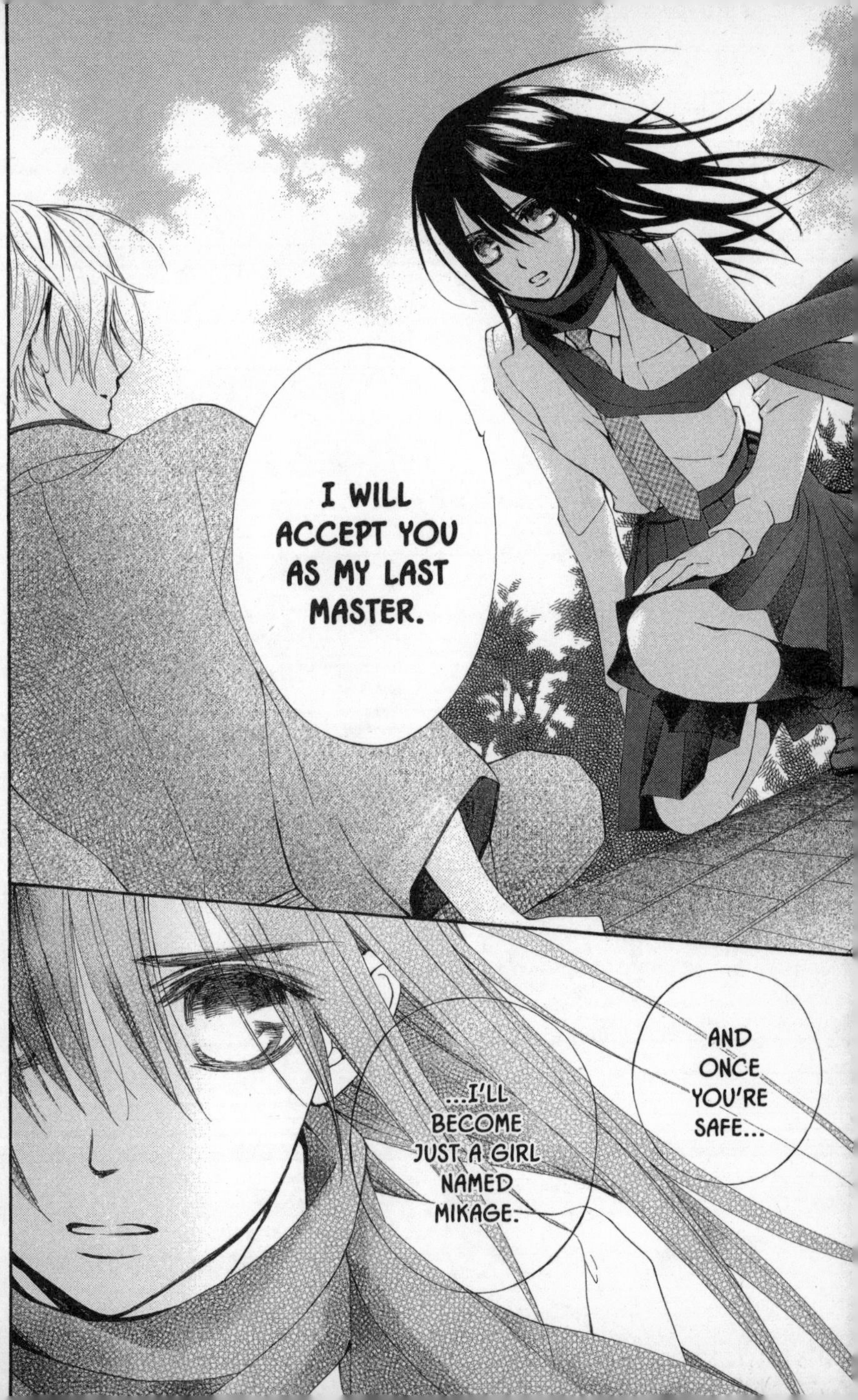
I WILL ACCEPT YOU AS MY LAST MASTER.
AND ONCE YOU'RE SAFE...
...I'LL BECOME JUST A GIRL NAMED MIKAGE.

Chapter 5

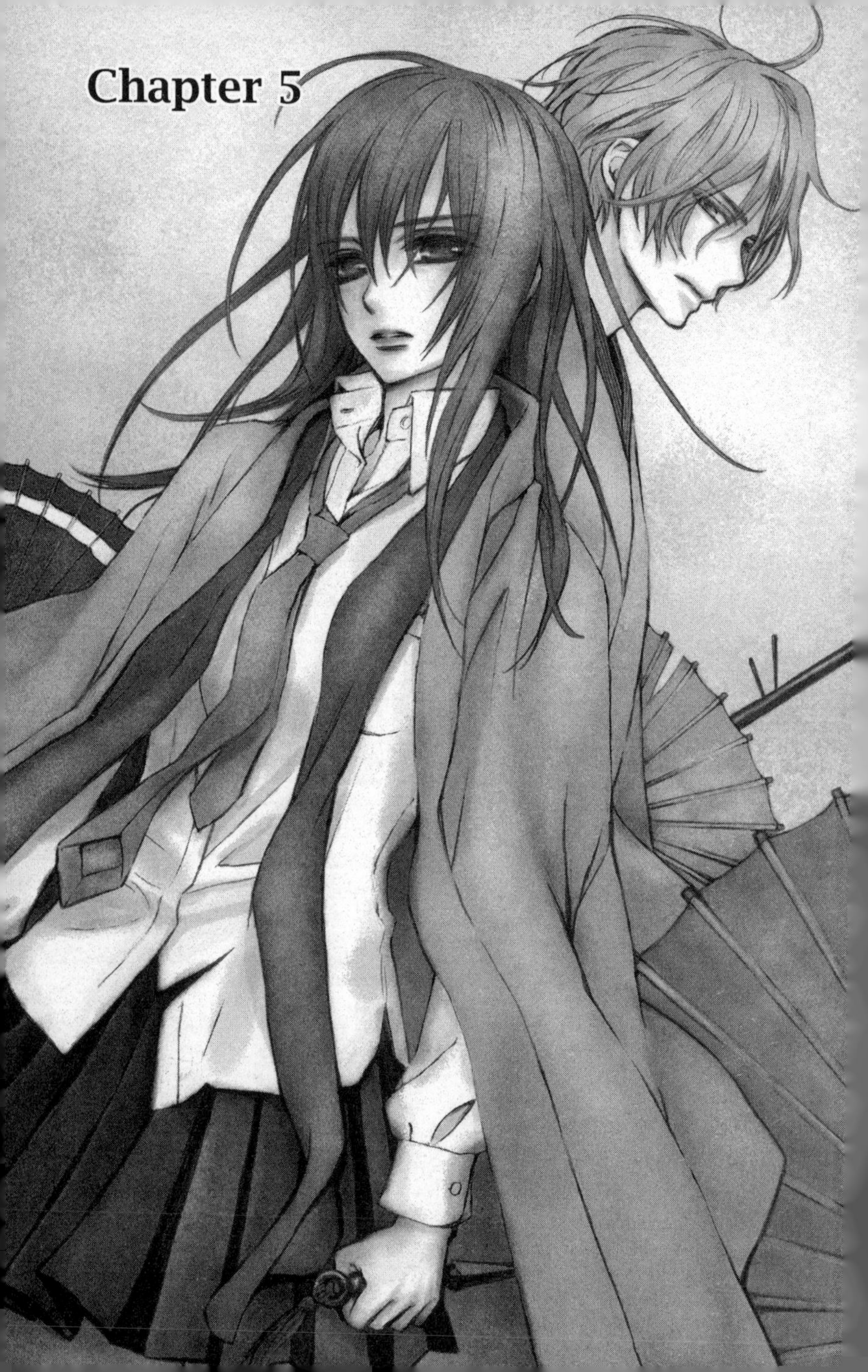

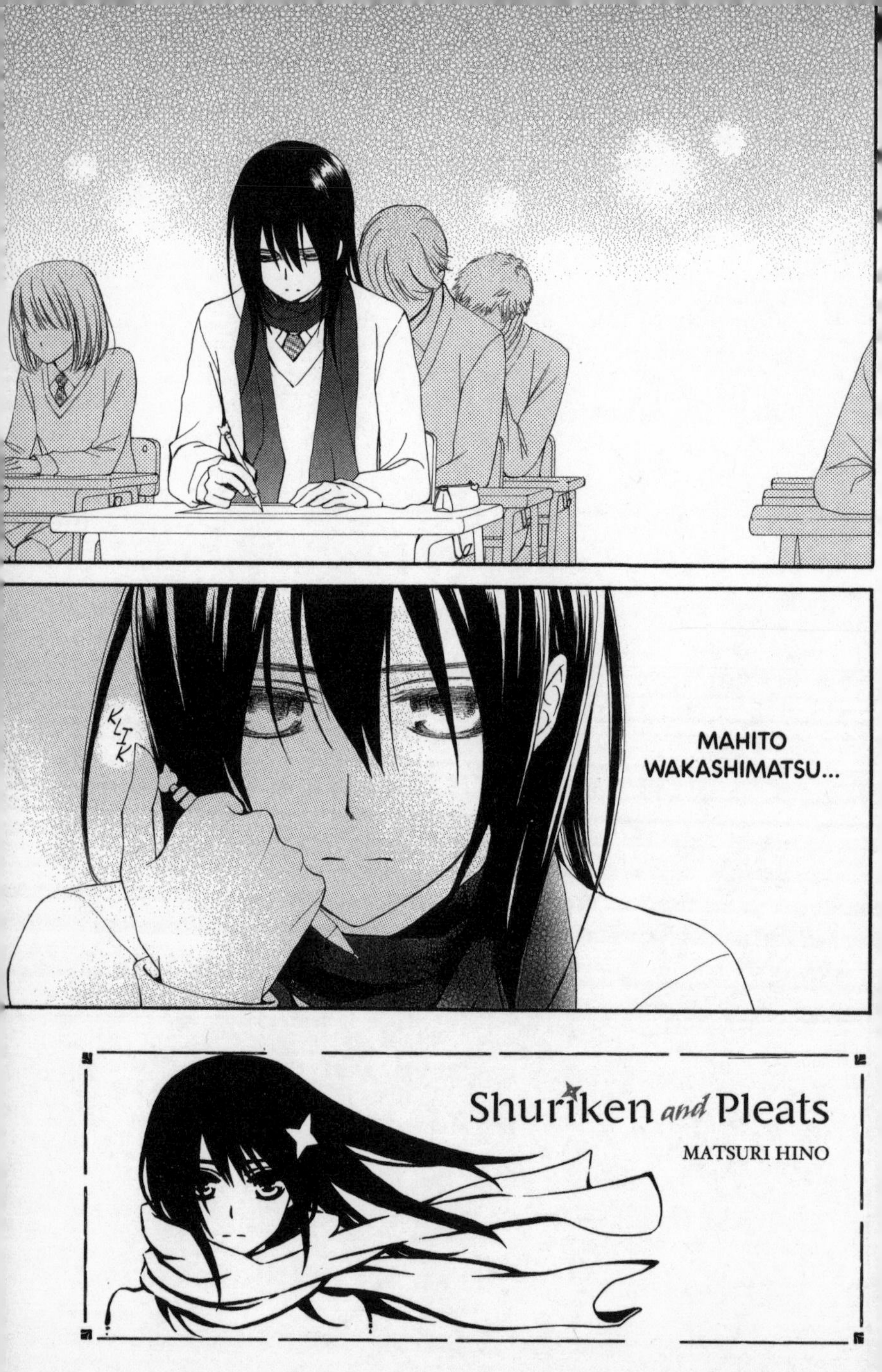
MAHITO WAKASHIMATSU...
KLIK
Shuriken and Pleats
MATSURI HINO

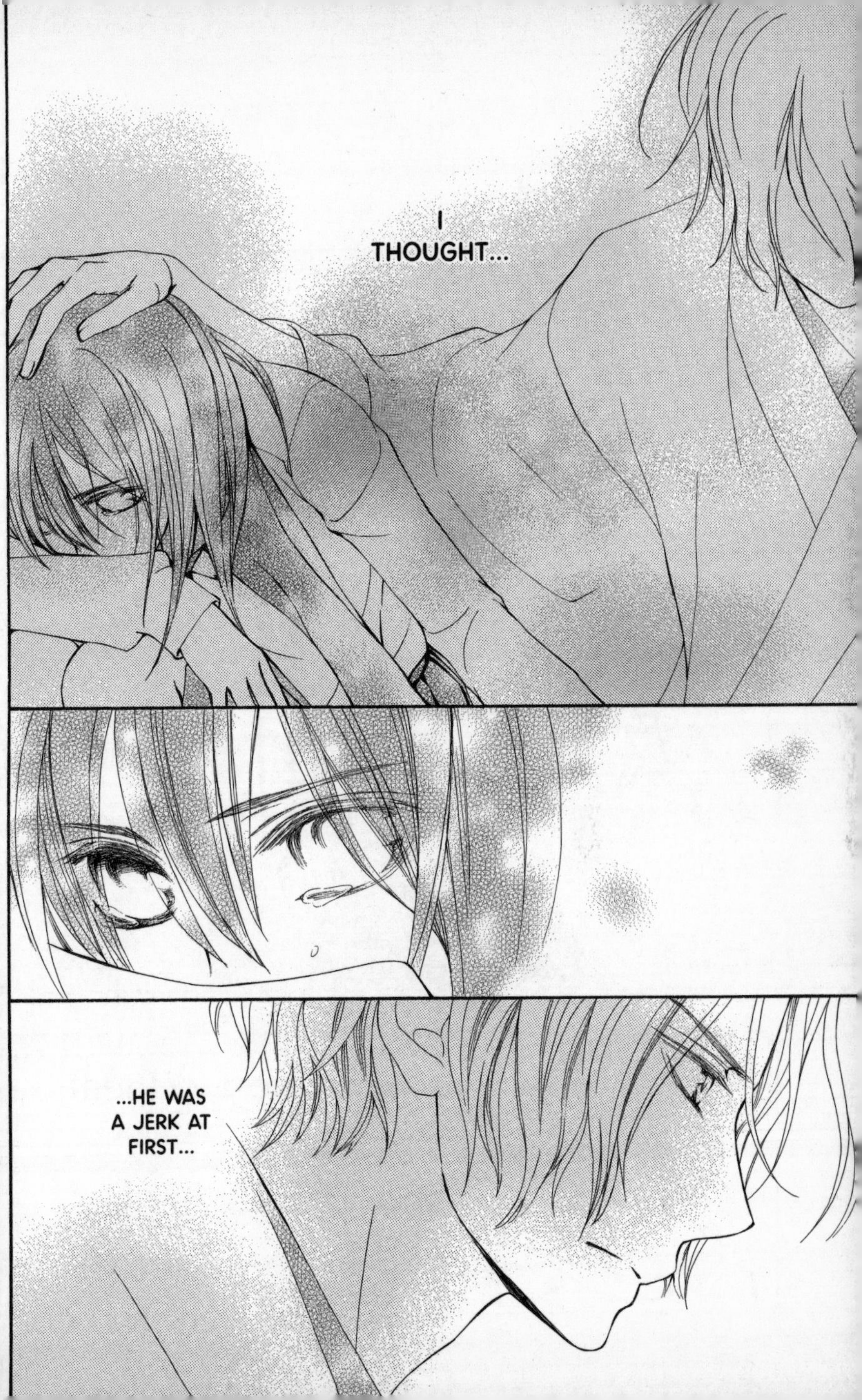
I
THOUGHT...
...HE WAS
A JERK AT
FIRST...

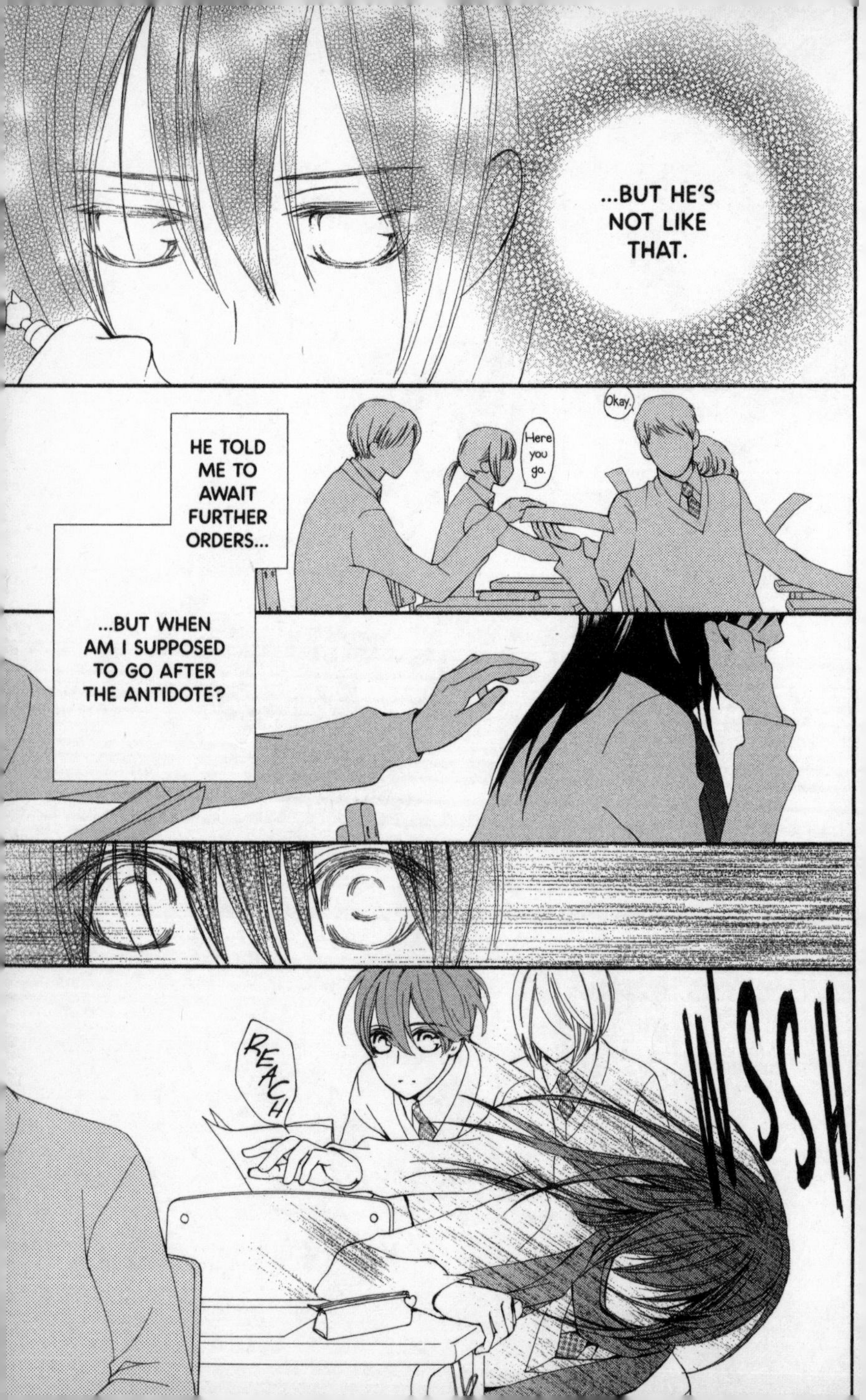
...BUT HE'S NOT LIKE THAT.
Okay.
Here you go.
HE TOLD ME TO AWAIT FURTHER ORDERS...
...BUT WHEN AM I SUPPOSED TO GO AFTER THE ANTIDOTE?
WSSH
REACH

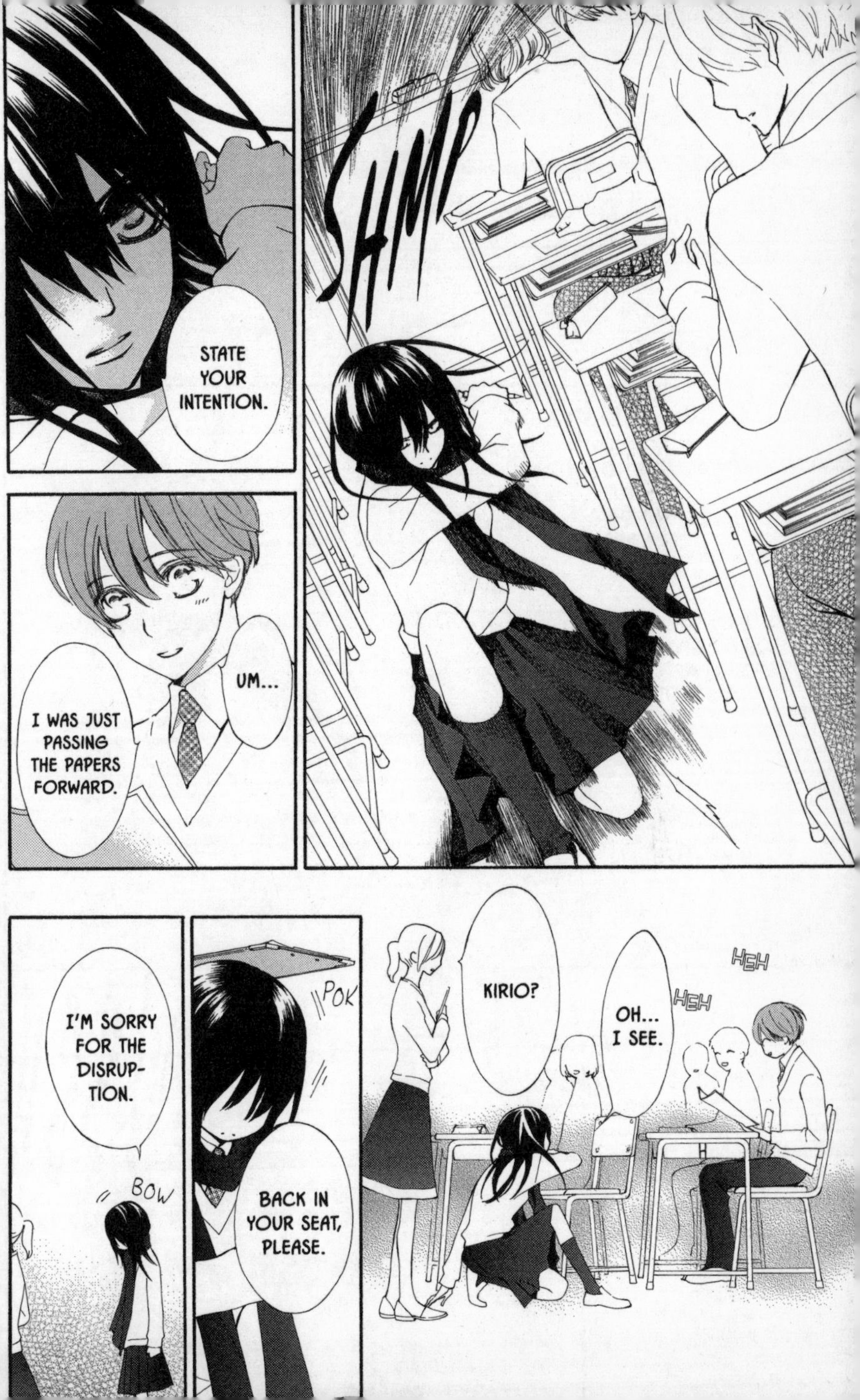
SHMP
STATE YOUR INTENTION.
UM...
I WAS JUST PASSING THE PAPERS FORWARD.
KIRIO?
OH... I SEE.
HEH
HEH
POK
BACK IN YOUR SEAT, PLEASE.
I'M SORRY FOR THE DISRUP-TION.
BOW

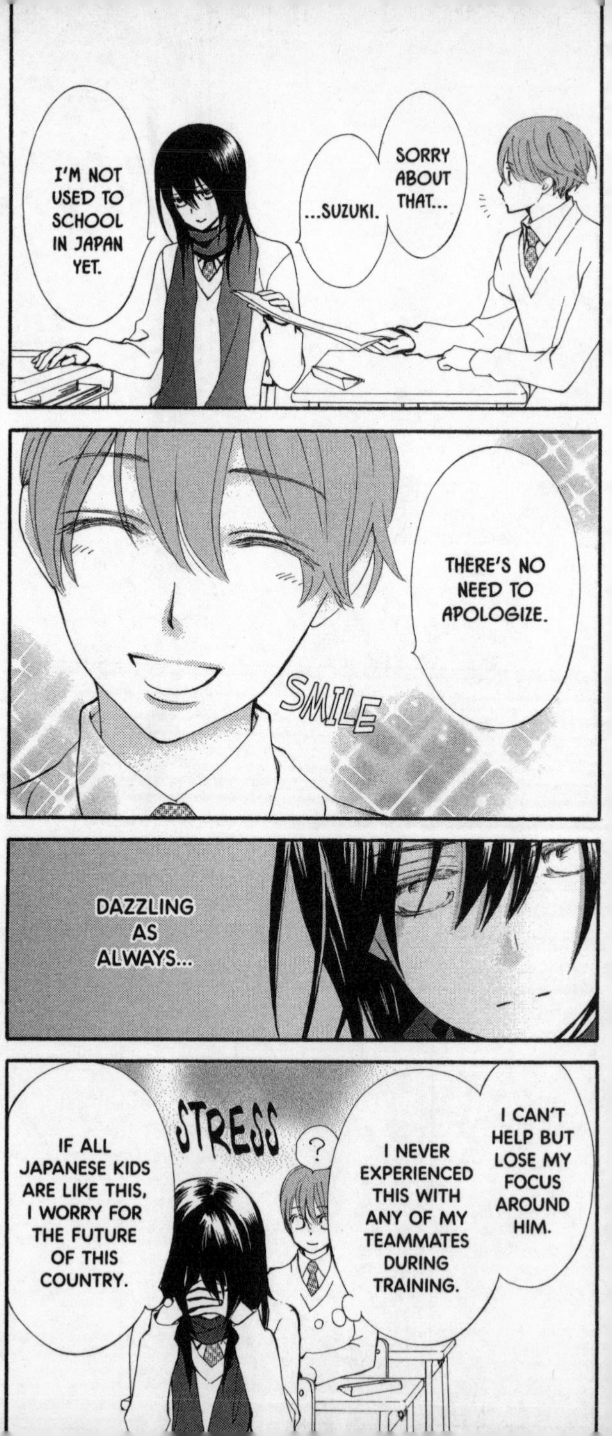
SORRY ABOUT THAT...
...SUZUKI.
I'M NOT USED TO SCHOOL IN JAPAN YET.
THERE'S NO NEED TO APOLOGIZE.
SMILE
DAZZLING AS ALWAYS...
I CAN'T HELP BUT LOSE MY FOCUS AROUND HIM.
I NEVER EXPERIENCED THIS WITH ANY OF MY TEAMMATES DURING TRAINING.
?
STRESS
IF ALL JAPANESE KIDS ARE LIKE THIS, I WORRY FOR THE FUTURE OF THIS COUNTRY.

♡

Here's a shout-out to all my assistants who have stuck with me even after *Vampire Knight*:
Miki O.-sama
Midori K.-sama
Ichiya A.-sama

Thanks also to my new editor, I-sama, and everyone involved.

Thanks to my friends, and to my mother.

And thanks to all my readers.

It's because of all your support that volume 1 of *Shuriken and Pleats* was released! Thank you so very much!

樋野まつり
Matsuri Hino

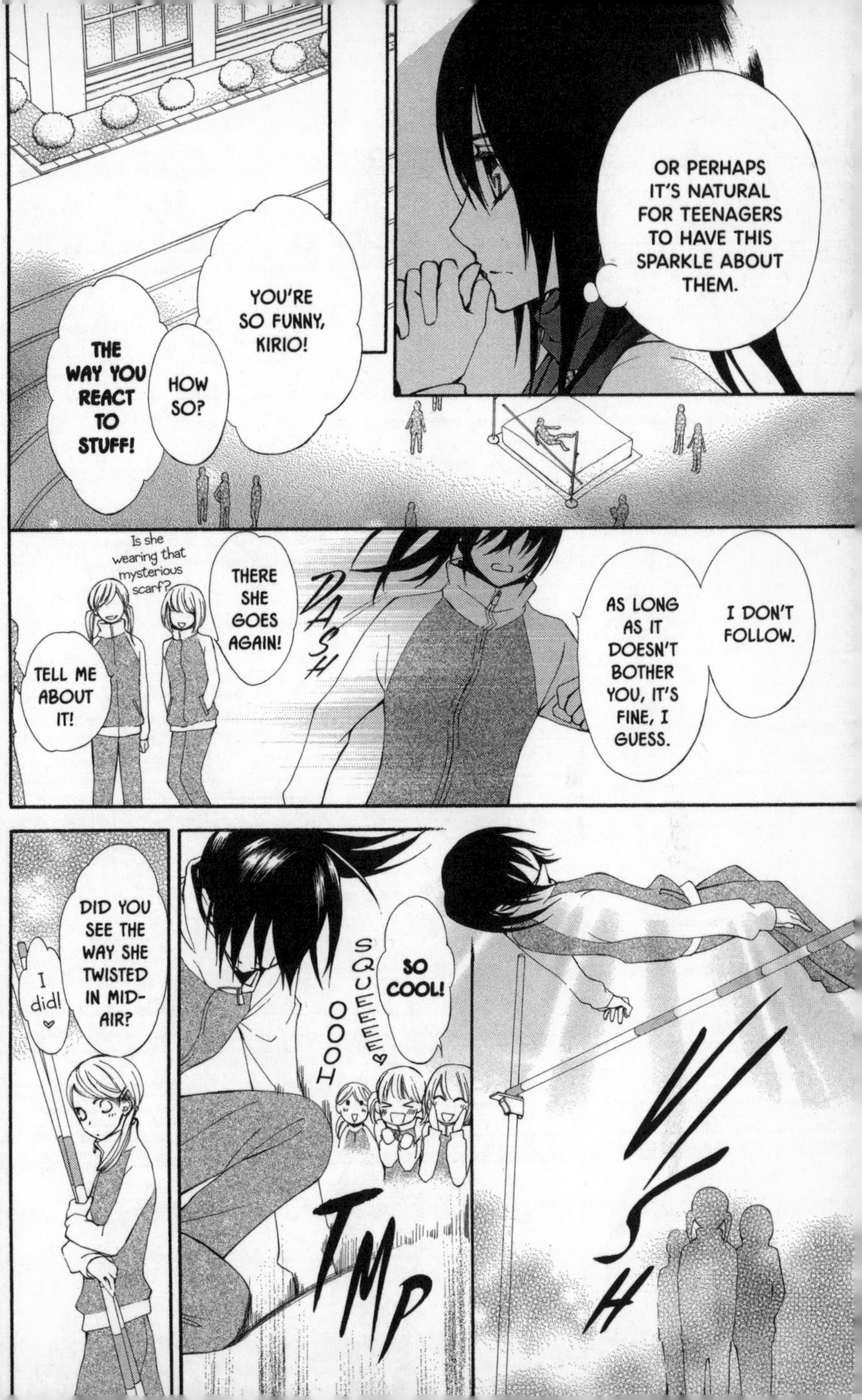
OR PERHAPS IT'S NATURAL FOR TEENAGERS TO HAVE THIS SPARKLE ABOUT THEM.
YOU'RE SO FUNNY, KIRIO!
HOW SO?
THE WAY YOU REACT TO STUFF!
I DON'T FOLLOW.
AS LONG AS IT DOESN'T BOTHER YOU, IT'S FINE, I GUESS.
DASH
THERE SHE GOES AGAIN!
Is she wearing that mysterious scarf?
TELL ME ABOUT IT!
WISH
TMP
SO COOL!
SQUEEEE♥
OOOOH
DID YOU SEE THE WAY SHE TWISTED IN MID-AIR?
I did!♥

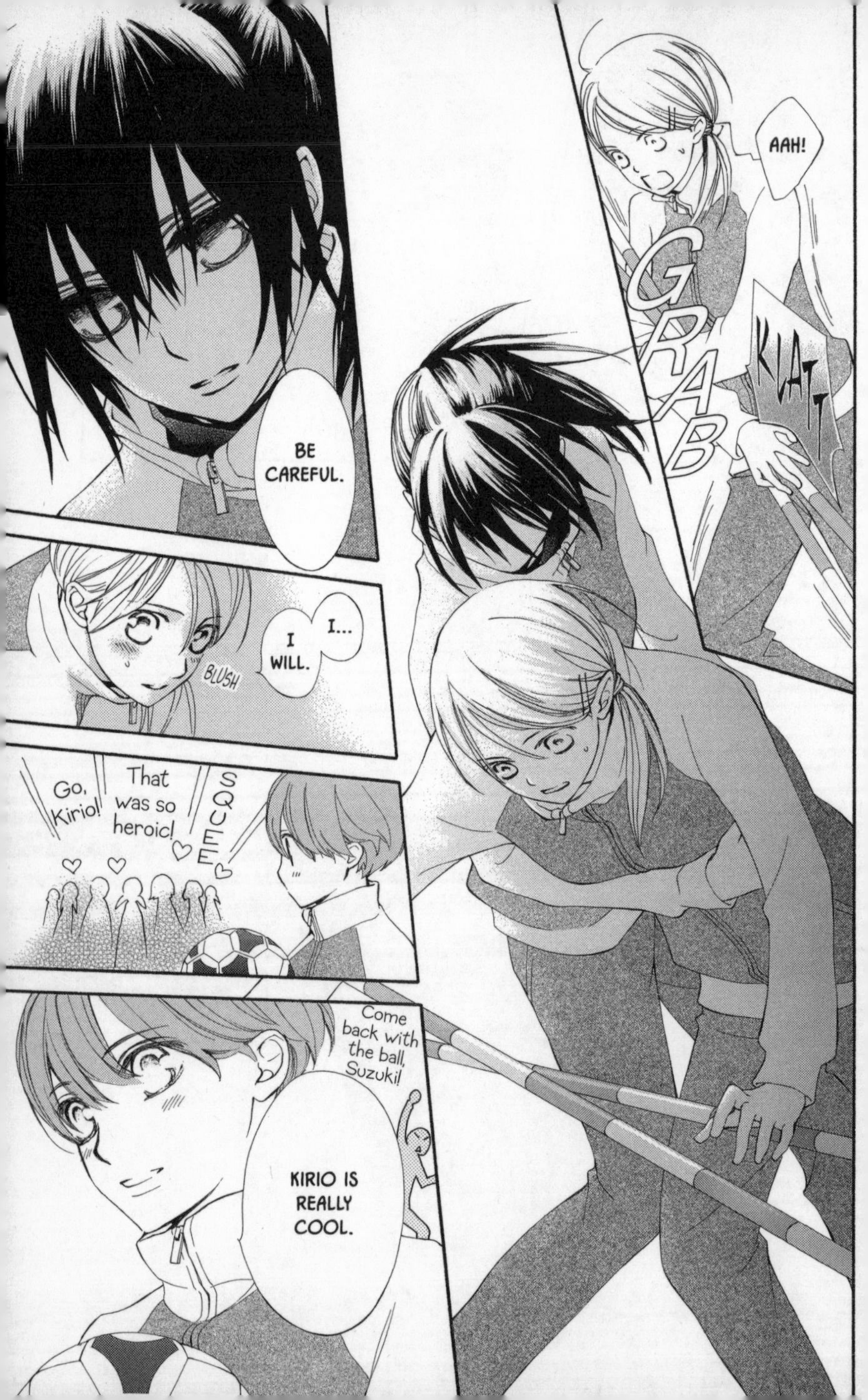
AAH!
GRAB
KLATT
BE CAREFUL.
I...
I WILL.
BLUSH
SQUEE
That was so heroic!
Go, Kirio!
Come back with the ball, Suzuki!
KIRIO IS REALLY COOL.

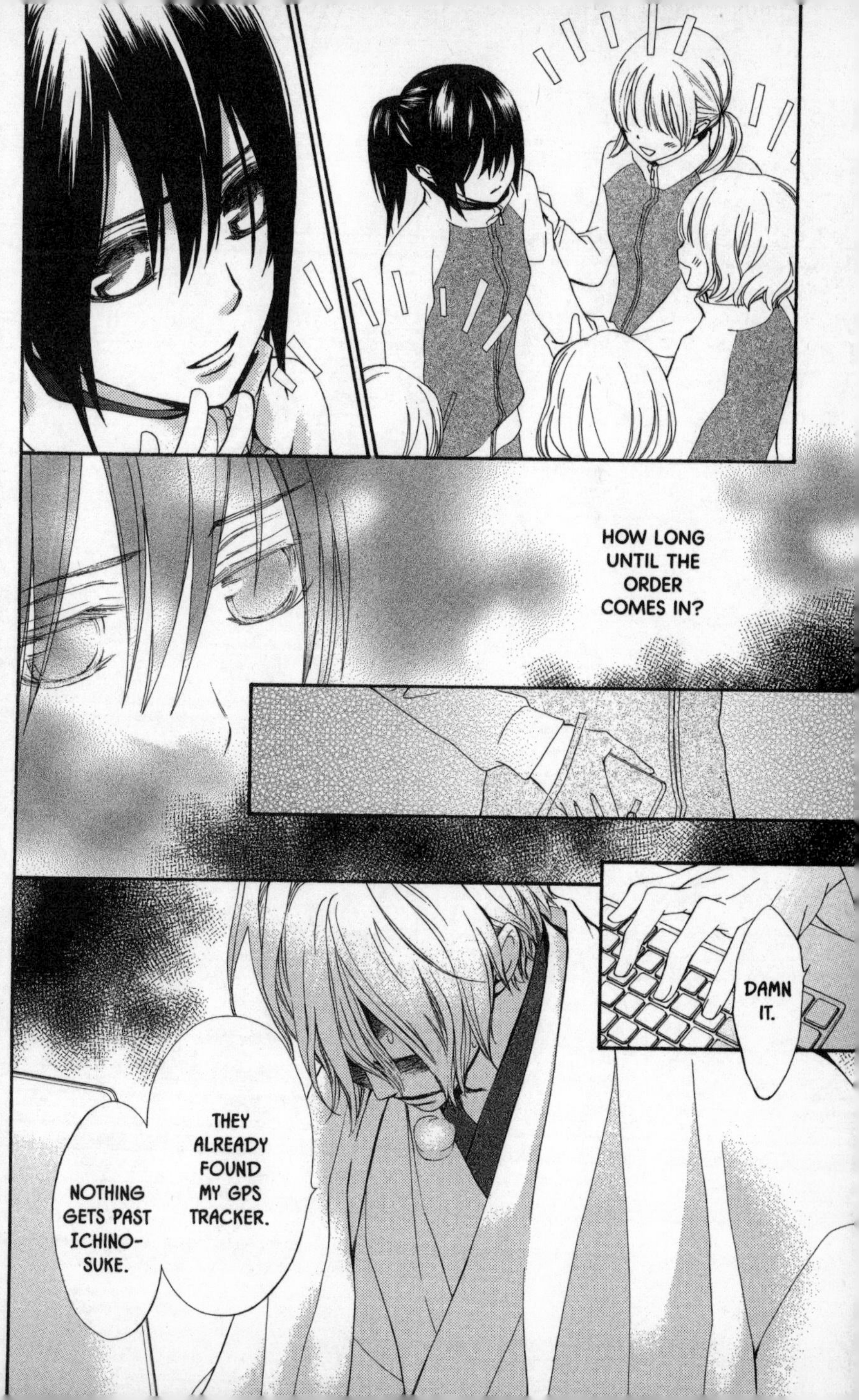
HOW LONG UNTIL THE ORDER COMES IN?
DAMN IT.
THEY ALREADY FOUND MY GPS TRACKER.
NOTHING GETS PAST ICHINO-SUKE.

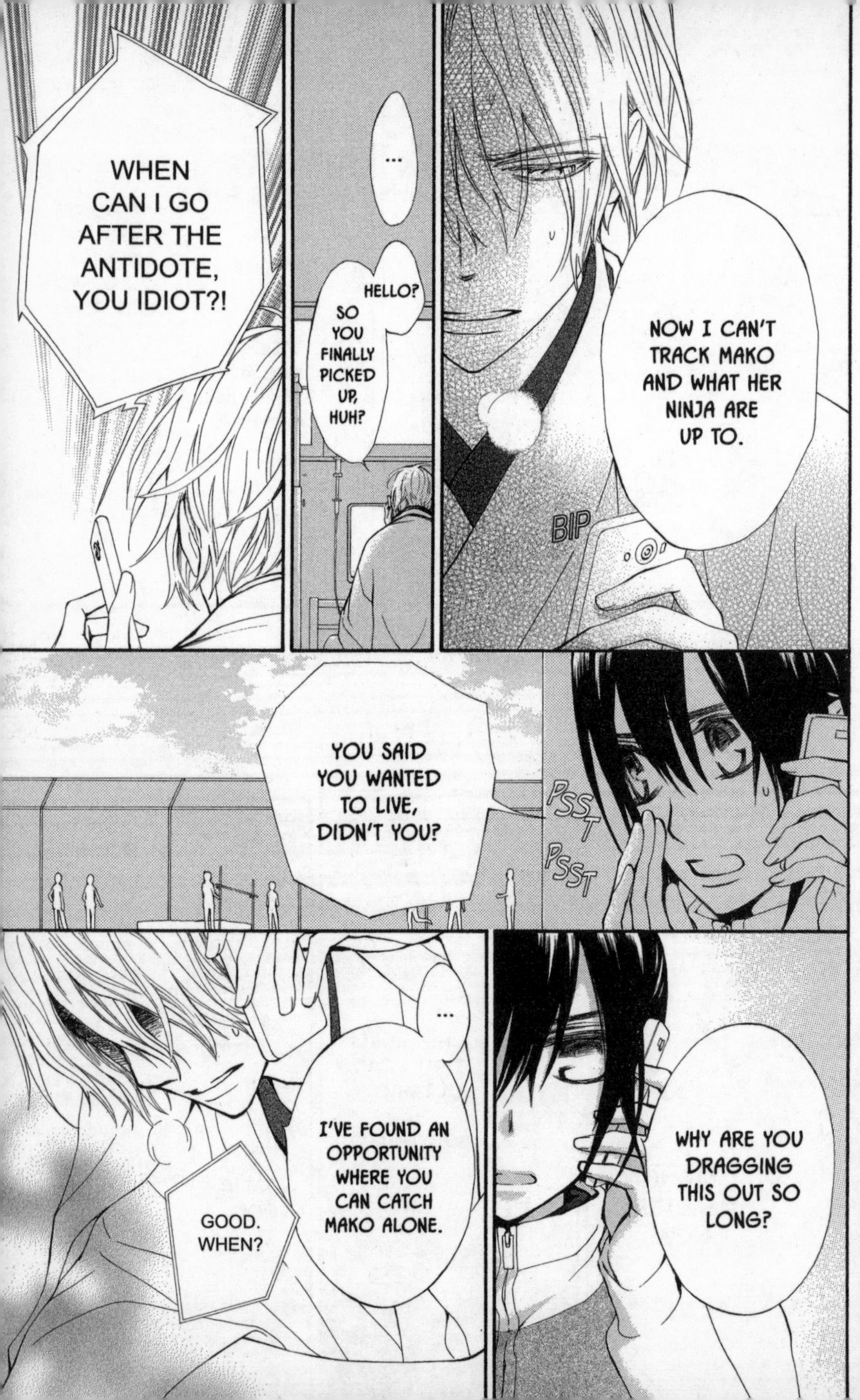
NOW I CAN'T TRACK MAKO AND WHAT HER NINJA ARE UP TO.
BIP
...
HELLO? SO YOU FINALLY PICKED UP, HUH?
WHEN CAN I GO AFTER THE ANTIDOTE, YOU IDIOT?!
PSST PSST
YOU SAID YOU WANTED TO LIVE, DIDN'T YOU?
WHY ARE YOU DRAGGING THIS OUT SO LONG?
...
I'VE FOUND AN OPPORTUNITY WHERE YOU CAN CATCH MAKO ALONE.
GOOD. WHEN?

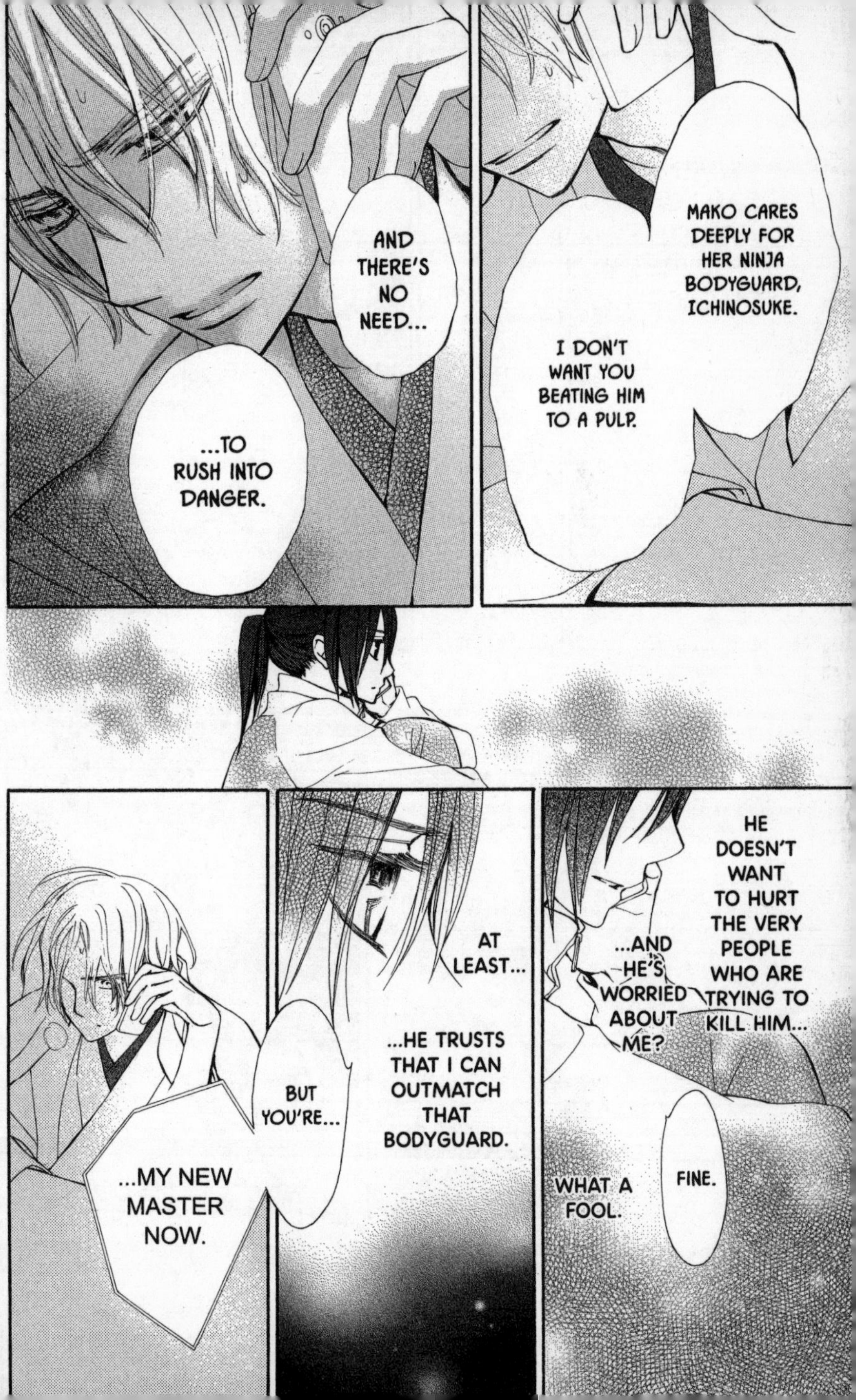
MAKO CARES DEEPLY FOR HER NINJA BODYGUARD, ICHINOSUKE.
I DON'T WANT YOU BEATING HIM TO A PULP.
AND THERE'S NO NEED...
...TO RUSH INTO DANGER.
HE DOESN'T WANT TO HURT THE VERY PEOPLE WHO ARE TRYING TO KILL HIM...
...AND HE'S WORRIED ABOUT ME?
FINE.
WHAT A FOOL.
AT LEAST...
...HE TRUSTS THAT I CAN OUTMATCH THAT BODYGUARD.
BUT YOU'RE...
...MY NEW MASTER NOW.

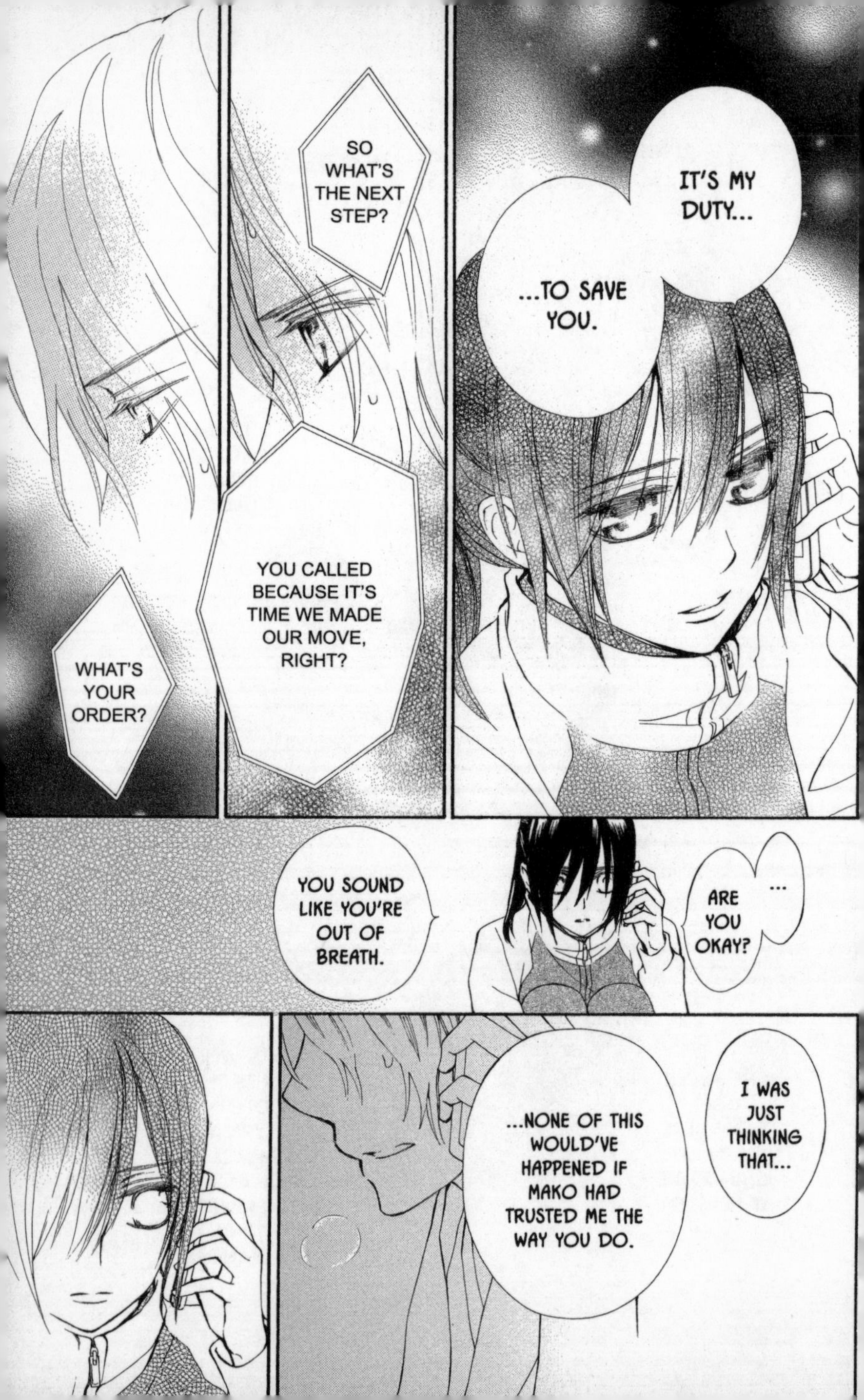
IT'S MY DUTY...
...TO SAVE YOU.
SO WHAT'S THE NEXT STEP?
YOU CALLED BECAUSE IT'S TIME WE MADE OUR MOVE, RIGHT?
WHAT'S YOUR ORDER?
...
ARE YOU OKAY?
YOU SOUND LIKE YOU'RE OUT OF BREATH.
I WAS JUST THINKING THAT...
...NONE OF THIS WOULD'VE HAPPENED IF MAKO HAD TRUSTED ME THE WAY YOU DO.

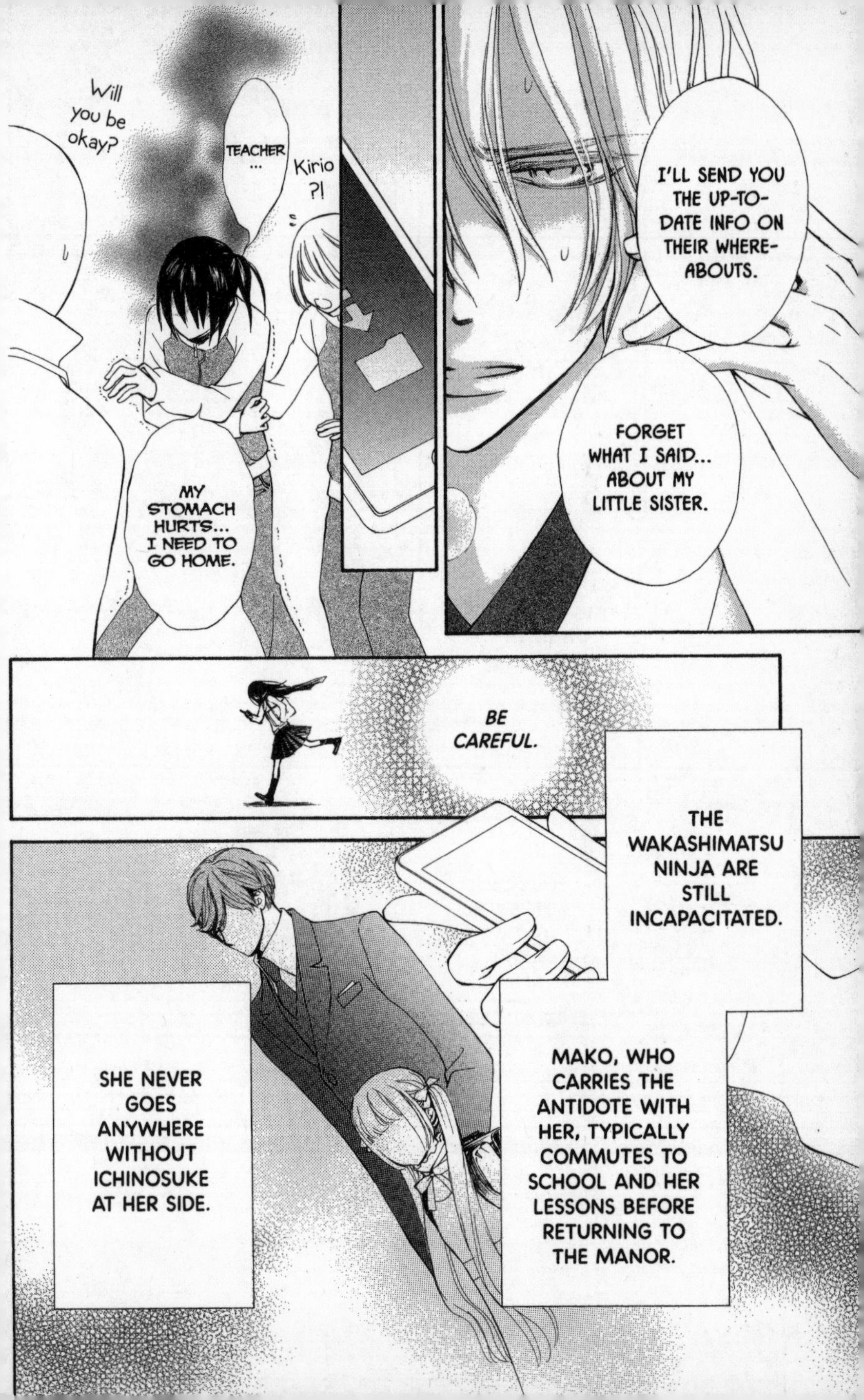
I'LL SEND YOU THE UP-TO-DATE INFO ON THEIR WHERE-ABOUTS.
FORGET WHAT I SAID... ABOUT MY LITTLE SISTER.
TEACHER ...
Kirio ?!
Will you be okay?
MY STOMACH HURTS... I NEED TO GO HOME.
BE CAREFUL.
THE WAKASHIMATSU NINJA ARE STILL INCAPACITATED.
MAKO, WHO CARRIES THE ANTIDOTE WITH HER, TYPICALLY COMMUTES TO SCHOOL AND HER LESSONS BEFORE RETURNING TO THE MANOR.
SHE NEVER GOES ANYWHERE WITHOUT ICHINOSUKE AT HER SIDE.

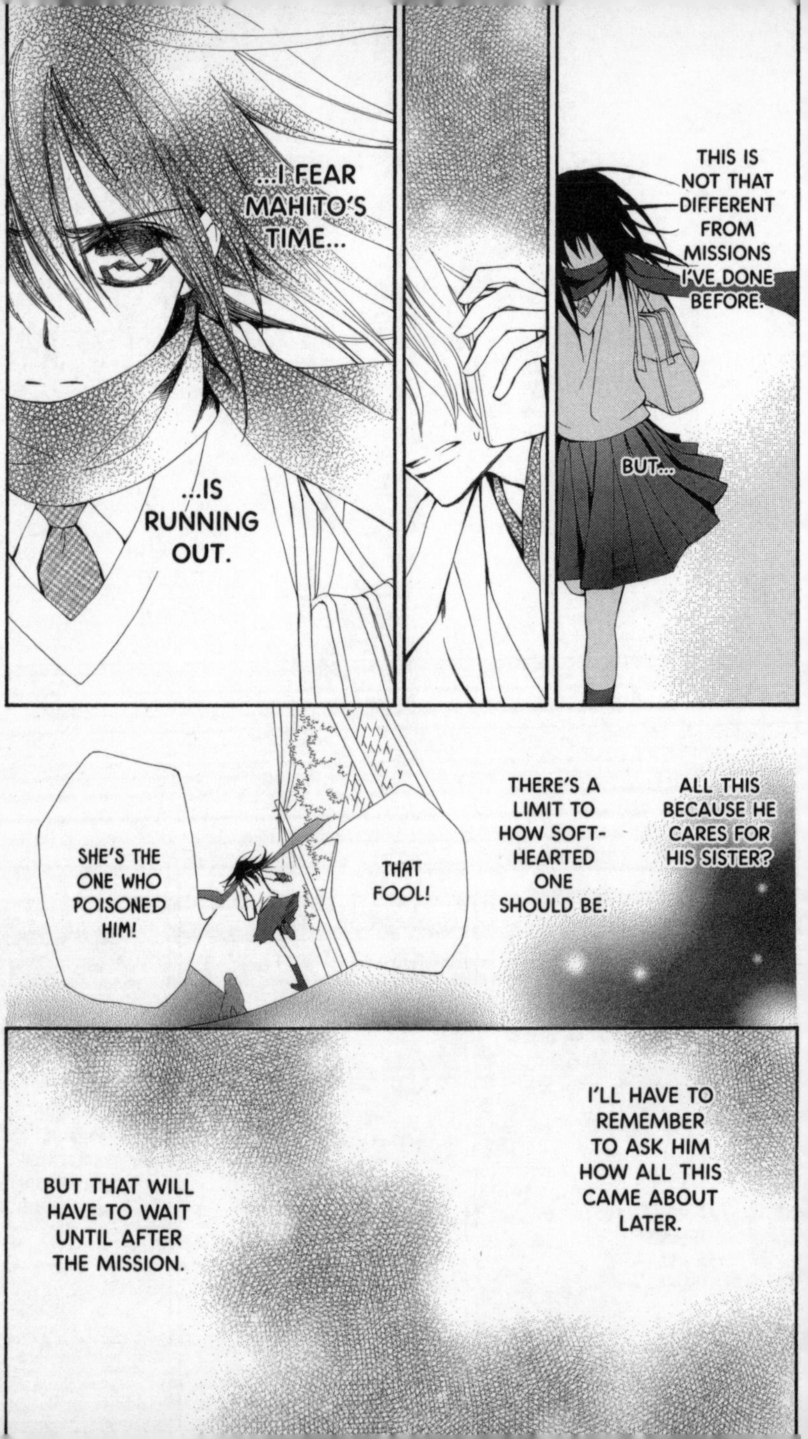
THIS IS NOT THAT DIFFERENT FROM MISSIONS I'VE DONE BEFORE.
BUT...
...I FEAR MAHITO'S TIME...
...IS RUNNING OUT.
ALL THIS BECAUSE HE CARES FOR HIS SISTER?
THERE'S A LIMIT TO HOW SOFT-HEARTED ONE SHOULD BE.
THAT FOOL!
SHE'S THE ONE WHO POISONED HIM!
I'LL HAVE TO REMEMBER TO ASK HIM HOW ALL THIS CAME ABOUT LATER.
BUT THAT WILL HAVE TO WAIT UNTIL AFTER THE MISSION.

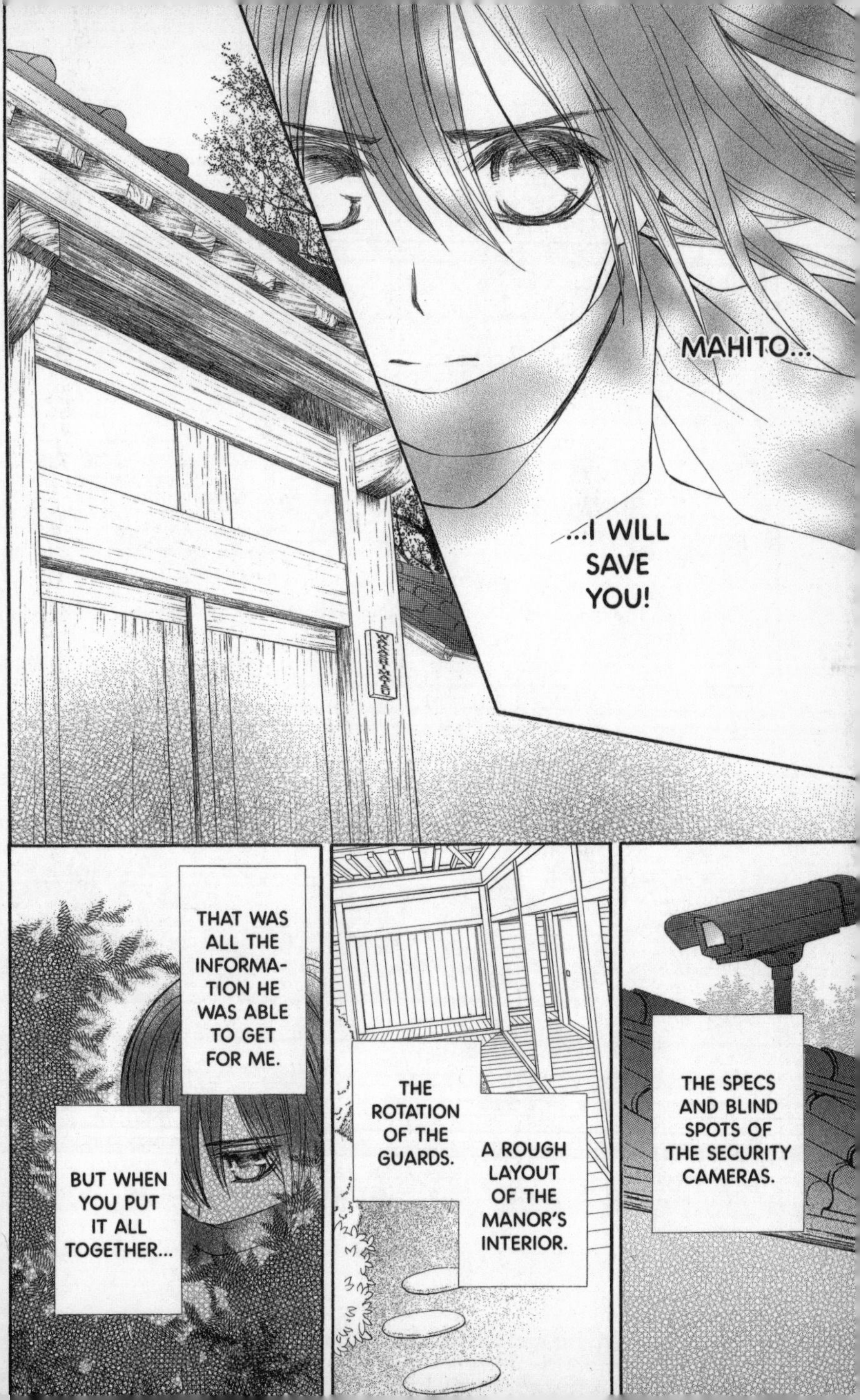
MAHITO...
...I WILL SAVE YOU!
THE SPECS AND BLIND SPOTS OF THE SECURITY CAMERAS.
A ROUGH LAYOUT OF THE MANOR'S INTERIOR.
THE ROTATION OF THE GUARDS.
THAT WAS ALL THE INFORMATION HE WAS ABLE TO GET FOR ME.
BUT WHEN YOU PUT IT ALL TOGETHER...

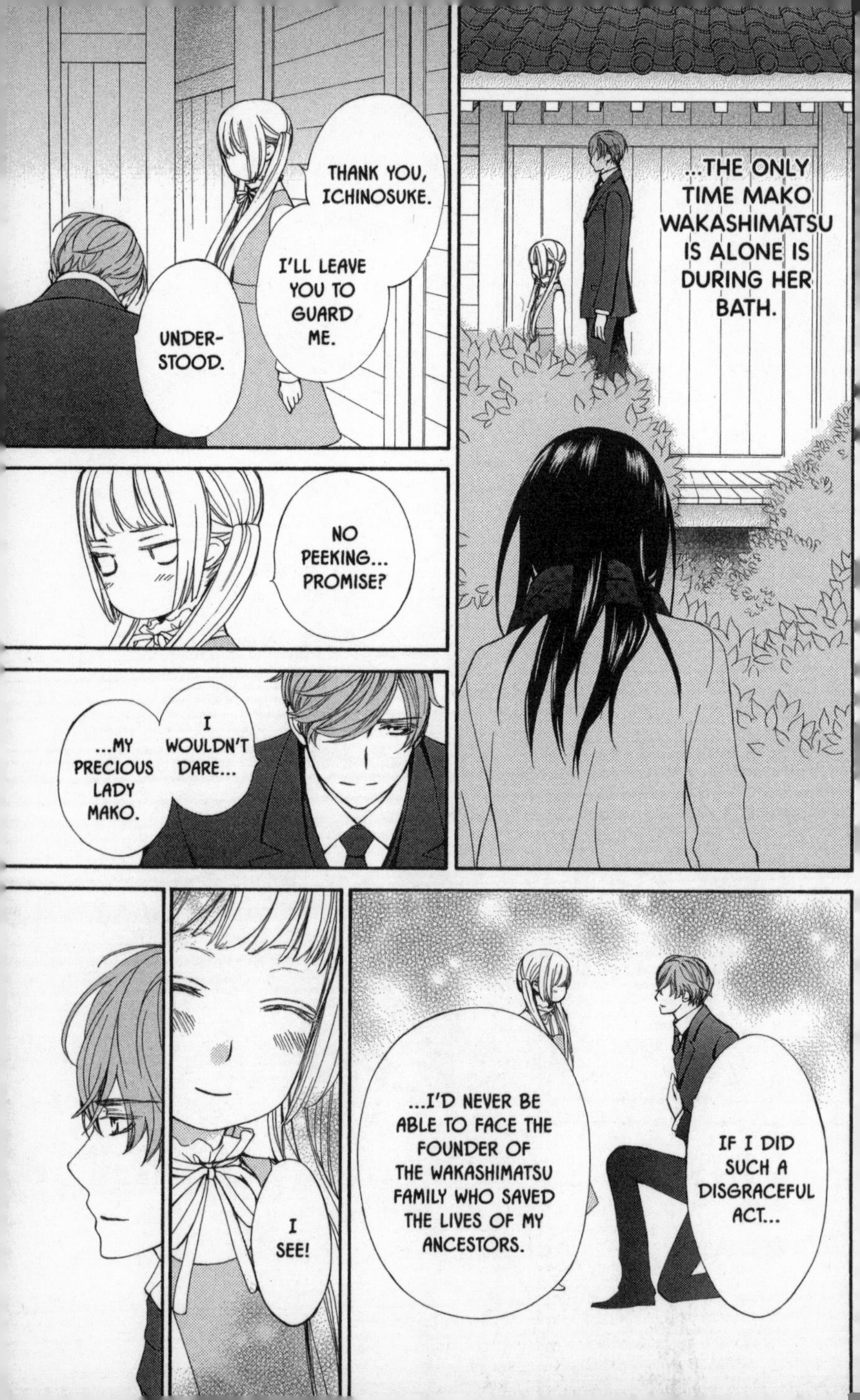
...THE ONLY TIME MAKO WAKASHIMATSU IS ALONE IS DURING HER BATH.
THANK YOU, ICHINOSUKE.
I'LL LEAVE YOU TO GUARD ME.
UNDER-STOOD.
NO PEEKING... PROMISE?
I WOULDN'T DARE...
...MY PRECIOUS LADY MAKO.
IF I DID SUCH A DISGRACEFUL ACT...
...I'D NEVER BE ABLE TO FACE THE FOUNDER OF THE WAKASHIMATSU FAMILY WHO SAVED THE LIVES OF MY ANCESTORS.
I SEE!

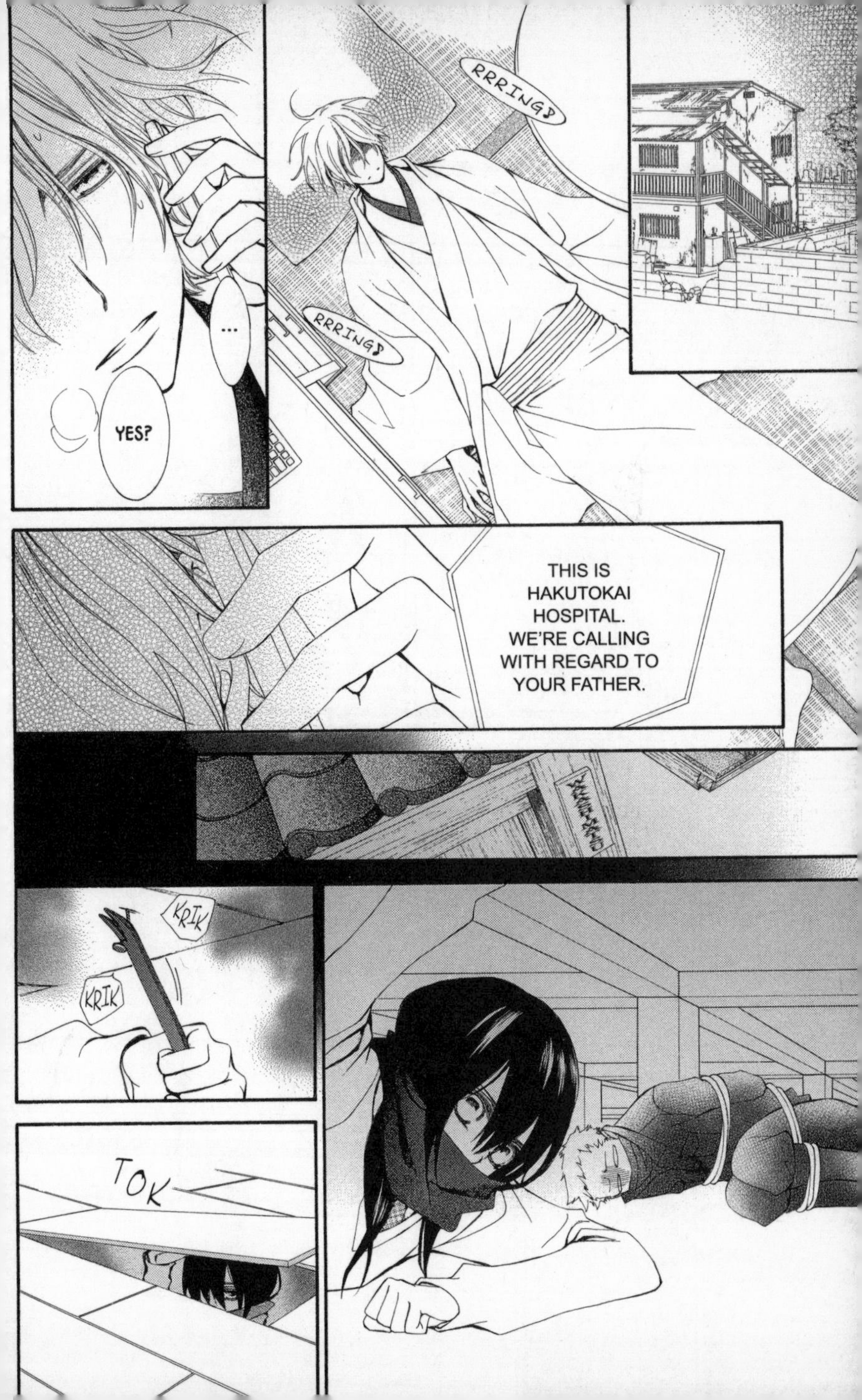
RRRING♪
RRRING♪
...
YES?
THIS IS HAKUTOKAI HOSPITAL. WE'RE CALLING WITH REGARD TO YOUR FATHER.
KRIK
KRIK
TOK

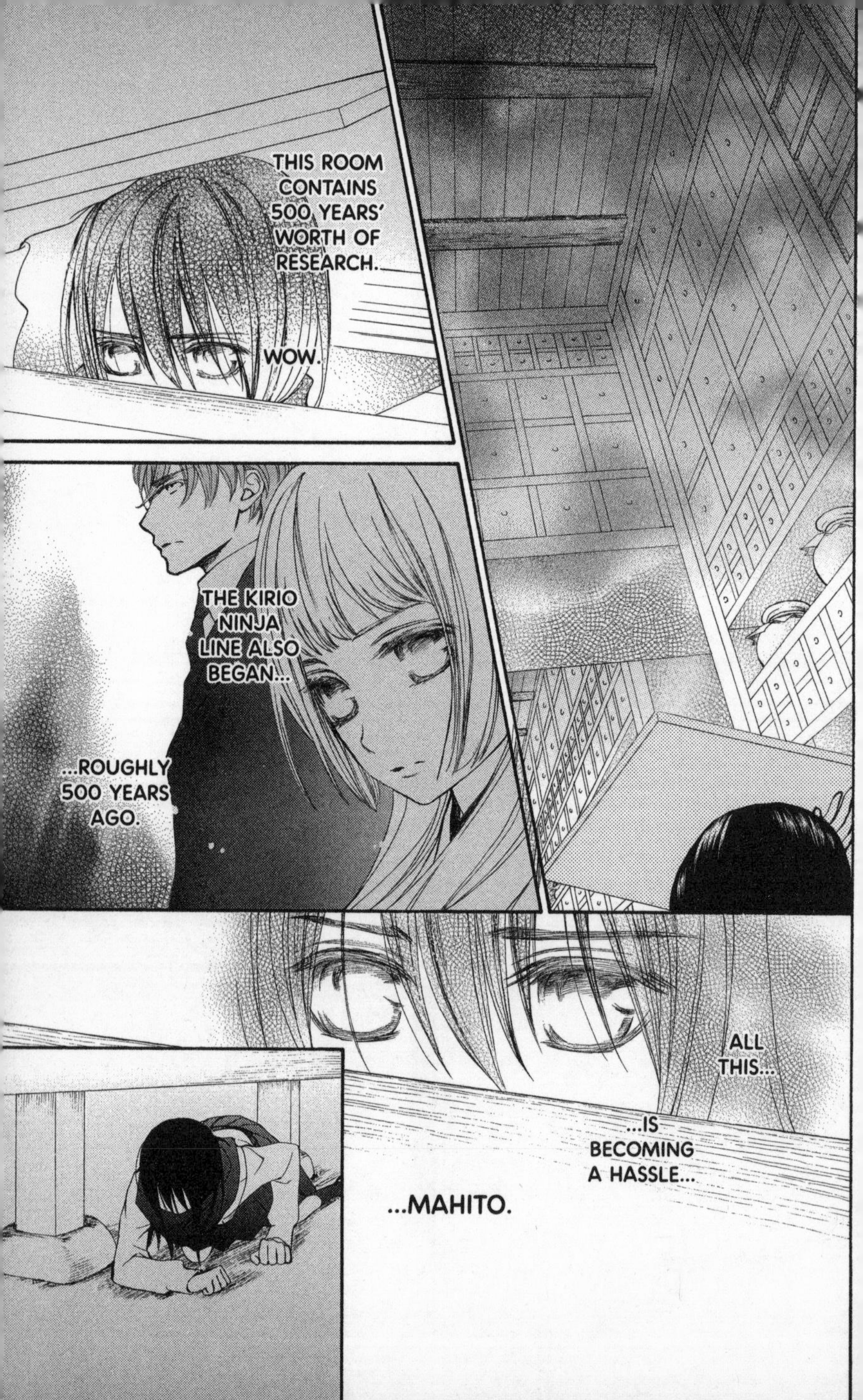
THIS ROOM CONTAINS 500 YEARS' WORTH OF RESEARCH.
WOW.
THE KIRIO NINJA LINE ALSO BEGAN...
...ROUGHLY 500 YEARS AGO.
ALL THIS...
...IS BECOMING A HASSLE...
...MAHITO.

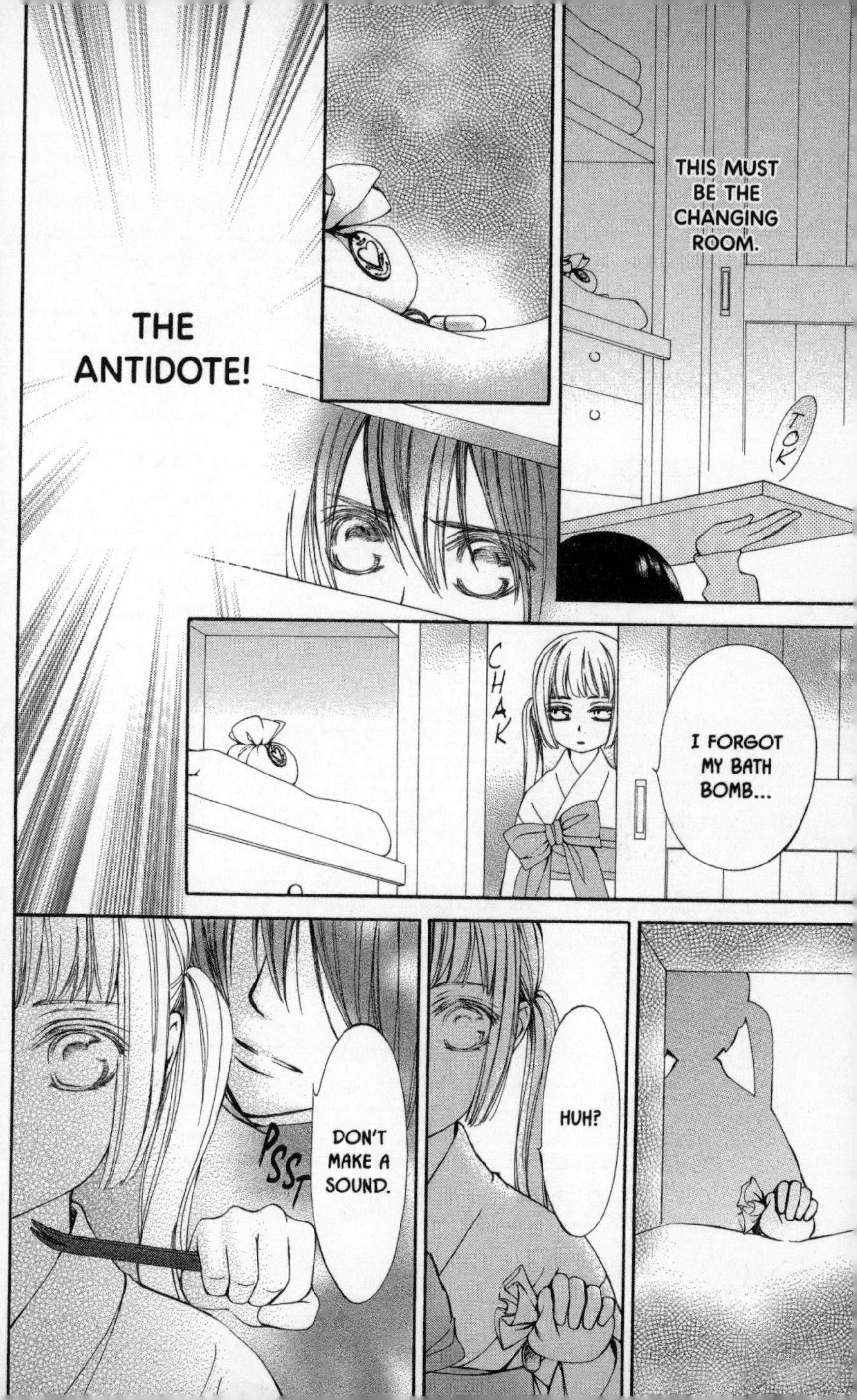
THIS MUST BE THE CHANGING ROOM.
TOK
CHAK
I FORGOT MY BATH BOMB...
THE ANTIDOTE!
HUH?
DON'T MAKE A SOUND.
PSST

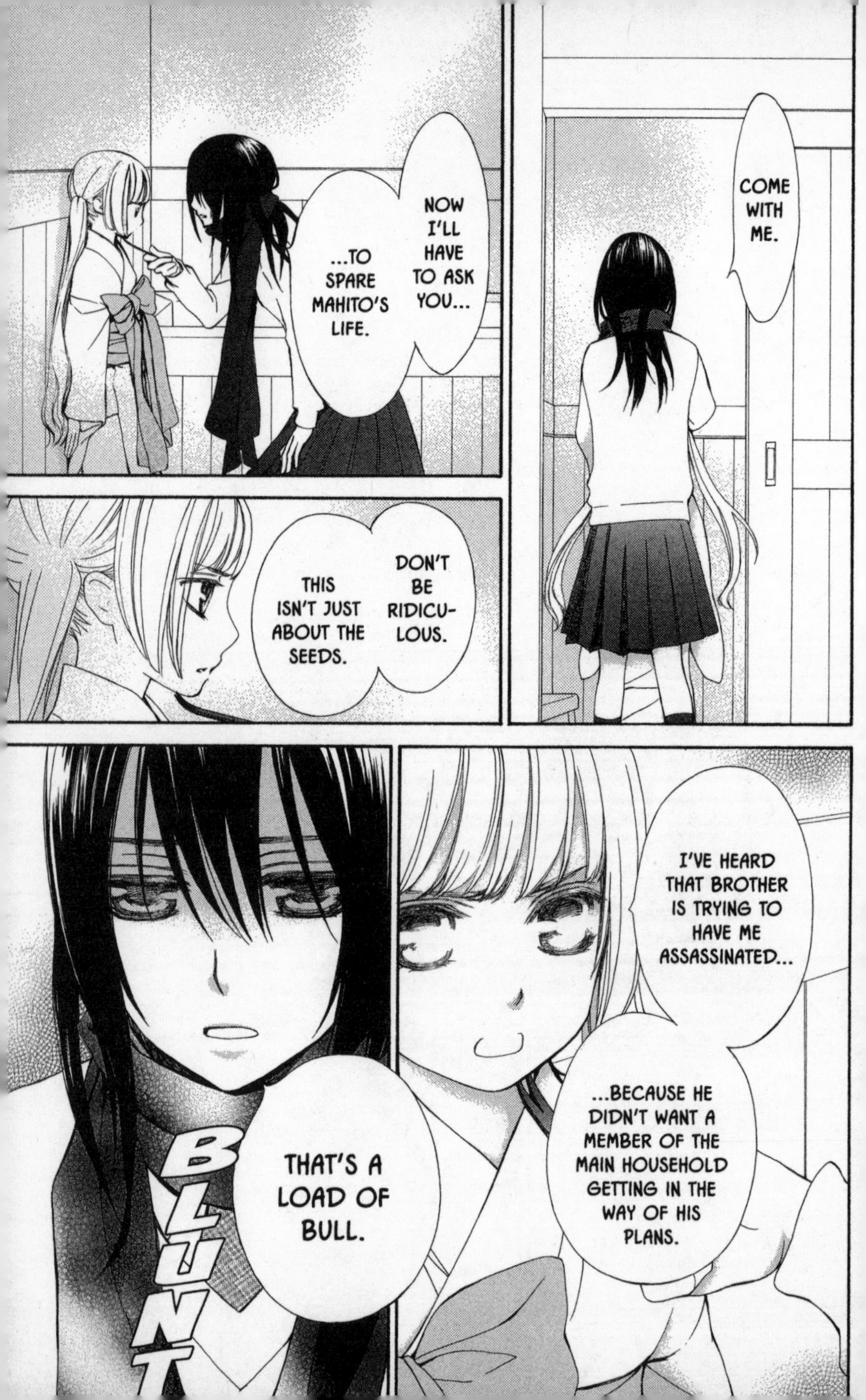
COME WITH ME.
NOW I'LL HAVE TO ASK YOU...
...TO SPARE MAHITO'S LIFE.
DON'T BE RIDICU-LOUS.
THIS ISN'T JUST ABOUT THE SEEDS.
I'VE HEARD THAT BROTHER IS TRYING TO HAVE ME ASSASSINATED...
...BECAUSE HE DIDN'T WANT A MEMBER OF THE MAIN HOUSEHOLD GETTING IN THE WAY OF HIS PLANS.
THAT'S A LOAD OF BULL.
BLUNT

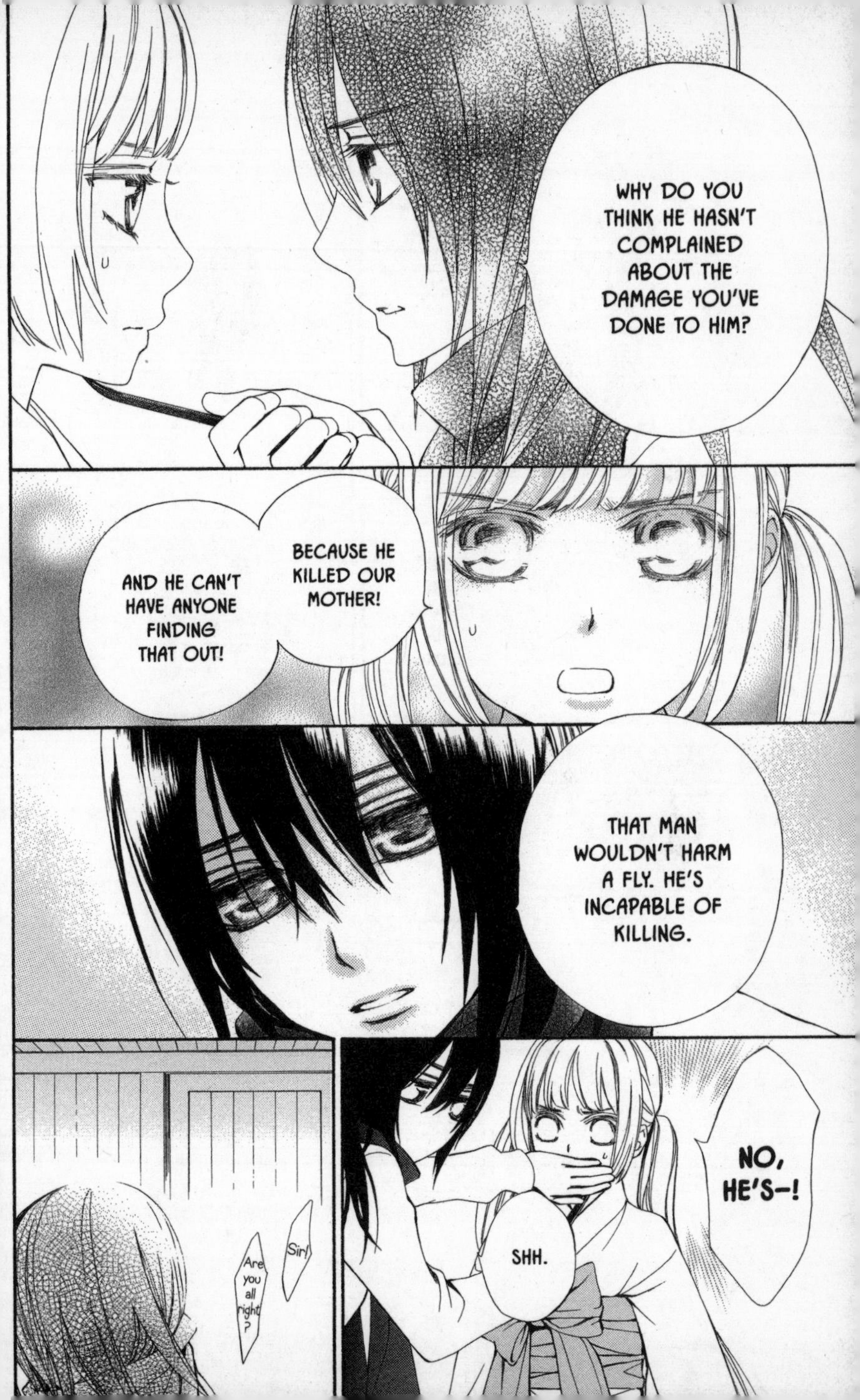

WHY DO YOU THINK HE HASN'T COMPLAINED ABOUT THE DAMAGE YOU'VE DONE TO HIM?
BECAUSE HE KILLED OUR MOTHER!
AND HE CAN'T HAVE ANYONE FINDING THAT OUT!
THAT MAN WOULDN'T HARM A FLY. HE'S INCAPABLE OF KILLING.
NO, HE'S—!
SHH.
Sir!
Are you all right?

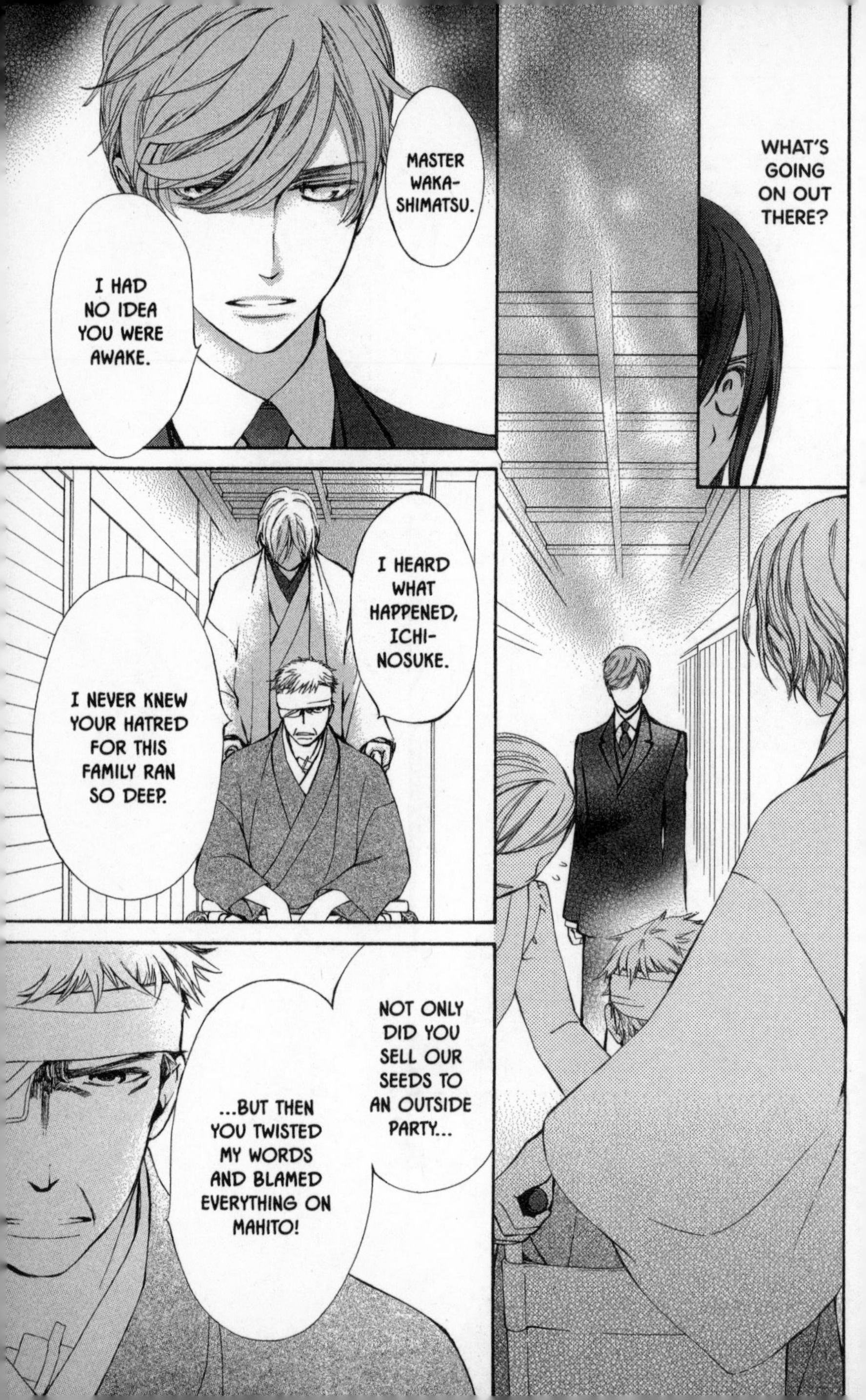
WHAT'S GOING ON OUT THERE?
MASTER WAKA-SHIMATSU.
I HAD NO IDEA YOU WERE AWAKE.
I HEARD WHAT HAPPENED, ICHI-NOSUKE.
I NEVER KNEW YOUR HATRED FOR THIS FAMILY RAN SO DEEP.
NOT ONLY DID YOU SELL OUR SEEDS TO AN OUTSIDE PARTY...
...BUT THEN YOU TWISTED MY WORDS AND BLAMED EVERYTHING ON MAHITO!

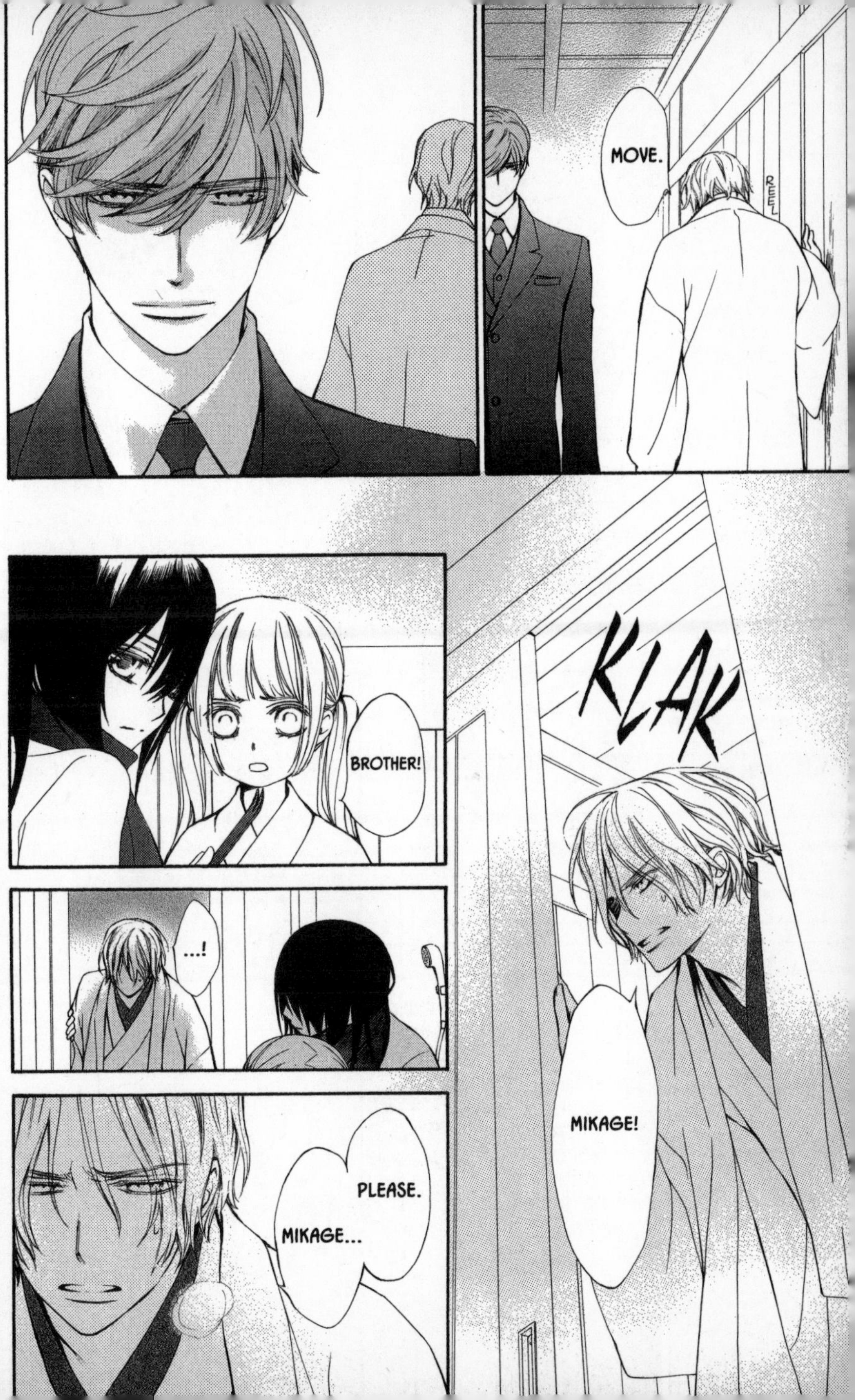
MOVE.
REEL
KLAK
MIKAGE!
BROTHER!
...!
PLEASE.
MIKAGE...

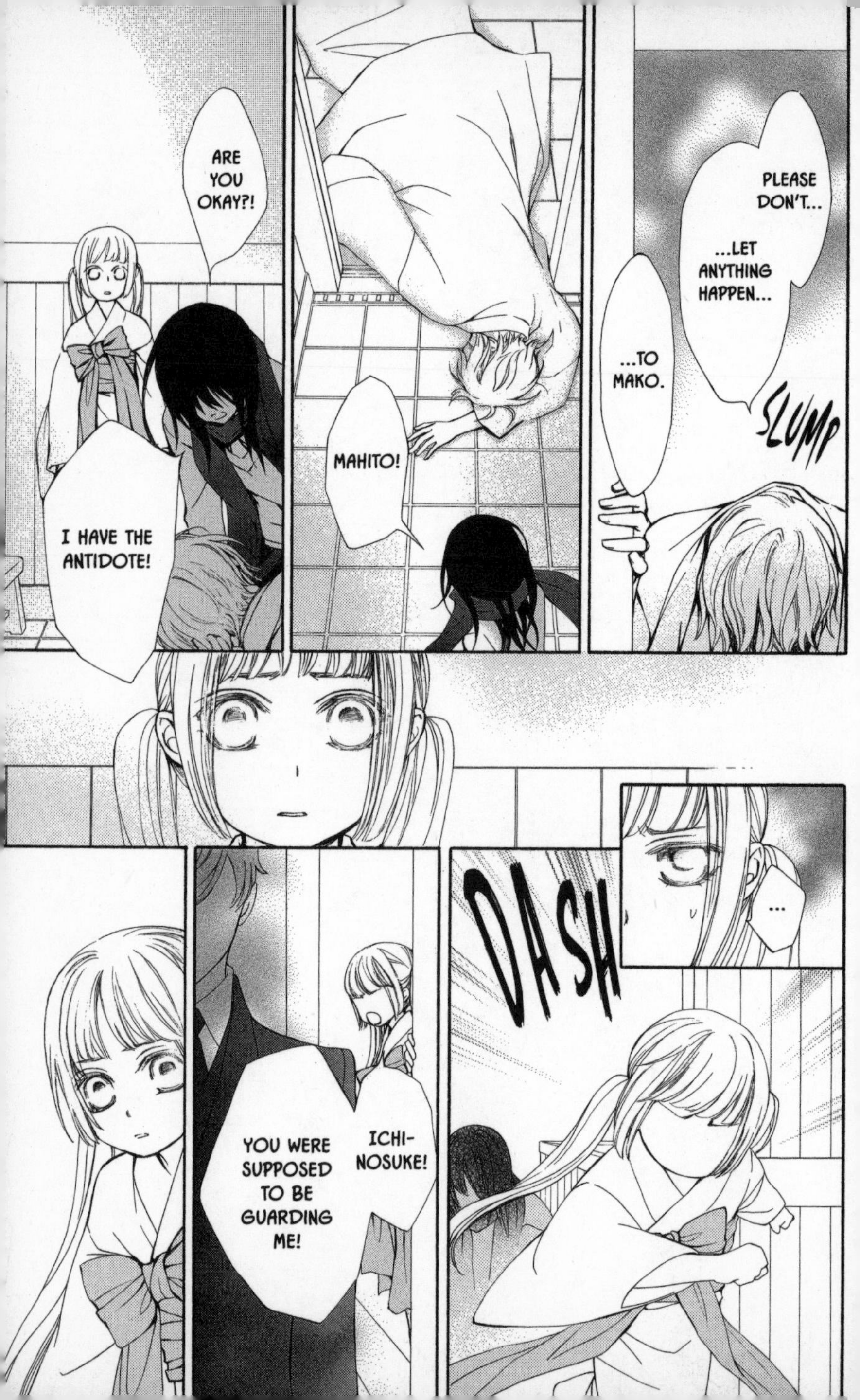
PLEASE DON'T...
...LET ANYTHING HAPPEN...
...TO MAKO.
SLUMP
MAHITO!
ARE YOU OKAY?!
I HAVE THE ANTIDOTE!
...
DASH
ICHI-NOSUKE!
YOU WERE SUPPOSED TO BE GUARDING ME!

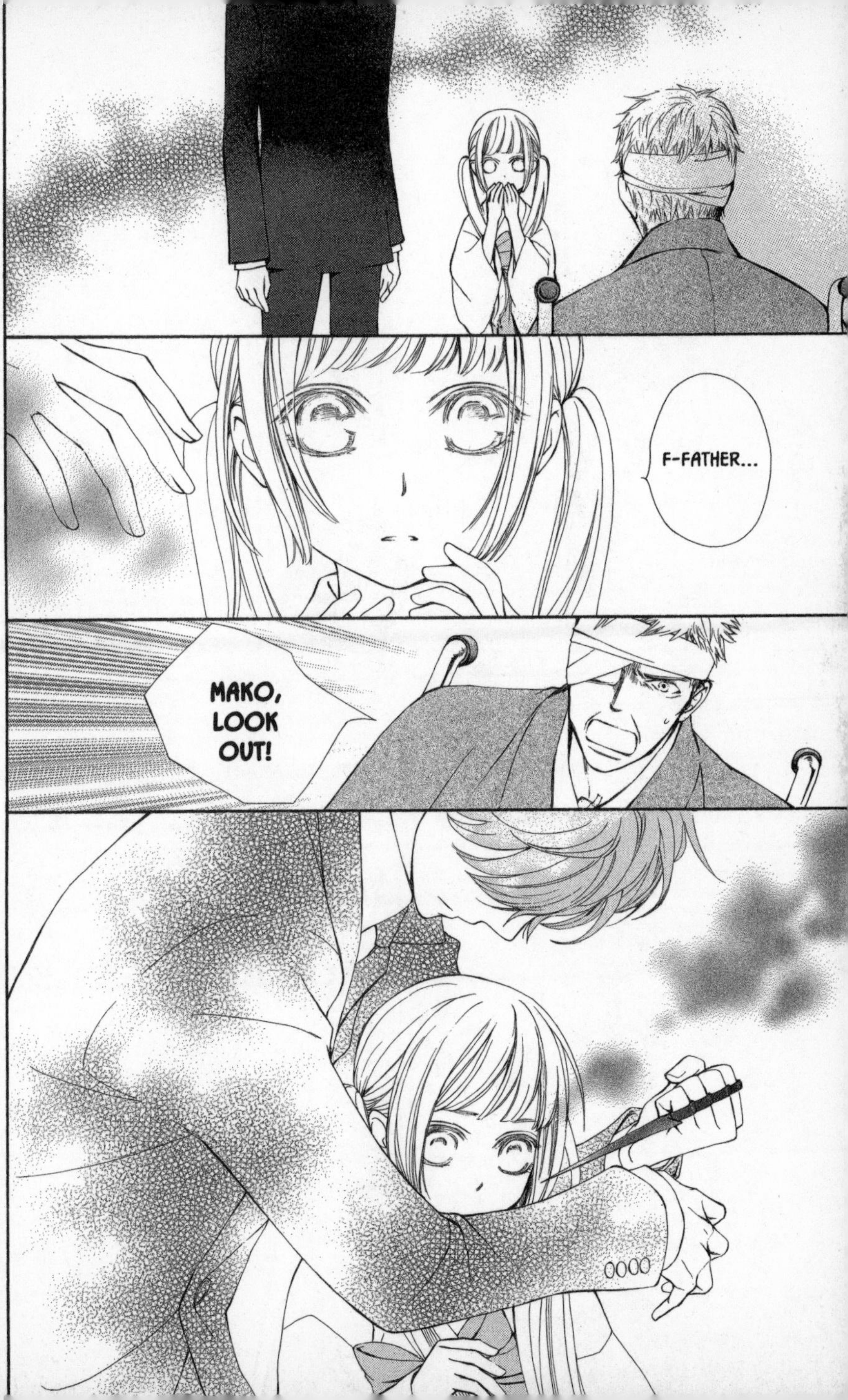
F-FATHER...
MAKO, LOOK OUT!

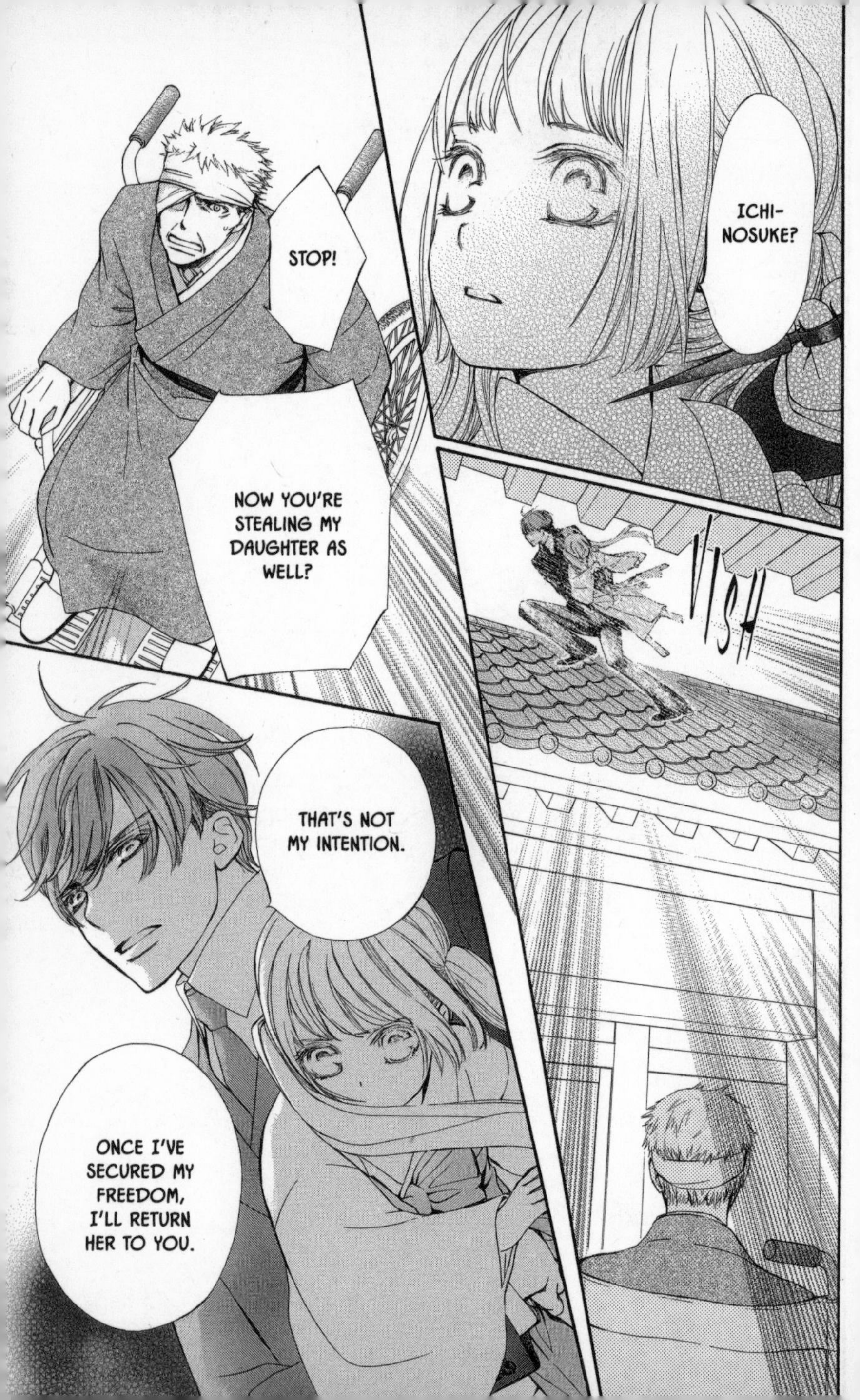
ICHI-NOSUKE?
VISH
STOP!
NOW YOU'RE STEALING MY DAUGHTER AS WELL?
THAT'S NOT MY INTENTION.
ONCE I'VE SECURED MY FREEDOM, I'LL RETURN HER TO YOU.

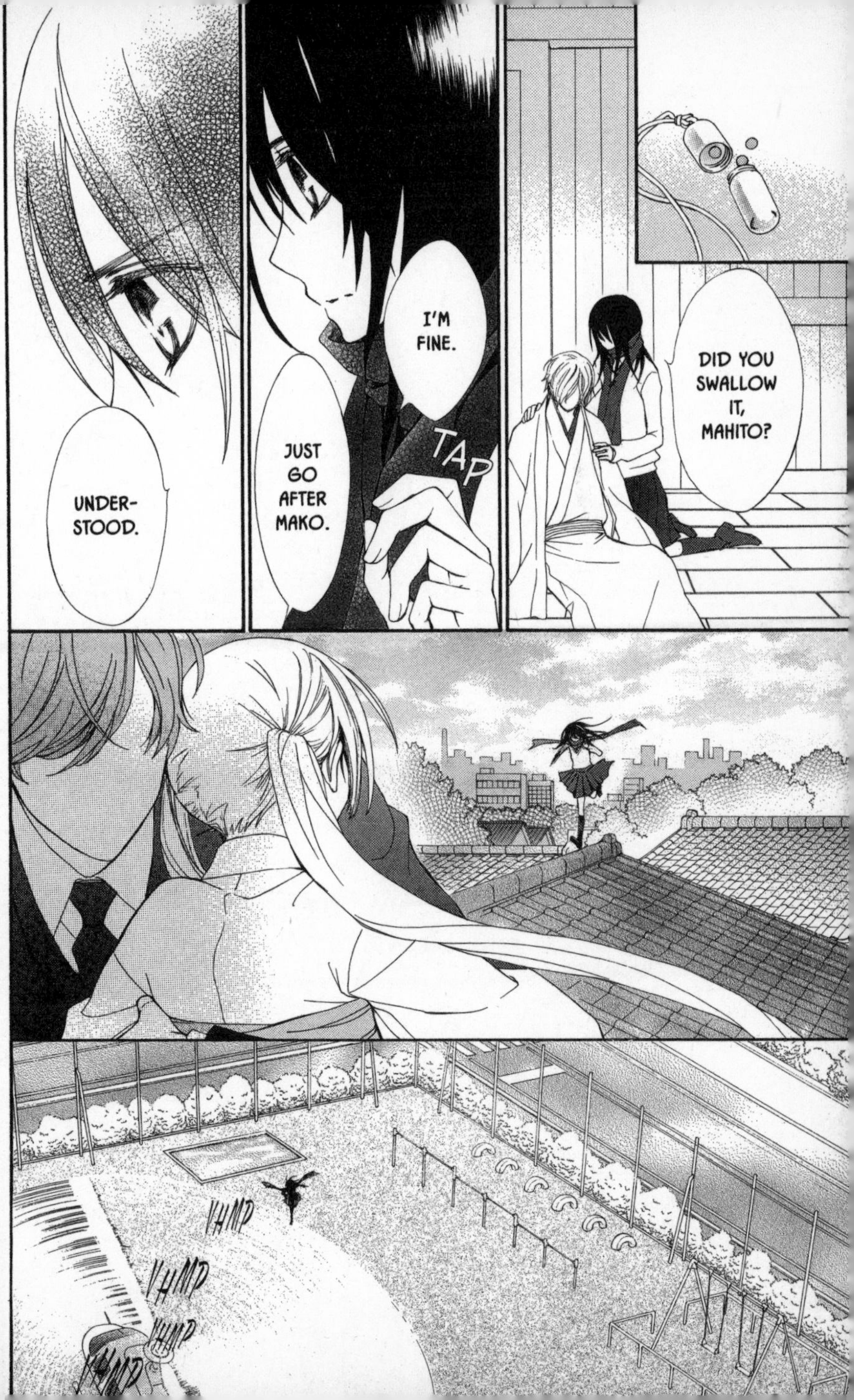
DID YOU SWALLOW IT, MAHITO?
I'M FINE.
JUST GO AFTER MAKO.
TAP
UNDER-STOOD.
VHMP
VHMP
VHMP
VHMP

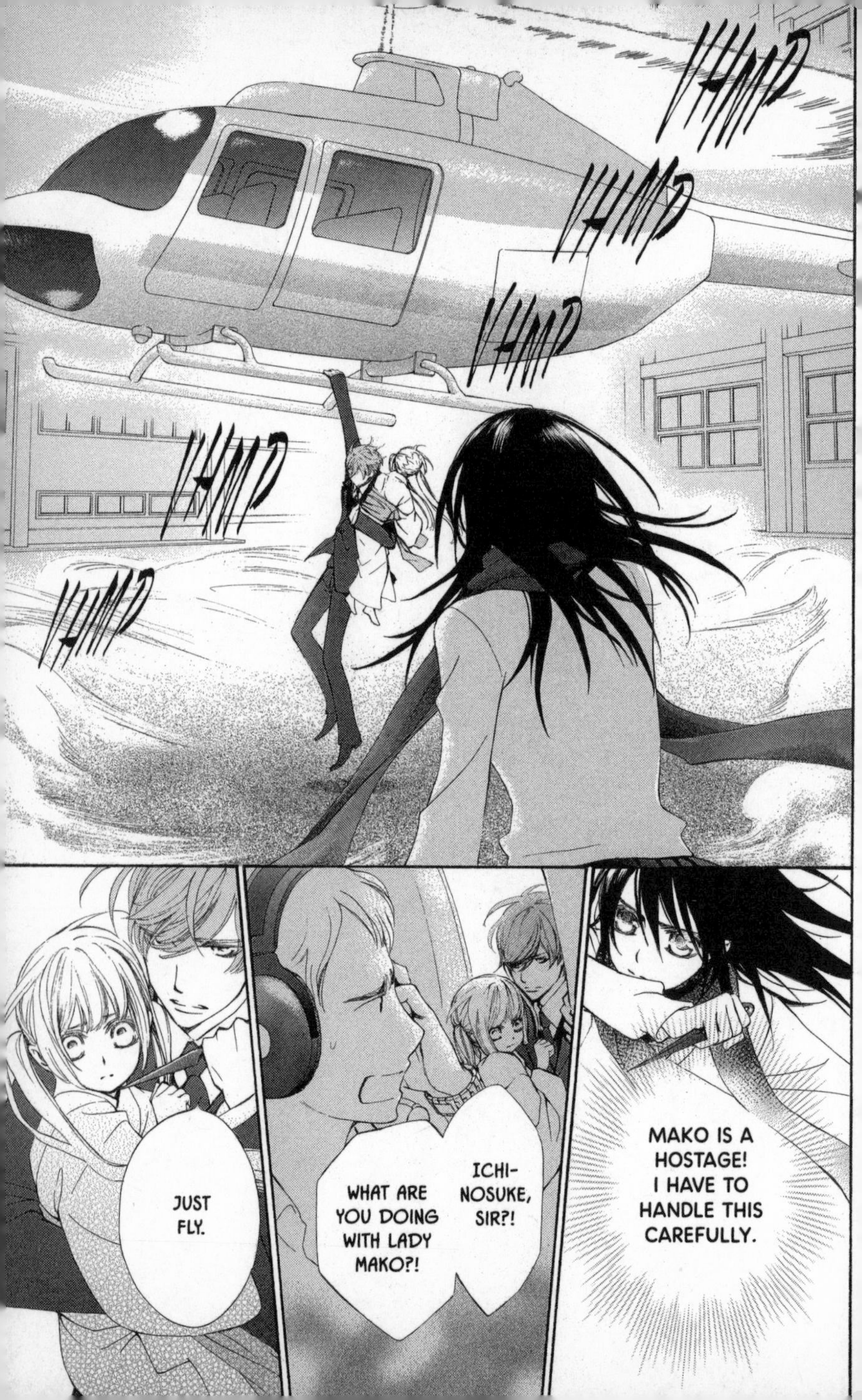
VHMP
VHMP
VHMP
VHMP
VHMP
MAKO IS A HOSTAGE! I HAVE TO HANDLE THIS CAREFULLY.
ICHI-NOSUKE, SIR?!
WHAT ARE YOU DOING WITH LADY MAKO?!
JUST FLY.

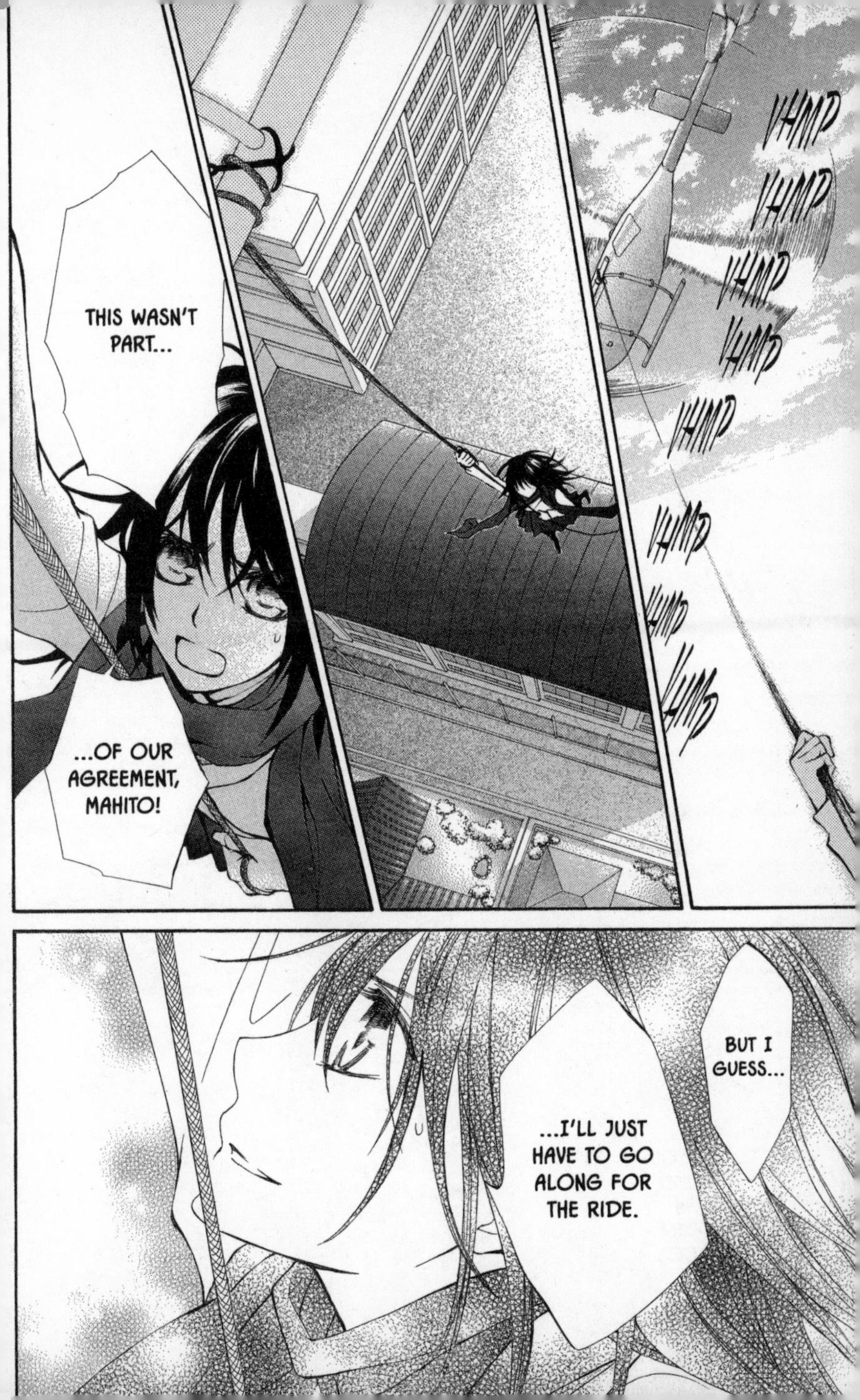
VHMP
VHMP
VHMP
VHMP
VHMP
VHMP
VHMP
VHMP
THIS WASN'T PART...
...OF OUR AGREEMENT, MAHITO!
BUT I GUESS...
...I'LL JUST HAVE TO GO ALONG FOR THE RIDE.

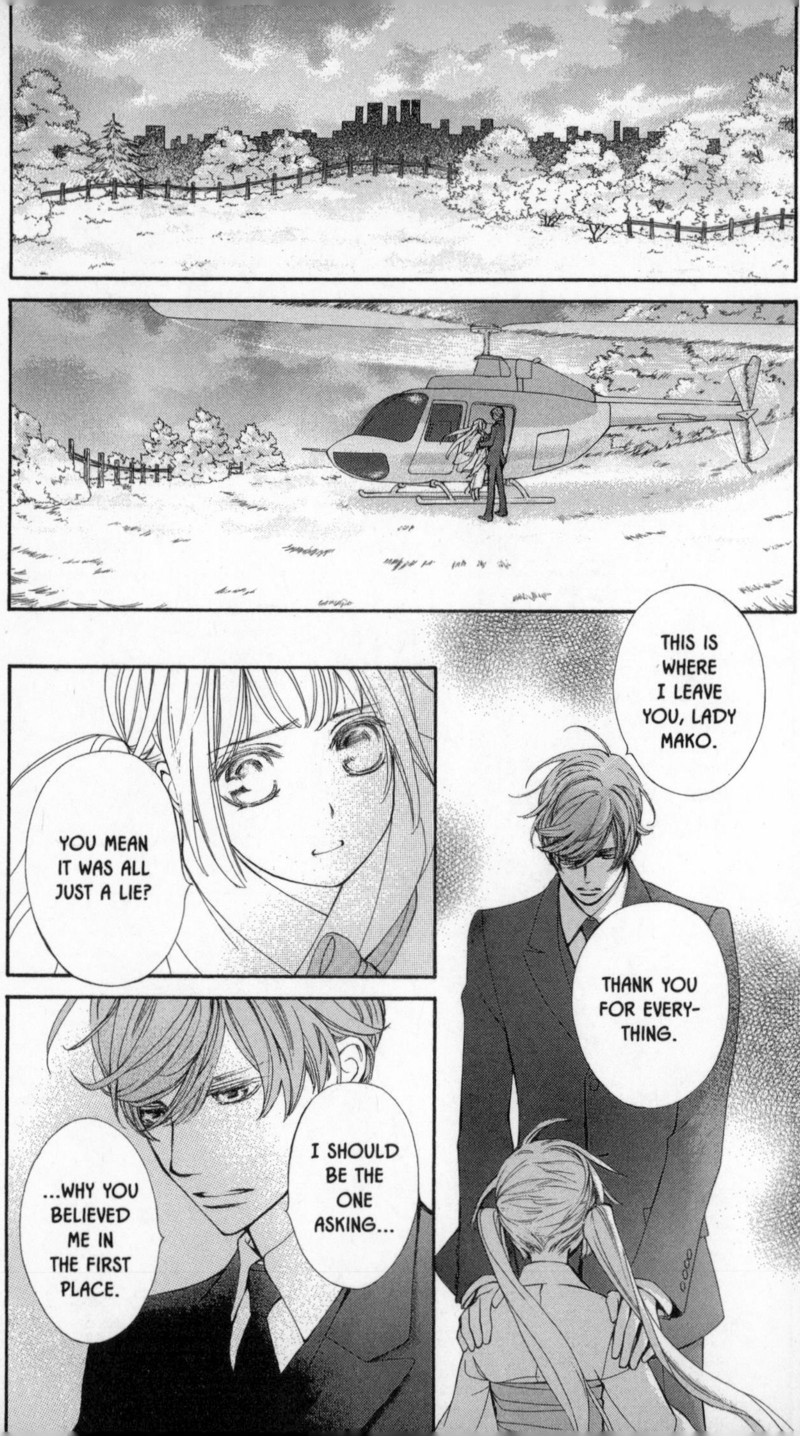
THIS IS WHERE I LEAVE YOU, LADY MAKO.
THANK YOU FOR EVERY-THING.
YOU MEAN IT WAS ALL JUST A LIE?
I SHOULD BE THE ONE ASKING...
...WHY YOU BELIEVED ME IN THE FIRST PLACE.

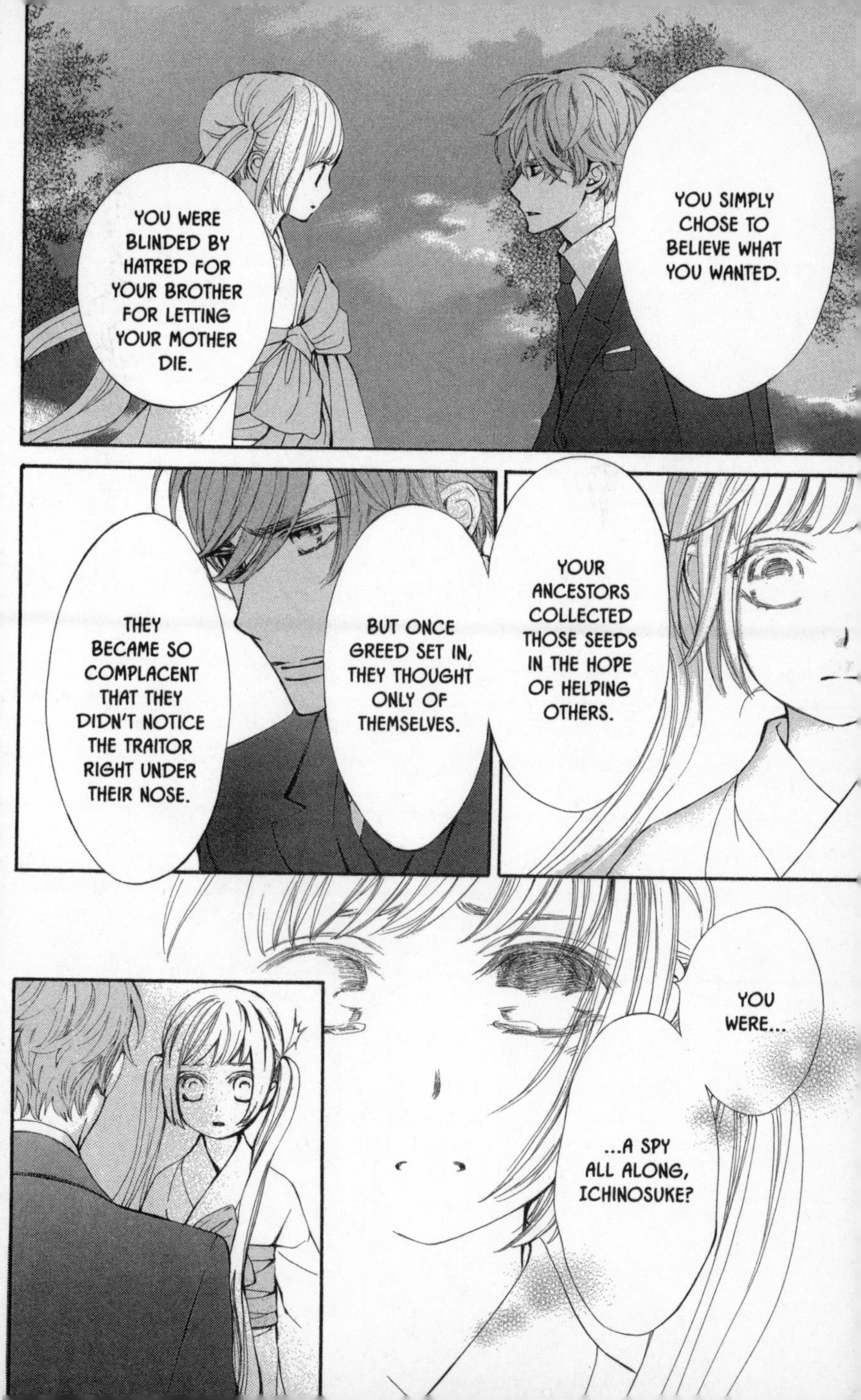
YOU SIMPLY CHOSE TO BELIEVE WHAT YOU WANTED.
YOU WERE BLINDED BY HATRED FOR YOUR BROTHER FOR LETTING YOUR MOTHER DIE.
YOUR ANCESTORS COLLECTED THOSE SEEDS IN THE HOPE OF HELPING OTHERS.
BUT ONCE GREED SET IN, THEY THOUGHT ONLY OF THEMSELVES.
THEY BECAME SO COMPLACENT THAT THEY DIDN'T NOTICE THE TRAITOR RIGHT UNDER THEIR NOSE.
YOU WERE...
...A SPY ALL ALONG, ICHINOSUKE?

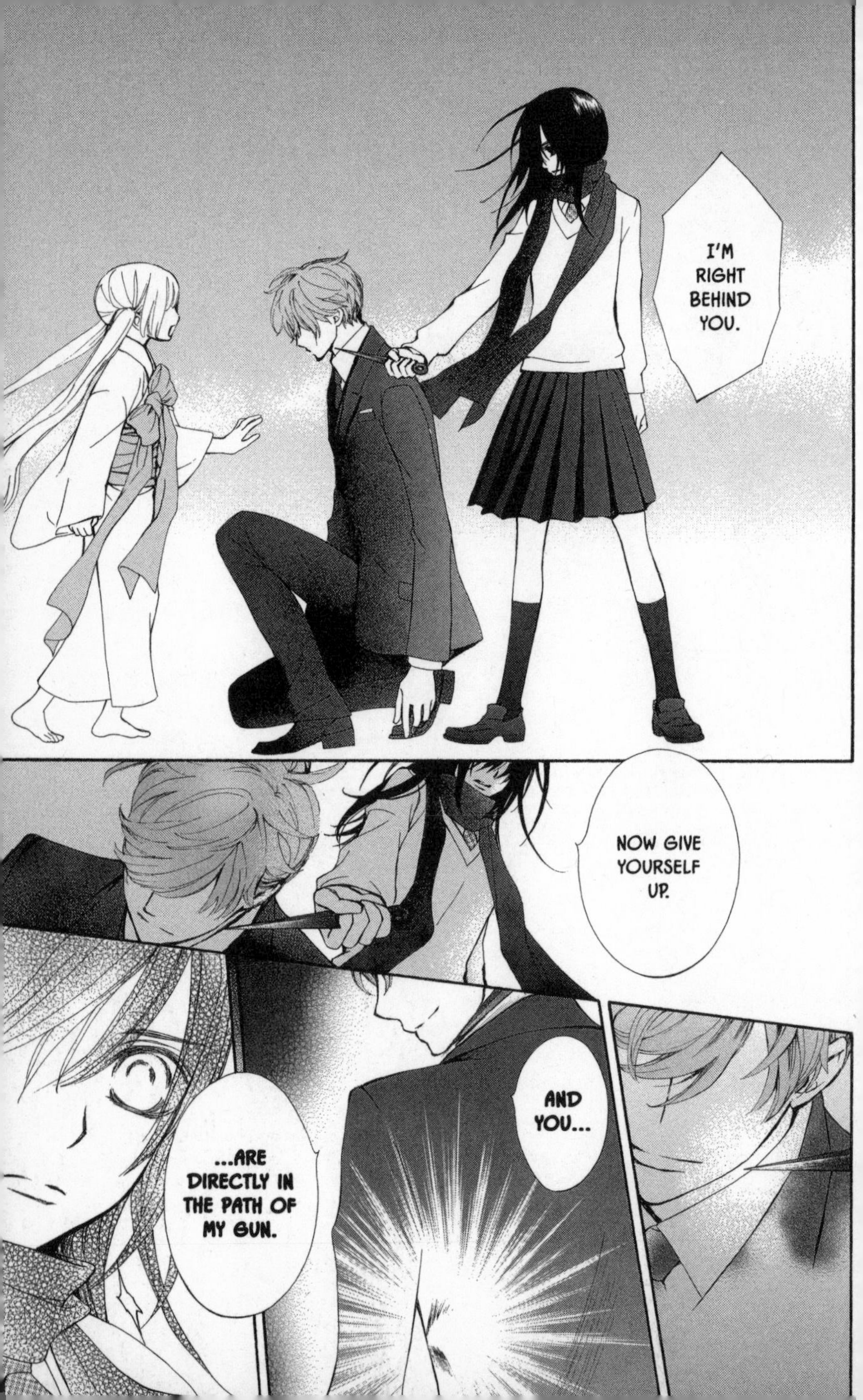
I'M RIGHT BEHIND YOU.
NOW GIVE YOURSELF UP.
AND YOU...
...ARE DIRECTLY IN THE PATH OF MY GUN.

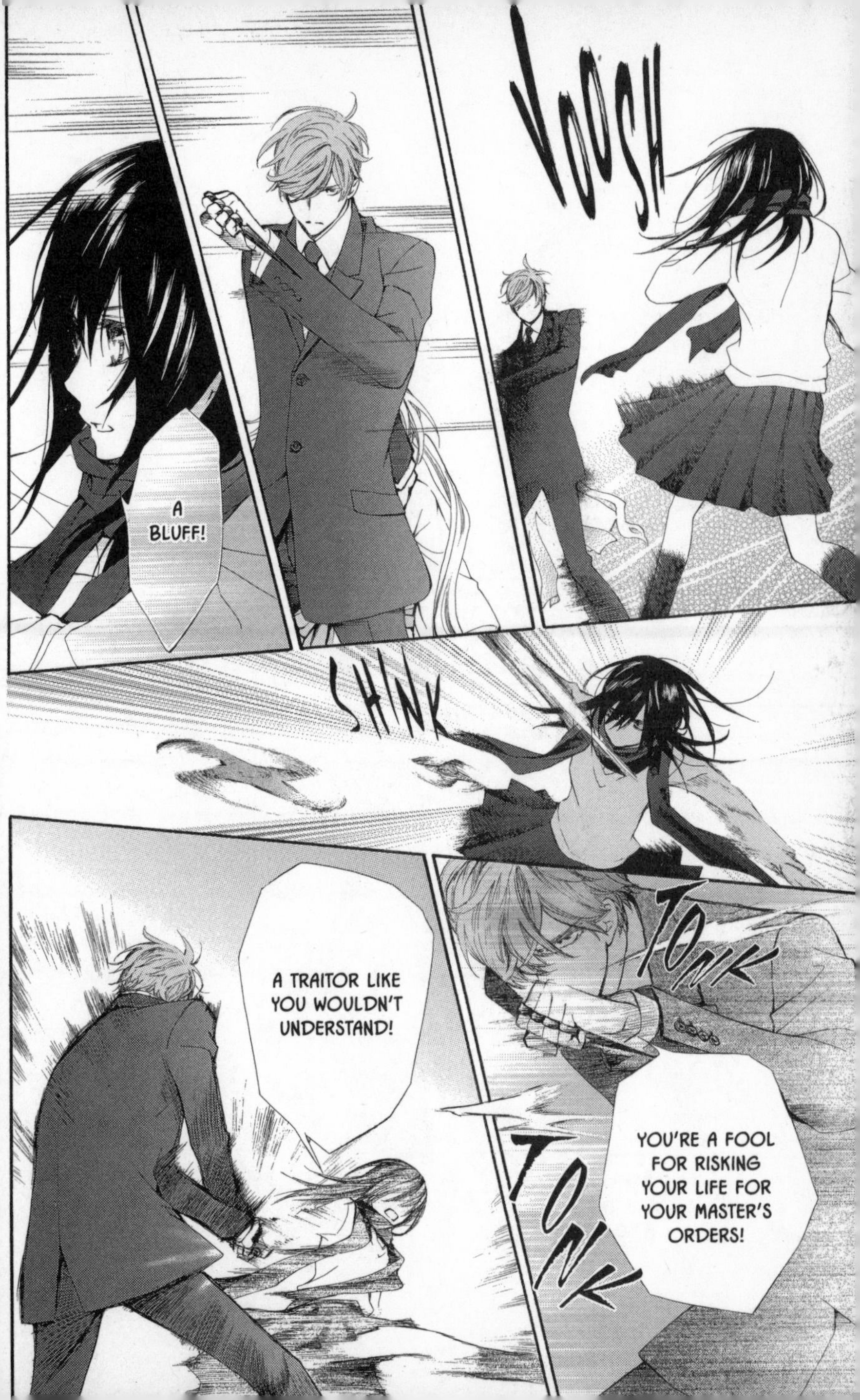
VOOSH
A BLUFF!
SHINK
TONK
TONK
YOU'RE A FOOL FOR RISKING YOUR LIFE FOR YOUR MASTER'S ORDERS!
A TRAITOR LIKE YOU WOULDN'T UNDERSTAND!

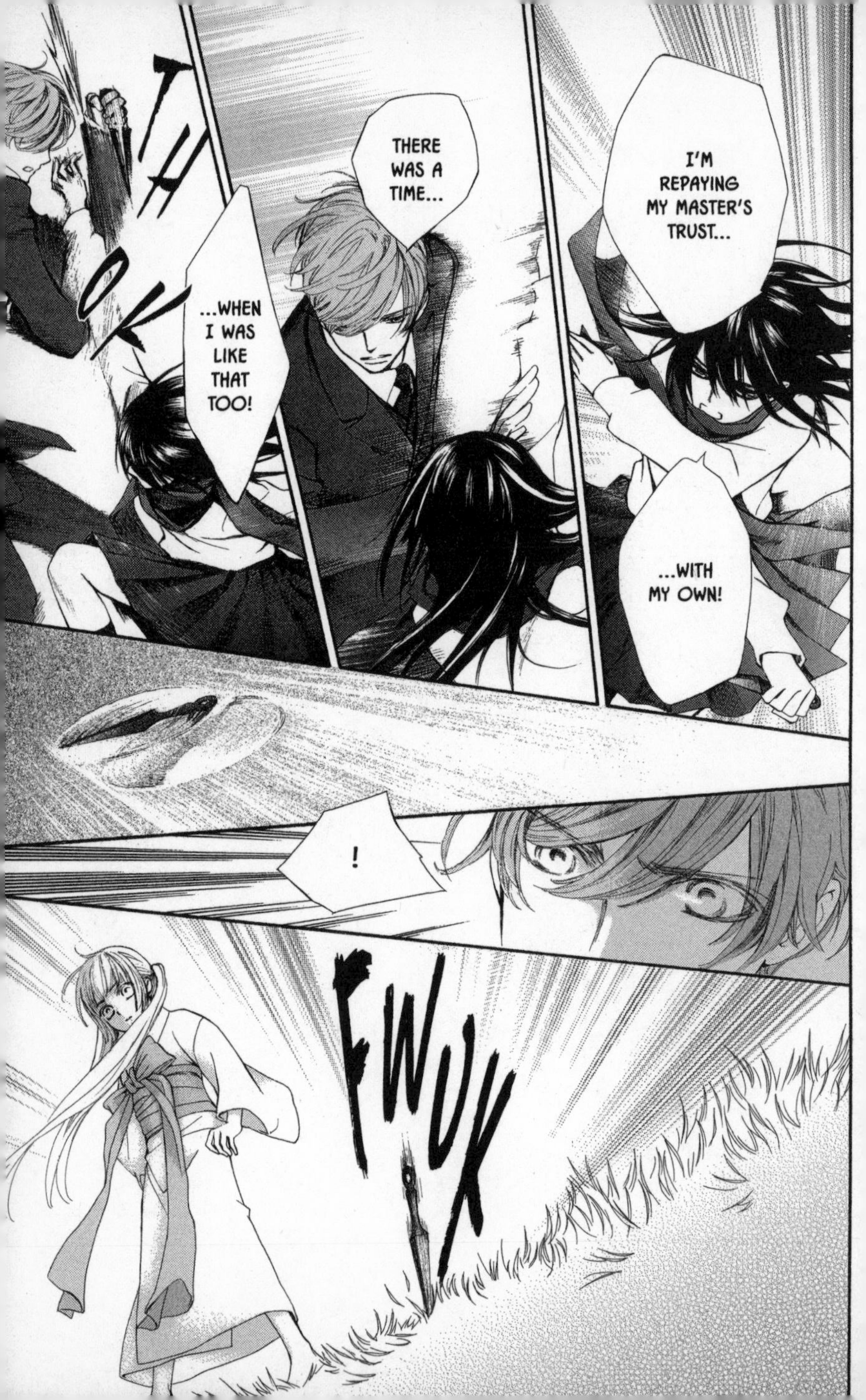
I'M REPAYING MY MASTER'S TRUST...
...WITH MY OWN!
THERE WAS A TIME...
...WHEN I WAS LIKE THAT TOO!
THOK
!
FWUK

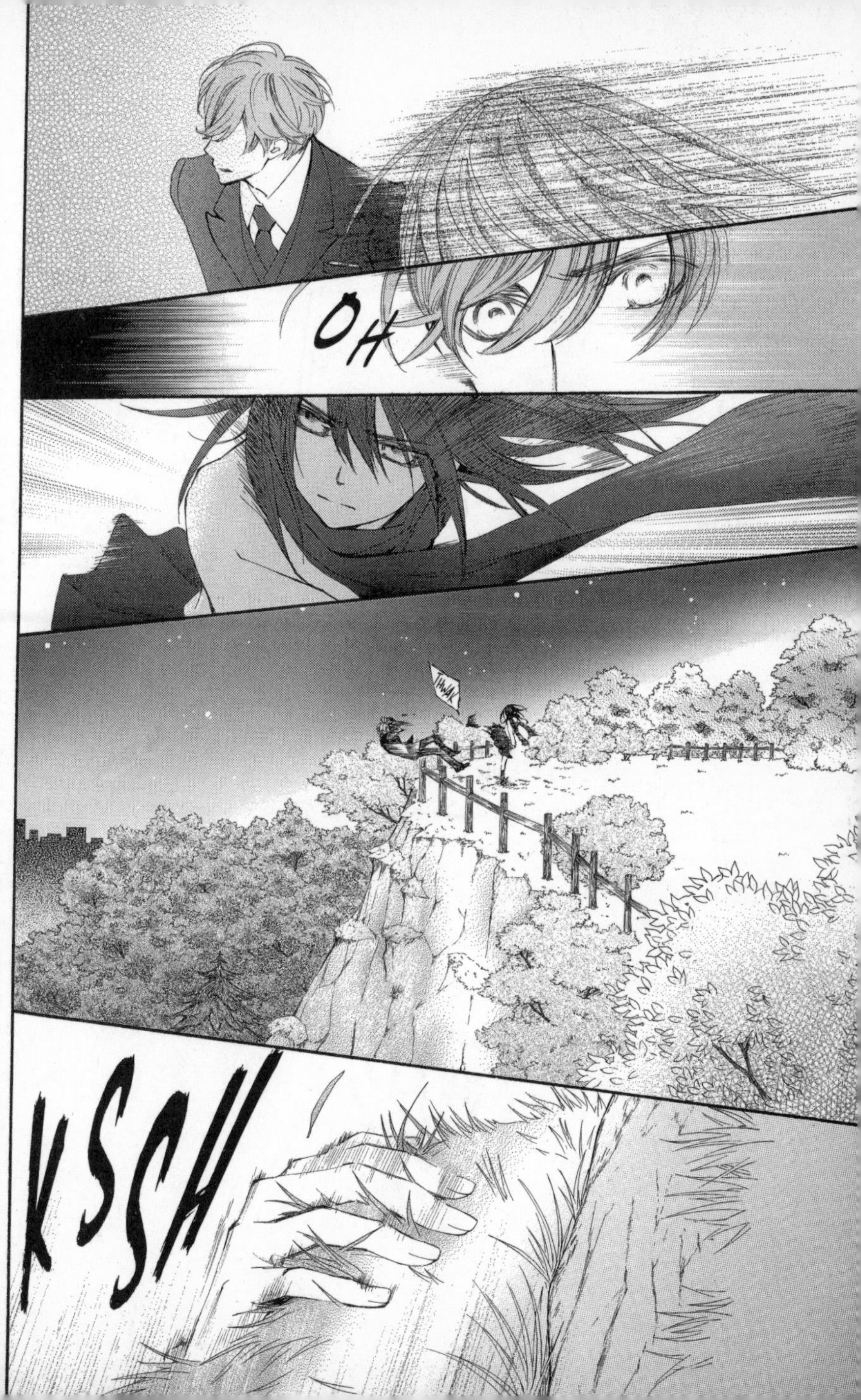
OH
THWAK
KSH

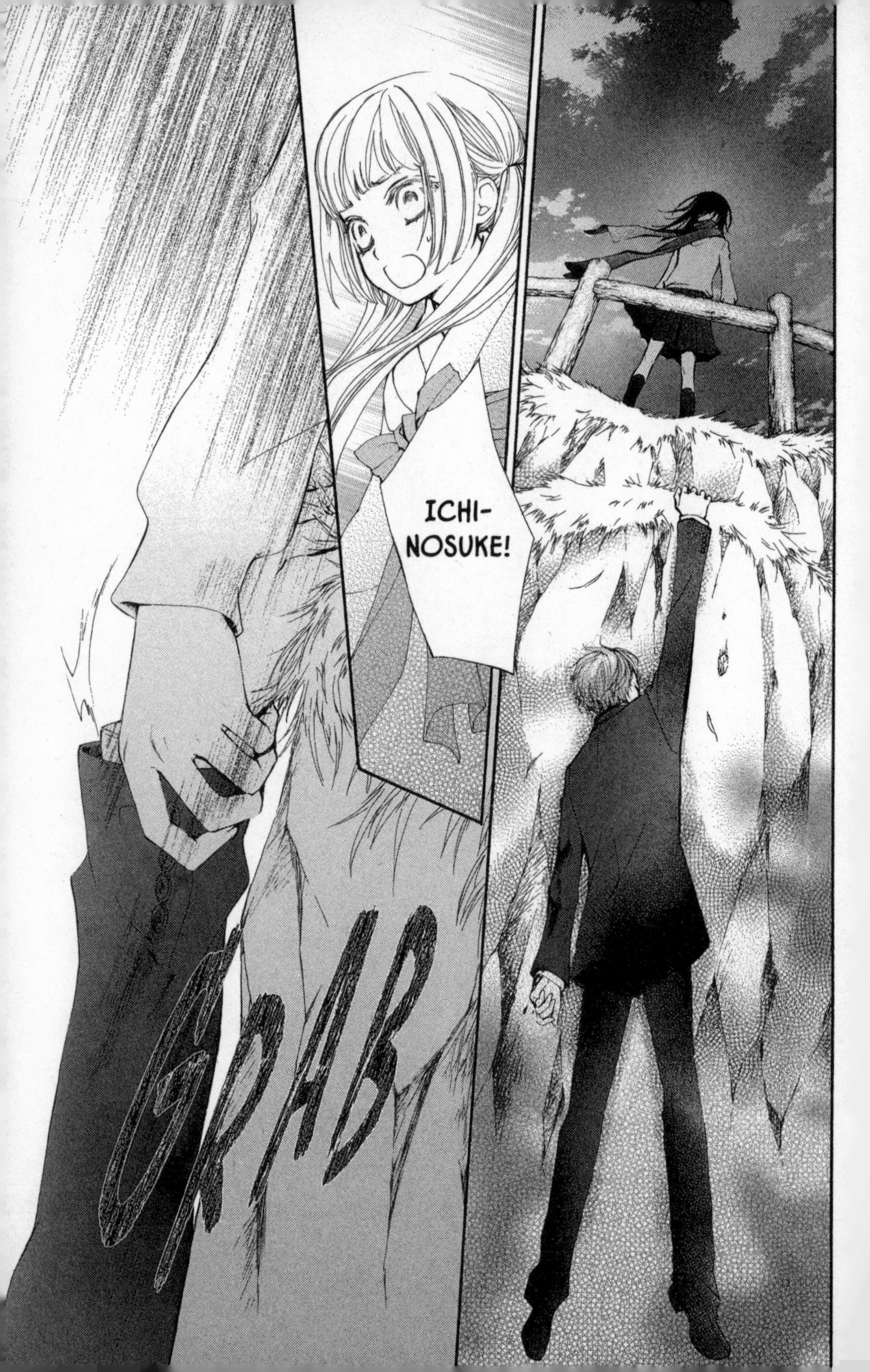
ICHI-
NOSUKE!
GRAB

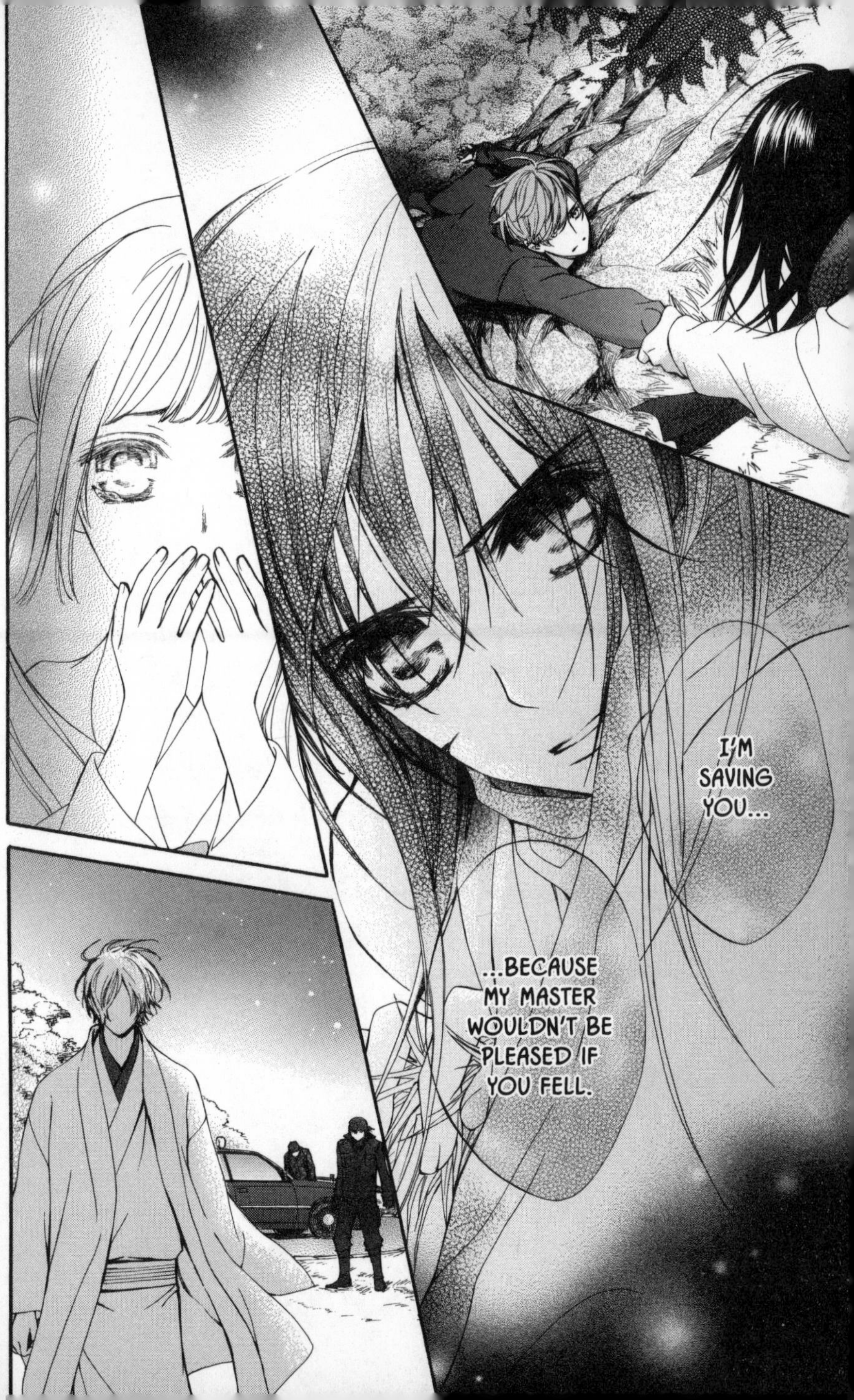
I'M SAVING YOU...
...BECAUSE MY MASTER WOULDN'T BE PLEASED IF YOU FELL.

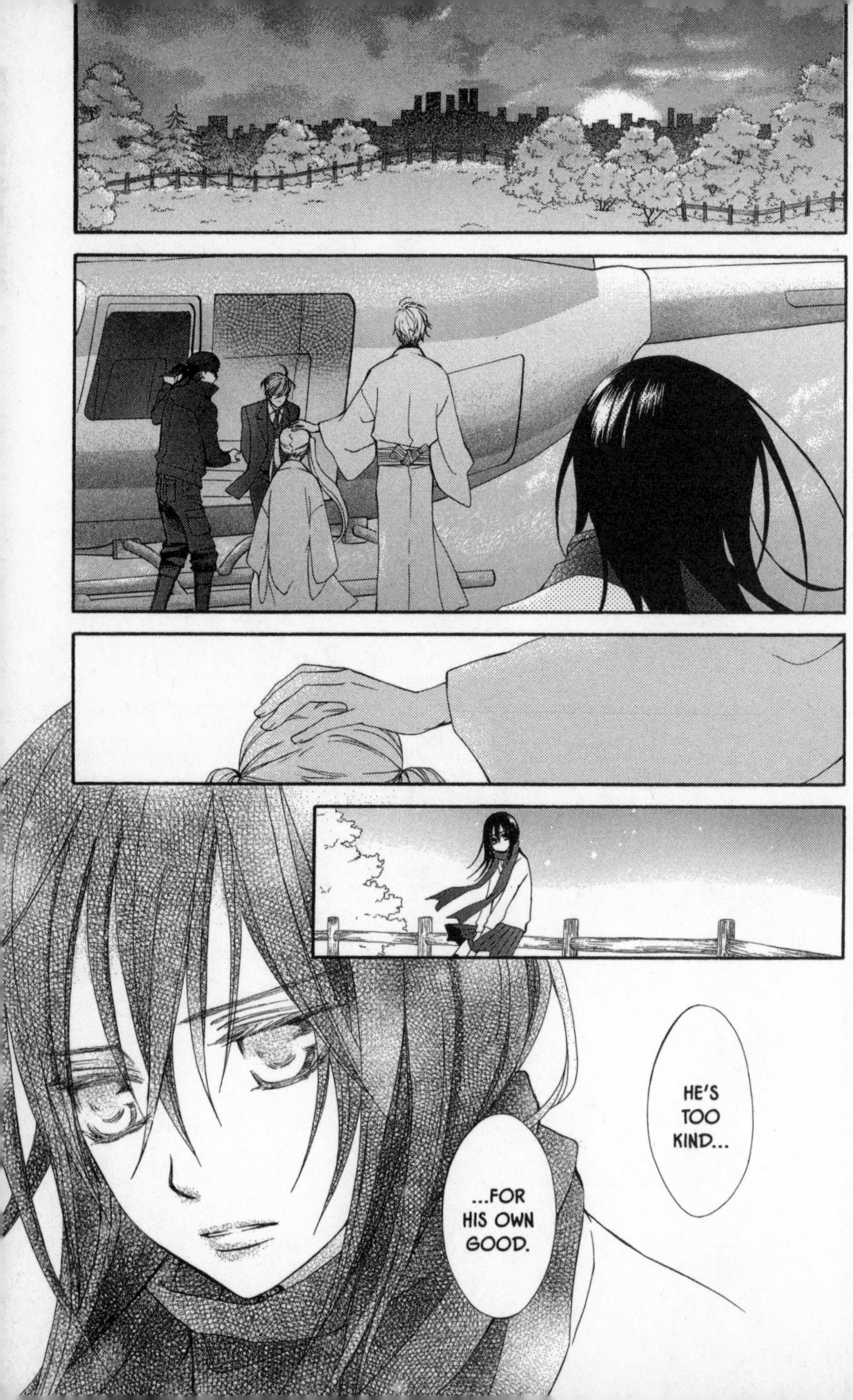
HE'S TOO KIND...
...FOR HIS OWN GOOD.

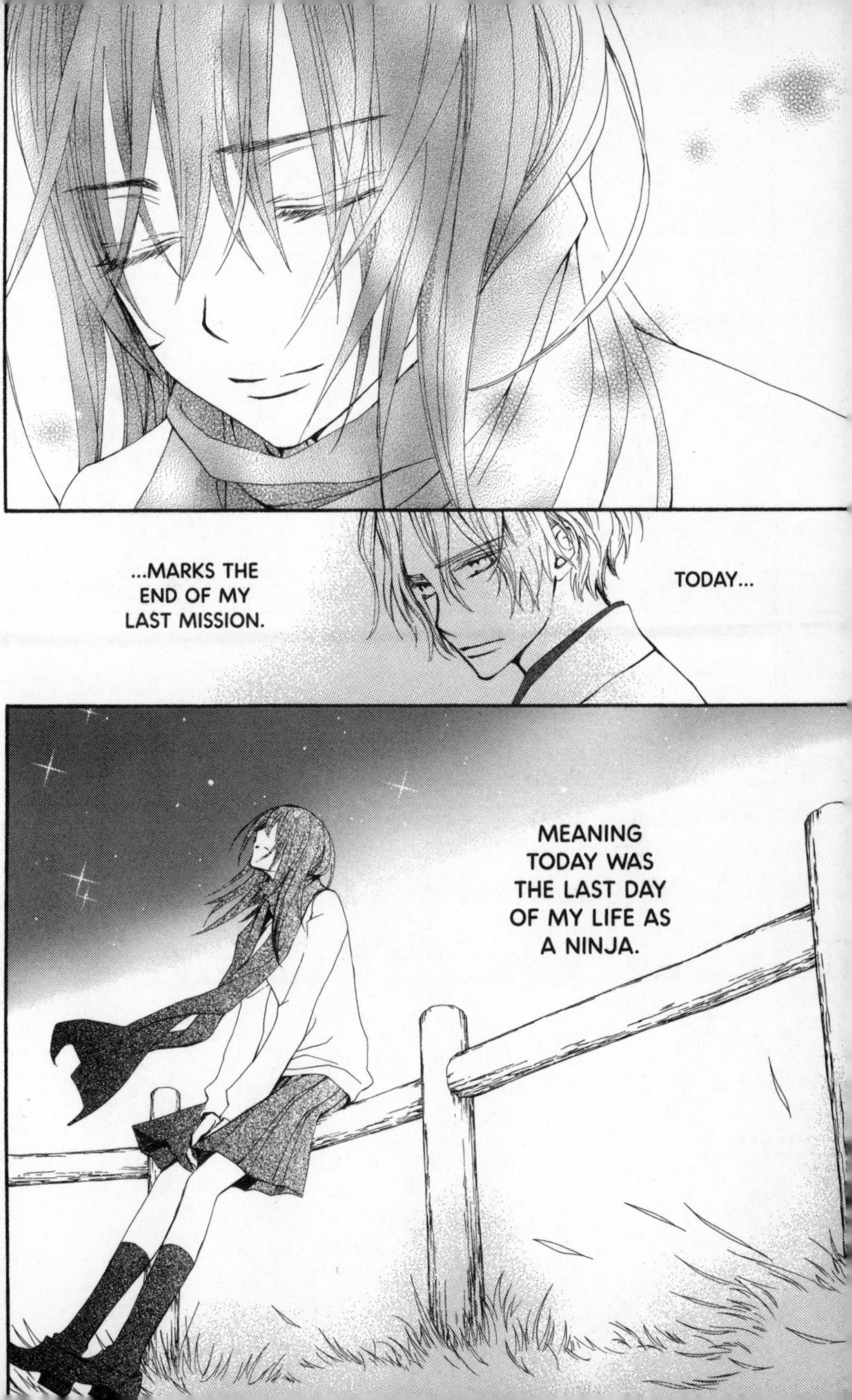
TODAY...
...MARKS THE END OF MY LAST MISSION.
MEANING TODAY WAS THE LAST DAY OF MY LIFE AS A NINJA.

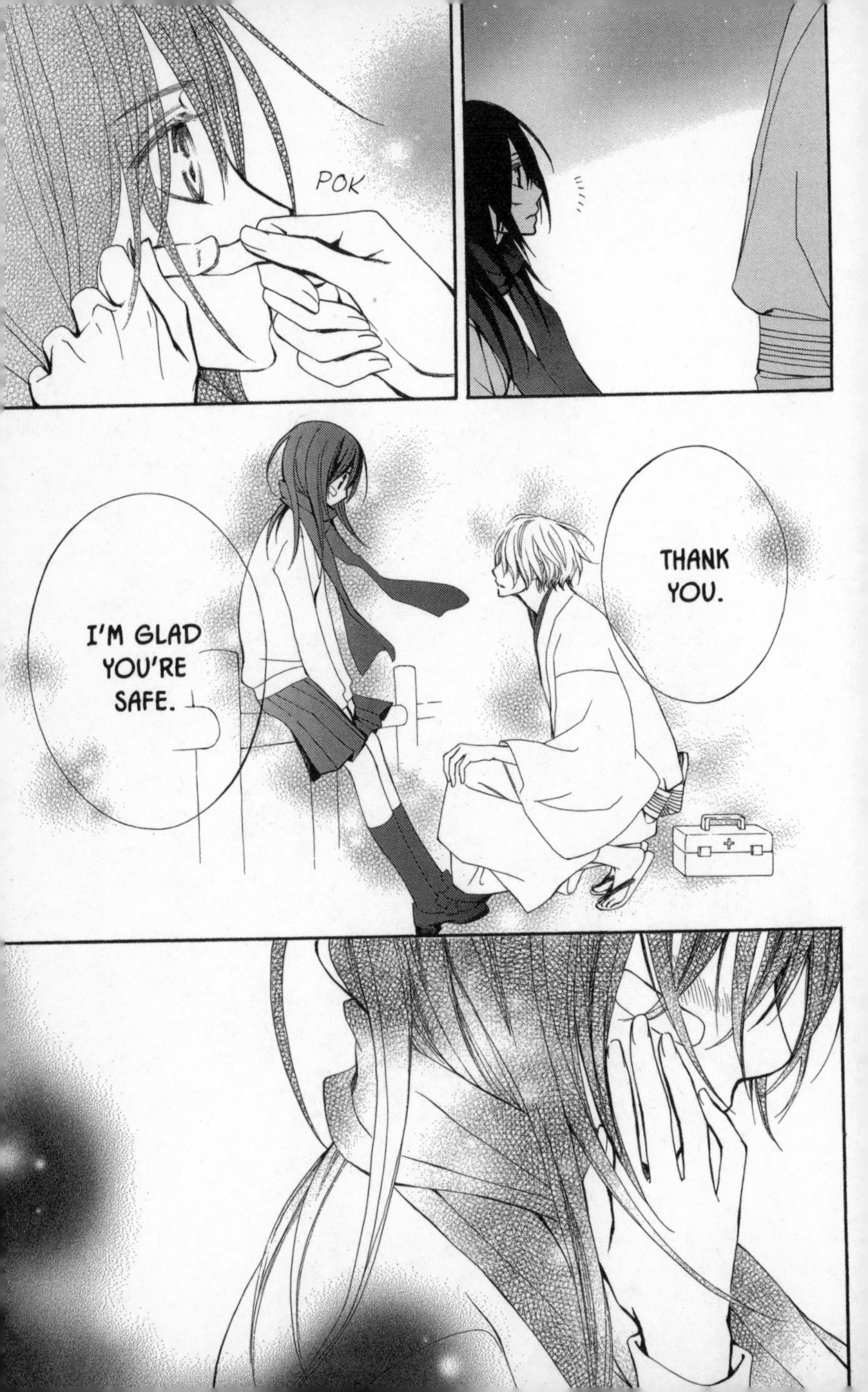
POK
THANK YOU.
I'M GLAD YOU'RE SAFE.

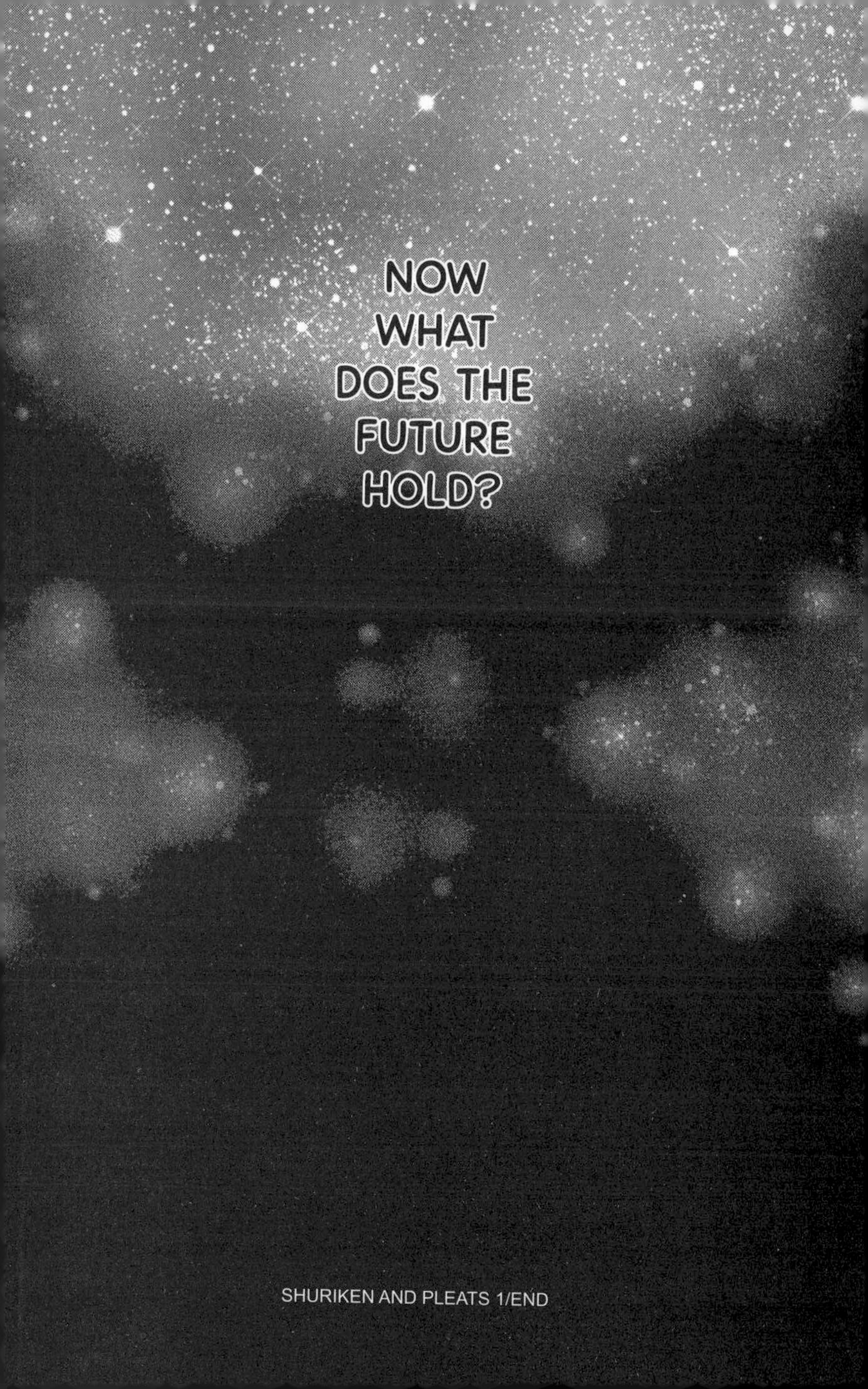
NOW WHAT DOES THE FUTURE HOLD?
SHURIKEN AND PLEATS 1/END

Shuriken and Pleats

I brush my hair...
...tie my bow...
...and open the door.
This is the life I've chosen.
But a ninja's life is never peaceful.

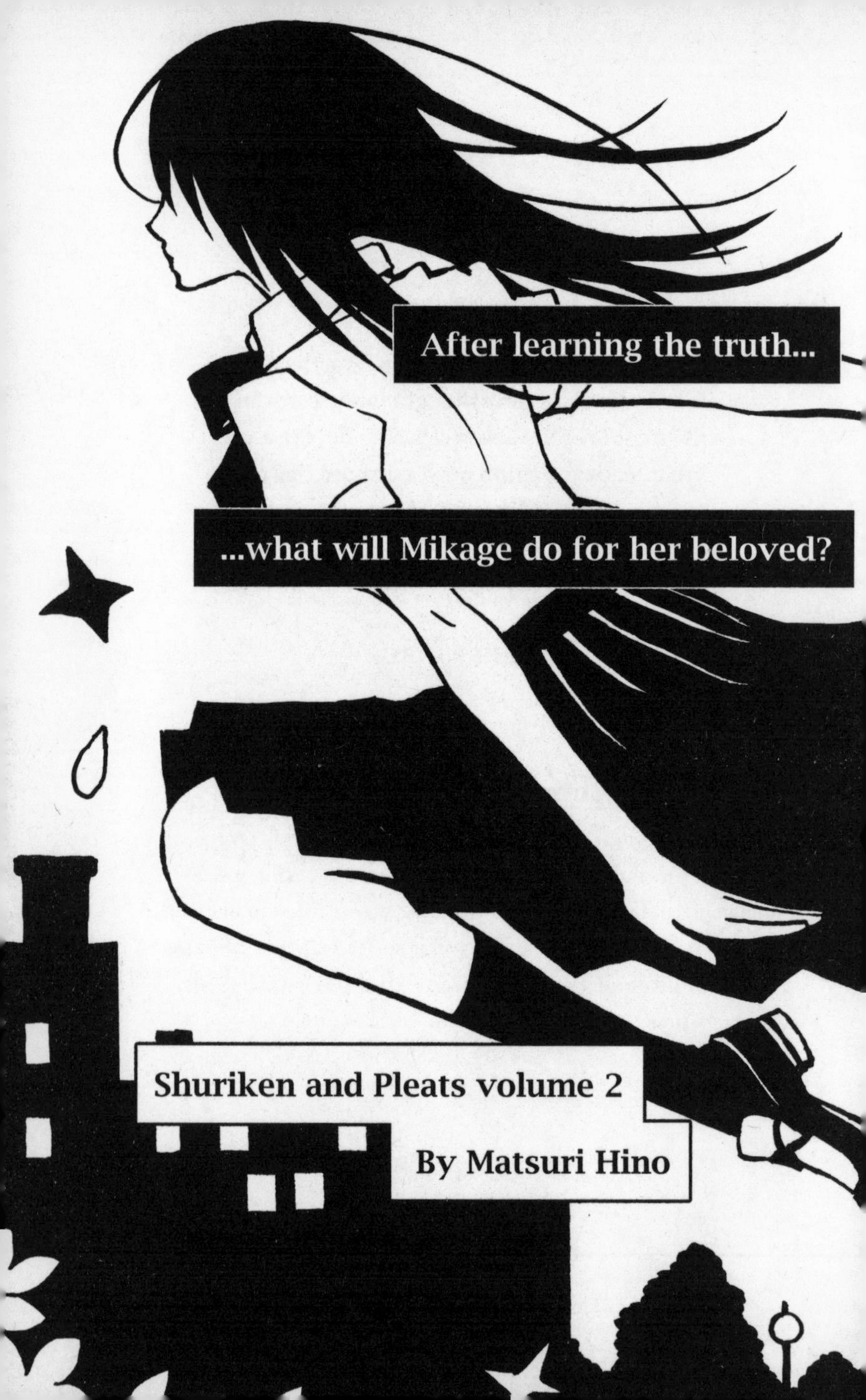

After learning the truth...
...what will Mikage do for her beloved?
Shuriken and Pleats volume 2
By Matsuri Hino

"I don't think I can write a new series."
That's what I secretly thought while I was in
the middle of my last series. The only thing
that made me think maybe I could was a
ninja girl named Mikage. I hope you enjoy this
story about a faithful and strong high school
girl who's trying to find her place in the world.

— **MATSURI HINO** —

MATSURI HINO burst onto the manga scene with her title
Kono Yume ga Sametara (When This Dream Is Over),
which was published in *LaLa DX* magazine. Hino was a
manga artist a mere nine months after she decided to become
one. With the success of her popular series *Captive Hearts*,
MeruPuri, and *Vampire Knight*, Hino has established
herself as a major player in the world of shojo manga.

Shuriken and Pleats 1

SHOJO BEAT EDITION

STORY & ART BY
Matsuri Hino

TRANSLATION **Katherine Schilling**
TOUCH-UP ART & LETTERING **Inori Fukuda Trant**
DESIGN **Shawn Carrico**
EDITOR **Nancy Thistlethwaite**

First published in Japan in 2015 by HAKUSENSHA, Inc., Tokyo.
English language translation rights arranged with HAKUSENSHA, Inc., Tokyo.

Printed in the U.S.A.

Published by VIZ Media, LLC
P.O. Box 77010
San Francisco, CA 94107

10 9 8 7 6 5 4 3 2 1
First printing, March 2016

www.shojobeat.com
www.viz.com

PARENTAL ADVISORY
SHURIKEN AND PLEATS is rated T for Teen and is recommended for ages 13 and up. This volume contains realistic violence.
ratings.viz.com

STOP!

You may be reading the wrong way!

In keeping with the original Japanese comic format, this book reads from right to left—so action, sound effects and word balloons are completely reversed to preserve the orientation of the original artwork.

Check out the diagram shown here to get the hang of things, and then turn to the other side of the book to get started!

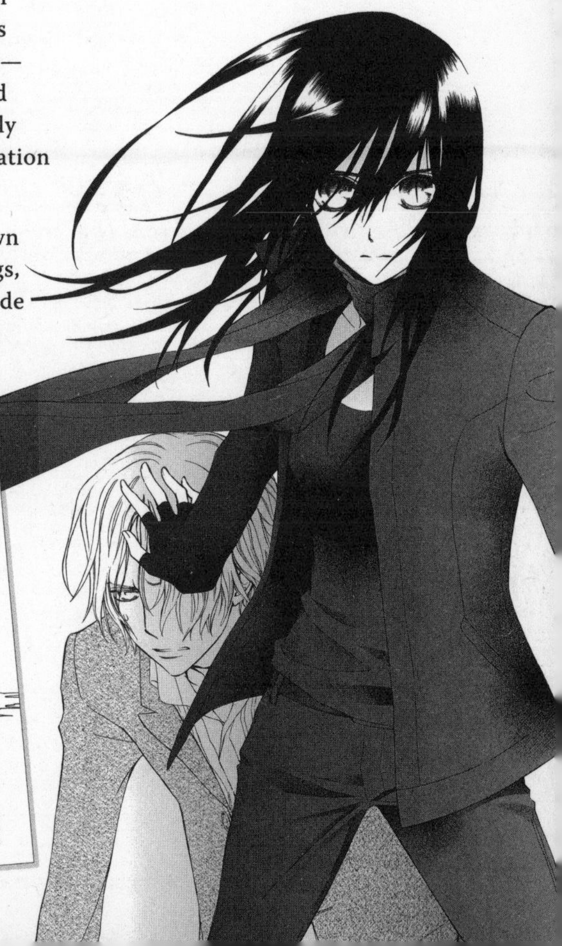

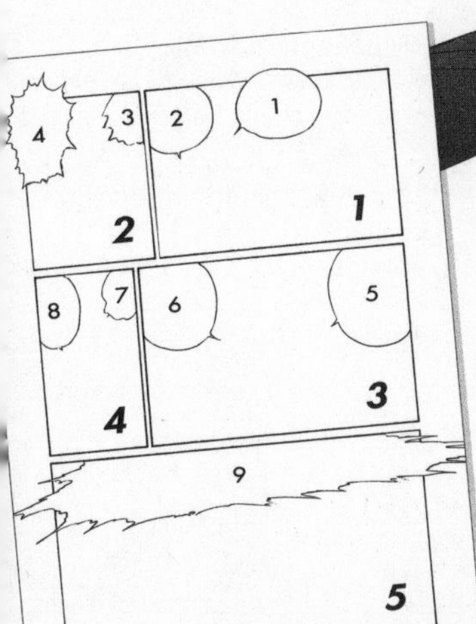
1
2
3
4
1
2
5
6
7
8
3
4
9
5
142

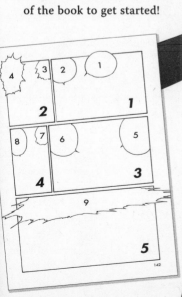